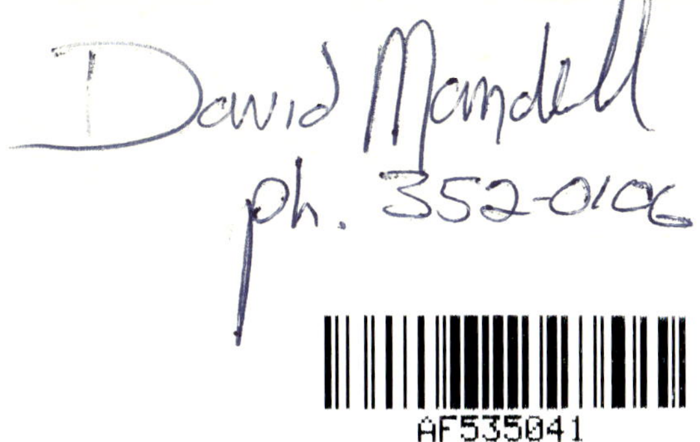

SOLID GOLD

Also by R. Serge Denisoff:
Great Day Coming: Folk Music and the American Left
Sing a Song of Social Significance
Sounds of Social Change (with Richard A. Peterson)
An Introduction to Sociology (with Ralph Wahrman)

SOLID GOLD

THE POPULAR RECORD INDUSTRY

R. SERGE DENISOFF

ta

Transaction Books
New Brunswick, New Jersey

Library of Congress Catalog Number: 74-20194

ISBN:0-87855-586-2(paper)

Printed in the United States of America

To the unsung heroes of the record industry:
the much unappreciated folks in the
promotion and publicity bunkers

If they make it through, that's why we pay them so much money, the odds against achieving all of that, of turning on that audience consistently enough, so that people love you and want to buy and are thrilled by your voice, are so against it happening that when you finally make it, if you do, that they pay you hundreds of thousands of dollars . . . everybody knows how hard it is.

—*Roy Silver, agent*

Consider the awful fact that of every hundred records produced, only six really catch on . . . leaving ninety-four nasty smells around the place.

—*Mickey Most, producer*

A group faces odds, 1,000 to 1 of making it.

—*Bill Graham, promotor*

. . . why one artist succeeds in a medium where another with similar talent does not has always been an impenetrable mystery.

—*Mark Stern, publicist*

CONTENTS

FOREWORD

Several years ago, writing in a volume entitled *American Music*, edited by my friend and colleague, Charles Nanry, I pointed out that "my starting point will be the place where artist and audience interest meet most significantly—the market, the recording. The record is to the musician what the book is to the academic scholar. It is the recognition of his importance to a wider public. It is the focus of his musical energies, all directed toward making the recording different from all others, or at least different enough to be purchased. Beyond that, the recording represents the transformation of an ephemeral idea into a copyrighted product; a musical moment into a durable commodity." Little did I know at the time that this marketing vision of the sociology of music was not only being shared but also exceeded by far in the work of R. Serge Denisoff. He has perhaps done as much for the sociology of music as anyone anywhere else, save perhaps the aforementioned Professor Nanry at Rutgers University's Institute of Jazz Studies.

At the risk of carrying this incestuous and perhaps self-congratulatory note one step further, I took the liberty of showing Denisoff's manuscript to my son Carl on the outside chance that perhaps I was merely reflecting a sociological prejudice on behalf of the book. Gratefully, this proved not to be the case, and the review I received back from Carl is something of a preface in its own right. Therefore, I take the liberty, with permission from my number-one son, of incorporating his remarks into my own remarks.

Out of the many so-called rock books published in recent years, there have been few as thoroughly analytical as *Solid Gold*. It is unconventional in the sense that it does not follow the usual course of such books, stating that rock began as a form of teenage innocence in the fifties and then showing how, through greater self-awareness, rock musicians made great creations.

This book covers all aspects of rock as a form of pop music. Here, pop is used in the sense of a cultural denominator of the masses, particularly American youth. All people involved in the creation of rock have influence in creating or altering the shape of pop culture, be it the musicians themselves, producers, the record-company hierarchy, radio stations, the press, various political factions or the fan. The book contains a few weaknesses; often it does not take a strong enough stand against the "commercializers" and sometimes it goes somewhat overboard in categorizing the various forms of pop. However, these are minor objections. The author's analysis of the rock scene is so complete, especially in terms of the record companies' frame of reference, that even the most knowledgeable student of the music scene cannot help but profit from it. By using direct quotes from innumerable individuals the reader is able to get a first-person view of exactly what goes on in the music industry. The author employs quotes more than any other book of its kind that I have read.

The key to understanding popular music is the idea of commercialization. We live in an economic society where competition for the consumer dollar is intense. Obviously, the goal to strive for is a quality product that maximizes one's profit. The music industry is no exception to this rule. When one speaks of commercialized music he literally speaks of music that is commercially orientated. However, this definition has an important connotation. In order to maximize one's profit one must achieve the greatest possible consumer buying force. Since a wide mass audience consists not of intelligent aficionados of music and does not grasp the various cultural dynamics behind music, it simply will not buy music which is too emotionally inaccessible for them.

Various record companies, musicians and radio stations are painfully aware of this fact and subsequently try to orientate their product so as maximize profit. Often this means dilution of the musical quality.

Economic success with artistic integrity—this is the ultimate goal of musicians. I feel, for this reason, that this book will be of greatest value to unknown, aspiring rock musicians. These people have musical ability but too often are unaware of the countless pitfalls which stand between the music itself and the musician's ultimate dream fantasy—to be a rock and roll star. Just to examine the obstacles facing an unknown band on the verge of getting a recording contract can boggle the mind. Before reaching that magical state of stardom the musicians must pass through the taks of finding an honest, reliable manager, having money for various equipment, finding a record label willing to promote them properly, knowing the stipulations of a recording contract, finding the "right" producer who will maximize the group's strength while not imposing ideas of his own on them, pleasing the "biggies" at a press conference, getting radio airplay on both AM and FM, attaining approval from the keen ears of the critics, surviving criticisms—often hysterical—from both extreme Right and Left political elements and pleasing the audience who buys records. All of these tasks are vital links in fulfilling the dream of the rock and roll star. If any of these obstacles or factors is mishandled or ignored, it can often mean a failure of the dream.

It is a cruel, mean world and the unfortunate fact is that good music alone cannot guarantee an artist's popularity. Commercial pressure on an art form is a twentieth-century phenomenon, and this is precisely why pop music did not emerge before then. There had to be sophisticated technology (radios, stereo, records, wide range of literature and automobiles) before a pop culture could emerge. This is the basis for Denisoff's *Solid Gold.*

I must add that *Solid Gold* exhibits an impressive acquaintance with popular music from the 1950s to the present. It represents an attempt to define popular music in terms of the recording industry's "performance." In effect, the interaction between commerce and esthetics is what enables popular music to become part of mass culture. In so doing, Denisoff makes a fundamental contribution to the theory and practice of mass culture and mass communication.

He identifies popular music, not as one kind of music but as a composite of many taste cultures. The sum total of these taste units creates the genres which coalesce among certain tastes and a preferential axis in a given space and time. He refers to this as a cultural artifact shown by specific subgroups in the social system. The cultural phenomenon is not esoteric but exoteric, and in its sum total is aimed not at a minority but a majority of the people. Beyond that, he appreciates the degree to which popular music feeds from and contains esoteric forms. These forms also have an independent existence, and the ability to transcend genres is a major determinant of its success as popular music.

Populism of the kind expressed by Denisoff differs quite markedly from Marxism as a form of cultural analysis. For although both share a theory that music and art belong to the people, only a radical populism assumes that the tastes and judgments of the people are in some way genuinely represented and reflected in what they are hearing or playing on their recording machines. The Marxist view begins with the distorting impact of bourgeois needs and, more often than not, ends with an a priori conviction of what mass culture or popular culture should be. As a result, many inherited forms of *Kulturwissenschaft* have failed dramatically to link up with the sociology of American music. One must appreciate Denisoff's work as an effort to get beyond the "isms" and into "actions." He does not avoid the commerce and politics of musicmaking as an industry or assume that what is commercial by its nature must be decadent. This healthy balance between audience demands and commercial constraints marks this as a book apart.

As a whole, *Solid Gold* demonstrates the life cycle or, perhaps more modestly, the social system within which the musician operates. Denisoff, despite his obvious understanding and appreciation of the business side of the record industry and the audience aspect, is deeply and profoundly concerned with art itself, with performer and performance. By taking for granted, in a sense, the performer and the process of creation, he is able to show the context within which that evolutionary process must operate if it is to be successful. For this reason his book has a unique focus: the process by which the artist achieves legitimacy; that is, the process of being signed by a recording company. This is followed by a discussion of major record-making companies and independent producers and the characteristics of each. In turn, the major arms of a record company are examined in terms of their critical capacities of marketing and distribution. This analysis of how the recording industry works and what it takes to have a successful recording is itself a crucial piece of sociological research. Nuts and bolts, rather than arts and crafts, are the key to this book: the relative merits of independent versus house producers; the cost of studio time measured by the equality of the product; items which suffer from a lack of promotion versus items which suffer from overpromotion; the whole matter regarding record clubs, remaindering and so on. But again, Denisoff never forgets his main interest, the creative arts, and he realizes fully well that distribution and merchandising are joint obstacles to the introduction of new arts and new musical forms.

Denisoff's work ranges far and wide beyond the recording itself to what he calls the gatekeepers of the music industry: radio station disk jockeys and program directors, the rock press, which helps determine and define the success or failure of a recording, festival promoters and rock 'n' roll radicals, all of whom seek in their own way to exploit the new music and the new culture of the new youth. The book is in fact the history of the youth culture up to the present moment. Culture has dynamics and a motion all of its own. Denisoff well appreciates the fact that the dynamism of musical culture, linked as it is to its commercialism, survives better than any political ideology which attaches to the culture. Thus, the end of student radicalism in no way signified the end of the rock and roll revival. The forms of the music change, the lyrics reflect new conditions, but the beat goes on—for reasons of commerce and industry no less than art and society.

As far as I am concerned, this is *the* major book thus far in the sociology of American music and not just a sociological analysis of rock and roll. Professor Denisoff has provided what many of us had hoped for but had not labored long enough in the field to produce ourselves: a carefully rendered appraisal of how music is made in America by whom and for whom. *Solid Gold* is sure to produce in its afterglow other efforts along the same direction, but I seriously doubt that the pioneering nature of this volume can be denied.

Irving Louis Horowitz
—Rutgers University

PREFACE

In a *Creem* review, I once wrote, "What the world does not need is yet another rock book." This is not such a book. Instead, *Solid Gold* is an effort to explain how popular music is created, beginning with the singer or musician, and how this art is rapidly transformed into a "product" to be bought and sold like shoes or automobiles. The transformation occurs in that corporate world loosely called the "record industry." This book is about that industry and its friends, employees and enemies.

The record industry has been characterized in many ways. The "makers of plastic ware" sang the Byrds. Stan Cornyn likes to think of his company as mere "ticket sellers" in the tradition of the Globe Theater. It is both of these things and more. The record industry is a music machine which engages in some practices that their corporate executive counterparts would shy away from. Yet, despite columnist Jack Anderson's charges of "drugs, sex and payola," the fascination of record conglomerates transcends the occasional sensations. What is more exciting and interesting is the nature and structure of the record business itself. Despite what its critics say, the industry is not an oligarchy that can predetermine hits at its whim, nor is it a creator of taste. However, it is not the total victim of consumer capriciousness. Instead, the industry is akin to a jigsaw puzzle where all of the pieces must fit together if the monster hit is to happen, an event which rarely happens.

The reason for the high mortality rate of most singles is the subject of this book. The labyrinth from the singer through the record company past the radio station to the "folks out there" is lined with failures. This is because each link in the chain exhibits dissimilar interests. Artists want to "do their thing." The controllers at Columbia, Capitol and United Artists all wish to make money. Radio station program directors want to play songs that will create a loyal audience for their stations. Consumers have a variety of tastes, as manufacturers and broadcasters are well aware, but there is no guarantee that a song in any particular idiom will sell. Why did Jefferson Airplane and Grateful Dead survive the late-sixties San Francisco scene while Moby Grape or Wildflower, considered by many to be groups of equal prowess, fail? *Solid Gold* will try to provide answers to this type of question.

This book is a consequence of the cultural debate of 1970. Charles Reich, in *The Greening of America*, joined other writers in presenting popular music as a revolutionary force. How can an artifact called "product" in a billion-dollar industry run by the minions of corporate America be revolutionary? In the popular music press the record-industry executive was presented as an insensitive fellow clad in mod clothing with dollar signs in his eyes. The evidence supported this image: artists were being stifled at every turn; content fights between acts and their companies are legend. The suppression of Bob Dylan's "Talking John Birch Society Blues" is but one example. Trade papers such as *Billboard*, *Cashbox* or *Record World* presented a totally different picture. Here the conglomerate was seen as a helpless giant attempting in the most unsophisticated way to sell its product. The two sources appeared to contradict each other. As a record critic and writer, I conducted numerous interviews with artists on how to "make it." In the spring of 1972, and winter of 1973, with the help of my friends, I was able to interview company presidents, production people, publicists, agents and various functionaries in the record business. What emerged was a far cry from my initial impressions. With this new model of reality, many of the statements in the trade and the rock press took on new meaning. Other materials were integrated into the model. Some statistical data clarified the nature of the record buyer, who turned out to be a multiheaded beast.

Given its rather ambitious and iconoclastic nature, this volume will no doubt raise many more questions than it will answer. Still, these questions and hypotheses need some kind of structuring if anyone, fan or scholar, is to make any sense of the social anomaly labeled "popular music."

ACKNOWLEDGMENTS

In order to produce a concert a symphony conductor relies almost totally upon his musicians. Their skills make the symphony happen. This book is the product of the thoughts and actions of a multitude of people. Jack Arnold, a music-book editor, spawned the idea. James Coffman kept the notion alive. Jerry Hopkins, Lewis Segal and Claire Brush transformed a curiosity into a viable research project. They opened many a door to the studios and executive suites at Capitol, Warner Brothers, Columbia, A&M, United Artists, ABC-Dunhill and many other companies. As they say at the Grammy awards ceremonies, "without them this would not have been possible." It may sound like a cliché, but it is completely true. Many performers, managers, producers, deejays, PDs, distributors, dealers, writers, promotional and publicity folks and company presidents gave of their valuable time and energy to explain the crazy workings of the record business.

I also wish to acknowledge the help of those who took the time to criticize and comment upon earlier drafts of this work. The insights offered by Jann Wenner, Dennis Killeen, Grelun Landon, Robert A. Rosenstone, Jerry Rodnitzky, Paul Hirsch, Bob Garcia, Ron Jacobs, Greg Shaw, Bill Ivey, Mark Levine, Don Weller, James Harmon, Bill Schurk and many others were invaluable. The secretarial staff at Bowling Green State University's Department of Sociology, Phyllis Eaton, Lauretta Lahman and Audrey Shaffer provided their usual high quality assistance. Ms. Lahman, especially, spent an entire summer transcribing boxes of tape. Finally, I wish to thank Charles and Dawn McCaghy for their assistance.

SOLID GOLD

1.

WHAT IS POPULAR MUSIC: A SILLY QUESTION?

> I'll tell you 'bout the magic and it'll free your soul
> But it's like tryin' to tell a stranger 'bout a rock and roll
> © *1965 Faithful Virtue Music Co.*

Popular music is like a unicorn; everyone knows what it is supposed to look like, but no one has ever seen it. Such music connotes a rhythmic idiom—songs, instrumentals, novelties or what-have-you—which reflects the musical preferences of the people. According to this definition, popular music exists for the enjoyment of listeners found in the "general public"; its alleged deficiencies mirror inadequacies in the popular taste. Neither of these definitions is appropriate.

Since the advent of the Beatles, Bob Dylan and other intellectually acceptable artists, few writers have insisted that popular music is kitsch, declassé or somehow without merit. This is a quantum leap from the view of popular music presented in previous decades. S. I. Hayakawa, for example, has insisted that popular songs were "diluted, sweetened, sentimentalized and trivialized . . . the product of white songwriters for predominantly white audiences tending towards wishful thinking, dreams and ineffectual nostalgia, realistic fantasy, self-pity and sentimental clichés masquerading as emotion."[1] The popular music of the 1960s retained many of these elements, but it was not dismissed in its entirety, as the wave of serious articles and books on the subject illustrates. However, high points of rock and roll such as *Sgt. Pepper*, *Surrealistic Pillow* or *Highway 61 Revisited* are by no means representative of popular music.

The more things change, the more they remain the same. The components of popular music are in constant flux. Different sounds, personalities and favorites dart on and off of the popular music charts. Certain styles dominate specific historical periods. These are complemented by other genres. Even when the Beatles and other English bands ruled the charts, novelty songs and big band crooners shared in the bounties of public acceptance. Popular music is not typified by any generic style. Marty Cerf, editor of *Phonograph Record* magazine, notes that just as "society is made up of many specialty, racial and mixed backgrounds, so is music, and the pop charts are made up of minorities." He continues, "On the pop charts you find 20 percent singles from albums; progressive albums 35 percent; rhythm and blues 25 percent; very straight middle-of-the-road and pop records 20 percent." Ron Saul, once the Warner/Reprise promotion head, concurs, "You look on the chart and all the records aren't the same." Consequently, it is less than accurate to say that rock 'n' roll in the 1960s or swing in the 1930s constituted the entire popular music spectrum of the time.

Quantitatively, popular music is a recognized product. The number of records sold is measurable and observable. *Billboard*, *Cashbox* and *Record World* charts define what is being played on radio stations and in part selling in record stores. This amorphous market is quite distinct from others attuned to particular musical forms. Popular music is a much larger and eclectic idiom. Capriciously it takes from specialty areas and momentarily provides an unfamiliar sound its place in the Top 40 sun. Popular music not infrequently is a blending of several specific musical forms. Rock, for example, is a wedding of country music and black blues. However, an important distinction must be made between the sum total of all musical forms and popular music.

Popular music is not just the sum total of all musical styles. It does not include all forms of music. If it reflected all the people's tastes popular music would then have to include a multitude of styles and all of the esoteric genres enjoyed by hundreds of preference groups. This, of course, is not the case.

Popular music is not beamed at all of the public but at a self-selected audience. This audience elects what is called popular with its listening time and dollars. Popular music then is a specific subcategory of the entire spectrum of music; what is referred to in the everyday language as "pop" is not ipso facto "popular." As will be seen, popular music is a medium addressed to a particular segment of the American and overseas public. Generally this audience consists of persons under the age of 24; however, some preferences of people past that generational watermark do manage to sneak onto the pop charts. Still, popular music is primarily designed for people between the ages of 9 through 24, the courtship years, and whoever else cares to listen.

An ever-growing number of people seem to fit this latter group. Quantitatively, popular music consists of whichever musical style sells sufficient numbers to be deemed successful or representative of an exoteric audience. Success is determined by indices of the music industry such as radio play and over-the-counter sales. Consequently, sufficient purchases by the youth audience, the main consumers, define what constitutes popular music at any specific time. The actual mechanics of the delineation of the youth market are highly complex. Adolescent and college tastes are not monolithic; they are shaped and influenced by numerous social forces around them ranging from age, race, marital status and sex to geographical location.

POPULAR QUA PEOPLE'S MUSIC

Any teenager who has heard the cry of "you don't call that music," will testify that some people—particularly parents—do not enjoy or even tolerate popular music. Feelings and attitudes notwithstanding, it is almost impossible to avoid popular music. Whether one is passing a record rack at the local supermarket or flicking the car radio dial in search of the most up-to-the-minute commuter report, it is usually present.

Popular music *is* everywhere. Some would call it a symptom of "noise pollution." Americans operate over 372 million radio receivers in both car and home. A hundred million color and monochrome television sets transmit "In Concert," "The Midnight Special," Dick Clark's transplanted Hollywood "American Bandstand," local music shows and the myriad of variety programs that occasionally present, with an eye on the youth market, performers deemed in the "pop" medium. The late Ed Sullivan, hardly a supporter of the new music, in the "now for the youngsters" segment of his now-defunct Sunday night show featured acts that appealed to his younger viewers but alienated many of his older viewers. But he also presented "crooners" like Andy Williams, Dean Martin or Doris Day, who appealed to both groups. Owners of television sets are potential popular music listeners, but they are not necessarily consumers.

More significantly, there are 61 million phonographs distributed throughout the United States population, a figure which becomes terribly important in treating record sales as an index of the universality of the popular music medium. In addition, 1967 saw 10,774,000 tape recorders in use in homes, cars and commerce. Three years later, 8,459,000 tape players of all types were sold.

In 1955, 4,542 pop singles were released and 1,615 long-playing albums vied for success. In that year Americans had access to 120 million radio receivers and 24 million phonographs. Nearly 15 years later the number of outlets for recorded music had doubled. In 1967 the record industry passed the billion-dollar mark in annual sales. And in 1968, the banner year of record sales, 6,540 singles were issued. In that same year, 4,057 long-playing albums were released and grossed over $1 billion, while 183,000,000 singles were sold through stores, jukeboxes and other sources. Americans also purchased 196 million long-playing records during 1968. An undeterminable number of bootleg records swelled this number. With these figures the pop *qua* people's music thesis seems almost plausible, since nearly every man, woman and child *statistically* could have bought an LP and a large part of a single. This is not the case.

There are less optimistic aspects of this flood of recordings. Murray Rose, president of an advertising marketing agency, observes: "In a business that saw the release of 4,000 albums and 5,700 singles in 1970, where only 10 percent even smelled 'break even,' you almost have to be an egomaniac just to think you can crack those odds."[2] A year earlier Henry Brief told a *Forbes* magazine reporter: "At last count, 74 percent of the 45s, 61 percent of the pop LP's, and 87 percent of the classical LPs failed to break even."[3] In 1973, 75 percent of the LPs released bombed. Most releases never even get to the public. Only a small portion of the public usually buys a pop record.

The music industry itself places inordinate emphasis upon success as epitomized by the gold record. "A gold record is the success symbol for the youth of the seventies," wrote *Look*'s senior editor Ernest Dunbar.[4] The mark of achievement in the music industry is the gold record, awarded for the bona fide gross of $1 million and on the basis of units sold. The single far outsells the album, of course, since the price of the single is about a dollar in many parts of the United States. Long-playing albums are much more expensive.

In practice, an album which finds about 502,000 buyers in the United States qualifies for the coveted gold record. An album is certified gold when net domestic sales of LPs and tapes values at one-third list price amounts to $1 million. Thus, at $5.98 list price, each sale counts $1.99 toward the gold record. Yet, considering the potential market, the figures are relatively small and certainly representative of only a small portion of the public. A baseball player with a batting average of less than 20 percent would not move past the first rung of sandlot ball. Joe Smith, executive vice-president of Warner Brothers and Reprise Records, underlined this point to *Roll-*

ing Stone: "I'm talking business, because there are 70 million homes in this country, of that 56 million, i.e., 78 percent, have record players or some means of playing a record. Why should we jump up and down to sell a million records?"[5]

The popular *qua* people's music notion is further shaken by musical taste and preference surveys conducted over the past decade. The National Family Opinion firm, in a study for Columbia Records, reported from its nationwide panel of consumers in 1969 that "rock and underground" constituted 29 percent of the record market. Country music was second with 16 percent, followed by easy listening or "middle of the road" (MOR) with 15 percent. Pop instrumentals received 14 percent, with classical, jazz, rhythm and blues, folk, Broadway shows and motion picture soundtracks capturing 14 percent. All other genres attracted 12 percent of the market. I sampled a middle-class "bedroom" community of British Columbia and found that musical tastes are very diverse when the generational factor is discounted. Given overrepresentation of adolescents in the sample categories considered, rock was favored. A closer examination of the data suggests that this preference is by no means equally distributed throughout the sample.

Adults predominantly chose speciality categories as their first musical choices. Jazz, show tunes, country and western and symphonic material account for 74 percent of adult preferences. Few in the sample like what is generally being aired on the local Top 40 and semiprogressive radio stations. Pop music, then, is generally the province of youth.

POPULAR QUA YOUNG PEOPLE'S MUSIC

Popular music is virtually the exclusive playground of the young. A vast majority of the records sold in North America are purchased by youths. In the North Vancouver sample 77 percent of the students picked rock music as their favorite

Exhibit 1.1

FIRST CHOICE OF MUSICAL PREFERENCE BY GENERATION

	High School Students and Dropouts	Parents and Teachers
Jazz and instrumentals	13 .03	16 .10
Folk and folk-rock	74 .17	8 .05
Rock and roll	195 .45	3 .02
Rhythm and blues (soul)	66 .15	11 .07
Country and western	7 .02	10 .06
Broadway shows, movie themes	0 .00	38 .24
Classical, religious	26 .06	54 .34
No answer	55 .13	17 .11
	436 .100	157 .100

idiom with only 11 percent echoing the tastes of their parents and teachers. When comparing generation on the variable of support or appreciation for "rock and roll" as either their first or second choice, a significant 87.9 percent of those adolescents sampled made this choice. Their elders followed suit only in 4 percent of the cases. In discussing the genres of "show tunes" and classical, a combined 96 percent of the adults indicated a strong preference for this material.

Taste and record-buying habits are strongly influenced by age. Bubblegummers or prepuberty females between the ages of 9 to 12 buy a lion's share of singles. After the age of 16, white youths begin to concentrate upon long-playing albums. Blacks, without comparable economic power, continue to buy singles for a longer period of time. As the courtship process begins teenage males become increasingly involved in record consumerism. By the age of 25 record buying begins to decline, much to the consternation of retailers. In a sample of a college population, it was discovered that preference for popular music fades with age. To illustrate, at a commuter college in Southern California it was reported that 38 percent of the respondents 29 years of age (one short of the magic "over 30") and older chose genres in popular music, while 52 percent preferred other more esoteric genres. Thirty-two percent expressed a liking for the classics. At the other end of the age continuum, of those below the age of 20, 86 percent favored the "pop" idioms with only 5 percent expressing appreciation for the classics.

The question of adult membership in the popular music constituency is a thorny one. The passing of the statistical watermark of 24 does not push a person into the "square" or "out-of-it" category except in record-buying figures. People over 24 *buy* fewer popular records than those half their age. Charts reflect this. Most acts on the Top 40 or *Billboard* Hot 100 are not performers known for their adult appeal. Nonetheless, radio programmers and record-company executives are aware that housewives who take care of the kids listen to daytime radio and occasionally buy a record. After age 24, the female makes most of the family record purchases.

The type of music supported by this group is called "easy listening" or "middle of the road" (MOR). It is a part of the popular-music idiom, but it is also a very large specialty area. MOR ranges from the piped-in Muzak heard in a dentist's waiting room to the soft strains of Andy Williams or The

Exhibit 1.2

AGE AND MUSICAL PREFERENCE (17-30)

	17-19	20-22	23-25	26-28	29+	TOTAL
Folk	20 .24	104 .36	58 .30	29 .25	25 .18	236 .29
Motown	19 .23	34 .12	29 .15	17 .15	22 .16	121 .15
Rock	32 .39	74 .26	40 .21	20 .17	6 .04	172 .21
Jazz	3 .04	25 .09	18 .09	14 .12	19 .14	79 .10
Classical	4 .05	27 .09	30 .15	23 .20	44 .32	128 .16
Other	5 .06	26 .09	20 .10	12 .10	22 .16	85 .10
TOTAL	83 (1.01)	290 (1.01)	195	115 (.99)	138	821

(N = 821)

Lettermen heard on the car radio. MOR material frequently "crosses over" into popular music, yet a good deal of popular music is totally banned from easy-listening stations. "If I played Alice Cooper or Black Sabbath at 10 in the morning," said one MOR program director, "100,000 women would find another station . . . I'd be looking for another job." Easy listening as it exists in the 1970s is generally a mix of traditional ballad and crooner styles doing love songs with lush string sections. Some "folk-rock" and novelty material also makes its way from the Top 40 charts onto MOR listings. Nostalgia in the form of "golden oldies" is an important aspect of MOR radio, as it is in Top 40 programming. Top 40 stations will program "solid-gold weekends" in order to lure MOR listeners. The bait of nostalgia is designed to alter the stations normal demographic profile of 9 to 18. By attracting older listeners the station's 18 to 49 category balloons, and that is "where the advertising money is."

For record-company executives, easy listening is really a postpop audience. The postpop audience generally consists of those people who have stuck to popular music as they enjoyed it as teenagers. A 40-year-old person can easily "get into" a contemporary ballad when performed by Andy Williams or Ray Coniff and yet detest the original version of the song. Indeed, many acts popular in MOR like Johnny Mathis, Johnny Mann or 101 Strings have made it a practice to "cover" or copy the current hits in their more traditional styles.

This group can and does buy 100,000 units of an album; attends night clubs and concerts; and watches their favorite acts on Johnny Carson's "Tonight Show." But, as Joe Smith of Warner Brothers indicates, one Jimi Hendrix would sell five million records, as opposed to Frank Sinatra's 200,000. Nearly all of the major record companies, while exhibiting a few "easy-listening" artists, spend most of their time, money and energy on performers who appeal to those under 24, because that's where the money is.

Popular music appreciation is along generational lines, but it is also not exclusively favored by all of the young. David Riesman, writing in *American Quarterly,* was one of the first postwar social scientists to explore the relationship of "radio music" to adolescents. The Harvard professor indicated that popular music was a monopoly industry which handed down material to the young who accepted it without question. In his awareness of this manipulative aspect of the music industry he dichotomized the teenage audience on the basis of "majority" and "minority" taste units. The majority was characterized as an amorphous unit with rather uncertain tastes that reflected peer-group pressures. This teenager typified what the author would term the conformist "other-directed personality":

> most of the teenagers in the majority category have an indiscriminating taste in popular music: they seldom express articulate

> preferences. They form the audience for the larger radio stations, the "name" brands, the star singers, the Hit Parade, and so forth. The functions of music for this group are *social*—the music gives them something to talk or kid about with friends . . . coupled with a lack of concern about how hits are actually made; an opportunity for identification with star singers or band leaders as "personalities" with little interest in or understanding of the technologies of performance or of the radio medium itself.[6]

The minority group was delineated as being small, comprised of more involved listeners "who are less interested in melody or tune than in arrangement or technical virtuosity." Riesman added the racial or declassé factor, indicating that this esoteric group was commonly interested in jazz and blues. He could also have easily included in this list the folk music enthusiasts of Greenwich Village, New York, and Berkeley, California. A key to the recognition of this minority group was its dissent from mass-produced culture:

> The rebelliousness of this group might be indicated in some of the following attitudes toward popular music: an insistence on rigorous uncommercialized, unadvertised small bands rather than name bands; the development of a private language and then a flight from it when the private language is taken over by the majority group; a profound resentment of the commercialization of radio and musicians.[7]

The majority taste culture was at this time dominated by six major recording companies—Columbia, Victor, Decca, Capitol, MGM and Mercury—who produced dreamy love songs, novelty and specialty numbers, which British rock historian Charlie Gillett pictures as featuring singers of "conventional expectations . . . their styles were bland, pleasant, and in effect suburban. The styles of female popular singers . . . were even more respectably pleasant."[8] The general tone of this style and the songs reflecting it denied the physical nature of sex and expressed trite emotions about simple events with almost no reference to any shared experiences.

Until the serendipitous successes of Bill Haley, The Crew-cuts and, finally, Elvis Presley, majority tastes were defined and catered to by Tin Pan Alley, the American Society of Composers, Artists and Publishers (ASCAP) and the major record manufacturers. The minority and esoteric cultural groups were dependent upon specialty labels, which in some instances were subsidaries of the majors, such as Okeh of Columbia Records. Businessmen, in both cases, produced for the youth culture and their parents. In the majority category the popularity of the crooning style mirrored the tastes of the mid-1930s. Singers such as Tony Martin, Johnnie Ray, Frankie Laine, Joni James, Kay Starr and quartets such as the Ames Brothers, the Four Lads and the Four Aces were musically closely related to the big-band crooners and quartets.

Only the minority, given their declassé overtones, in fact clashed with majority taste. Jazz clubs of the 1950s, now peopled by intellectuals and college students, for many people remained in the historical context of dens of illegitimate behavior ranging from narcotics to prostitution. Rhythm and blues was considered "race music"—unsuitable for the white middle class. One religious publication claimed that "Rock and Roll [is] a Disease." Frank Zappa recalls, "They did everything they could to make sure their children were not moved erotically by Negroes."[9] When rock and roll dominated pop music, the "minority" of the early 1950s merged with a large segment of the "majority" to create a new plurality that the record industry could not or would not immediately accept. While the quartets and crooners still led the music parade, the tune was changing and so was the audience, but not as drastically as Frank Zappa or White Panther John Sinclair would later suggest. Rock and roll did not comprise all of popular music, and even in the heyday of Elvis Presley not all teenagers were into his music as many rock histories seem to imply.

In 1955 only one song, "Only You," broke into the coveted circle of the *Billboard* top 25 sellers from a minority taste category. The years 1956 through 1958, customarily described as the original rock and roll epic, exhibited more authentic black rhythm and blues although much of it was designed for a white audience. By 1959 the transmogrified product of the Philadelphia school and other pseudo rhythm and blues products joined the usual "easy-listening" fare on the *Billboard* charts. While Elvis Presley and "rock riots" attracted news headlines and parental attention, the youth culture was not in fact following suit en masse. In a sample of Chicago high school students conducted by James Coleman in 1958, 43.5 percent of the girls and 45.2 percent of the boys chose Pat Boone as their favorite singer. Elvis Presley placed third, behind Perry Como, gaining 21.5 of the boys and a surprising low 17.5 percent of the girls. Studies of taste, while more supportive of the rock *qua* pop notion, did not indicate uniform adolescent backing of the new sound.[10]

Exhibit 1.3

FAVORITE TYPES OF MUSIC—1957

	Boys	Girls
Rock and roll	51.6	48.1
Calypso	7.1	5.5
Other pop	17.5	17.5
Jazz	10.1	5.2
Classical	6.5	9.4
Country and western	6.3	3.8
No answer	0.8	0.5
	100.0	100.0
N	(4,020)	(4,134)

SOURCE: James Coleman, *Adolescent Society* (New York: The Free Press, 1961).

If this Chicago sample was representative of national tastes, it would appear that only half of the teenage market was then attuned to rock and roll as their favorite musical form. Another study undertaken during the same period, while not conclusive, did point to fragmentation of taste by peer-group influence and geographic propinquity, that is, neighborhood of residence. Even during the so-called golden years of rock, it is impossible to speak of a musically homogeneous taste culture.

Paul Hirsch and his associates, reporting from a national survey conducted in the winter of 1969, indicate that the "widespread hypothesis of homogeneity of music taste preferences among teenagers is untenable."[11] Their sample, conducted by the Opinion Research Corporation, found that 18 percent of the teenagers preferred "message" songs such as "War, What Is It Good For" and "Give Peace a Chance." They also included so-called drug songs in this category. The "square" category encompassing mood music, country and western and classical music polled 7 percent (N = 560). With the categories set as they are, it is arguable that the Top 40 classification was favored; nonetheless, this sample does suggest that what is popular does not in toto mirror the youth culture. A study of collegiates on the West Coast in the same year exhibited a parallel heterogeneity in musical preferences.

Measurements in the two studies were somewhat different. Hirsch and his colleagues labeled "square" to include jazz, classical and others. Soul and "old-style hits" are the same as categories two and three in Exhibit 1.4. Only "folk-rock" and message songs overlap, that is, much but not all of folk-rock can be listed as containing a "message," as they define it. On the other hand, so-called drug songs such as "Journey to the Center of the Mind" and "White Rabbit" are not connected to folk-rock.[12] While different, the two studies underline the heterogeneity of the youth market.

The 1970s have witnessed even a greater differentiation of musical tastes within the youth audience (see chapter 9). Pre-

Exhibit 1.4

MUSICAL PREFERENCES OF COLLEGIATES, WEST COAST—1969

Folk, Folk-Rock	Soul	Rock	Jazz	Classical	Other
236	121	172	79	128	85
.29	.15	.21	.10	.16	.10

N = 821

puberty girls continue to swoon over the current teen idol. Teenagers, three or four years older, have much different tastes, usually preferring hard rock or "heavy-metal" bands such as Mott the Hoople, Black Sabbath, Deep Purple, Uriah Heep or Grand Funk Railroad. People a few years older seem to fall into assorted taste groups. One group follows Alice Cooper, David Bowie, the New York Dolls and other seemingly "outrageous" "glitter-rock" acts. Others remain wedded to the quasi-folk-country balladeers such as Kris Kristofferson, John Denver, John Prine and Arlo Guthrie. Still others prefer the blues-rock material of Carole King, Leon Russell and a legion of imitators. Country music has made a significant dent in the pop music market. Fifty-one percent of singles released in 1973 were country and western products. Indeed, some record companies seem convinced that country and western music will become the dominant popular music style of the 1970s.

While young people and adolescents do not as a bloc prefer popular music, they remain its major consumers. There is little doubt that popular music is largely the property of every passing generation and its particular preferences. However, the popular music audience over the past 20 years has expanded considerably. This is largely a function of the character of the American population in 1975. Sixty million persons will be under the age of 25, a statistic which brings joy to the hearts and pocketbooks of record-company executives. The increase is also due to more over-25 adults staying with popular music. Despite this trend, popular music, especially those songs and acts supported by those under 25, is frequently the subject of generational conflict. While styles have changed over the years the points of contention have remained remarkably similar. Jitterbuggers, whose music in the 1930s was termed "syncopated savagery," three decades later would label rock as a destructive force in society.

TURN DOWN THAT NOISE! GENERATIONAL CONFLICT AND POPULAR MUSIC

Plato's often-cited admonition to the effect that "music corrupts youth" highlights the timeless quality of this generational struggle. It did not begin with Frank Sinatra, Elvis Presley, Mick Jagger or Alice Cooper. Only the degree and form of generational difference appears to have been altered. The folk culture featured its rhythms and play party songs and courtship ballads primarily directed to the young. Elders had their own bawdy and drinking songs. The advent of the printing press and the ensuant rise of the broadside ballad further dichotomized songs suitable for children and those designed for their parents. The coming of industrialization and professionalized songwriters and publishers somewhat diminished the age cleavage since Tin Pan Alley produced material suitable for all—men, women and children. Sociologists Richard Peterson and David Berger have characterized the so-called Tin Pan Alley era as both monolithic and Puritan in nature:

> Tin Pan Alley procedures emerged in the 1880's on the wave of a rising popular demand for sheet music to be played on the home piano, the newly fashionable adornment of middle-class living rooms. To be acceptable for this market, tunes and rhythms had to be kept simple and rigidly uniform. *What is more, lyrics could not offend Victorian sentimentalities*.[13]

In this period the more earthy or deviant elements in the music were confined to jazz and country or "hillbilly" music. Following World War I, some elements of jazz were blended in recordings, but this mixture rarely challenged middle-class conventions. As H. F. Mooney put it:

> Commercial orchestras of the period around 1920–50 followed more or less the "safe bet"—the aesthetic aspirations of the middle-class market—as did, indeed, most of the big Negro bands. They presented a music which despite solo variations emphasized precise, lush, ensemble harmony.[14]

The music of the depression era idealized the romantic love ethos of "June, spoon, moon," although some guardians of the public morality did object to a few songs from the Broadway stage such as "Love for Sale." Most popular songs were from the newly discovered "talkie" motion pictures and radio. The songs were traditional both in content and style, even in the heyday of the fox trot. One apt description said it was customarily "orchestrated like symphonic tone poems," such as "The Night If Filled With Love." The classics were injected into the fox trot formula with "Tonight We Love" (Tschaikovsky) and "Reverie" (Debussy). Big bands, such as Freddie Martin's, simply "jazzed up" other well-known symphonic themes with great success. It was all good, clean middle-class fare, stressing self-improvement, which adults, who in fact were the major consumers, and adolescents alike could enjoy. The two generational units, it seems, were not attuned to the same aspects of the music. The songs played by big bands were lyrically, in the main, innocent; the rhythms, however, generated considerable generational conflict.

As with the rock-a-billy phenomenon of the 1950s, swing was a hybrid of a black musical style, jazz, with a style middle-class whites would accept and purchase. It was also a musical form many adults perceived as "garbage," a sentiment their children often did not share. The deviant aspects of the music stemmed not from the lyrics but from the structure and the loudness of the riffs performed by Benny Goodman, Artie Shaw, the Dorseys and Jimmie Lunceford, and the dance steps enacted by teenagers to "swing." William Allen White of the America First Committee attacked swing as "blood raw emotion, without harmony, without consistent rhythm, and with no more tune than the yearnful bellowing of a lonely, yearning and romantic cow in the pastures or the raucous staccatic meditation of a bulldog barking in a barrel."[15] A Barnard College professor termed the dance music "musical Hitlerism."[16]

The second objection went beyond the realm of musical taste or propriety into that of morality in the framework of the Puritan fathers. More than the music, the dance, given its physical nature, was subjected to attack. At one time the Spanish throne prohibited the waltz for several centuries due to its supposedly "immoral" requirement that males and females actually touch. Centuries later the moral entrepreneurs of the 1930s viewed the fox trot and especially the jitterbug in a similar light. According to Frank Zappa: "Our story [evolution of rock] begins in . . . the good old days, at the recreation centers, no levis or capris please. . . . The kids would be holding onto each other desperately and sweating. The chaperon would come along and say 'Seven inches apart, please,' and hold a sawed-off ruler between you and the girl."[17] Jitterbugging in the aisles of the Paramount Theater, or indeed, at Benny Goodman's Carnegie Hall appearances were indicted in the press as riotous behavior and roundly condemned by clergy, teachers and parents. The focus of the condemnation was the time-worn symbolic figure—the fiddler. Throughout Puritan demonology, the fiddler has been portrayed as a tool of Ole Lucifer. In 1938, it was the "jitterbugger" who was performing the latest version of St. Vitus's dance while the Devil fiddled. Satan, in this instance, took the unlikely form of Benny Goodman and the countless other big band leaders who paced the dances with riffs, interludes and exhilarated from solos. Critic George Simon related the interaction between band and audience:

> There's nothing to match it today. The whining electrified guitars and the flabby-sounding electronic basses of the sixties have power, all right—they can virtually steam-roller you. But hearing big bands in person was completely different . . . they lifted you high in the air with them, filling you with an exhilarated sense of friendly well-being; you joined them, emotionally and musically, as partners in one of the happiest, most thrilling rapports ever established between the givers and takers of music.

The bandleader was not alone in the disapprobation of segments of the adult world. The bobby-sox idol or the boy band vocalist was yet another target. Simon in comparing the singers of the swing period to rock stars, recalls: "The hysteria that greeted boy singers during the forties almost matched that spewed on the vocal groups of the sixties. Mobs would wait for them outside stage doors. In the theaters they'd howl and scream—perhaps not as blatantly as the kids in the sixties did in the presence of their idols."[18] It must be remembered that the worried parent of the late 1930s did not have the comfort of historical comparison to quell his fears. In a delightful twist of irony the Tommy Dorsey band named its singing quartet the Pied Pipers. At one time it featured Frank Sinatra, who was later to become the symbol of the idolatry of the swing era. With swing the generational cleavage was established: "for the first time in American history teenagers were very much a social reality."[19]

World War II solidified this esthetic gap, leaving the adolescents on the home front as separate entities without young adults to serve as role models and with increasing buying power. Jitterbugs, bobby soxers and Victory Girls were all identifiable generational units within the American populace.

The war years found radio a central source of immediate battle information and propaganda. Kate Smith and Gene Krupa, Bing Crosby and Frank Sinatra all appeared on broadcast marathons to heighten support for the Allies and to sell war bonds. Appeals by Sinatra and other teenage favorites were directly aimed at this age group. The tag "youth listening" began to appear in newspaper radio logs. One study undertaken during this time reported that "the pleasure of 72 percent of radio listeners under 30 in popular music is shared by only 22 percent of those over 50 years of age." Conversely, one observer reported, " 'Old, familiar music' is more popular with older listeners."[20] While the nation was united in common cause, generational differences along cultural and esthetic lines continued to increase.

The music of the postwar era was a retreat from the big-band era into the sentimentality of the ballad and the baritone crooner. Swing had, through the war years, become too complicated and "difficult to dance to!" The costs of studio recording and of maintaining a traveling band became prohibitive. By 1947 most of the "big-name" bands had been dismantled. Some bands continued but the world was, in jazz writer George Simon's words, becoming the "property of a group of their most illustrious graduates—the singers."[21]

Following the war, popular music reflected what appeared to be an intragenerational appeal. In the late forties most of the top sellers were either studio bands or crooners. By 1950 the singers clearly dominated the charts. The *Billboard* top sellers of 1950 found 21 groups or individual song stylists in firm control of the chart. The remainder were either instrumentals or novelties. The Weavers' watered-down versions of folksongs, "Goodnight Irene" and "Tzena, Tzena, Tzena" and Red Foley's swing version of "Chattanoogie Shoe Shine Boy" were the only songs from a nonpopular base. Their swinglike arrangements made them totally suitable for the pop market. As reported by *Billboard* the top ten singles of the early 1950s, a form predominantly directed to adolescents, found few songs not in the quasi-operatic style of the "number-one songs." Only novelties such as Jimmy Boyd's "I Saw Mommy Kissing Santa Claus," "Doggie In the Window," "St. George and the Dragonet," "The Thing" and several others broke the increasing monopoly of ex-band vocalists like Joni James, Eddie Fisher, Perry Como, Tony Martin and Patti

Page. The television show "Your Hit Parade" highlighted these years with four ex-band singers—Dorothy Collins, Gisele MacKenzie, Russell Arms and Snooky Lanson—taking turns singing, after the drum roll, "the song that's Number One all over America!" The inability of this show to cope with rock in time drove it from the nation's television screens.

For many an adult, the popularization of rock and roll symbolized "overt rebellion," as did movies such as *Rebel Without a Cause* and *The Wild One*. Yet, interestingly, neither used rock music in any manner. Teenagers accepted the new genre as a symbol of their "new" status. According to Frank Zappa: "I didn't care if Bill Haley was white or sincere . . . he was playing the Teenage National Anthem and it was so LOUD I was jumping up and down. *Blackboard Jungle* . . . represented a strange sort of 'endorsement' of the teenage cause: 'They have made a movie [*Blackboard Jungle*] about us, therefore, we exist.' "[22] Zappa's concluding phrase is taken from Camus's brilliant essay *The Rebel,* which in the original read "I rebel—therefore we exist." Rock and roll, its Negro and country origins notwithstanding, was placed within the context of juvenile delinquency and "bopping gangs" which had attracted headlines in Los Angeles and New York.

"Rock Around the Clock" was the theme from *Blackboard Jungle*, a movie depicting the struggles of a teacher in an urban ghetto school. The transposed Evan Hunter novel was a classic statement of generational and social conflict—disrespect for tradition, authority and learning—all values in especially high regard during the Eisenhower years. In the film, even the musical tastes of the older generation are not spared. Richard Kiley, as a teacher in the ghetto school, makes several futile attempts to reach his rowdy charges. One involved introducing his valuable collection of jazz and swing 78s' to his students. Placing Bunny Berigan's "I Can't Get Started With You" on the phonograph, he explains the esthetic of jazz. The students listen for a moment, then overpower the instructor and proceed to destroy his entire collection. The theme "Rock Around the Clock" interdicts, underlining the rejection. As with the jitterbuggers and jazz fans, rock became the nexus of generational conflict, one that was eventually reified into struggle over the playing of the music itself.

Elvis Presley was the personification of evil for those who saw rock as "inflaming youth." Unlike Haley, who was somewhat overweight and looked like everyone's "older brother," Presley epitomized the "bike hero." David Riesman presented the dynamic singer as generating a "a definitely 'anti-parent' outlook. His music—and he, himself—appeared somewhat insolent, slightly hoodlum."[23] The long sideburns, ducktail haircut, black slacks and pink sports jackets were accentuated by the defiant curled upper lip and motorcycle. The overt sexuality of the singer's early television appearances only compounded his image as "child corrupter." Jack Gould, television critic of the *New York Times*, warned: "When Presley executes his bumps and grinds, it must be remembered by the Columbia Broadcasting System that even the twelve-year-old's . . . [sexual] . . . curiosity may be overstimulated." *Billboard* writer Arnold Shaw recalled:

> Presley's impact was troubling to adults because his influence seemed more nonmusical than musical. . . . The intensity of teenage reaction suggested that youngsters were responding to him for deeper psychological, emotional and social reasons. To them, he was in fact the first rock symbol of teenage rebellion—made so in part by adults because they did not like him, and condemned him as depraved. Anti-Negro prejudice doubtless figured in adult antagonism. Regardless of whether parents were aware of the Negro sexual origins of the phrase "rock 'n' roll", Presley impressed them as the visual and aural embodiment of sex.[24]

Various campaigns and polemics were directed at the rock-a-billy star. One district attorney is quoted as saying, "Rock and roll gives young hoodlums an excuse to get together. It inflames teenagers and is obscenely suggestive." Evangelist Billy Graham, when asked about the singer, expressed an opinion widely held: "From what I've heard, I'm not so sure

I'd want my children to see him." Listening to the songs popularized by Elvis or many of the other rockers climbing the charts was another matter; the pop lyrics of the 1950s were usually innocent as the driven snow.

Donald Horton's (1957) content analysis of popular song lyrics of 1955, taken from fan magazines such as *Hit Parade, Song Hits*, *Country Song Roundup* and *Rhythm and Blues*, suggests the conflict was more symbolic than real.[25] Horton found that 83 percent of the lyrics in these song magazines dealt with boy-girl relationships. Of these, 39 percent address the traditional courtship theme, 9 percent the honeymoon, 17 percent the disintegration of the relationship and 30 percent the "loneliness" syndrome. Lyrically, this is not far removed from the sentimental ballads and torch songs of the previous generations. They were, as Greg Shaw, editor of *Who Put the Bomp*, quickly observes, more intense, emotionally direct and aimed at the teenager as lover. Even the lyrics of the much-maligned Presley songs were simply reflective of the "boy meets/loses girl" syndrome.[26] Only his early Sun label covers such as "Milk Cow Blues Boogie" and "Baby, Let's Play House" evidenced verbal sentiments mirroring his "provocative" stage presence, and none of these was a hit. The late Gene Vincent, a Presley imitator, included the controversial Anglo-Saxonism in "Women Love," the flip side to his only great hit, "Be Bop A Lula." Still, the lyrics of the 1950s in the pop market rarely transcended the values of romantic love so popular in the dominant American society.

The significance of the emergence of rock and roll and Elvis as a "superstar" in the 1950s was fundamentally one of perspective and focus. The generational-esthetic cleavage, as Frank Zappa's paraphrase of Camus indicates, was solidified both by the condemnations of adults and the basic ineptitude of segments of the music industry and Tin Pan Alley. Statements such as "I know it's only a phase" or Frank Sinatra's portrayal of rock as "a rancid-smelling aphrodisiac" all were proven wrong. Riesman's "minority" of the crooner years, in time seemed to become the majority—even for Mitch Miller.

Popular music—whatever it was—was "for the youngsters," to use Sullivan's tired introduction.

The conscription of Elvis Presley into the military and his ensuant image change from hoodlum to G.I., coupled with the advent of "American Bandstand," defused much of the hostility to rock and roll. Dick Clark and his coterie of Philadelphia teenagers did little to offend adults.

The payola controversy provided a forum for several congressmen and industry personnel who disliked rock and roll, but it had little to do with teenagers' musical tastes (see chapter 5 on the payola hearings). The morality of Dick Clark, Alan Freed and a host of other deejays was the issue. Some critics did maintain that rock and roll had bought its way into the hearts of America's teenagers, but very few fans took this accusation seriously. *Billboard* replied to the allegation: "The cancer of payola cannot be pinned on rock and roll. Payola was rampant in the music business during the vaudeville era of the 1920's." This editorial went on to cite the generational aspect of the charge, indicating that the accusers were those who "sigh for the good old days, blame their plight on rock and roll, and construe that rock and roll is an outgrowth of payola."[27] Most of the industry concurred and the hearings did not curtail the number of rock records being released. The rise of Chubby Checker and other go-go singers found adults joining teenagers in gyrating to the "twist," the "swim," the "frug" and other variations on that theme.

Beatlemania, prior to John Lennon's "more popular than Christ" remark, was received by adults as a continuation of the Davy Crockett and hula-hoop crazes. Signs saying "Stamp Out the Beatles" and "Bach Not Beatles" were more in fun than in protest. "I Want to Hold Your Hand" or "I'm Happy Just to Dance" certainly lacked any of the threat or sensuousness of Elvis "The Pelvis" or the black rhythm and blues artists of the 1950s. David Riesman compared the Beatles to Elvis, observing:

> My impression is that the Beatles have none of this somewhat sinister quality that Presley represented for adults. They don't have the quasi-sexual, quasi-aggressive note that was present in Presley . . . it's very safe for a young girl to admire these Englishmen. Then, too, there are four of them, and there's safety in numbers.

The sociologist concluded this interview on the prophetic note saying. "If I were the Beatles' press agent, I'd work to have ministers and professors and the press all saying, 'Oh dear!' "[28] With the advent of the "Jesus remark" and *Sgt. Pepper* they would indeed say this, but in 1964 even the radical Right, to be discussed later, generally ignored the Beatles. One English psychologist concluded a clinical report expressing a prevailing attitude toward the Liverpool four: " 'Beatlemania' is the passing reaction of predominantly young adolescent females to group pressures of such a kind that meet their special emotional needs."[29]

Only the association of rock and roll with the flowerchild phenomenon and the hippie movement revived outcries of "brainwashing" and "corruption." Much of this attack was ideologically inspired and a continuation of the Right's thesis that popular music was subverting the flower of American youth for an expected Kremlin takeover. The charge that song lyrics were on open invitation to "turn on, tune in and drop out," attracted more support. Sunday supplements ran headlines announcing "Songs Have a Double Meaning." Nearly all of these articles focused upon two or three obvious examples and a number of songs open to various interpretations. The Byrds' "Eight Miles High" was reported to mean "high on LSD." Bob Dylan's "Mr. Tambourine Man" was characterized as "describing a dope pusher and a drug-induced dream."[30] The Association's "Along Comes Mary" and other songs invoking the name Mary were linked to marijuana. Later songs such as the Jefferson Airplane's famous "White Rabbit" were cited to support the pop-as-advocate hypothesis. The Beatles' album *Sgt. Pepper* sparked considerable controversy after a *New York Times* reviewer decided that "Lucy in the Sky with Diamonds" meant the acronym LSD. Some segments of American society took these allegations seriously, harassing radio stations not to play "drug-oriented" songs. The bedroom community sample from British Columbia taken in 1969 indicates that the largest portion of both adolescents and their parents found popular music to be addressed to romantic love themes and love for humanity. A smaller percentage believed songs were topical and concerned with social protest.

Exhibit 1.5

INTERPRETATIONS OF THE MEANING OF POPULAR SONGS—1969

	Adolescents	Parents
Love theme	35.9 %	27.6 %
Topical-protest	20.3 %	11.7 %
All of these	21.5 %	5.3 %
	(N = 389)	(N = 94)

Ironically, not one adult in the entire sample felt that the basic theme of popular music was drug-oriented, despite a deep concern in the community over this issue. Fourteen (3.6%) of the teenagers, however, did feel that pop was advocating drug use. This clearly was not a major bone of controversy between generations.

A portion of the popular music of the 1960s can best be labeled punk-rock, sometimes termed shock-rock. Its lyrics are not terribly profound or protest oriented. The music is simple and loud. It is primarily a visual form. Punk-rock challenged the norms of social etiquette. Performers appear to be championing those aspects of life which society considers perverse, deviant and grotesque. Violence, homosexuality, transvestism and infanticide all may be props in the act.

Rolling Stone Mick Jagger probably originated punk-rock; he pranced about a stage assuming various poses and making seemingly "obscene" gestures. Iggy and the Stooges expanded on Jagger's stage presence. Iggy would mimic sodomy with his microphone then leap into the audience, taunt, shout and challenge the spectators. Writers labeled this punk-rock, since it expressed social defiance in the most unsophisticated manner. One critic described it as embodying "the essence of a street gang."[31] It was giving society "the finger." In the context of the late 1960s, Iggy's act seemed to be "political." Critics merely assumed he was "putting down the system" in the usual Detroit MC 5 manner. He wasn't as intellectual as either the Mothers of Invention or the Fugs. But Iggy gained little popularity outside of the Motor City area; the youth audience was not yet ready for shock-rock right on the heels of the 1967 Summer of Love and the Woodstock Festival.

Alice Cooper, an all-male band, popularized the glitter version of punk-rock. Some people stumbled into Alice Cooper thinking "she" was a folk singer with a repertoire of Child ballads. What they found instead was a band in homosexual drag. The music they played was high volume and unsophisticated. One patron leaving a Los Angeles night club told Ben Edmonds, "I've never seen anything like it. The very thought of it is enough to make me *vomit*. Alice Cooper . . . I thought it was gonna be like Judy Collins or something. It was the most revolting thing I've ever seen. You shoulda been there. . . ."[32] Revulsion became Alice Cooper's ticket to pop-music fame. Kinky sex and violence became important parts of the band's act. *New York Times* and *Billboard* critic Ian Dove describes a typical Cooper concert:

> Alice Cooper went about cutting up mannekins, impaling babies, being laser-beamed (with James Bond film music in the background), being caught in a strobe-lit gang fight (shades of

> "Clockwork Orange"), singing to a boa constrictor, being guillotined (hardly a far, far better thing for the audience), wielding a 6-foot toothbrush and only in America—sending off stage for a couple of beers.

In 1970 Alice Cooper's single "Eighteen" became an instant hit on CKLW, a 50,000 watt Canadian outlet which also serves as Detroit's favorite popular music station. Going to see Alice became the thing to do. Several other acts either imitated or did variations on the Alice Cooper gimmick. A lesser-known veteran English rock artist, David Bowie, was repackaged by RCA Victor as a bisexual. A *Rolling Stone* writer labeled him "a brittle powdered flake of hermaphroditic humanity."[34] On stage Bowie continued Iggy's practice of simulated homosexual acts, this time with members of the band. After a major and expensive promotion campaign stressing Bowie's "deviance," a successful American tour was launched. The latest version of "punkitude" is the New York Dolls. They have been called "transsexual junkies" whose songs talk about violence in the subways, drugs, sex and various forms of "thrill seeking." They wear lipstick, black leather, pantyhose, drag outfits and wigs. Their theme is "ultradecadence."

Punk-rock has many meanings. As Arthur Kaye of the Dolls suggests, "People have the wrong idea about us. They think we're a bunch of transsexual junkies or something."[35] Some people see them as merely gay liberationists flounting the "straight" world. For some music fans they are merely a good rock band in the Rolling Stones tradition.

Outside of its natural habitat of the concert hall or club, punk-rock has encountered some opposition. Alice Cooper's appearance on the first "In Concert" found Lawrence H. Rogers II, president of Taft Broadcasting, calling his Cincinnati television station, after watching Alice for 15 minutes, and ordering the show off the air. Alice was replaced by an old episode of "Rawhide." A Philadelphia station postponed "In Concert" until 1:30 A.M. WPVI-TV explained their action as making sure "not too many kiddies would be watching the

Alice Cooper rock program."[36] Nielson figures indicated that while the show got excellent ratings its audience was primarily under the magic age of 24. WABC-TV Vice-President Bob Shanks complained to *Billboard*. "We must attract more than our target audience of serious rock fans in order to keep this show on the air. The hope here is that good rock has become acceptable to television viewers outside of the 1930 age range."[37]

The reason for adult indifference to much of the shock-rock genre may simply be lack of exposure. Most parents, and the traditional guardians of public morality, are generally unaware of the phenomenon. It is only on exhibition at concerts. Indeed, when asked about Alice Cooper, Black Sabbath and other punk-rock bands not one member of the audience at a Popular Culture Association meeting in 1972 had heard of these acts. If this totally unrepresentative sample of people interested in popular music is any indication, punk-rock remains a mystery to most people over 24. Considering the material and the stage acts of many shock-rock bands, only ignorance can explain the lack of moral indignation leveled at Alice, Bowie and the Dolls.

Numerous studies of generational conflict and popular music have found that it is caused by misinterpretation and lack of understanding rather than actual threat. Interest in popular music is customarily one of the first independent steps taken by a child. The first major purchase for many little girls is a record by the current "fave" idol. The taste preferences of teenagers are their own, not their parents'. Young people in the main view "their music" as just fun—"you can dance to it"—while adults may, as did Plato, impune more sinister motives.

Popular music is fundamentally an idiom of the young but it is not monolithically standard with all young people. Segments of the youth audience exhibit differing tastes and preferences. Only when these preferences coalesce can we say that a song is popular. The merging of these diverse tastes and preferences is in part that magical process which makes a song a "hit" rather than a "miss" or a "stiff," as unsuccessful records are called.

WHAT IS POPULAR MUSIC? A DEFINITION

A frustrated moviegoer, after standing in line for nearly an hour, glared at the sign of the box-office window reading. "Popular Prices—Admission $5.00," cursed and muttered, "popular with who?" and left. The retort is fairly simple, of course: "popular with the management." So it is with music. Record sales, taste cultures and social differences in musical preferences suggest "popular" is a term which enjoys currency with those who produce and manufacture records and in the everyday vernacular, but is difficult to locate in the real world.

There are few definitions of popular music of any substance. Most writers join with Carl Belz in the sentiment that "any listener who wants rock [a segment of the pop of the sixties] defined specifically is probably unable to recognize it."[38] There is, of course, truth in this statement, but experience alone does not help clarify the maze called "popular music." British writer Richard Mabey outlines popular music as being "concerned with participation, with parties, dances, outings, demonstrations and any other social gatherings where camaraderie and simple shared emotions are important. . . . The music, in fact, acts as a further binding force on the group, and the observed responses of the other members are a way of clarifying your own."[39] Popular music, therefore, is a cultural artifact shared by specific subgroups in the social order. Music may represent the taste of a subculture within a culture or that of a "contraculture" which exists in opposition to the dominant one. Jazz is a subcultural genre, while so-called punk-rock is perhaps indicative of Theodore Roszak's "counterculture." Mabey distinguishes pop music as a "subdivision" of popular, in that it operates as a mode of communication to "satisfy teenage tastes." This refinement has considerable merit as popular music does contain a number of sounds and styles which do not appeal solely to teenagers. Still, persons under the demographic cut-off point of 24 comprise the major constituency for popular music. So popular music is not "pop" but many parts of "pop" are found in popular music.

Ray Browne of the Center for the Study of Popular Culture, while not directly concerned with music, adds another element to clarifying the nature of its popular manifestation. Browne argues that "popularity" comprises "all those elements of life which are not narrowly intellectual or creatively elitist and which are generally though not necessarily disseminated through the mass media."[40] In the field of popular music this is especially true, since media exposure is imperative. A cardinal tenet in the record industry is the necessity for "radio play" or "exposure." Browne's definition also transcends the specialty areas and suggests a differentiation between the exoteric and esoteric, majority and minority and large and small taste groups. Popular music is exoteric, supported by a large majority of record buyers.

The exoteric unit is by its very nature large and highly unstable both in taste and artistic personnel. The esoteric is customarily, though not always, small, stable and relatively homogeneous. The jazz market, while containing many subgenres, is a specialty field with an identifiable audience and record companies, concert promoters and clubs service. Entrepreneurs have definite expectations in respect to this audience. Few jazz acts sell over 100,000 records. Errol Garner's *Concert By the Sea* and Dave Brubeck's *Take Five* were pleasant surprises. Consumers of classical, romantic and modern symphonic music equally constitute an esoteric taste unit, which responds in a relatively predictable manner.

Characteristic of esoteric genres is the homogeneity of consumers and their loyalty to specific artists and styles. Records on the country-music charts at one time remained there much longer than their Top 40 counterparts. Country-music performers have also exhibited a durability and stayingpower rare in popular music stars. Ernest Tubb, Hank Snow, Eddy Arnold and Bill Monroe are but a few of many artists with a firm faithful following. Jazz performers, at least those that are considered stars, also command a following for many decades. The classics are an even more stable market.

The larger the esoteric taste group the less stability and predictability. In years past, country and western and so-called race music was aimed directly at specific audiences defined by geography and race. For many years country music was distributed only in the southern states. "Race" records were generally confined to the same geographical area as well as stores in urban ghettos outside of the South.

The out-migration of white southerners and the growth in the black urban population expanded the audience for both genres. Therefore, while country and soul music remain esoteric styles they appeal to relatively large numbers of people and also supply records which cross over the Top 40 charts.

Middle-of-the-road records are the ultimate extension of an esoteric genre tied to sex and age factors. MOR is predominantly the taste preference of married women over the age of 24. This music, which stresses nostalgia and styles of the recent past, frequently enters the popular music arena simply because tastes of many women in this category are not far removed from the dominant youth market. A number of artists are capable of appealing to both the MOR and college audiences. John Denver, James Taylor, Andy Williams and the Carpenters are but a few examples. The larger the esoteric public the more chance of its tastes entering into the exoteric world of popular music.

Being exoteric, the producer of popular music must address a generally amorphous, fluid, heterogeneous and unpredictable collectivity of people. Popular music is in fact an idiom designed to cut across a number of taste cultures predicated upon age, education, class, geography and race. Loyalties here are fickle. Consumer demand is difficult to measure because of the varied interests of those comprising the audience. Yet popular music remains popular, even if its internal parts change, as they frequently do. Some esoteric genres become exoteric or popular and then return to their previous status. Sociologists Rolf Meyersohn and Elihu Katz report: "Every few months a new 'content' in the form of new hits flows through the same network of distributors (disk jockeys, etc.) and consumers (primarily teenagers and other radio audiences), while an occasional song may attract some distributors or consumers who are not regularly a part of the system.[41] Esoteric elements may enter popular music such as "Amazing Grace," "Take Five," "Moritat" or "Duelin' Banjoes.' " However, they generally must take second place to the style of the period. The popular-music idiom, as a structure, remains the same with industry, promoters, cultural gatekeepers and distributors producing a "continuous cycle of discontinuous hits."

The discontinuity of popular music is an important element in its makeup vis-à-vis age. The songs and artists preferred by the so-called bubblebummers and teenyboppers change nearly every two years. Heroes of the pubescent set have ranged from Fabian, Frankie Avalon and Mark Lindsay to Donny Osmond. Chuck Laufer, editor of numerous teenage magazines and the proprietor of the Partridge Family Fan Club, observed. "There *has* to be teenage idols, but the girls outgrow them. When they're 11 to 14, they can have a nice, safe love affair with somebody like Davy Jones, Bobby Sherman or David Cassidy. By the time they're 16 they're having dates and they don't need them anymore."[42]

At this level musical tastes are generally established. People outgrow an idol, but not the style. The screaming girls who discovered Elvis Presley stuck with the rock-a-billy style through 1958 when their hero and his imitators disappeared from the scene. The abandoned fans did not flock to Dick Clark's army of pretty teenage vocalists. Consequently, a popular-music fan is generally wedded to a specific style current in the idiom in his adolescence. As time progresses, taste publics loyal to a specific popular-music form proliferate—to the point that within any two decades a vast number of rock fans can be identified. Yet there is a vast difference between them. Only a few years can separate musical style preferences. A nine-year-old may "like" her idol. A twelve-year-old detests the idol and prefers a punk-rock band. Collegiates have more esoteric musical preferences than secondary-school students. The success of many so-called easy-listening formula stations which feature stylized versions of current youth-market hits and "oldies but goodies" further suggest that some carryover from adolescent tastes occurs. Older people tend to prefer more traditional genres or none at all. People who were teenagers in the days of Glenn Miller still like crooners in the swing genre. Older blacks have been reported to have tastes different from their soul-oriented adolescents.[43] Older country-music buffs attend fiddle conventions and mock the mod musicians from Nashville. Those people who do maintain a strong interest in any form of music after their courtship days are statistically unusual. If they do, the preference is usually more likely to be in an esoteric style than in an exoteric one. People in their sixties, seventies and older, for example, remain ardent country and western fans.

While age remains the crucial factor in popular music tastes, other social characteristics also have an effect. Sex and marital status complement age. Social class may be important. Paul Hirsch observed that the sons and daughters of upper-class and lower-class parents exhibit more unique musical tastes than those in the middle.[44] Geography further complicates the situation. Polka fans are more likely to reside in Minnesota and Wisconsin than in New York City or Tennessee. Race has a great deal to do with musical preferences and record-buying habits. A composite of black and Latin music tastes would find a strong commitment in soul and ethnic material. Even in their early twenties, blacks buy more singles than whites, who predominatly favor albums after 16. Age is certainly the most important factor determining a person's allegiance to music. Race and geography further complicate the identification of taste units. These three factors help determine esoteric and exoteric taste groups and establish the individual's relationship to popular music. Some taste units are totally divorced from the Top 40 sound. Others, to their peril, do contribute to the *Billboard* Hot 100.

An esoteric genre that enters the popular-music arena must satisfy the demands of an exoteric audience while remaining unique to its original supporters. Its failure to accomplish the latter may lose its supporters. "Rhythm and blues," for example, was far from new before it was "popularized" in the 1950s "Race" records had long been produced by promoters for consumption by a black audience. In 1955, portions of this minority taste unit entered the majority world of the Hot 100. The envelopment of rhythm and blues by the pop market, in turn, watered down the original product creating a vacuum into which a quasi-gospel sound labeled Motown and soul would enter.

The hootenanny craze and the folk-music revival followed a remarkably similar pattern. In the urban areas from the 1930s to the Kingston Trio in the 1950s folk music was an esoteric form generally catering to folklorists and some Marxist sympathizers who interpreted the genre as a "cry for justice." *Sing Out*! magazine and recording companies such as Disc and Folkways serviced this small group during the 1950s. The soaring success of "Tom Dooley" changed the status of the music as well as its audience. The revival lasted approximately six years, undergoing two phases, and finally was overwhelmed by the invasion of rock music. The excess of the revival in turn had so transformed the genre itself that many original supporters were driven to an entirely different esoteric "blue-grass" medium.

Although it is a minority or small portion of the total music audience, an esoteric taste unit is in fact a "fashion feeder"; it attempts to preserve its genre while remaining part of the crazy-quilt pattern of popular music. Rhythm-and-blues stations continued to broadcast "purist" material while many of their artists were being coopted into the white market. As some of the stars left, others with different sounds took their place. The Platters were replaced by the Supremes, and Smokey Robinson and the Shirelles displaced the Five Satins and a multitude of other "street" groups. Folkniks, during the revival, generally disdained the revivalists and continued to collect Carter Family records and make "knowing" allusions to old-time country pickers such as the Stanley Brothers or the political folk group the Almanac Singers. Bob Dylan, however, lured many of the politically oriented into the revival and then left them empty handed in 1965. Still, while popular music feeds from and contains esoteric genres, they also have an existence independent of popular music.

Meyersohn and Katz, when discussing the "fashion-feeder" aspect of esoteric genres, also maintain the tenure of each in the exoteric or popular sphere is transitory. One genre in capricious manner replaces another. A genre never totally dominates the best-selling or most-played charts in purist form. The first rock era (1955–58) found nonrock selections placing number one. "Cherry Pink and Apple Blossom White" (1955), "Singing The Blues" (1956), "Love Letters In The Sand" (1957) and "It's All in The Game" (1958) were the top singles. During the second era of rock, English groups dominated the top position with "Satisfaction," "To Sir With Love" and "Hey Jude." The Monkees' "I'm A Believer" pushed the British "invaders" into second place in 1966. The rock revival (1964–68) was not a musically similar phenomenon. The basic rock instrumentation was wedded with numerous esoteric genres creating "hyphen-rock" such as folk-rock, jazz-rock, sympho-rock, ad infinitum. Once the genre experimentation had been exhausted rock moved increasingly into the visual arena. Arthur Brown with his "Flaming World" of pyrotechnics, hoists, masks and eccentric costumes began what has been titled glitter. Other acts followed suit, donning snakes, lipstick, and paroding homosexuality. Fads come and go; some, very few, develop into a trend.

The existence of these diverse genres and taste cultures makes popular music unpredictable, since every record must be directed to a taste culture sufficiently large to promise a profit on the record. In a homogeneous taste culture such a return is relatively safe; however, a popular song must appeal to the parent taste culture as well as others. For example, the Blind Lemon Jefferson classic "Matchbox" was originally recorded for a black rural audience. Another version retitled "Little Wheel" by John Lee Hooker in the 1950s was directed at blacks living in cities. The Carl Perkin's Sun label adaptation of the same song was a rock-a-billy piece aimed at the youth and country-and-western market. The Beatles' Mersey interpretation of the rock version transcended all of these boundaries, thus assuring its popular success. It may not be coincidental that the few superstars such as Elvis Presley, the Beatles, the Rolling Stones, and Chicago all introduced hybrid musical forms which attracted a number of diverse musical subtastes. Indeed, the operational definition of a superstar may well hinge on his ability to cross over or to place on other charts besides the Top 40. The ability to transcend genres is a major determinant of popular-music success. Most popular singers in the esoteric sphere travel the road from success in one genre to the nebulous arena of middle-media in an attempt to maximize their exposure and in the process disassociate themselves from their roots. The Platters, Diana Ross, Roberta Flack and Glen Campbell are but a few examples. Campbell's trek from being a country singer and studio-guitar musician to that of a song stylist assured the success of his national television show. Johnny Cash, whose forte was more country than most popular music fans could take, failed dismally when he attempted a similar transition. Cash's style was too "purist" to hold the attention of a popular audience for long. His attempt to do "citified" or "uptown" material only alienated his original constituency.

The success of a given taste or style ultimately is determined by its popular acceptance in other taste clusters. Success depends on either attracting support from a small number of large taste units or by eliciting support from a large portion of small groups. A single, such as "I Think I

Love You" by the Partridge Family, by appealing to a significantly large portion of the "bubblegum" audience, is an immediate success. The Monkees, with a regular television series, commanded an equally large segment of the same group. The size of Elvis Presley's fan clubs and followers still guarantees that all of his records will near the million-seller figure. Lesser-known and more esoteric artists are not afforded this cushion. Joan Baez's version of "The Night They Drove Ole Dixie Down" relied upon a much larger number of groups such as underground, country and folk, to finally make the Top 40 play list. The problem for record-company executives is precisely how these combinations operate. The comments of an industry advertising executive sum up the dilemma:

> To be in the rock 'n' roll record business today, you've got to be a "total-crap-shooter" with a good instinct for money management. You've got to have enormous faith in your A&R people and your own ear. . . . You'll have a better shot playing black jack in Las Vegas with a stake of $10,000 using the house rules and an arithmetical progression money system.[45]

In 1972, Amos Heilicher, an important record retailer and rack jobber, commented that this chance factor was declining while picking a hit was becoming more complex. "At one time, 80 percent of our volume was done from 20 percent of our inventory. Now it's done from 35 to 40 percent of the product we carry."[46] In the same year, the Warner/Reprise bulletin *Circular* ran a headline announcing "This Time the Big Trend Is No Trend." Passing years have not contradicted the announcement. Considering the ever-expanding pop music audience some observers feel that no one trend will take over the charts.

The music industry is not quite as subject to Adam Smith's "invisible hand" as they would have others believe; nonetheless the formula for a hit popular record remains elusive. Yet this element more than others distinguishes popular music from its nonentertainment sister conglomerates and also from the specialty labels who by and large know what their audiences want—at least most of the time. The very nature of popular music is dynamic change and all that it implies; however, it should be kept in mind that while parts of popular music are transformed, other properties remain relatively unchanged. The industry itself has not greatly changed over the years. Promoters, disk jockeys, critics and other functionaries are not as fluid as the music and the artists.

Popular music is a whole that is different from the sum of its many diverse, static and dynamic parts. Keeping this in mind, we can attempt a loose definition of popular music. *Popular music is the sum total of those taste units, social groups and musical genres which coalesce along certain taste and preference similarities in a given space and time.* These taste publics and genres are affected by a number of factors, predominantly age, accessibility, race, class and education. As such the designation of popular music is more a sociological than a musical definition. People select what they like from what they hear. The reasons for this selection are influenced by many factors some of which have little to do with the esthetic quality of a song or instrumental piece.

Record companies, much to their dismay, must orchestrate this demographic cacophony in order to earn a profit. Unlike the classics, country music or jazz, the record company must deal with a mosaic of dissimilar genres and taste and age groupings. Kal Rudman's statement, "it is easier to get a bill through Congress than a record on the *Billboard* chart," is a correct assessment.

The following pages trace, beginning with the artist, the life cycle of a record from the studio until it reaches the "folks out there." The path of the artist through the record-company bureaucracy is hazardous. Few artists ever successfully traverse the obstacle course and achieve a hit record. Mere possession of talent hardly dictates success for a guitar picker, singer or a band. The manager, producer, company, distributor, merchandiser and the media also play roles in the scenario of a hit record or the success of an artist. In the best Horatio Alger tradition, it all begins with stage struck performers who in acting out their dreams of stardom become another Elvis Presley, John Lennon or Janis Joplin.

Notes, Chapter 1

1. S. I. Hayakawa, "Popular Songs vs. The Facts of Life," in Bernard Rosenberg and David Manning White, eds., *Mass Culture: The Popular Arts in America* (New York: Free Press, 1957), p. 393.
2. Murray Ross, "The Record Business: What Makes It Run," *Record World*, July 24, 1971, p. 230.
3. Henry Brief quoted in "$2 Billion Worth of Noise," *Forbes*, July 15, 1968, p. 26.
4. Ernest Dunbar, "Music Is Where the Money Is," *Look*, August 25, 1971, p. 13.
5. Jann Wenner, "The Record Company Executive Thing," *Rolling Stone* 86 (July 8, 1971): 34.
6. David Riesman, "Listening to Popular Music," in Rosenberg and White, eds., *Mass Culture*, p. 411.
7. Ibid., p. 412.
8. Charles Gillett; *The Sound of the City* (New York: Outerbridge and Dienstfrey, 1969), p. 10. See Howard Junker, "Ah, The Unsung Glories of Pre-Rock," *Rolling Stone* 72 (December 1, 1970): 46–47.
9. Frank Zappa, "The Oracle Has It All Psyched Out," *Life*, June 28, 1968, p. 85; see also Jonathan Kamin, "Taking the Roll Out of the Rock: Reverse Acculturation," *Popular Music and Society* 2 (Fall 1972): 1–18.
10. James Coleman, *Adolescent Society* (New York: Free Press, 1961).
11. Paul Hirsch et al., "A Progress Report on an Exploratory Study of Youth Culture and the Popular Music Industry," (Ann Arbor: Survey Research Center, Institute for Social Research, University of Michigan, 1971), p. 28.
12. A 1965 poll of San Francisco State College students supports these findings. David Brice notes that 43 percent of those questioned customarily listened to music classified as "general popular." Twenty-four percent regarded themselves as classical listeners and

16 percent as folk enthusiasts. Jazz accounted for 11 percent and rock and roll for only 6 percent. These figures should be treated with care considering the manner in which the data was gathered, the small size of the sample (N=100) and most significantly the time of the report. Rock music did not capture collegiate interest until the popularization of *Sgt. Pepper* and in San Francisco until the local bands began to record. David Brice, "Students Favor Dylan," *San Francisco State Gator*, October 1, 1965, p. 1.

13. Richard A. Peterson and David Berger, "Three Eras in the Manufacture of Popular Music Lyrics," in R. Serge Denisoff and Richard A. Peterson, eds., *Sounds of Social Change: Studies in Popular Culture* (Chicago: Rand McNally, 1972), p. 286.

14. Hughston F. Mooney, "Popular Music Since the 1920's: The Significance of Shifting Taste," *American Quarterly* 20 (Spring 1968): 68.

15. "A Sage Looks at Living," *Time*, May 20, 1940, p. 41.

16. Cited in J. Frederick MacDonald, "Hot Jazz, the Jitterbug, and Misunderstanding: Generation Gap in the Swing Era, 1935–1945," *Popular Music and Society* 2 (Fall 1972): 44.

17. Zappa, "All Psyched Out," p. 84.

18. George Simon, *The Big Bands* (New York: The MacMillan Co., 1967), p. 35.

19. D. Duane Braun, *The Sociology and History of American Music and Dance, 1920–1968* (Ann Arbor, Mich.: Ann Arbor Publishers, 1969), p. 48.

20. Charles Siepmann, *Radio, Television and Society* (New York: Oxford University Press, 1950), p. 99.

21. Simon, *Big Bands*, p. 32.

22. Zappa, "All Psyched Out," p. 85. John Sinclair, the creator of the concept of trans-love energy, the catalyst for the revolutionary potential of rock, also views *Blackboard Jungle* as the turning point in generational conflict (see chapter 7).

23. David Riesman, "What the Beatles Prove About Teenagers," *U.S. News and World Report*, February 24, 1964, p. 88. Also Jerry Hopkins, *Elvis* (New York: Simon and Schuster, 1971), pp. 141–47.

24. Arnold Shaw, *The Rock Revolution* (New York: Crowell-Collier Press, 1969), p. 16.

25. Not all of the songs included in these magazines are in fact taken from the best-selling charts. Approximately 30 percent are

not from *Billboard* or *Cashbox* reports, but rather reflect the picks of the magazine editors.

26. Donald Horton, "The Dialogue of Courtship in Popular Songs," *American Journal of Sociology* 62 (May, 1957): 569–78.

27. "Lame, Halt, and Blind," *Billboard*, November 30, 1959, p. 2. Also, "Ford Doubts Payola Made R&R Popular," *Billboard*, May 9, 1960, pp. 1, 27.

28. David Riesman, "What the Beatles Prove," p. 88.

29. A. J. W. Taylor, "Beatlemania: A Study in Adolescent Enthusiasm," *British Journal of Social Clinical Psychology* 5 (1966): p. 81.

30. "Songs That Have a Double Meaning," *San Francisco Sunday Examiner and Chronicle*, September 25, 1966, p. 13.

31. Joe Fernbacker, "Days of Blood and Peanut Butter," *Punk Magazine* 1 (May 7, 1973): 4.

32. Quoted in Ben Edmonds, "Alice Cooper Blows His Wad: Sciences from An Impending Conquest," *Creem* 5 (June 1973): 38.

33. Ian Dove, "At Alice Cooper's Show, Tunes Don't Get in Way of the Action," *New York Times*, June 5, 1973, p. 42.

34. Ed McCormack, "New York City's Ultra-Living Dolls," *Rolling Stone* 120 (October 26, 1972): 16.

35. Robert Christgau, "In Love With the N.Y. Dolls, All-American Boys Into Ultra-Decadence," *Newsday,* February 18, 1973, p. 18.

36. "Alice Cooper Rock Group Rocks Viewers," *TV Guide*, December 9, 1972, p. A–1.

37. Nat Freedland, "1st ABC Rock Special Ratings Spawn 3 More," *Billboard*, December 9, 1972, p. 6.

38. Carl Belz, *The Story of Rock* (New York: Oxford University Press, 1969), p. VII.

39. Richard Mabey, *The Pop Process* (London: Hutchinson Educational, Ltd., 1969), p. 41.

40. Ray Browne, "Popular Culture: Notes Toward a Definition," in Browne and Ronald Ambrosetti, eds., *Popular Culture and Curricular*, (Bowling Green, Ohio: Bowling Green University Popular Press, 1970), p. 11.

41. Rolf Meyersohn and Elihu Katz, "Notes on a Natural History of Fads," *American Journal of Sociology* 62 (May 1957): 595.

42. Leslie Raddatz, "Dear David—I Am 9 Years Old," *TV Guide* , May 22, 1971, p. 24.

43. See Charles Keil, *Urban Blues* (Chicago: University of Chicago Press, 1966).

44. Paul Hirsch, "The Structure of the Popular Music Industry: An Examination of the Filtering Process by Which Records Are Preselected for Public Consumption," (Ann Arbor, Mich.: Survey Research Center, The University of Michigan, 1970).

45. Ross, "The Record Business," p. 230.

46. Quoted in John Sippel, "Major Retailers Prophesy Boom." *Billboard*, August 12, 1972, p. 1.

2.

IN THE GROOVES: THE PERFORMER

You're a little insane
Playing the game for public acclaim
© *1966 by Tickson Music Co.*

God help the Troubadour
That tries to be a star
© *1968 Barracade Music*

"You either have it or you don't." This simple statement defines talent, but talent alone cannot guarantee recording success. It all hinges on the performer's ability to persuade others to recognize his talent. Discovery and appreciation are mercurial events. An artist evoking epithets of praise from Mo Ostin at Warner Brothers may only generate yawns from Goddard Lieberson at Columbia. To further complicate matters, appreciation for the artist's work must spread from the record company to the radio programmer, and finally and most importantly, perhaps, to the "folks out there," the consumers.

The odds against this happening are enormous. Promoter Bill Graham asserts that the chance of succeeding in the music business is approximately "a thousand to one." Only 17 new artists per year, it is believed, ever record a Top 40 hit, while in the same year 23 persons are statistically likely to be struck dead by lightning. (Of course, more people are exposed to lightning storms than try to achieve musical stardom. Still, the odds against "making it" are tremendously large.) With odds this monumental, it is not surprising to find a good deal of misinformation and superstition surrounding the "making of a star." Success almost becomes a product of luck, time, divine intervention or some other *deus ex machina*. Recall the case of America, a trio catapulted from obscurity in the spring of 1972. As one publicity sheet stated, "The story of America and their meteoric rise to the zenith of vinyl popularity has such an endearing fantasy quality that it would make the minds of many a script writer brighten."

Gerry Beckley, Dan Peek and Dewey Bunnell were three U.S. Air Force "brats" living in England. They played guitars, sang and drank together, writing songs in the confines of their automobile. In 1971 the trio decided to chance a professional career. As was to be expected, their original reception was minimal and the three were forced to work on the U.S. Air Force base in England washing dishes in the cafeteria and moving crates in a warehouse. In this dining room they gleaned the name America from a jukebox manufactured by the Americana Company. The trio finally generated some attention from Jeff Dexter, an English disk jockey and concert promoter, who agreed to manage the group. He proceeded to book the band in selected British clubs and produced the customary sample or "demo" record. The group was ultimately signed by the English branch of Warner/Reprise.

Their first album was a collection of songs in the Neil Young genre of country-folk-rock. Many listeners, especially critics, dismissed the record as a mere imitation of superstars Crosby, Stills, Nash and Young. *America* was perceived as yet another "wimpy" album. Several other songs were recorded. One was a single with a surrealistic lyric titled "Horse With No Name." When this song became a hit it was added to the original album. The group went on tour with a bevy of English headliners such as Family, Cat Stevens and Traffic. The tour generated several postive reviews, especially in the *New Musical Express*, a major fan and trade paper in the United Kingdom. In February 1972, the album and the single were released in the United States, as the group was beginning a poorly publicized tour of the United States at the Cellar Door in Washington, D.C. In three weeks' time the group was a "monster" with the number-one song and an appearance on the "Dick Cavett Show." Ron Jacobs, one of the parents of boss radio, observed, "If we had asked Warner Brothers executives to write down and put in a sealed envelope on January 1, 1972, what they thought would be a smash record, I doubt any of them would have written out 'Horse With No Name' had that record been in the company's catalogue at the time." Warner executives would not dispute this statement: "As a matter of fact, their ascendency to the heights of rock stardom is so rapid, atypical and unpredictable, that company executives are driven in their attempts to explain the success story."* The meteoric rise of America typifies the rags to riches mystique of the music industry. America was recognized and appreciated by a sufficient number of strategically placed people to achieve a dominant position in the record scene of 1972. However, as competitors were quick to note, "They must repeat 'Horse With No Name' with their next single." The group did with "Ventura Highway." The percentages against this are rather great even if radio people see the group as having momentum and therefore are apt to play their next effort. Yet, despite the ethos of success, people don't just make it. Certain things do happen that are essential to the emergence of a successful performer. The first step is the recognition of talent by influential people and the emergence of a professional performer or act.

WONDERLUST

A basic principle in the music business was articulated by Warner Brothers executive Stan Cornyn: "You can send it up in a balloon, you can put it on the Goodyear blimp, you can send it up by rocket, etc. If it doesn't have it in the grooves, it isn't gonna sell. You can't package and sell a piece of shit."[1]

---

*Throughout this book there are a number of unattributable quotes. Many are simply the function of unsigned press releases. Some are anonymous statements where the interviewee requested that his name or company not be used.

Looking at the English development of rock, musician-writer George Melly wrote, "Some initial magic [must be] inherent in the group or artist in the first place."[2] This magic must be apparent to those exposed to it. Peter Yarrow, contemplating his future after the breakup of Peter, Paul and Mary, evaluated the notion of magic in his performances saying, "In show business terms it may be my undoing . . . because I have the feeling you need at least an ounce . . . of mystique." He continued, "There has to be a bit of a mystery and there is nothing mysterious at all about me." How an artist is perceived by an audience is a critical factor in his success. Talent must be recognized by someone in a position to bring further scrutiny to the artist. A college student under an elm tree picking out Bob Dylan strums on a Martin guitar and singing his own songs is not considered "talented" unless he is able to generate some excitement. If he turns on enough people he may move into the attention sphere of others. He must eventually be brought to the attention of someone in a position to label him a performer. Ry Cooder recalls, "They used to have party nights at the Ash Grove when people would get up out of the audience and play. And it seemed like when I was 16 I was good enough, and somebody said 'Get up, get up,' and they pushed me on stage. I got up and I was so scared I was petrified. I played and sweated and people laughed and clapped." This initial appearance did not establish the guitarist as a performer. He remained unemployed until later, for none of the audience treated him as a serious performer. For the aspiring artist, generating the label of performer, let alone star, is a monumental task. He must attract the attention of a sufficient number of people in a position to legitimate him as a performer. Corb Donohue, creative services director at ABC Records, observes, "Anything that rises above the mire is a success. Anything that draws attention to itself and continues on without some sort of great preposterous hype involved is a success." The labeler, the guy who can "make it happen," is a person already within the music business, such as a manager, agent, critic, executive or performer. Preparation for an audition is essential; an artist must be sufficiently developed to elicit a desired response. This maturing can only occur through performing, usually as local artists on campuses or as weekend bands playing at small towns, colleges and high schools. This is as true in the Midwest and Southwest as it was in the Cavern Club in Liverpool or at the Matrix in San Francisco or in Laurel Canyon in the hills of Hollywood. Many of these local artists, while dreaming of a "break," rarely get it due to the lack of recognition. The few that do make it refer to this period as "dues paying." Ironically, the rare act that does get to national prominence following such a start only adds to the mythology of future stardom which permeates the dingy clubs and old ballrooms. Despite this mythology, there are numerous ways of reaching someone in the music industry who is in a position to appreciate and reward a performer.

One shortcut to recognition is through the "over-the-transom" or unsolicited demo tape which is either mailed to a recording company or to an agent. While these tapes are treated somewhat cavalierly, especially by successful companies, they do receive a hearing. Aspirants customarily receive the verdict in six weeks. Leo Kottke was signed to a Takoma Records contract on the basis of a tape he sent John Fahey, who detested Leo's voice but admired his dexterity with a guitar. The Doobie Brothers similarly were picked up by Warner Brothers as talent on the strength of a tape. According to a company spokesman, "An orphan tape arrived, devoid of hype or contacts. It was played and deemed worthy. The group was met with and signed shortly thereafter—the first time in company memory that a band was signed on the basis of sound and sound alone." The rarity of success using this attention-getting device is sufficiently unique to generate considerable excitement and lore. Barry Drake was advertised by Capitol Records as a case in point. Drake was one of many college dropouts turned wandering minstrel and singer-writer-guitarist. He played traditional songs and his own material, occasionally appearing in Village coffee houses, the Bitter End, the Gaslight and sitting in whenever and wherever he could. In 1965 a professional musician befriended him and convinced Barry to make a tape, which was sent to Capitol Records. The rest, as this promotional handout illustrates, is nearly fantasy:

> This is where the old Godmother and wand situation enters the scenario. As usual with unsolicited material, Barry's tape eventually languished in Capitol's Out Tray. But working late one night, a secretary put the tape on, just to have a little music as she typed. Exactly as in an old movie musical, Terry Knight, Capitol Records' star-guiding producer, came walking down the hall as the tape was playing, and stopped cold to listen.

The result was a management contract and a record, *Happylanding*, which economically bombed. There was no second album. The fabled shortcut to recognition is a rarity because tape senders lack the experience to turn executives on. Most successful acts go through a difficult apprenticeship in which they obtain proper management and eventually develop professionalism.

Recognition of one's talent, while essential to status as a performer, does not guarantee further success. There are literally thousands of "one-record wonders" who are never heard or seen by those outside the music industry. Music critic John Mendelsohn's song title aptly describes this phenomenon, "There's a Broken Heart for Every Rock and Roll Star on Laurel Canyon Blvd."

WITH A LITTLE HELP FROM MY FRIENDS

The question as to why people aspire to be popular music performers is almost unanswerable. Glamour, fame and fortune are all attractive to varying degrees. Tammy Wynette, when asked why so many great singers all came from a 30-mile radius of Tupelo, Mississippi, replied half-jokingly, "Just to get out of there." Rock musicians have echoed this sentiment about other places or social conditions. Black musicians, especially, have found the entertainment business a ladder by which to escape the ghetto. Gordon Friesen, the editor of *Broadside* (NYC), indicates:

> The black kids, and I'm talking of boys and young men, were continually forming and reforming quartets with the aim of somehow breaking out of the ghetto into the bigtime music world of records. They rehearsed endlessly, into the wee hours of the morning. It was generally on the streets, but not by choice. They were always begging for someone to provide them a place to rehearse in.

This phenomenon is not limited to blacks. Waylon Jennings explained, "It's kind of like they say sports is with black dudes. It's a way to get up and away from something that's bad . . . I'll tell you what it is: either music or pull cotton for the rest of your life . . . you'll learn to do something if you've ever been to a cotton patch." Kids growing up in the shadow of Detroit factories have contributed to what has become known as punk-rock. Texas rock-and-roll band members have an equally deprived background. Other musicians have a more affluent background. The Carly Simons, James Taylors and Art Garfunkels have some college classes and come from middle- and even upper-class backgrounds. The sheer expense of becoming involved in popular music in the 1970s almost negates the possibility that a "Johnny B. Goode" may emerge without either some economic cushion or tremendous drive to escape poverty. Whatever the desire, the performer must have talent in order to "make it." But, despite mythology, "talent is not sufficient" according to Roy Silver, a successful agent who has managed Bill Cosby and Tiny Tim. The artist must also have "the ability to perceive who's right and who's wrong; the ability to choose good people; ability to sustain performing regardless of emotional crises; to continue to work ahead because it's a long hard grind and continue to pay those dues. All those things have to be there. The talent aspect of it is not sufficient." The people who transform the individual into a successful performer have to be professionals.

Pat Carr, a *Crawdaddy* writer, cautions: "Choosing a manager is the single most important career decision a musician has to make. Pick the wrong man, and you may end up with holes in your shoes, howling creditors and a bundle of legal/financial problems difficult enough to send you back to pumping gas—and just when you thought that you were just about to move on to a house in Woodstock."[3] Cat Stevens, while a student at the Hammersmith College of Art, began writing his own songs and singing them for his friends. A cigar-smoking entrepreneur heard him and announced, "I'm gonna make you a star." Being a novice in the music industry, the businessman planned a movie career for the singer. A Stevens tape, which was heard by producer Mike Hurst of Decca Record (UK), catapulted Stevens into the recording industry. Van Morrison, recalling the early days of Them, states: "I don't want to mention any names or offend anybody in the business, but it just put me in some awkward positions, because they were *unreal*. . . . Like lip-synching to the record on a television show. I can't lip-synch, 'cause every time I do a song I do it differently. I just can't sing any song the same way twice. Obviously it was what *they* wanted, but they didn't want *me*. They had some kind of singer in mind for that, but it wasn't me. I just couldn't do that kind of thing."[4]

A band with a large following and recognized potential for superstardom not infrequently experiences the same dilemma. The Grateful Dead, one of the top acts in the acid-rock scene in San Francisco, was contracted by Warner Brothers and given a $10,000 advance—$3,500 for signing, $6,500 when they sold 10,000 records. Two years later the band was $180,000 in debt. Of this $80,000 was wasted on the preparation of *Aoxomoxoa*, their third album. Jerry Garcia explained to *Rolling Stone* how this all happened:

> See, our managers were Rock Seully and Danny Rifkin who were really our friends and they were a couple of heads, old-time organizers from the early Family Dog days and they agreed to sort of manage us. . . . They weren't too experienced at it and we weren't too experienced at it and so all we really managed to do in that whole world was get ourselves incredibly in debt, just amazingly in debt in just about two years.[5]

The next manager of the Dead was dismissed for misappropriation of funds. In 1972, some five years after the Warner signing, the Dead were finally free of debt. The original Byrds experienced parallel problems. Very few stories of this kind have a similar happy ending, as most acts rarely had the staying power and willingness to work of the Dead or the Byrds.

Picking the right management and a willingness to work for exposure are essential to an act with aspirations of success. ABC Records philosophy of a marketable act hinges upon these two variables:

> It's the management and the direction of the agency affiliation that give an act the mobility and flexibility of approach that help the record company and the agency and management people and the artist *themselves perpetuate the energy*.

ABC Records has a pink 5"-X-8" index card which allows them to rate a performer. The card contains spaces for the names of the artists' manager, booking agency, public relations office and producer, as well as a place for an evaluation. ABC and other companies such as Warner Brothers and A&M all insist upon professional management if at all possible. Joe Smith, at Warner Brothers, explained:

> Everybody used to have managers before, and then when you got rock groups, some kid who was their friend was their manager, and it didn't seem to be terribly important who managed them, if they had a hit or their records made it. But it soon became very competitive and good management made a difference. I think we have a group, Fanny, here that to whatever heights they've risen,

to whatever off-the-market position they've taken, is to a large part due to Roy Silver, their manager.

Veteran publicist Billy James describes a similar attitude, "Record companies now want to have as much support around the musicians as is available. By support I mean are they good live, are they professional live, do they have an employment agent booking for them, do they have a personal manager for advice and council and baby-sitting, do they have a bondsman, just how together are they." In the eyes of record-company executives, "It's the management's responsibility to get that act booked, to get him touring, to get him working."

Most agents and managers, according to musicians and record-company spokesmen, are in one voice "incompetent" and "unprofessional." Some musicians might add "dishonest" to the list. Kristina was a struggling hard-rock band from West Virginia. They had signed three managerial contracts. None of these agreements have worked out. The girl singer, after whom the act is named, explained: "Once they get ahold of you they don't want to do anything for you. . . . As soon as they signed us to a contract it seemed like the momentum died." Jim Henshaw, the bass player, adds, "They expect it to happen right away for the group. The group knows it can't happen right away. But these people come and they see a group and say 'wow, they're really good, they should really go.' So they take a group and do a little bit of work and nothing happens and then they just sort of lay back and don't do anything else." Most artists, especially at the lower rungs of the music business, if asked "What did your manager do for you today?" would no doubt reply "Nothing." Going in and out of managerial contracts seems to be a part of industry dues paying. In the wake of the Beatle boom, friends, equipment movers, devotees and even girl friends of musicians not uncommonly began managing, usually with disastrous results. Bob Garcia, an A&M executive, outlines his company's problems with managers and agents by saying:

> When they start trying to buck it [the company] then that's really hurting themselves. "What are you, crazy? Hey this isn't going to get you anywhere; it's not going to get your artist anywhere. And everybody's doing as much as they can for that particular artist and what else do you want us to do." We'll listen. If it's within the realm of possibility, we'll do it. But if it's not, forget it.

A&M, which prides itself on having a smooth-running cohesive company, especially resents agents' unprofessionalism. Garcia continues:

> We have gotten a lot of managers here that started in this office and moved on to graphics, and then promotion, and then to merchandising, and they've got a different story and a different approach to each department. But what they don't realize is that immediately after they've been in here, we call ahead and let the other department know that so-and-so's on his way over and the situation.

At every level from A&R (artists and repertoire) to marketing and publicity, an executive has a horror story about an agent. Some of these stories, as Dennis Killeen at Capitol aptly states, are "cop-outs" for some other company failure, but many have substance. David Anderle, an independent producer, tells of the agent who demanded to "mix" his act's record. Brown Meggs, Capitol's vice-president of marketing, recalls the manager who insisted upon designing his performer's jacket cover. Joe Smith observes:

> You sign an act, the management gets all over you, and it will make you crazy right from the start. Everybody's pushing and pressing and they create a law of diminishing returns right here. By their pushing, people respond less. By terrorizing kids who work here writing ads and things, they've now got those kids so they'll write crappy ads . . . and all the life juices will be sucked out of them. Roy Silver would say, hey, whatever you guys want to do, go do.

Conversely, a publicity director at Shelter Records notes that many agents are not "on top of it," because they do not follow the progress of their artist's record. More commonly, agents are seen as actually inhibiting the direction of a performer's career. Mauri Lathower, Capitol's former head of A&R, laments, "Managers are on the most part lame. Very unprofessional. . .We just had a case of a group working at a club and the group should have been grateful that they were working. The group was so loud that people almost ran out, this was not a small club. And the manager says, the club was wrong. And I say hey, you have to adjust to the club. The club cannot adjust to you. You're not being professional about it. So what happened, you'll never go back there again." Refusing to adjust to a club or not working in a club that is not "right" strongly violates the work-exposure ethic of the industry. The artist in question is no longer with Capitol. Yet numerous agents have done just that. Some agents and management firms such as Roy Silver and CMA have been singled out as exceptions but, overall, performer management is a sour note to nearly everyone in the music business. Part of the reason is that many agents are in the same age bracket as the act itself. They lack the experience and the ability to communicate with much older and philosophically far-removed business executives. Bill Graham, since the opening of the Fillmore Auditorium in San Francisco, has screamed that agents and managers are not professional. Joe Smith again adds: "So many older people are promoters. . . . So if some straight kid isn't able to establish any level of dialogue with that, then he's less than a good manager." Attorney Richard Schulenberg also points to the communication problem of the artist and agent at Columbia Records: "You have the corporation being faced with this long-haired freak who mumbles jargon and his language is incomprehensible to them saying that he's being ripped off because he didn't get paid for something and the company doesn't understand . . . is unable to develop the emotional understanding that that artist relies on us to support him."

The scarcity of qualified management is a hindrance to many neophyte performers in that without them upward mobility in the industry is quite hazardous. Successful agents such as Roy Silver prefer acts with new and novel approaches that provide challenges to them. Silver will sign an act such as the female rock band Fanny or the long-haired 47-year-old ukelele player Tiny Tim but prefers not to work with competent talents without an original sound. The lack of experienced management leaves many aspiring artists in a position of either having mediocre agents and managers or none at all. Although the quality of management seems to be gradually improving, many consider it the weakest link in the chain to success. Consequently, recording companies have increasingly become involved in management.

PAYING YOUR DUES

Bill Roberts of United Artists observed, "It's no longer the day that you can walk into a major record company and hand them a record and say, 'hey, make me a hit record.' The record company, in turn, says, what are you going to do for us? What are you going to do to help us break that record? If he says, 'well, I don't know what to do,' then we refuse that act. We have no interest in that act. If they can't help themselves, then they shouldn't be on our label, and they won't be." This sentiment permeates the record industry. Corb Donohue: "They need to be out to work because then we can begin to generate around air play the additional attraction and interest in them that they can build. Humble Pie is a great example of that. . . . They were out grinding it out. And they worked and worked and were seen and were playing and people were seeing them." Tony Ashton said, "I think we have to just keep playing *at* people and we'll persevere." In response to the notion that touring and playing clubs was the vehicle for success, Ashton replied, "Yeah, I can't think of any other way, really. And of course doing interviews and trying to get across and all that." An act must constantly work, originally to attract the initial recognition that will place them in the professional ranks of the business. An established artist must also work to maintain public interest and further his potential for success. "Working" simply means getting the right equipment, rehearsing, touring and giving live performances before media and public.

Joe Smith, president of Warner Brothers, estimates it costs from $20,000 to $25,000 to launch an act. The money is for "whatever they need for equipment, to live, to get it together, to pay old bills, to be able to allow themselves the luxury of rehearsing without pressures on them and playing gigs."[6] Few neophyte groups begin with such a lavish operating budget unless one of the members is a spin-off from a successful group. The initial investment is for electronic equipment and instruments. Good electric guitars run from $300 to $700. A Fender Stratocaster, a favorite with rock musicians, costs $367. A Hofner bass (500/1), popularized by Beatle Paul McCartney, retails for $345. Even a fairly low-priced Harmony bass costs more than $100. Electric instruments and the human voice require amplification. A good microphone is priced at about $75 to $100. Most units have at least two of these. Amplifiers and power speakers constitute an act's major investment. The Fender Super Showman is $1,569, while the more popular Marshall systems with two bottom speakers run from $1,495 to $2,000. Professional bands usually have additional speakers. The Yardbirds at one time used 14 eight-foot speakers. A set of quality drums made by Ludwig, Grestch or another brand, costs from $800, minus cymbals, to $1,500. Several music shops estimate that a beginning rock-and-roll band would in the course of time expend $1,200 for a bass and amplifier, double that for a good guitar, $1,000 for an organ, and approximately $1,000 for drums. This totals over $5,000. Microphones, public-address systems and other paraphernalia all add to the cost. Furthermore, some form of transportation capable of moving all of this equipment is necessary.Professional acts rent U-Haul trucks; the neophytes all too frequently cram their equipment into a used Volkswagen bus. Even at the most primitive level the average rock or country band has several thousand dollars invested in the tools of their advocation. Touring bands usually have $15,000 to $20,000 in equipment. Having made the initial investment, the act must begin to work.

Working begins at a very early level. Initially, it may just be for personal pleasure. High-school bands such as Bob Zimmerman's quartet in Hibbing, Minnesota, were begun as a lark and then started getting serious. It became serious because of the leader's desire for success. "Beginning bands," as they are called by musicians, are an important initiation and training ground for musicians, although they rarely last. Members come and go and regroup in amoebalike fashion. A member of the Raspberries recalls, "When you're young and try to play in a band together there are a lot of hassles coming about. Ego things and who wants to run the show and who doesn't and different outlooks. When you're young, it's hard to cope with things like that." But these fluid units are training grounds. Group membership frequently motivates people to take up supportive rather than lead instruments. A guitarist can practice as a solo and have a self-contained sound. For a bass player, and particularly the drummer, a group is essential. Many drummers and bassists with "name" rock bands of the mid-1960s were converted guitarists. Skip Spence, the Jefferson Airplane's first drummer, was recruited since, according to Marty Balin, "I was looking for a drummer and I saw Skip Spence. I'm very struck by images of people. And I saw him and I said 'that's my drummer.'"[7] Skip was a guitar player. Mike Clarke of the Byrds similarly got "on-the-job" training. At every level, rehearsing is the most elementary form of working. "Getting your shit together" is essential for recognition and appreciation. "Tightness," "being together" all revolve around the timing of a group, and synchronization is only possible through hours and hours of practice. Most successful acts are "tight." A new band is always compared to those that are on top and have been. Most acts, despite the beliefs of the performers, are not original in sound. Their music is patterned after a successful prototype or some variation of that theme. Practice, originally, is little more than repetitive imitation. The copying of the Kinks' bass line to "You Really Got Me" or the runs to "Sunshine of Your Love" as played by Jack Bruce of Cream were musts for rock bassists. As the skill becomes greater the unit is left with two options. It can emerge previously established styles and produce a "new sound." This is rare. Elvis Presley, the Beatles, the Byrds, the Buckinghams, Blood, Sweat and Tears, Chicago and Waylon Jennings are a few of the acts which have successfully accomplished this feat. Normally, a musical act develops proficiency within an established style, as was the case with America, whose sound is nearly identical to that of Neil Young. The legion of Elvis Presley imitators—Conway Twitty, Gene Vincent, Eddie Cochran, Ronnie Self, Ricky Nelson and Jody Reynolds—all found some modicum of success within the rock-a-billy genre. The revolving army of lead guitarists within British blues bands such as Mayall's Bluesbreakers, Baldry's Hoochie Coochie Men and the Yardbirds provided a showcase for the growth and dexterity of artists as Eric Clapton, Mick Taylor, Jeff Beck, Jimmy Page, Peter Green and others. John Mayall explained the turnover saying, "They decided they've learned all they could or developed as far as they could in structure, and it gives them the inspiration to take it further."[8] Nearly all successful performers have patterned themselves after some model. Carlos Santana, Elvin Bishop, Keith Richard and other guitarists cite B.B. King as their prototype. Eric Clapton admits, "I copied most of my runs from B.B. or Albert King or Freddie King."[9] Bob Dylan copied Woody Guthrie and Jack Elliott prior to pioneering his own poetic sound. The Beatles and the Rolling Stones imitated Chuck Berry and the Chicago blues sound before venturing into "Sgt. Pepper" and "Sympathy for the Devil." Learning the riffs, runs and songs is the beginning. Tightness comes through arduous hours of practice. Then the artist must find an audience.

From a beginning band, the musician or group graduates to the world of the "traveling band." The traveling band is simply an act which plays everywhere and anywhere in order to gain experience, not to mention housekeeping money. Outside of the recording centers of America—New York, Nashville and especially Los Angeles—the aspiring performer is totally dependent upon visual performance for exposure and recognition. This essential fact has placed the concert promoter in the role of talent arbiter and sometimes agent. He is the person who provides the artist with his first audition and his debut before a paying audience. The expectations of promoters vary depending upon the market in which they do business. A night-club owner may well be hiring background noise rather than talent. Frank Zappa began playing in go-go bars in Hollywood. Sly Stone performed in North Beach topless bars before becoming a rock star. Carlos Santana practiced B.B. King runs in the strip joints on Revolutión Street in Tijuana. A good deal of dues paying is done in bars where the act is a human jukebox. They are expected to provide background noise for strippers and bartenders. Original material is frowned upon, so bands feature familiar, loud rock-and-roll songs.

Having gone through three managers, Kristina was still dues paying in the night clubs of the East Coast and Midwest. Market West in Lima, Ohio, is a typical midwestern club. It contains a bar with a small stage, tables, chairs and booths. Most people come to drink or find someone to pick up. Patrons sit at long cafeteria tables drinking 3.2 or watered-down booze in red, white and blue paper cups. The bandstand, nearly buried in wires and speakers, is nestled in the far corner of the club. A living-room sized area is reserved for dancing. Kristina plays 250 such clubs a year. Introductions to songs are muffled by crowd noise. Their material comes from Grand Funk, Mountain, Humble Pie and Cream. These are songs the patrons know. There is little audience reaction until late in the evening when a sufficient amount of alcohol has been consumed. A fight breaks out. The band continues its four-hour performance for which they recieve $200 to be divided between five musicians, a roadie, a sound or mix man and a manager. The next time they play Market West they will be paid $1,400 for five days, a $400 raise. Jim Henshaw, the spokesman for the group, recounts the evenings' events: "The road's hard and that's where you pay your dues, by playing on the road and meeting different people and playing different clubs." Steve Darling, then lead guitarist: "This was fairly typical. Like, some you get a worse reaction. Some you get a better. . . . You don't always have the fights and everything, but you know the drugs." The road is arduous. Playing for four hours a night at Market West is better than conditions at many other clubs. In other places they play seven hours weeknights and ten hours weekends. One club in West Virginia, Steve goes on, "was so bad that when you came in the door, they checked you for a gun and if you didn't have one they hand you one." The organ player, Jim Lewis, especially hates the Boston clubs, "That's some jungle, really a jungle, especially for groups . . . 'cause they're all types of people, just like a circus, zoo, whatever. The clubs we played in, they were all Mafia-owned, Mafia-supported . . . the riot squad was there mostly on the weekends." They play there because of the pay, "you have to go and do those things to get the money to continue in your career." Lewis interrupts. "It's gaining experience. Seeing what really the whole music business is like, you know. At the level that we're at—trying to make it." They talk about possible breaks. Their potential manager's brother has acts—Argent and Elephant's Memory. They are writing songs, working and hoping. "If it doesn't happen soon," starts Kristina, "it ain't gonna happen," replies Jim. Steve underlines the thought, "it's not gonna happen." They don't really believe that. They climb into their well-traveled cars to return again Sunday night for another club just like Market West. In two weeks it's the Agora in Cleveland, a step up on the ladder to success, maybe a recording contract, and perhaps fame. Until then the bars, small stages and audience noise will continue. Kristina's $16,000 investment in equipment, three years on the road and willingness to work suggests a recording contract will probably be forthcoming, although they must cater to club patrons' tastes while trying to develop their own material. This lack of new material is the major obstacle to earning a record contract.

Another arena for dues paying is the high-school or university fraternity party. Here college students and street people play music for exposure and experience. The problems are very much the same as in the rural and big-city night clubs and bars. The experiences of the now-defunct General Store, a Los Angeles band, illustrate the similarities of situations and also how acts may fold from the strain of competing demands.

The General Store, originally named the Great Society (until one member recalled the San Francisco band of the same name), began with five members. All had had experience in other bands. Two guitarists, a drummer, an organist and a bass player comprised the group. Most members were in college. Only one had any outside income besides playing dates. This was to become a major problem for the unit. The group began with the belief it might have "a chance at the big time." The group, using the bass player's past connections, hired a promoter. He in turn booked them to three nights a week at various jobs, primarily fraternity parties. The band received from $50 for a four-hour gig to $150 for a one-hour performance as a supporting act on a bill with a headliner. Their promoter received 10 percent of this amount. The income from these performances was the group's sole means of support and proved totally inadequate. One guitarist could not afford to buy his own instrument and was finally expelled from the group because he spent an inordinate amount of time borrowing an "axe" prior to each performance. One member spent over $2,000 on an organ. The band, according to one member, was "mostly in hock." Earning money and playing gigs became the immediate concern for most of the members: "Money was all important. Payments had to be made." The group invested some $4,000 in equipment. The demand for playing dates became dominant. The group slanted its music to the fraternity scene in Los Angeles. Most of their time was spent "getting it down so they don't complain." The group played standard popular pieces such as "Louis, Louis," "Money," "High-Heel Sneakers" and "Gloria." Mixed in with these party favorites were some country, blues and folk pieces. However, the main thrust of the group was covers of current hits. The group had no time and mixed desire to develop their own style. "We were too eclectic," says Mark Levine, "not proficient in any one. Not good enough in any one area."

The fraternity-party scene disillusioned the group. In 1967 many fraternity members were openly hostile to the long-haired musicians. Inebriated students were even worse. "Frat guys, they drink a lot and harass people." Some of the band's equipment was broken at these parties and beer was spilled on speakers and drums. The reaction on the part of several members was open contempt. The guitarist turned his back to the college audience in Miles Davis fashion. Levine said, "I refused to play anything that was requested, even if we planned to play it . . . for a damn $50. Why sell out for that amount?" The situation was one of stagnation. The band was not getting any better since there was "no time for improvement." In December 1967 the band decided to take six months off and develop their own sound; however, the demands of economics again interfered. Their promoter offered a $150 gig on New Year's Eve if the band appeared using another group's name on a bill with the Standells and the Box Tops at San Bernadino. The attractiveness of this offer recalled the unit to its subsistence posture. The General Store continued to function for several months after its decision to forego artistic growth. In March 1968, with only one of its original members still in the band, the General Store played at a peace rally along with Big Brother and the Holding Company and Blue Cheer. Shortly afterward the group was disbanded. The General Store's career is not atypical.

The price of survival is a major obstacle to success. Unappreciative audiences, the cost of electronic equipment and daily sustenance plague every new act. The ability to overcome these harassments is essential for success. Many groups such as the General Store have neither the commitment nor the ability to cope with these conditions. There are literally thousands of bands like the General Store which never get past the third slot on a concert billing, even with the name of another more successful act. Perhaps the Achilles' heel of such bands is best summed with the statement by one of the General Store's members: "I was willing to work, but I didn't like all this other crap." Putting up with this adversity is precisely what an aspiring act must do. Dues paying is exactly that. Groups in the mold of the General Store, according to Joe Smith, lack an essential ingredient for success: "Something with the group that wants to make it too, in addition to making music. They want to make it. There's got to be some ambition in a group. You would think that everybody has it, but they don't. So many are willing to do that number and play three on bills with no people watching, things like that." Conversely, Kristina had qualities applauded by Roy Silver: "You got to want to get out there and fight to turn them on. If I don't see that within the group, I will pass because I know that the odds are against your making it regardless of your ability as an artist and performer." as in the case of Bob Dylan, a former Silver client, it is the musician with self-generating motivation that survives the morass of semi-professional popular music. Dylan, besides talent, had another quality the General Store lacked. His hometown girl friend recalled: "Bob was sort of oblivious to the whole fact people were not turned on by his music. He lived in his own world, and it didn't bother him. There was this cat playing like they were clapping when they were really booing."[10] The dedication necessary to sustain the so-called dues-paying period is partially bolstered by the original euphoria of public performance; however, this is soon dissipated leaving the act with little but dogged determination in the best Horatio Alger tradition. Being a musician must be first and foremost. Eric Burdon explained:

> There is a very strong brotherhood of musicians, we talk about nothing else but music. A guitarist talks about nothing else but

> guitars, and when I meet a musician who talks about anything else but music . . . talks about anything else but creativity, I just avoid him because I know that he's no good, cause I know that he's playing a game, that he's being pretentious.

Capitol Records presented one of its groups as follows: "Nitzinger is a collection of purist musicians totally dedicated to their music and completely disinterested in the workings of the industry which supports them." The leader of the band, John Nitzinger, told the recording company, "When they are finished working out the details, and they tell us to come out and play, we'll be there. But all we want to do is make music." Eric Carmen, leader of the Raspberries, says, "We didn't want to get together to become a failure. . . . I looked at the potential of these three [members of band] and thought, God, if I could be put in that, we'd have a great group." Self-confidence is imperative for recognition. It is essential if a group is to survive the early stages of its career.

Almost as a defensive device nearly all bands define their sound as being unique. Any artist becomes hostile and defensive at the suggestion that his material is similar to a better-known artist. Tony Ashton, a British rock musician, objected to a review in the *Hollywood Reporter* saying, "It said we were trying to sound like an American group. Like trying to analyze what we're about, and we're just trying to entertain people and maybe make them feel good. We're not laying any numbers on anybody. . . . We've not borrowed from Chicago, we're not born from them, not consciously. We just got the band together, I wrote three songs, and there it is. . . . We can't possibly be doing a copy of anything." The Dillards, a folk-country-rock group, violently objected to this label and their relationship to the Byrds: "The Byrds sound like us. The Byrds got their harmony from us." Rodney Dillard claims, "We sound like ourselves." To this Mitch Jayne adds, "We've always been amazed when we found a sound that somebody would say 'do you know who that sounds like?' and they'd come up with something and it would knock us all dead because we'd felt we were doing our very own thing." The Dillards' influence on the Byrds is in fact correct; however, their belief in the uniqueness of their sound is a function of self-assurance and belief in the quality of their act. Colin Carter, lead singer of Flash, an English band, concurs: "The main reason that people get too defensive is the fact that musicians have huge egos that they need to prop up on stage . . . so when they are compared to someone else, it is an affront to their ego." Joe Smith elaborates, "I think the group has to believe it. You do run into monumental egos. The first time three girls scream in an audience some kids are stars right away in their own minds. I guess they believe they've refined it but that's crap. . . ." Smith continues, "I really think that anybody who has the guts to stand up on a stage and entertain people has got a quality that most of us don't have. An inner drive. Their ability to write songs and each song that they write, like James Taylor, is blood from the veins, and to hear it played and to sing it and try it on an audience and put it in an album wondering how somebody will receive it, those are things that you and I don't know about." This very same quality needed to achieve fame may, following an act's success, be its downfall. This contradiction most frequently manifests itself in the sphere of artist-company relations (see chapter 4). Billy James, once a publicist for the strife-torn Byrds, attributes "ego" as being one of the two prime causes for the dissolution of successful rock bands. Roger McGuinn's statement in *Fusion* about the original Byrds, considered by many critics one of the premier American bands, is illustrative: "We just had a bunch of amateur musicians who couldn't play live. . . . Ah, Hillman was a good bass player. Crosby wasn't a hot guitarist. Ah . . . Michael wasn't a hot drummer. And Gene Clark . . . didn't really know how to keep time . . . at all . . . at all . . . He was just spastic on the tambourine. . . . I'm glad he left, actually . . . I'm glad everybody left."[11] This quality is further illustrated by Janis Joplin's rebuke to her band, "When I'm out there singing, I don't need you guys upstaging. It's my act, man, I'm the one they paid to see, dig."[12] In the beginning this kind of self-esteem is imperative for survival and success. Teddy Bart, a Nashville television personality and author of *Inside Music City, U.S.A.*, describes the formula for success in the country music idiom as a mixture of "talent, desire, and perseverance." A healthy ego and notion of self-esteem are essential for at least two of these elements.

At the outset, ego is important as it can carry the artist through a number of difficult and sometimes unpleasant situations to, hopefully, his first break. The first break is the recognition and appreciation of an artist's talents by someone in a position to label the performer a professional. It usually is a billing of an act along with established artists or the rendering of a recording contract with a major company.

With the decline of the small coffeehouse and the night club, rock concerts have become the dominant form of "live" exposure for performers. Only large auditoriums can afford the expense of having popular artists appear. It is in this milieu that the emergent act must compete for public acclaim. In the case of a discotheque band, gigs may be simply a paying job, but at a large ballroom such as the Fillmore, Avalon or Grande, it can be a make or break situation. Promoters in smaller cities have volunteered to manage local acts they believed to be talented. Given the promoter's relationship with the industry, this offer frequently netted the act at least a look over by industry and management personnel. Many a record company has signed an act upon the recommendation of a promoter. So long as the promoter continues to book touring acts he has some leverage within the industry. Bill Graham, when managing several San Francisco bands, was able to bring immediate attention to them by virtue of his power to put acts into the Fillmore auditorium. His ability to follow up was severely hampered due to this responsibility. Groups such as the Jefferson Airplane left Graham's tutelage for this reason. Most managers lack these kinds of credentials. With luck, an act may generate enough attention as a "working" unit to transcend the inexperience of their management and be signed by a recording company or be taken over by an established management firm. A manager with several proven acts in the fold is of invaluable aid to a new performer. He knows the business but, more importantly, he has the leeway to negotiate with the recording company from a position of strength.

The signing of an act by a recording company is of immense significance because it is the hallmark of professionalism. The fluidity of the semiprofessional circuit becomes lessened. The commitment to the unit is increased. The potential for success is now a reality. The signing also predetermines the career of the group since the conditions of the contract outline the relationship of the act to the recording company.

A contract, according to the authoritative guide *This Business of Music*, indicates an artist is now a professional who is employed to render personal services as a performer on an exclusive basis for the purpose of making phonograph records and tapes. The contract specifies a certain number of records the artist is to provide the company. In return, the recording company will pay the performer a specified amount of money in compliance with American Federation of Television and Radio Artists (AFTRA) and American Federation of Musicians (AFM) scales. Monies above and beyond this amount are negotiated, as are other artist responsibilities.[13] It is in this sphere that adequate management and legal representation are essential. Most contracts include advances for signing as well as a percentage of the profits from record sales. These percentages range from 5 to 10 percent depending upon the terms of the legal document. Caution is in order, as Richard Robinson recently noted, for the finanical aspects of contracts are generally window dressing: "What most successful groups learn too late is that you can get a big advance and a big percentage and still, as they say in French, get nailed to the wall."[14] Many advances are against royalties, meaning that the $20,000 given an artist by Warner Brothers or Capitol Records will have to be repaid to the company before the act receives any income from a successful record. Other ex-

Exhibit 2.1

AGREEMENT

AGREEMENT made this __________ day of ____________ 1972 by and between GEE GOLLY PRODUCTIONS INC., Gollywood, California and SUPER STAR, USA.

NOW THEREFORE, in consideration of the foregoing and of the mutual promises hereinafter set forth, it is agreed:

1. Whereas Super Star agrees to the terms set forth in the ensuing agreement, Terms, for all services rendered (by Gee Golly Productions) a fee of 30%(per cent) shall be paid to Gee Golly Productions.

2. Whereas Gee Golly Productions shall be the management company for Super Star, for a period of not less than 10 (ten) years, according to the date above, and ten years thereafter.

3. Whereas Super Star shall be held responsible for all of his own equipment.

4. Whereas Super Star gives Gee Golly Productions the full power of attorney, in the event of his absence, for the signing of copyrights, etc., etc.

This agreement shall be binding upon and inure to the benefit of the respective parties hereto, and represents the entire understanding between the parties. If any part of this agreement shall be invalid or unenforceable, it shall not affect the validity of the balance of this agreement.

IN WITNESS WHEREOF, the parties hereto, have entered into this agreement the day and year first written.

penses such as studio, production and promotion costs, are frequently included in contracts as an advance against royalties. Advances vary from company to company and from artist to artist. MC 5 received a $50,000 advance followed by $20,000; like the Dead, they found themselves $128,000 in debt to Atlantic Records. It is quite possible that an act with a poorly negotiated contract can have a gold record and still not make any money. Another important aspect of a contract is the option clause, which gives the company from one to five years control over the act. The company has the power to renew its option annually with an artist. If the company is not satisfied with the act, it can drop the group. The performer has no such ability except to renegotiate—usually at his peril. Contract negotiations, consequently, are of dire importance, especially to the performer.

The stature of an act, even at this fundamental level, greatly determines the terms of an agreement. The Doobie Brothers, who were signed by Warner Brothers on the basis of an over-the-transom tape, originally had little power to exert their will in Burbank. Their chance for success was limited as the company rarely takes more than one or two chances with a new act. By the third album, if they have not demonstrated an audience appeal, they are apt to be cut out of the catalogue. Conversely, an act with potential—proven audience appeal and professional management—may receive a large advance, which makes the company less likely to be cavalier with the group. For example, Warner Brothers advanced the Grateful Dead approximately $75,000 against royalities over two contracts. In order to recoup the advance, the company invested a considerable amount in promotional fees and was patient with the group, which did not produce a gold record until *American Beauty,* some five years after they were initially signed. Other San Francisco groups, such as the Steve Miller Band and Quicksilver Messenger Service, received similar advances which reportedly were never recouped by Capitol. Columbia Records purchased Big Brother and the Holding Company's contract away from Mainstream Records for a reported quarter of a million dollars. Johnny Winter received $300,000 from Columbia to sign. Ironically, the lesser-known acts require the greatest handling and attention, but the company has the least stake in them. Peter Banks of Yes, indicates, "They don't want to put a lot of money into a new band unless they can see some return. As soon as they see a return coming in they start with the promotion. I think that was the problem with Atlantic. They sort of put us on one side. They had Led Zeppelin; we were on the bottom of the pile." Christopher Milk felt it received similar treatment at United Artists, a major label with a small roster. The act was new with one "name" member, rock critic John Mendelsohn. Proper handling of the act dictated that a certain time schedule be adhered to for maximum promotion and exposure. The small investment in the unit found the company pressing other more expensive and successful acts, thus placing the potentially successful act on a back burner. This decision was also abetted by the inexperience of the group's second manager. The recourse of the act's third manager was to try to raise the value of the act in the eyes of the company executives. This can only be accomplished through extraneous ploys outside the company, the most effective of which is reaching the people by touring. Press reviews of concerts and "plants" in industry trade papers all serve this function. Positive reviews, especially if the act already has a record out, are most persuasive. Michael Ochs, ABC Records publicity director, has noted that tearsheets and clippings were the best way to motivate people in the company to work for an act. Roy Silver has observed that getting the record company "behind an artist" was the most difficult task of an agent or manager. Publicity directors, especially at the larger companies, faced with competing demands from artists and agents, make decisions based upon "the bottom line," that is, based on profit or loss margins. Richard Schulenberg, a former Columbia executive, noted, "If you're selling a million units, at a lick, any album that comes out, no matter how much trouble you offer, for some reason you're not accounted to be a pain in the ass. If you're selling 40,000 units, and you're doing the same thing, no one wants anything to do with you, because you're not worth the trouble. Economics, again, is the deciding factor in who is and who isn't a pain in the ass."

ON THE ROAD AGAIN

Once an act is signed it is now a professional or "working" band. It is put on tour coupled with the release of a record. Since a hit single is improbable, the tour is used simply to introduce the group to the "folks out there" and to stimulate record sales. The more exposure the more recognizability, and increased appreciation. Roy Silvers's formula for the successful act centers upon this notion: "Air play means it's good. Audience clap for *familiar* pieces. If there is no air play, "the audience adopts an 'I got to wait and see for awhile' attitude." Furthermore, "you have to expose the group continually, look for air play, press coverage, and the more things you can get to sock it home . . . to that mass audience out there. 'They are good, they are good, they are good!' . . . so it ultimately sinks in." Besides the elusive Top 40 hit, touring is the best way to create a following. It is grueling, arduous work. One member of Flash said, "It's a real killer." Ray Bennett of the group added, "It's something you have to do if you're going to play music. You go into a group knowing that you have to travel and move around. You just have to accept it." Randy Bachman recalls his days with the Guess Who: "The worst I can remember is 93 one-nighters in a row. And its just no fun anymore. A job is a job, you tell me about a job where you work 20 hours a day for 93 straight days away from people that you're familiar with. . . . It's really hard on you, it's like being in solitary and working. Trying to look happy trying to groove with all these kids, it was such a false thing, it was unbelievable going out there trying to be cool and happy meanwhile you're crying on the inside. It was really, really tense; emotionally, physically, mentally *and sooner or later it catches up with most groups.*"

The road is a series of one-night stands, as exhibit 2.2 indicates. The acts travel from one Holiday Inn to another between jet flights. "It's all so horrible," says "Ozzie" of Black Sabbath, "flying around and around, landing again.

The hotel room's the same, everything's the same, the walls. It drives me mad."[15] Each stop involves the usual meetings with local radio people, deejays, writers, concert-hall managers and record-company promotion men. The new band generally plays its first album introducing each song, "This is from our first. . . ." The songs, the reporters' questions, all rapidly become identical. Audiences are frequently hostile. Bills are balanced with two styles of music, but the audience out front generally comes to hear only one style or group. Writer Jerry Hopkins observes, "today in concert situations, up to one-third to one-half of the audience is entering the theater during the warm-up act's performance." Free's first American tour was an admitted disaster because they came as the opening act for the widely heralded Blind Faith. According to an A&M spokesman, Free "on a number of gigs was literally booed off the stage by feverish Faith fans." The Raspberries, a band with a sound somewhat akin to the early Beatles, was ignored by a Toledo audience impatient for the hard-rock unit Flash. Eric Carmen, lead singer of the Raspberries, explained thc problems of being second on a bill: "When you're a number two act you really have to knock yourself out and knock out the crowd to get anything at all. It gives you a little bit of a challenge because if you can do really well you might be able to do better than the top act." David Smalley, the bass player, interrupted saying, "The odds are against you; it's a definite disadvantage. The people know you're the opening act, the warm-up act, and they accept you that way unless you really, really knock yourself out and pull things off to the best of your ability. And then, possibly, I'd say maybe 20–30 percent of the time, maybe 40, they'll give you a break. But other times it's really a disadvantage. I don't like it." Professional bands accept these conditions as part of the job. The lead singer noted, "These people are more of a challenge than people who are really with you . . . if you can get a crowd like this going then you've really done something. Crowds like this make you work harder." A member of Flash said, "It's man's work." Jim Messina, a veteran of many groups including the Buffalo Springfield and Poco, feels that the road is responsible for many acts breaking up. The confinement in motel rooms of volatile personalities usually results in somebody's leaving or the dissolution of the entire act. "That's exactly what happened to Poco," he remarks. Yet, he is a fervent believer this is the only way to reach people without a Top 40 hit. None of his bands had broken on AM radio until "Mama Won't Dance" in 1973 with Kenny Loggins. For Messina there is only one avenue to the public: the road. A concert in a midwestern university town aptly illustrated some of the immediate problems of touring. The affair was held in a large basketball arena. The floor had just been painted. The audience was forced to huddle around the sidelines. The intimacy of the crowd so important for performers was lost. The acoustics of the building rivaled a cheap three-dollar transistor radio. The appearance was a disappointment. But the Loggins and Messina band continued on to another auditorium—to experience more such situations.

With none of the luxuries and applause, the adjunct band on any tour must overcome hostility and sell itself to a captive audience waiting to see the main attraction. A case in point is the Dillards, a folk-music act, which in 1972 temporarily moved into the realm of country-rock. The Dillards had been in the business for some ten years. They had made at least six albums but had never traveled the rock circuit, just appearing in small clubs and colleges. United Artists booked the Dillards on a tour with British rock star Elton John. Bill Roberts outlined the problems facing the Dillards: "Imagine being in the business ten years having to play second billing to an artist who is so big that the people who are coming to that concert are there to see him, they're not there to see the Dillards, so you can imagine how they feel when they have to go out on stage first and they know the people are out there to see Elton John. So they have to do their best. The pressure is really on them to really turn that crowd on to them as a group. . . . They're paying dues to be exposed on a tour that they don't want to be on, so they can be seen." In a sense the Dillards

Exhibit 2.2

CAPITOL RECORDS: ARTIST ITINERARIES (JULY 14, 1972)

Flash

July 17	New York, N.Y. (Prospect Park)
July 19	Cherry Hill, N.Y. (Arena)
July 20	Georgetown, Wash. (My Mother's Place)
July 21	Bowie, Md. (Bowie Ice Rink)
July 22	Falls Church, Va. (Community Center)
July 24	Cleveland, Ohio (Agora)
July 25	Toledo, Ohio (Agora)
July 26	Cincinnati, Ohio (Reflections)
July 27	Columbus, Ohio (Agora)
July 28-30	E. Hampton, N.Y. (The Barge)
Aug. 2	New York, N.Y. (Gaelic Park)
Aug. 3	Charlotte, N.C. (TBA)
Aug. 15	San Diego, Calif. (Earth)
Aug. 16-20	Los Angeles, Calif. (Whiskey)
Aug. 26	New Orleans, La. (Warehouse)

Heads, Hands & Feet

July 3-4	Los Angeles, Calif. (Whiskey w/Hugh Masakela)
July 7	Lubbock, Tex. (Tex. Tech. Mun. Aud. w/Procol Harem)
July 9	Okla. City, Okla. (Civil Center w/Procol Harem)
July 10	Clarkston, Mich. (Knob Hill w/James Gang)
July 12	Philadelphia, Pa. (Spectrum w/Allman Brothers)
July 13	Syracuse, N.Y. (War Memorial w/Humble Pie)
July 14	Rochester, N.Y. (War Memorial w/Humble Pie)
July 16	Staten Island, N.Y. (Ritz Theater w/Procol Harem)
July 20	Milwaukee, Wis. (Summer Fest w/J. Geils, E. Winter, B.B. King)
July 21	Kansas City, Mo. (Musical Hall w/Procol Harem)
July 22	Rockford, Ill. (Peckatonica Frgnd. w/Edgar Winter)
July 23	St. Louis, Mo. (Kiel Aud. w/Procol Harem)
July 24	Crystal Lake, Ill. (High School w/Edgar Winter)
July 25	Niles, Ill. (Notre Dame H. S. w/Edgar Winter)
July 26	Villa Park, Ill. (Willowbrook High w/Edgar Winter)
July 27	Arlington, Ill. (Hersey H.S. w/Edgar Winter)
July 28-29	New York, N.Y. (Central Park w/J. Geils)

are fortunate in that their record company was able to place them on such a tour, as many acts are competing for the few slots on such excursions. Groups climbing the ladder of success are not the only ones exposed to the demands of touring. Even the so-called super groups dislike the demands of the road. The Beatles' film *Hard Day's Night* hinted at the pressures placed upon an act. Keith Richard of the Rolling Stones complains about the "hangers on" who clutter dressing rooms and make a general nuisance of themselves—representatives of small radio stations or contributors to obscure magazines. "It's hard to fuss if they want to know what's going on or if they just want to be around for a second-hand thrill." He also objected to the overenthusiastic audience reaction the Stones frequently received. At one point the band could not play more than three or four songs before the battle between fans and police broke out. "Chaos," he said. "Police and too many people fainting. . . . We'd walk into some of those places and it was like they had the Battle of the Crimea going on. People gasping . . . nurses running around with ambulances.[16]

George Harrison told biographer Hunter Davies:

> Then came touring which was great at first, doing an even shorter, more polished act and working out new songs. But it got played out. We got in a rut, going around the world. It was a different audience each day, but we were doing the same things. There was no satisfaction in it. Nobody could hear. It was just a bloody big row. We got worse as musicians, playing the same old junk every day. There was no satisfaction at all.

John Lennon adds, "It's like the Army, whatever the Army's like. One big sameness which you have to go through. One big mess."[17] For established artists the monotony of repeating their successes is the main displeasure of touring and a consistent source of conflict. Peter Townshend of The Who was expected to smash his guitar at every performance. He felt it detracted from his music. "The actual performance has always been bigger than my own patterns of thought. . . . I think with guitar smashing, just like performance itself, it's a performance, it's an act, it's an instant and *it really is meaningless.*"[18] Yet people come to see The Who smash their instruments after playing "My Generation." It was their trademark. The McCoys were similarly plagued by their hit songs. Johnny Winter recalled that promoters, "would hire us expecting 'Hang On Sloopy' and we'd do the new stuff and they'd get pretty flipped out."[19] The Velvet Underground, during the final months of their existence, refused to play their early songs like "Heroin," much to the displeasure of their audiences. Paul Simon echoes a similar sentiment, "I always felt weird on the road. I was in a state of semi-hypnosis. I went into a daze and I did things by rote. . . ." Moreover, "I didn't want to sing 'Scarborough Fair' again. I didn't want to sing all of those Simon and Garfunkel songs every night. When you've developed, it's harder."[20] Janis Joplin, in discussing the breakup of Big Brother and the Holding Company, gave an identical argument: "By the end we were shucking. We worked four, six nights a week for two years, man, doing the same tunes. . . . I was jumping and dancing and all, but I was lying, and I'd go off stage and feel like the world's biggest bullshitter."[21] Rick Nelson in "Garden Party" summed up this feeling: 'If memories were all I sang I'd rather drive a truck."

Corb Donohue sums up a feeling widely held in the industry on established artists and touring: "As an artist recording you have an obligation to your audience to at least be conscious of their desires. You've got to play your hit, whatever it happens to be . . . if a person comes and pays money which you are getting a piece of to see you work and you refuse to entertain him, then you are turning your back on the obligation as a popular artist." An agent said, "If people drive 150 to 200 miles to hear your hit, you'd damn better play it." While established artists may use the tour to increase their audiences and their bank accounts, newer acts must use the same avenue for recognition.

To facilitate a band's ability to reach the "folks out there," some companies have entered the field of bookings and tour financing. A former A&R director at Capitol explained, "We do support groups . . . there are so few places for them to work and get established. We've even supported whole tours. We would rather support a group that is touring. Some of them will be a second or third act on a major concert tour with Three Dog Night or whatever it may be." The third act on a bill receives little money, consequently it is necessary for the record company to pay many expenses of the tour. Lathower continues, "We'll support them as far as maybe transportation, money, lodgings, or if they're working in Chicago or whatever it may be, plugging them, and if they have an album out in what we call the 'marketplace' highlight the album, hoping that the act can catch on. Grand Funk probably would be the best example of that. They were a third or fourth act at one time." ABC Records promotes some of their lesser-known artists by sponsoring and underwriting concerts which the booking agencies refuse. One tour of seven dates in the New England states featuring Alice Coltrane, Pharoah Sanders and Michael White was underwritten by the company. All of the dates were sold out with 25,000 white college students attending. In Houston, the same company working through a local radio station put Bobby Whitlock in as the headliner with two other ABC label bands, Gladstone and Navasota. The company paid all of the expenses. "We pay for the date. We'll buy their hotel rooms, we'll pay them per diem, we'll give the musicians the money. We'll pay for the PA system, to get them up there to get that exposure." Warner/Reprise had very much the same philosophy concerning bookings. If they are not available through normal booking channels the company will bankroll the band. According to Warner Brothers executives, the functions of promoters, concert bookers, tour managers and press liaison frequently are now handled by the record company. In the case of Deep Purple, for example, Warner Brothers subsidized the transportation of the band's equipment from the United Kingdom and flew it around the country for them. The company paid for advertising on radio and in the press announcing the various concerts Deep Purple would give nationally. In the case of lesser-known acts, the company underwrites the entire tour. Joe Smith suggests this is totally essential for the exposure of his acts: "Acts that agencies can't get with—Beefheart, Mother Earth, T. Rex—we've run our own tours. . . . We don't share 5¢ in the personal appearances. We're the second beneficiary, maybe if they do good. Their record will sell in town. The promoter does well just by the very fact that the people are there. He abdicated much of his responsibility to us." In fact, Warner brothers provides many other services to facilitate exposure for their acts. Booking tours is but yet another way to garner recognition and perhaps appreciation. Invading the booking circuit provides these record companies greater control over the artist and his fate. By booking him into a series of college concerts and urban ballroom appearances, the performer is given "a shot" or a chance. The opportunity is not inexpensive. Frank Barsalona, a major booking agent, discussed the costs of handling an English act: "Led Zeppelin comes from England, so the band also has an American manager who gets 5 percent; the American agent receives 10 percent, and the English agent, who hasn't even picked up a phone also gets 10 percent."[22] The band's regular manager gets another 20 percent, leaving the act 55 percent with which to pay the costs of one road manager, three equipment movers and their salaries. Transportation, accommodations and expenses must be met. At a concert grossing $31,000, after commissions and expenses the group is left with $5,900 for a night's work. Led Zeppelin was, however, a super rather than average act. For new artists, touring is simply costly exposure. If he succeeds, the artist will pay for this promotional effort out of his royalties. Record-company executives do not spend money without some expected return, a point many artists—and their managers—frequently forget while relaxing in a Laurel Canyon house. Without exposure the odds for success are zero.

YOU'RE ON, BABY!

The end or beginning of a tour may be celebrated with a "press party" or opening. For the ardent music fan the occasion may have some of the elements of the 1,001 Arabian nights of pleasure. Few fans are ever invited. The exceptional AM radio station contest winner does, on rare occasion, penetrate these rites. Generally, these are functions for the media or "list people" rather than the public. These "list people" are writers, deejays, program directors and record executives in a position to help both the company and the performer. Landing a spot on a list is no simple matter. Two or three reviews in an obscure rock magazine will not place a writer on a party list. Lists reflect the judgments of a specific publicity or promotion director as to who is important and in town, as well as objective media status. For example, several companies in Los Angeles treat local record reviewers for high-school, college and university papers with greater deference than their more influential counterparts on the *Chicago Tribune* or *Washington Post*. Their mere attendance indicates to both company and artist the publicity director's ability. Every company determines the value of media, so variations do exist. A&M has staged many huge parties with more than 300 to 400 people in attendance—competitors have observed that these are "rent-a-crowd" parties. Other companies are more conservative. United Artists, with a philosophy and structure very similar to A&M, has a party list of from 30 to 40 people. According to Martin Cerf, then United Artist creative services director, the list contains 20 press people, 10 program directors and deejays, 10 record store managers and 4 to 5 publicists from other companies.

RCA Victor's party list is fluid and tied to numerous contingencies. Budget, newness of the act and type of returns all are figured into who is invited to an opening or press party. All give trade papers—*Variety*, *Hollywood Reporter*, *Billboard*, *Cash Box* and *Record World*—head the invitation list. Their importance is due to the immediacy of their coverage. They provide "instant print" for an act. The trades are followed by Los Angeles dailies, wire services, national magazines such as *Time* or *Newsweek*, *Rolling Stone*, columnists and outlying papers. For long-range features members of the rock press are present. Grelun Landon, RCA's public affairs director, feels that lists should be tailored to each event:

> We have to set lists, which I believe lock you in. For an opening at a local spot as the Whiskey or the Westside Room, you go different routes. For a concert, it's something else. Each of these things/events should try and persuade people to our point of view in the most favorable manner and also (also, also) motivate them into expressing this. That's what it should all be about. . . . We also, depending on the act, go after audacious approaches in addition to bread and butter things. We invited fashion editors to our Kinks party here (got good oh-gosh press, too) along with British Consular office . . . great people and a good wide-eyed time had by all. We covered Waylon out here with country-contemporary underground.

Local radio personalities, distributors and company executives also are occasionally found at RCA's affairs.

Elektra Records had three departments that host parties and openings, those of radio promotion, publicity or print media and sales. Each department invites those people it feels are important. Billy James, then publicity director, said that the parties host "never less than a hundred people." The number invited varies from act to act. Elektra, for example, does not give parties for new acts. Established acts are "hosted" but it is against Elektra's policy to "paper the house" with journalists and other media people. Professionals, according to Billy, create an artificial atmosphere which is disadvantageous to the performer. It is better to have paying customers who have come to see the act intermingled with the media, as professionals are quite different from the average audience.

The press party and the opening expose an act to the radio and press media. In exchange for their time, the media people and a few assorted hangers-on are entertained, fed and provided with an ample supply of alcoholic beverages and sometimes, discretely, drugs. However, the press party and the opening are structurally dissimilar. The press party is staged at a hotel, restaurant or suite of offices in a record-company building. Guests, by invitation only, are introduced to a new group via hors d'oeuvres and cocktails, followed by a performance. Parties for established artists involve the circulation of the performer from table to table, frequently with a company photographer in tow. At these tables sit deejays, program directors, writers for the rock press and record distributors and executives. The artist at the party is not selling his talents, but his personality. While providing the performer access to people in a position to give exposure to his product, the party also serves to impress him with the promotional abilities of his record company. Bill Yaryan, former Fantasy publicity director, now with Atlantic Records, acknowledges that parties are obligatory. "Sheer volume of product makes it necessary to give gimmicks. One company does it, they all do. It's an escalating thing. Artists expect parties." A record-company publicist adds: "I find myself traditionally bound into the opening night party type of thing. Partially from tradition, partially from ego on the part of the artist. Very frankly we do them often as an appeasement factor for the artist. It makes them believe that you're on their side and that you care about them and that there's some concern on the party of the company."

For the new act, the press party is ultimate exposure before opinion-makers. After a sufficient number of caviar-laden crackers with whatever alcoholic beverage one prefers, and a suitable amount of "street rap" or industry gossip, the performer is on. Unlike the audience the performer encounters while touring and paying his dues, the Hollywood media are antiseptic and critical despite the efforts of caterers, record-company publicists and the bartenders. Press parties and openings are nearly a daily event. The free booze, food and record with photo and biography are the rule rather than the exception. Indeed, many media people are forced into choosing which of two or three events to attend in a given evening. The event attended first or last is frequently predicated upon friendships, caprice and travel time. One publicist for a major company says, "The party goers are fat cats here in Hollywood in that they have been able to pick and choose luncheons, dinners, entertainment and whatever because of the plethora of parties." RCA Victor's policy because of this overabundance is to avoid parties in which one encounters the same people he saw the night before and will see the following night.

Despite the handicaps upon the artist, the press party is not an insignificant institution, but the new act's "moment in the sun." The hundred or so blasé opinion-makers can, on the basis of an extraordinary party, "break" an act. The ratio of such successes are exceedingly small but nonetheless legend and tradition perpetuates the rite. Actually, the press party is functional since in its context the artist is the main focus of attention. The gastronomical and alcoholic delights preceding the event—if served in moderation—can skew the receptivity factor. Appearing alone does give the artist somewhat of an advantage as opposed to the opening where the bill is shared with another performer.

The opening is virtually a New York—Los Angeles phenomenon, although Mercury spotlights its people in Chicago and country-music talent is displayed in Nashville and, less frequently, Bakersfield, California. It is simply the first night for an act in the city. The status of the performer is important; it determines who will come. When Peter Yarrow, Carly Simon or any other artist opens at a club, the media are nearly always invited to the nine o'clock first show. The record company pays for the drinks, but not for the food. Two companies will split the cost if the artists are on different labels. Normally the second act, lacking the drawing power of the headliner, will be on the same label or under the tutelage of the manager or public relations firm handling the headliner. Performer peril, especially for the neophyte, is great, since appearing at the Ash Grove, Whiskey or Troubadour is psychologically as trying as a Broadway opening. Consequently, only the most polished and poised artists can adequately cope with the situation. Knowing that an acerbic critic for the *Los Angeles Times* or *Rolling Stone*, is sitting in the front row along with some of the most influential writers and program directors in the medium sorely tests how well an act has paid its dues. Nervousness not infrequently negates much talent. The highly extroverted Todd Rundgren blocked out the lyrics to one of his own compositions. Elton John nearly forgot much of his finale song because Leon Russell was at his highly publicized opening. Less-experienced artists have suffered similar lapses.

As on tours, the warm-up act both suffers the onus of opening and being compared to the headliner, who is the draw. The editor of a major rock publication observed: "The second act/headliner does not come on 'till 10:30, so don't worry about the time." We did not see the opening act.

The party and opening audience sees the act through physicians' eyes. Various mental checklists come into play. There is little they have not viewed before. New acts all bear the burden of what has preceded them. The ability to compare favorably with the mythical yardstick will curry favor with the opinion-makers. Established performers with a niche in the music scene obviously come off better at these affairs. A good blues band must stand up to the quality of Butterfield, Cream, J. Geils and several other acts—no minor task. Yet, occasionally lightning does strike thus justifying the rite. The most cited event used to warrant the opening as an integral aspect of the industry is the "Elton John thing."

Reginald Kenneth Dwight is from the English county of Middlesex. He began playing piano, if his press agent is to be believed, at the age of three and studied at the Royal Academy of Music. At the age of 18 he briefly backed bluesman Long John Baldry. Answering an ad in an English pop-music magazine, Dwight met Bernie Taupin and Dick James and a band was formed. In 1970, he crossed the Atlantic for his American debut as Elton John, MCA recording artist.

Norman Winter, a publicist for the record company, orchestrated John's arrival in Los Angeles by chartering an authentic English double-decker bus displaying a bold banner reading "Elton John Has Arrived." Correlated with this grandiose gesture was a massive promotional campaign encouraging local FM stations and record stores to play the album, thus assuring some artist familiarity the night of the opening.

At his opening at the Troubadour, Winter hired a photographer to snap pictures of various MCA executives in the audience. The practice highlighted the significance of the event as such frivolity is uncommon at openings. The stage was set. By common consensus what followed was one of the "great opening nights in Los Angeles rock." Robert Hilburn, resident *Los Angeles Times* critic, wrote:

> John finished his round check and went back to the hotel to get ready for the show. *At the special press party that night, almost all the UNI* Records executives—from head man Russ Regan to publicist Norman Winter—were on hand to greet arrivals. Bill Graham dropped by to look at his investment, some writers from *Rolling Stone*, some critics from the San Francisco dailies, lots of radio people. It was a "show me" audience, toughened in part by the glowing raves from Los Angeles.
>
> But Elton John was equal to the task. By the third song, even the Troubadour employees from the kitchen were in the room watching. Rising to the challenge, John did a vocal of "Honky Tonk Woman," a daring piece of programming considering the almost definitive versions by the Rolling Stones and Joe Cocker. But it went fine and he returned to his own songs.[23]

Another participant reported: "Every time he started to play a cut off the album, the audience gasped and applauded . . . Odetta, to everyone's delight, got up in the back row and danced, strutting and twirling that famous huge body like a matronly dervish."[24]

The morning after found KPPC-FM, a local progressive station, buying a full-page ad in the Los Angeles *Free Press* in appreciation of John's appearance. That Sunday, Robert Hilburn published an extraordinary three-newspage review announcing, "A Super Rock Star Arrives on Scene." "Elton John," he wrote, "was being welcomed like a new bit of magic." After a lengthy biography and interview, the critic concluded, "no one I met in Los Angeles or San Francisco doubts that success will happen. Elton John has arrived."[25] In keeping with social historian Daniel Boorstin's definition, John became a celebrity, "a person who is known for his well-knownness." The application of the "superstar" label in fact made the performer a bone fide star. John's stage demeanor, concluding with Keith Emerson and Jerry Lee Lewis acrobatics, certainly helped his image. His resplendency at the Troubadour, where he appeared in red bibbed corduroy overalls, aluminum-colored boots and a Donald Duck button only added to the celebrity mystique. However, the handstand on the piano during his traditional final number "Burn Down the Mission" by itself did not transcend others who use the same stunt without success. Some have argued that in September 1970, Elton John—or somebody like him—had to happen. However, John did possess a number of ingredients necessary for success. The opening did evoke nervousness, but John "thought it would go well." His drummer and bass player were not terribly sure.

Elton John attributes his success to his publicist. He said, "Norm Winter—well that really sums it all up, doesn't it. Actually, he's worked bloody hard. They really worked hard."[26] On the other hand, Corb Donohue does not attribute the opening's success to Winter's promotional efforts: "He wasn't really as responsible for all that flash as the press was. The press and the radio were so desperately looking for a super hero. . . . You couldn't have bought that kind of publicity. The timing was perfect." Donohue's view is given support by the condition of the music scene in the fall of 1970. The long-awaited Beatles two-album set had failed to chart the new directions many had anticipated. Established acts like the Cream and the Yardbirds had disbanded. There was, as Hilburn acknowledged, "little to dig one's artistic teeth into." The magic was gone and the economy was becoming tighter. The press was increasingly faced with a gaggle of singer-guitarists, unsuccessful rock festivals and uninspiring bands. At the time, any spark was welcome. Roy Silver explained, "Those people are breathlessly waiting there whose lives are involved with yours and all they want to do is applaud." All the artist has to do is turn them on. A repetition of the Elton John happening is remote, but the ideology perpetuates the rite.

It is totally possible for record and press people in New York and Hollywood to attend over a thousand such events a year. For these *aficionados*—many of whom work for other companies—the fare only serves to dull the senses. For some, attendance is obligatory. One well-established publicity director and rock critic explained his reason for attending a rather second-rate opening as "X is a nice guy and this is his first party." Mr. X was the publicity director of a new record label. The "favor" no doubt would be returned at some future date. This interdependence partially explains the attendance at press parties by even the most jaded of "list people." Some record-company executives are somewhat skeptical about the efficacy of openings and press parties. As will be seen in chapter 6, the mere attendance of a writer at one of these events does not guarantee a review or article; the sheer number of aspirants operates against this happening. Several executives strongly question the value of press parties and openings. Bob Regehr of Warner Brothers' artist relations department says: "I believe that most of the little buffet receptions companies keep throwing for their artists are a waste of money. I'd rather spend my budget on one or two big parties a year and make them events which are really memorable. I figure, if it's not a party I'd look forward to going to myself, then it's just one of 20 things that week that the media has to force themselves to attend because it's part of their job."[27] Billy James believes that the invitation of publicists from the other record companies serves no useful purpose for the artist. Another executive stated, "To me, there's 50 writers in America that mean a . . . thing to me, and I refuse to indulge the other 4,000 with free trips, parties and bullshit. I would rather spend $100 a head per day on the people I know are intelligent and interested and passionate reviewers whether they take my act apart or not, than spend $5 or $50 a head on all the freeloaders that are in this business." While privately many media representatives would echo this sentiment, the parties and openings remain an integral rite in the business.

The recognition of talent is relative and time bound. "The time of an act," to paraphrase Proust, "must have come" for it to be a success, at least according to many observers in the music industry. Dennis Killeen, advertising director at Capitol Records, argues that the phenomenal success of America was one of timing. "Crosby, Stills, Nash and Young," he says, "didn't have a record out for a year and a half." The logic is that America filled the void. Elton John's Los Angeles success was explained in similar terms by Donohue: "The press and radio were so desperately looking for a super hero. And when a guy who came very close in a lot of ways. . . . " *Guitar Player*, a magazine addressed to amateur and professional guitarists, advised its readers:

> One of the most crucial factors of a group's success is timing. It is the most ambiguous as well as the most mysterious factor in music. If your group had entered the scene a little too early (the original Byrds) or a little too late (Dave Clark Five), your chances for survival were few. Whether or not you liked the Top 40's groups or top underground stars of the day, you still studied their style and songs, not so closely as to let them completely influence you, but just close enough to know what their sound was doing on the market; whether it was rising on the charts or not. You also learned to tell whether or not a group would succeed, with reasonable accuracy.[28]

Program directors at radio stations, especially those with formulas like the Top 40, generally support this notion, for they only have three or fewer vacant slots in their play lists and these are filled by different genres of songs. Three singles by folk-rock acts or Motown stars would find two of them being discarded. The mystique of timing and luck is weighed by many industry spokesmen against hard work and perseverance, in the best sense of the Protestant Ethic, as the key to success. One writer said, "Horatio Alger is not dead, he is alive and well in Hollywood." Roy Silver, with a track record that lends credibility to his argumentation, insists that, "It's all very logistical. We want to make it into some great esoteric mystery mystique. Nobody wants to do the work." Silver's argument has considerable merit in that a group's longevity increases its probability of success. Recognition must occur in the early phases of an act's career. The leap from being a supporting act on a bill to stardom is more a product of working than it is at the development level.

The apprenticeship for the popular-music performer is long and arduous. Most begin in their teens with high-school bands, later graduating to clubs and college dances. Groups form and dissolve, and throughout this process many fall by the wayside, as was the case with the General Store. Others such as the Raspberries, grow stronger and more self-confident. To survive the rigors of the early years, performers must have the desire to make it, exhibiting many of the straight-world virtues lauded by Horatio Alger. As the act rises the demands to work become greater. Landing a recording contract is but a small step on the road to success. Touring is essential and the road is hard. Starting from second place to the top of the bill also requires long, hard work. Coupled with all of these demands are many conditions over which the performer has no control. As one experienced rock musician put it. "The only thing that we can control is our performance." The perception of the audience, media appreciation and, indeed, timing and the state of the industry, are all beyond the power of the musician. He is the product and the beginning of the chain. His voice and sound constitute what is in the grooves. Before his talent can be evaluated by the record-buying public he must go through a number of channels over which he has little or no authority, beginning with what many ironically feel is the major obstacle to stardom: the record company.

Notes, Chapter 2

1. Quotations unless otherwise indicated are taken from interviews conducted by the author with industry personnel.
2. George Melly, *Revolt Into Style* (Garden City, N.Y.: Anchor Books, 1971), p. 42.
3. Patrick Carr, "The Manager: Da Guy With Da Money," *Crawdaddy*, August 1972, p. 30.
4. Happy Traum, "Van Morrison: The Interview," *Rolling Stone* 62 (July 9, 1970): 31.
5. Charles Reich and Jann Wenner, "The Rolling Stone Interview: Jerry Garcia," part II, *Rolling Stone* 101 (February 3, 1972): 32.
6. Jann Wenner, "The Recording Company Executive Thing: Rolling Stone Interviews Joe Smith," *Rolling Stone* 86 (July 8, 1971): 31.
7. Quoted in Ralph J. Gleason, *The Jefferson Airplane and the San Francisco Sounds* (New York: Ballantine Books, 1969), p. 91.
8. Fred Stuckey, "John Mayall Interview," *Guitar Player* 4 (December 1970): 43.
9. Fred Stuckey, "Eric Clapton Interview," *Guitar Player* 4 (June 1970): 47.
10. Quoted in Anthony Scaduto, *Bob Dylan* (New York: Grosset and Dunlap, 1972), p. 22.
11. Quoted in Bud Scoppa, *The Byrds* (New York: Scholastic Book Services, 1971), 96.
12. Quoted in Michael Lydon, "Every Moment She Is What She Feels," *New York Times*, February 23, 1969, p. 37.
13. Sidney Shemel and M. William Krasilovsky, *This Business of Music*, rev. ed. (New York: A Billboard Book, 1971), pp. 1–15, 545.
14. Richard Robinson, "The Record Company: How-to and What-for," *Crawdaddy*, August, 1972, p. 27.

15. Quoted in Robin Green, "How Black Was My Sabbath," *Rolling Stone* 94 (October, 28, 1971): 41.

16. Robert Greenfield, "The Rolling Stone Interview: Keith Richard," *Rolling Stone* 89 (August 19, 1971): 29.

17. Harrison and Lennon quoted in Hunter Davies, *The Beatles: The Authorized Biography* (New York: A Dell Book, 1968), p. 241.

18. "The Rolling Stone Interview: Peter Townsend," *Rolling Stone* 17 (September 14, 1968): 10.

19. Quoted in John Morthland, "Johnny Winter: On Music, Hype, and Happiness," *Rolling Stone* 68 (October 15, 1970): 24.

20. Jon Landau, "The Rolling Stone Interview With Paul Simon," *Rolling Stone* 113 (July 20, 1972): 33, 38.

21. Lydon, "Every Moment," p. 44.

22. Quoted in Ritchie Yorke, "Pop Music—A Mecca for Money Makers," *Los Angeles Times Calendar*, December 14, 1969, p. 50.

23. Robert Hilburn, "Elton John—A Super Rock Star Arrives on Scene," *Los Angeles Times Calendar*, September 13, 1970, p. 51.

24. David Felton, "Elton John," *Rolling Stone* 84 (June 10, 1971): 29.

25. Hilburn, "A Super Rock Star," p. 51.

26. Felton, "Elton John," p. 35.

27. "He Handles a Lot of Chores for Acts," *Billboard*, October 14, 1972, p. 10.

28. "On Making It," *Guitar Player* 4 (April 1970): 23.

3.

THE VINYL CRAP GAME: THE RECORD COMPANIES

> Sell your soul to the company
> Who're waiting there to sell plastic ware.
> © *1966 Tickson Music Co.*

Creating a hit record or a headline act is akin to constructing a jigsaw puzzle. Unless all of the pieces are in their proper place the effort is futile. Some of the most important parts of the puzzle are the province of the record companies, large conglomerates which handle nearly every aspect of the business. Bhasker Menon, president of Capitol Records, sees the record company as having three capabilities: "*manufacture* efficiently to get product to those who choose to demand it; *persuading* purchase by consumer and customer; and for lack of a better word is the capability of *management.*" The company makes records, distributes them and attempts to motivate the "folks out there" to buy the "product," as records are called in the music industry. Over $2 billion worth of product is sold each year. Stan Cornyn adds another element to the definition:

> A record company is truly nothing but a ticket seller. It can be a good ticket seller, but Mo doesn't go around singing, and I don't go around singing. I've often had a feeling just because I'm interested in spending my life intelligently and fruitfully, of—and ticket selling is not my idea of being the most fruitful thing in the world—of doing it better than other people have done it before.

Records—act, disk, skin cover, notes, lyric insert—are the tickets, and the record company sells them to the public.

Record companies are first and foremost large business enterprises governed by laws of profit and loss. In fact, they are much more attuned to the canons of laissez faire than their counterparts in the shoe or steel industries.

Record companies lack the market control of their corporation counterparts, adroitly described by economist John Kenneth Galbraith in the *New Industrial State.* A record company cannot "control the markets that it is presumed to serve and beyond, to bend the *customer to its needs.*"[1] General Motors, Ford and Chrysler can and do project their design models several years in advance. Record companies only dream about such luxuries. A publicist notes, "The people who work for record companies are really no more informed or enlightened in their tastes than is the general public." Stan Cornyn feels, "There is no formula." The lack of any sure guideline has made the industry as uncertain of success as any of its artists. Obviously the Capitols, CBSs, RCAs, Warnerses and MCAs will survive long after their current crop of "superstars" are gone. Still, very few billion-dollar corporations in America would openly compare their efforts with dice-throwing. Think of the stockholders! A former West Coast director of business affairs for CBS Records argues:

> Our industry is a classic example of crap shooting. When you win, you win big. You can afford to take a 70 percent stiff ratio. On the three that make it you more than make up your cost and profit on the entire 10. And if you spend on 10 records, say a million dollars, and 7 of these records earns back $50,000 but on the other 3 you earn back one million dollars, you still have a $100,000 profit over the million. That's still a 10 percent profit. I would think that is one justification why record companies can operate the way we do without having outraged anguish from the stockholders.

The crap-shooting analogy is widespread in the record business. Producer Phil Spector uses it. Joel Vance, a former Buddah Group publicist said: "The record business is a gambler's business . . . if you're not willing to gamble, then you shouldn't be in the business."[2] Murray Ross, a promoter-producer, told *Record World*, "To be in the rock and roll business today, you've got to be a 'total crap-shooter' with a good instinct for money management. . . . "[3] In dice-rolling, winners and losers emerge. So it is in the music business. At each level, the element of chance, the futuristic imponderable is present. Each segment of the puzzle must jell. Otherwise, the ticket becomes a loss in the 59-cent discard or "close-out" bin at Woolworth's. The elements of luck and timing are enormously important, yet it would be a mistake to treat record companies as the innocent victims of the caprices of Adam Smith's "invisible hand." The companies' business orientations and philosophies greatly color their performances at the vinyl crap table.

A company's ability to succeed determines its status in the industry. This status in turn accounts for its approach to record making and selling. Several companies, partially due to tradition, are believed to be "majors"; other companies, due to their corporate birthdays, are not. Nonetheless, the designations of "majors" and "independents" or "nonmajors" are commonly used in the record business.

THE MAJORS AND INDIES

Ticket sellers are usually divided into several categories based on the nature of their roster of artists and the portion of the sales market they control. The larger companies with their own plants and branches are called majors. The majors include CBS Records (Columbia, Epic), RCA Victor, Warner Communications (Warner/Reprise, Elektra, Atlantic), Music Corporation of America (Decca, Kapp, UNI) and Capitol Records. All are owned by conglomerates. The majors have traditionally serviced over 50 percent of the market. In 1968 five majors enjoyed 55 percent of the record sales leaving the remaining 45 percent to 90 percent of their smaller competitors. Columbia alone that year had over a fifth of the market to itself. In recent years the major label could not be applied solely on the basis of sales, for independents have successfully captured portions of the cherished top five places in the marketplace. In 1970 Motown attracted 11.4 percent of the *Billboard* singles action and 6.9 percent of the Top LPs. In 1971 Motown was joined by ABC-Dunhill in the singles category, while being replaced by A&M in the LP winner's circle. In overall chart action in 1972 and 1973, A&M and Motown performed better than so-called majors. A better barometer is the size of the record catalog and artist roster. CBS, Capitol and RCA, had lists which numbered over 2,000 entries. A&M's list is around 250 to 300. A&M carries some 65 artists on its books, while some majors have nearly two or three times that number. When he took over Capitol's A&R department Art Mogull found 247 artists on his roster. Columbia and Warner/Reprise have at least that many. The majors, with the notable exception of Warner Communications, catalog a large amount of nonpopular material—classical, country and western, jazz, gospel, soul and even polka. During bad times in the pop market, a company may rely upon these other genres to keep sales up. Country and western literally provide the economic foundation for Columbia and Capitol during business slumps.

The nonmajors lack these advantages. They are generally smaller in size and lack the economic power of the majors. Today these companies include Motown, MGM, United Artists, A&M, ABC-Dunhill, Janus-Chess, Famous Artists Records—including Blue Thumb, Paramount and Dot Records—Vanguard, Fantasy, Polydor and many others. The smaller companies frequently parallel the majors in sales. United Artists is owned by TransAmerica Corporation and has its own distribution set up, a feature generally attributed solely to majors. Other companies have moved in that direction. A&M's portion of the popular-music market far exceeds its size and rivals the majors. The size of the majors tradition-

Exhibit 3.1

BRANCHES AND RECORD COMPANIES—1973

	London	WEA	UDC	Capitol	Colum-bia	ABC-Dunhill	RCA	MCA
Boston	SB	W	SO	W	SO	SB	SO	SO
Hartford			SO		SO	I		SO
New York	SO	W	SO	SO	W	SB	SO	W
N.J. Plant					W		W	
Philadelphia	I	W	SO	SO	SO	I	SO	
Springfield								SO
Buffalo						I	SO	
Balt.-Washington	I	SO	SO		SO	I	SO	SO
Bethlehem, Pa.				W				
Cleveland	SO	W	W	SO	SO	I	SO	W
Detroit	I	SO	SO	W	SO	I	SO	SO
Indianapolis							W	
Chicago	SB	W	W	W	W	SB	SO	W
Terre Haute					W			
Cincinnati		SO	SO		SO	I		SO
Minneapolis	I		SO	SO	SO	I	SO	
St. Louis	I	SO	SO		SO	I	SO	SO
Pittsburgh							SO	SO
Pickneyville								W
Dallas	I	W	W	W	W	I	W	SO
Houston	I	SO	SO		SO			
El Paso	I							
Phoenix	I	SO						
Memphis	I		SO				SO	
Atlanta	W	W	W	W		W	W	W
Charlotte	I		SO			I		
Miami	I	SO	SO	W	SO	SO	SO	SO
New Orleans	I					I	SO	SO
Los Angeles	SB	W	W	W	SO	W	W	W
Santa Maria, Calif.					W			
San Francisco	SO	SO	SO	SO	SO	SO	SO	SO
Seattle	I	SO	SO		SO	I		SO
Denver	SO	SO	SO		SO		SO	SO
Great Falls	I		I					
Honolulu	I	I	I	I	SO	I	I	SO

Source: *Billboard*, March 3, 1973, p. 3. SO = locations in the 50 states with sales offices; SB = stocking branches; W = warehouse-depots; I = independent distributors. The labels included in the chart did 66.9 percent of LP-tape business in 1972 and 56.1 percent of the singles action. It should be noted that few if any of these companies are directly involved in "soul" music.

ally has been a key factor in their approach to corporate dice playing. Unlike their smaller counterparts, they have greater resources to spend and consequently try more often to win. A $50,000 gamble with possible winnings in the millions means little to corporations with annual earnings of $200 million or more. Parent companies in conglomerate structures are sometimes only too happy to subsidize such activities for tax purposes. Yet, despite the obvious advantages of size these bonuses are not as decisive as one might expect.

THE BUCKSHOT THEORY OF RECORD RELEASING: GOLIATH VERSUS DAVID

CBS Records, with its plant and catalog, must produce an enormous amount of product to keep its various bureaus, agencies and departments busy. Of every 10 records released, only 2 or 3 will sell. Consequently, large companies must produce massive amounts of product to sustain their larger corporate bodies. Huge investments are made and must be maintained. A concentration upon proven talent, coupled with the 7 to 3 ratio, motivates the larger companies to treat newcomers indiscriminately, at the same time competing with each other for sure-fire sellers. According to Mike Ochs:

> They need that, they have to have that. Columbia owns all their own distributors. They've got like hundreds of hundreds of people employed. So that the guy in St. Louis works only on Columbia product. So to keep that kind of major overhead up, it's got to have a lot of superstars. They can't afford not to have like 10–20 acts that sell a million out because they have all that *machinery that has to keep going.*

Brown Meggs argues, "A company the size of Capitol Records needs 20 LPs per month to support the overhead." "Or," David Lawhon, the marketing chief adds, "4,000 people get spooky." Capitol operates on what Meggs calls Formula 10, which is nearly identical to Columbia's 7 to 3 ratio. Capitol's advertising department head believes that in 10 releases at least one should be gold with several others bringing in a sizeable return. Companies with a smaller overhead, like A&M, can be more selective about when they wish to challenge Lady Luck.

Still, companies with their own distribution systems (branches) appear to have a tactical advantage in servicing radio stations and retail outlets. Richard Schulenberg recalls:

> I was with two other companies before coming to Columbia, and my first week was right at the height of Johnny Cash's "Boy Named Sue." I was amazed to find out that every week, "Boy Named Sue" had sold over 750,000 units, the single, which completely blew my mind because I had come from a company where when we had sold 30,000 or 40,000 total on a single, we had gotten very excited, we figured we were on the way. The idea that Columbia had just sort of opened up the pipeline and the three-quarter million units of one record had moved through that pipeline very easily without any returns in that week was a complete mind blower to me.

The "throw it up against the wall, and see if it sticks" or "buckshot" philosophy of the larger companies is highly controversial. Many majors, including Columbia and Warner/Reprise, officially condemn the practice. Conversely, artists, agents and many company executives, all for different reasons, decry the vast amount of product released each year. Roy Silver, whose concern lies with artists, claims that the major obstacle in the music business is getting "the record company behind the artist." Many artists feel lost at major companies. A United Artists executive observed, "There's no way of having 200 acts and keeping artists happy." "Do you know how many people from Columbia Records were here when I opened the other night?" asked blues singer John Paul Hammond. "There were none . . . not one person from my own company . . . they didn't bother to advertise either."[4] Ironically, Hammond's father is one of the most important producers in the Columbia hierarchy. Michael Lutz of Brownsville Station, an act which left the biggest selling pop label for the serenity of a smaller company, said: "Warner Brothers released like something like 47–48 albums in one month's release. And my God let's say they hit over of 6–7 albums. Okay; 6–7 albums and everybody goes 'My God, they're the hottest company in the world!' But what about those other 42 acts? See, nobody ever hears about those 42 acts. Everybody else forgets about those other groups." Publicists and promotion executives both acknowledge that size and a substantial release schedule do hamper their abilities. Billy James recalls:

> We used to complain a lot at Columbia when we would have 25 releases, and all of a sudden we'd have 30 for the Christmas release. Our feelings were that we couldn't do them all justice, the buckshot system. Throw them all out there, hopefully some of them will hit.

Marty Cerf:

> The hardest job in a company like UA or Columbia or RCA or Capitol is to convince their own people. Cause they are the greatest allies. If you get your own people turned on out in the field, they'll do their numbers vocally. I mean I can tell you about it and play the record and you'd get into it, imagine if there was 40 people doing that all around the country. That's what you gotta do; you gotta turn your own people on and forget about what they think is good.

He adds, "No company can work on more than 3 or 4 recordings at a time anyway." Publicists are especially aware of product volume. Claire Brush, then with Warner Brothers exclaimed, "What do you do when Jethro Tull, Van Morrison and Peter Yarrow are in town—all at the same time?" Other publicity and promotion people solve the size situation by pushing those acts they personally like as opposed to others. The artist in the disfavor of a publicist may have only the usual bio-promo photo and review record mailing, unless his contract or agent dictate otherwise. Mike Ochs when with Columbia: "It's a weird thing; it's a problem you get with the big companies. How do you get the whole company unified behind one act? I had that problem with Grin." As for pushing groups, Mike continues: "I pretty much ignored the major groups. I figured any group that was big could afford their own publicist. I zeroed in on the people who needed the work, like Johnny Otis, Firesign Theater, Grin, the Byrds, because they weren't selling then." Ochs succeeded in breaking Firesign Theater and reviving the Byrds for a fleeting moment. Other acts did not fare so well. Their chances at the roulette wheel were skewed from the beginning. Indeed, the relationship of the artist to the record company is quite similar to the conglomerate's posture toward its consumers. But acts do not have the autonomy, economic clout or staying power of RCA, CBS or MCA.

ARTIST DEVELOPMENT

Smaller companies, where size is determined by the number of acts and releases, place a greater stress upon the development of individual acts. A&M, is one model of success. Bob Garcia, an executive, describes the firm:

> It's a family company. There's a tremendous interaction between all the departments on all levels. From stockrooms to president to vice-president to maintenance people. It's not a role-playing company. There are no shut doors, there are no high-level conferences. So in comes an artist off the street. We sign this particular artist. Then we get all together and pool our particular talents. We like an artist and we sign the artist and we deliver the artist.

Elvis Presley on the "Steve Allen Show" (courtesy of NBC)

THE BEATLES (courtesy of Capitol Records)

Kristina (courtesy of Kristina)

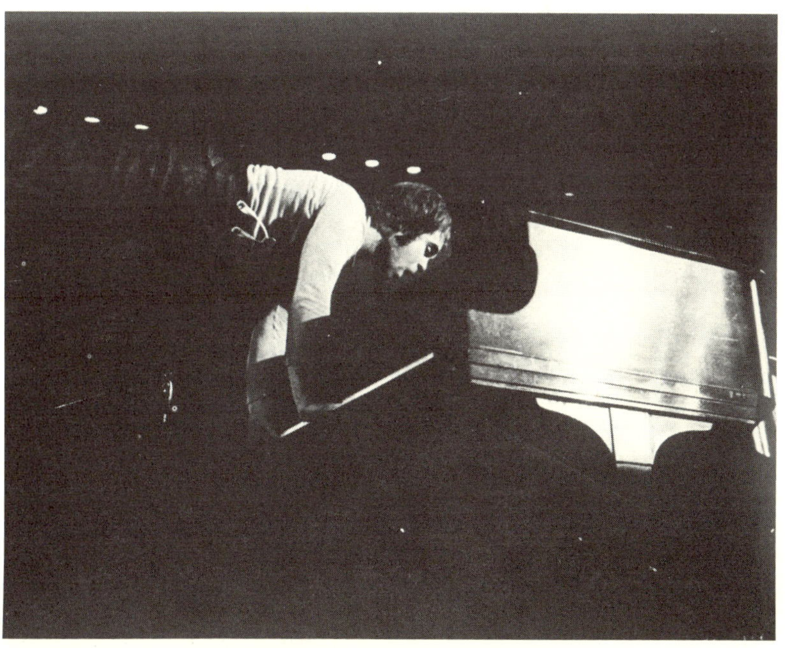

Elton John (courtesy of MCA Records)

Bob Garcia (courtesy of A & M)

Bhaskar Menon (courtesy of Capitol Records)

Joseph Smith (courtesy of Warner Brothers)

Herb Alpert (courtesy of A & M)

Mitch Miller and the Sing Along Gang (courtesy of NBC)

Jerry Moss (courtesy of A & M)

Stan Cornyn (courtesy of Warner Brothers)

Dennis Killeen (courtesy of Capitol Records)

The size of the company, located in Charlie Chaplin's old studio, allows for this kind of interaction. Small size has its problems, especially at the promotion and distribution level. One artist's manager explains:

> You go into say Philadelphia, and the jobber [independent distributor] there carries like A&M and ten other labels. So A&M can't exert much pressure on them. Like "X" is coming in and we go to the local distributor that is handling A&M, and he's got two records in stock in the whole company. He's got two records in stock! "X's" doing a major concert there, like 3,000 seats, and he has only got two records. I mean what do you do. You call A&M and complain and A&M calls them and complains, but there isn't that much power.

There does seem to be an element of truth to the complaints about A&M's distribution and promotion system. Record-store managers say they are unable to get some A&M products. One month after the release date, a retailer I interviewed complained that he still had not gotten Status Quo's *Hello* album.

Arranging press contact with A&M artists on the road frequently is a Herculean task. Writers regularly receive invitations from Andy Meyer, the A&M press chief, to interview or review a touring act. The press contact is always the local promotion man. In some cases, the local people either do not know about the tour or get dates and schedules totally mixed up. While this is not totally endemic to A&M, many media people would prefer to work with WEA or Columbia where the chain of command seems more coordinated.

With the advent of Cat Stevens and Carole King, A&M gained more power, yet jobbers only carry highly charted material as opposed to potential hits. United Artists, a company with its own distribution chain, United Distributing Corp., also stresses the selective handling of artists. United Artists's promotion director, Bill Roberts, outlined their philosophy:

> We believe in operating small. Not putting out albums or a single just to have them out there to catch volume or create volume. [And] so we have to keep our artist roster quite small. It basically begins at A&R at deciding what artists we're going to sign to the label. We will turn down an artist if he's very good, if he's great, we'll turn him down maybe because he doesn't have a good producer. We'll talk to him about everything, but we won't consider him for our label because he won't fit on this label because it's a total organization.

As with A&M, UA stresses the act rather than the record itself. As Martin R. Cerf suggests, "our job here is to exploit an act to the best of our ability and not lose it. If we can promote an act and get them known without losing an album having an unsuccessful LP, that's great." UA's distribution system provides the advantages of both unit dispersal and special promotion of product. Whether they can maintain this precarious balance without falling into the trap of "throwing it up against the wall" remains an open question.

ABC Records, while primarily a singles "bubblegum" type of label, has expanded into the more sophisticated market. It also has embraced the artists development philosophy. Steve Barri, a producer of a long line of hit singles and A&R director told *Billboard*, "We cut down on the amount of acts that we sign; hold it down to a select few so that we can put enough promotion behind them, enough excitement behind them, and go with quality instead of quantity. I want to hold it down to a smaller amount of releases but get the best out of them."[5] The company is also setting up its own chain of branches.

Compact organization should not be lauded as a universal panacea. It can be totally disadvantageous, as it is with Fantasy Records, located in Berkeley, California. Originally, the company was a specialty label producing jazz quartets, Lenny Bruce discs, and "Peanuts" soundtracks and one hit single, Vince Guaraldi's piano version of "Cast Your Fate to the Wind," from the film *Black Orpheus.* Fantasy entered the rock-music field late in 1967 with a second generation San Francisco band, Creedence Clearwater Revival. Beginning with "Suzy Q," the unit produced a long string of Top 40 albums. All were solid golds. Creedence's earnings reportedly accounted for over 80 percent of the company's annual earnings. While occasionally signing acts such as Clover, Fantasy did little to highlight its roster. Most companies support publicity lists of 600. Fantasy's was 200, according to Bill Yaryan, formerly its publicity director. Relying on Creedence, the label made only half-hearted attempts to break new acts. The dissolution of Creedence in 1972 effectively removed Fantasy—at least temporarily—from participation in the crap game of popular music.

The size factor colors that artist-company relationship. A large company with its own branches or distributors can move products and receive special field promotion. They need not share their field people with competing labels. The artist—unless he is an established headliner—will in any case have his record in competition with all the others on the same label. The odds of success are much greater when the performer is in the branches than when the act's record is collecting dust in the bins of an "indie" distributor. The rule of thumb in the industry is that established artists enjoy an advantageous position with the major companies. As one record-company executive put it:

> A lot of artists who are with other companies who have been broken by them, as they become more popular, they expand past the capabilities of that smaller label to really do commercial justice to them in terms of the number of units they can sell. . . . I know a number of artists who have ended up at Columbia after initial SUCCESSES elsewhere because they felt on an album elsewhere that sold 3,000 copies, that Columbia would have sold 6,000 to 8,000 copies.

Columbia has lured headliners such as Neil Diamond, Donovan, Ian and Sylvia, Crazy Horse and the Association with these arguments. Given Columbia's unofficial policy of "guaranteed act," established artists *are* afforded special treatment. RCA Victor, a company of comparable economic size and a traditional rival in recent years, has followed suit. When Rocco Laginestra became president of the record division he signed headliners away from other labels, among them Cass Elliot, the Everly Brothers, the Kinks, David Bowie and Lou Reed, formerly of the Velvet Underground. He explained, "You don't create a Guess Who or a Jefferson Airplane overnight."[6] Buying superstars is the safest bet in the popular music business, but it also presents its set of built-in problems. Bill Roberts, discussing Neil Diamond's reported $5 million signing with Columbia, cautioned, "The longevity of an artist might be five years. Now if he already had four years of his career, extremely strong at selling records and being exposed, then maybe he only has a year left. . . . They [Columbia] may not just be able to do anything with him. He may fall completely on that label." There is that risk, but Neil Diamond is a star and his odds of success are great. The deejay still plays proven product rather than risking his job. An executive assessing the value of the Association to Columbia said, "Rather than trying something new, they'll go with the Association record because they know the name. 'They did "Windy" we'll see what their new thing is.' Rather than taking a chance on an unknown." Buying stars is not a guarantee of success because the market can shift, as Roberts indicates, leaving both the transferring act and the company out in the cold.

For the new or lesser-known act a smaller company may be the best avenue to success. Jac Holzman told Jay Ruby, "I'd rather sell more records of fewer artists and still retain that kind of closeness. . . . No record's ever going to be made and released out of Elektra that I'm not a part of in some way. It may be only that I'll just get to hear it and say, 'Wow, that's really great.' . . . I think our people have been so well chosen that that's liable to happen."[7] The closeness of the smaller company is an attractive magnet for disenchanted acts.

Brownsville Station explained why they signed with Bell Records and Big Tree Productions: "They believe in us. The smaller company is believed to devote time and energy to breaking an act. ABC Records has what is called a "bull-pen theory," which takes one act at a time directed to a specific audience. Jay Lasker's "formula" was to break into Top 40 radio with Barry McGuire, followed by the Mamas and Papas, then Three Dog Night, then Steppenwolf and Grass Roots. Each was pyramided upon the other. In 1973 ABC opted for more of the album market, enlarging its vision to include the more specialized philosophy of artist development, the dominant ideology of the record industry of the 1970s. With loaded dice a few throws are as good as 20 honest ones.

In the waning months of 1973, Americans were introduced to the "energy crisis." The dominant component of the alleged crisis was petroleum. First home-heating oils and then gasoline became in short supply. A by-product of petroleum is polyvinyl chloride (PVC), the main ingredient in the making of long-playing records. This shortage, coupled with the rising cost of paper, impacted the buckshot theory of production. *Billboard* announced, " 'Selectivity' was the key word in planning future LP releases. . . . " Carefully planned releases, of course, were standard practice for the smaller labels. Logically the majors would be most affected by the "crisis," but this has turned out to be only partially true.

Some major labels cut back the number of albums released. *Billboard*, in January 1974, reported slashes in product up to 50 percent by some companies. This new-found caution or "selectivity" compounded several trends. Established artists "would go to the post more often." Concert performances and *Best Of* albums would be used more often. Major companies increasingly attempted to lure "name" performers to their labels. The buying and using of superstars grew by leaps and bounds. Even Bob Dylan began touring again, while his album *Planet Waves* climbed to the number one position on the charts.

For the majors the vinyl crisis has meant a consolidation. Marginal artists were quietly removed. Recording contracts for new acts became almost nonexistent. Numerous economies were undertaken, some of which were ineffective, cosmetic or just plain foolhardy. As with gasoline, a number of observers questioned the severity of the crisis, as well as the motives of some of the majors. It was noted that as record-company executives decried the situation, in January 1974 CBS released some 41 rock, easy-listening, soul and country LPs. The next month, Warner Brothers announced 22 new albums for release. These figures implied that the majors, while protesting the crisis, were not cutting back product or necessarily abandoning the buckshot theory.

The companies most hurt by the vinyl crisis appeared to be the smaller independents. The majors, of course, have always pressed and manufactured product for their smaller counterparts. In order to preserve the production schedules of the majors the independents were cut off. George Hocutt, the president of the National Association of Independent Record Distributors (NAIRD) complained: "Some of our member labels were shocked when RCA canceled custom operations early this year. One label had been with them since 78 rpm days and we understand it is contemplating legal action. Capitol stopped pressing for their firms in early fall, crippling fall business for some small labels who had difficulty making other arrangements on such short notice." He continued, "The situation is getting worse."

Some mutterings were heard in the retail end of the record industry about the coincidence of the vinyl crisis and a projected $1.00 per unit price rise in albums. One retailer observed, "Once albums are all $6.98 list, then the crisis will be over." George Hocutt seems to agree: "The shortage of vinylite and pressing plants is certain to be inflationary. It quite possibly is a combination in restraint of trade and the problem will worsen if proper government action is not taken." If the critics and the skeptics are correct then the basic marketing ideologies have not changed.

WHEN YOU'RE HOT, YOU'RE HOT

From 1948 through 1955, four companies (Columbia, RCA, Decca and Capitol) placed over 75 percent of the records listed on the *Billboard* top sellers chart. By 1958, they had less than 36 percent of the market. The reason for this slump was that the majors were not producing what record-buying youth wanted. Black independents such as Chess, Atlantic, Imperial and Vee Jay moved into the void.

The record industry during the early 1950s was characterized by company pre-eminence over artists. Singers had five-year contracts and were tied to the dicta of the record company. The companies determined style, song, recording date and in some cases the artist's stage name. Record companies took over what had previously been the function of the big band. Orchestra arrangers during the swing era put words and music together. Frank Sinatra, Helen O'Connell and others came as part of the total package along with Tommy Dorsey, Harry James or Benny Goodman. The demise of the big band altered this relationship, with the balladeer becoming more dependent upon the record company for orchestration, material and direction. The artists and repertoire director became an increasingly important figure. He was, as David Lawhon of Capitol observes, "the man with the feel of the public pulse." He picked the songs the artist would record. Stan Cornyn, then employed by Capitol, describes the power of the A&R director. "The company would pick out 12 songs for Peggy Lee and tell her to be at the studio Wednesday at 8, and she'd show up and sing what you told her. And she'd leave three hours later and Capitol'd take her songs and do anything it wanted to with them. Her art was totally out of her—the artist's—hands. . . . That was a time when the artist was supposed to shut up, and put up with anything the almighty recording company wanted."[8] Five or six A&R men dominated popular music during the early Eisenhower years —Gordon Jenkins (MCA), Art Talmadge (Mercury), Hugo

Winterhalter (RCA), Ken Nelson (Capitol) and Mitch Miller (Columbia). All of these men were musicians steeped in either the classics or big-band swing. The most successful A&R director was the goateed oboe player whose songs appeared on "Your Hit Parade" and record-sales charts.

Mitchell William Miller was the prototype A&R man of the 1950s. A graduate of the Eastman School of Music, Miller became the highest-paid oboe player in classical music history. In 1947, John Phillip Hammond recruited the oboist to Mercury Records as a contributing A&R director. Producing Frankie Laine, he turned out successive hits: "Lucky Ol'Sun," "Mule Train" and "Cry of the Wild Goose." Columbia Records lured Miller to its ranks with a contract for $25,000 a year plus expenses. At Columbia, Miller could do no wrong. *McCall's* characterized him as "The Man Who Makes Money Records." *The Saturday Evening Post* introduced him in a fea-

Exhibit 3.2

TOP 30* SONGS PER YEAR BY "MAJORS"

	1950	1951	1952	1953	*1954	*1955	N
Capitol	3	5	3	6	5	4	26
Columbia	1	7	11	5	6	2	32
MCA†	11	2	3	0	2	6	24
Mercury	4	4	2	3	5	1	19
RCA	4	4	6	9	5	2	30
Others	6	4	5	8	4	9	

* *Billboard* lists only Top 25 after 1954.
† Then Decca and Coral.

ture story as "The Shaggy Genius of Pop Music." *Post* biographer Dean Jennings, who normally reported on movie celebrities, wrote, "Miller's snap judgment on hidden talent is almost as *infallible* as a Geiger counter."[9] Between 1950 and 1956, Columbia sold 80 million records with the Miller imprimateur. At one point he had eight songs on the *Billboard* Top Ten. He defeated Columbia's arch rival RCA in the pre-rock-and-roll 1950s, placing more songs on the top 25 annual sellers. The selection of a Pittsburgh night watchman's song "Cry" for an equally obscure singer Johnnie Ray, earned Columbia $2 million. He transformed Anthony Benedetto into Tony Bennett and moved 1,500,000 units of "Because of You." He revived the innocuous Confederate marching chant, "Yellow Rose of Texas," earning a gold record. Norma Jean Speranza became Jill Corey and sold millions of records on the basis of an over-the-transom tape. He did similarly good things for the Four Lads, Jimmy Boyd, Guy Mitchell, Rosemary Clooney and the one-hit sensation, Joan Weber. In a 1955 *New York Times Magazine* article Miller elaborated on his "keep it sexy, simple and sad" formula of success. Acknowledging that there are "still mysteries and miracles" to producing hits, Miller outlined the basic ingredients for successful records:

> 1. *Self Identification*. The song says to the listener what the listener has in his own mind but can't quite put into words himself. It speaks for him of his own love, or sorrow. It recalls nostalgically an episode of the past, sweet or bitter. Thus, the listener identifies with the song.
>
> 2. *Universality*. In articulating his own emotions, the song makes the listener aware that he is not alone, that the singer too has the same misery or joy. And so do the millions of other people who rush out to buy that song.
>
> 3. *Simplicity*. The ability of the listener to hum the tune, and to pick up the lyric quickly is essential.[10]

The ideal songs to reflect those elements were about love, "boy longs for girl, girl longs for boy" and optimism. In the same article, Miller defended the then-emerging genre of rhythm and blues. He felt it was a youthful reflection of a concern with the plight of southern "colored people" as well as generational rebellion: "I would rather have a teenager express his defiance of authority by listening to a rhythm and blues record than by going out and knocking someone over the head." This lukewarm endorsement was offset by a statement of concern over singers like Doris Day, Jo Stafford and Tony Bennett "singing in this frenetic style once belong[ing] wholly to the Negro singers."

The following year, according to several Columbia executives, Miller was offered a singer who was considered a possibility for the country-and-western catalog. "No singer is worth an advance over $25,000," Miller told Colonel Tom Parker. Elvis Presley was consequently signed by Miller's arch rival, RCA Victor. Several years later, Norman Petty, a Columbia artist, approached Miller with a demo record. Miller told the instrumentalist, "Don't waste your time on a group like this; they'll never make it." He was wrong again. The group in question was Buddy Holly and the Crickets, and the song was "That'll Be The Day." Rock impresario Don Kirshner recalls, "In those days Mitch Miller had a strong position in the business. If he turned down a song you were in trouble. I brought 'Will You Still Love Me Tomorrow' to him and he turned it down. But I wouldn't accept that. I felt it was a terrific song and a sure hit if it was done right. So I gave it to the Shirelles [and Phil Spector] and it became No. One."[11]

The deviant and foreign strains of 'Sh-Boom" and "Rock Around the Clock" were originally hailed as fleeting novelties soon to join "The Thing" and "Doggie in the Window." To cope with the new fad, A&R people resorted to a practice called "covering." Covering basically refers to the recording of a song doing well in a specialty market such as rhythm and blues or country by a headliner in the pop idiom. Despite what some rock historians have written, covering was standard practice in the recording industry long before rhythm and blues. Top-name artists frequently copied songs of their lesser-known contemporaries. A number of Hank Williams's songs were covered by Tony Bennett ("Cold, Cold Heart"), Polly Bergen ("Honky Tonkin' ") and several other pop stars. Copying Negro material, however, added the dimension of racial exploitation. A *Los Angeles Times* writer, Mike Greshman, noted: "The prevailing racism on white-owned radio stations could never permit a black blues artist the time to communicate his music to white audiences. Only safe Negroes like Nat (King) Cole and Ella Fitzgerald were given that privilege. None of that 'dirty music' could be allowed to sully the ears of young white females."[12] This sentiment has been echoed by many diverse writers of different ideological persuasions, ranging from Eldridge Cleaver and Leroi Jones to English rock writer Charles Gillett. Nonetheless, there are many more persuasive arguments beyond the racist charge. Censorship has been popularly pointed to as a prime reason for the practice. Charles Calhoun's "Shake, Rattle and Roll," for example, was originally designed for a black audience. Bill Haley changed the lyric "You wear low dresses, the sun comes shining through—I can't believe my eyes, all of this belongs to you," to "You wear those dresses your hair done up so nice —you look so warm, but your heart is cold as ice." Most white teenagers originally thought the song was about a dance. The Midnighters' very straightforward song "Work With Me, Annie"—followed by "Annie Had A Baby (Can't Work No More)"—was transformed to "Dance With Me, Henry" by Negro singer Etta James and popularized by white vocalist Georgie Gibbs. The connotation given to the designation "rock and roll" by singers such as Teresa Brewer, Pat Boone, Georgie Gibbs and the "Your Hit Parade" staff was one of dancing. When Shirley and Lee sang "Let The Good Times Roll" or "Rock All Night," they did not mean "I Could Dance All Night." The sexuality in some rhythm and blues numbers perhaps justified covering, but a cursory examination of other songs copied indicates that it could not have been the sole consideration.

Many rhythm and blues songs by Negro artists that were copied did not contain "offensive" lyrics. Totally innocent songs such as "Dance With Me, Henry" (despite its origin) and "Ko-Ko-Mo" were covered. Nearly all of the majors, with the notable exception of Columbia, developed their own rhythm and blues and rock-a-billy singers when the sales of covers no longer surpassed the original version. When the

Exhibit 3.3

Song	Original	Cover
"Dance With Me, Henry"	Etta James	Georgie Gibbs
"Ruby, Baby"	Drifters	Dion
"Jim Dandy"	LaVern Baker	Georgie Gibbs
"Tutti Fruitti"	Little Richard	Pat Boone
"Shake, Rattle and Roll"	Joe Turner	Bill Haley
"I Hear You Knockin'"	Smiley Lewis	Gale Storm
"Wheel of Fortune"	Cardinals	Kay Starr
"Sh-Boom"	Chords	Crewcuts
"Earth Angel"	Penguins	Crewcuts
"Ko-Ko-Mo"	Gene and Eunice	Perry Como
"Seven Days"	Clyde McPhatter	Dorothy Collins
"Sincerely"	Moonglows	McGuire Sisters
"Good Night Sweetheart"	Spaniels	McGuire Sisters
"Eddie My Love"	Teen Queens	McGuire Sisters
"Corrina, Corrina"	Joe Turner	Ray Peterson
"Ain't That a Shame"	Fats Domino	Pat Boone

Penguins' "Earth Angel" outdistanced the Crewcuts and LaVern Baker surpassed Georgie Gibbs's "Tweedle Dee," then, as Danny and Juniors would later sing, "Rock and Roll Was Here To Stay."

During this period, Columbia used Johnnie Ray to cover a Sun recording by the Prisonaires, "Just Walking in the Rain," but did little else in the rock and roll genre. In 1958, at a disk-jockey convention sponsored by Todd Storz, the father of Top 40 programming, Miller launched an all-out assault upon the radio format and rock music. He lectured the 850 deejays assembled:

> You carefully built yourselves into the monarchs of radio and then you went and abdicated your programming to the 8 to 14 year olds, to the preshave crowd that makes up 12 percent of the country's population and zero percent of its buying power—once you eliminate pony-tail ribbons, popsicles and peanut brittle. Youth must be served—but how about some music for the rest of us?

> Does the demand for the record come because you play it first, or do the kids demand it because they heard it first on Top 40? If Top 40 is an election, will somebody please blow a whistle for the Honest Ballot Association. . . . The 75 percent of the nation over 14 years old is buying hi-fi record players in unprecedented numbers, setting them up in the living room, shutting off the radio and creating their own home-made programming departments.

Dick Clark, at the beginning of his tutelage of "American Bandstand," shrugged off Miller's protest saying the Columbia executive was "entitled to his opinion." Alan Freed, who originated the term rock and roll, replied to Miller with equal passion:

> It sounds like sour grapes to me. I believe Mitch knows little about rhythm and blues and native American music. He's always been classically minded and my feeling is that he's a musical snob.

> How can he talk out of both sides of his mouth? On the one hand he's condemning rock and roll. On the other he has such rock and rollers as Otis Blackwell, Leroy Kirkland and Jessie Stone doing writing and managing jobs. . . . Let's face it, rock and roll is bigger than all of us. As my personal protest against Mr. Miller's speech, I'm hereby banning all Columbia and Date Records from my show.[13]

Freed's threat was an idle one, as the Columbia roster had little to interest the rock jock. History, of course, has proven Freed the winner as Capitol, Decca, MGM, Liberty and many others attempted to find country singers who could emulate the distinct Presley style. Capitol signed Gene Vincent and Tommy Sands. Even Columbia went south, recruiting Johnny Cash as the "New Elvis." Later, Ronnie Self ("Bertha Lou") became their "new hope." Liberty discovered Eddie Cochran and Jody Reynolds, while MGM transformed Harold Jenkins into Conway Twitty. RCA hoped lightning would strike twice and spent $100,000 promoting David Houston as the successor to Elvis. Most of these singers lacked, at least for traditional A&R people, the professionalism attributed to the older crooners. Many record executives used this charge to validate their disdain of the new sound. Nonetheless, the ticket-selling function went on. Young teenagers were scooped up from the sidewalks of Philadelphia on the basis of their personal appearance and transformed into overnight idols on "American Bandstand." Some could not even sing. Billy Parsons's "All American Boy" was recorded by Bobby Bare and then played on the Dick Clark program as the real thing. Echo chambers and other production devices became the rule. The widespread practice of payola in the late 1950s transformed promotion into image building as the act would be introduced by $20.00 bills or "presidents" handed to the deejay and program director. All a company had to do was contract numerous deejays and the producer of "American Bandstand" and a hit record was believed soon to follow. The majors, observing their smaller competitors succeeding with this technique, joined in. The payola period, followed by the years of the twist, were not especially kind to those companies referred to as the majors. The smaller labels with black roots still benefitted from the majors' inability to cope with the rock and roll phenomenon. The advent of the Beatles further complicated the role of the major companies.

SHAKIN' THE TOWER

Capitol Records was founded in 1942 by songwriters Johnny Mercer and Buddy DeSylva and record retailer Glenn Wallichs. Beginning with band singer Ella May Morse's "Cow Cow Boogie," the independent grew into one of the majors basically on the strength of such ex-band singers as Al Martino, Kay Starr, Peggy Lee, Les Paul and Mary Ford. In 1961 most of the company's stock was taken over by Electric and Musical Industries (EMI), a British conglomerate. Through this association the label acquired the recording rights to the Beatles. Ironically, the company's president, Alan Livingston, originally turned them down twice because, "English groups just weren't selling here in 1962."[14] With the Beatles, Capitol adhered to the policy of having superstars carry the company supplemented by the sporadic "one-hit" wonders. The Beatles paid the bills, occasionally aided by a monster hit such as "Ode to Billy Joe" or the late Senator Everett Dirksen's reading of "Gallant Men." The "one shots" cost the company little money to promote and publicize. As the Beatles sold their usual 5 million units per release, the company began to "throw out" material. The occasional hit was nearly pure profit, especially when the artist's advance money and studio costs were deducted from his royalty check. The roster grew to 247 acts. "As long as they keep going 'Yeah! Yeah! Yeah!' Capitol has nothing to worry about," so wrote *Forbes*, the financial magazine in 1968. "People got lazy," commented Claire Brush, a five-year Capitol veteran. The Beatles required little promotion. All that was necessary was to tell the people a new album was out. An executive recalled, "What more can you do for the Beatles except give them their billboard on Sunset Blvd?" The affluence from Beatles product also allowed Capitol to buy and carry a number of so-called middle-selling artists such as The Band, Steve Miller, Quicksilver Messenger Service, the Stone Poneys, Sea Train and approximately 15 other acts which sold in the neighborhood of 60,000 to 150,000 albums returning a bare profit when advertising and production expenses were subtracted. In several cases, as with the San Francisco bands, the company bid excessive amounts to secure the services of unproven acts. The disbanding of the Beatles and the defection of the Beach Boys to Warner Brothers, along with a sales slump by Buck Owens, impacted both economically and psychologically upon the company causing massive personnel and policy changes.

In 1967, enjoying the success of a $100 million fiscal year, Alan Livingston told *Newsweek*, "It's impossible to be the leader for any length of time. Asking who's Number One is like asking what day it is."[15] Five years later when Capitol's fortunes appeared bleakest, Mauri Lathower looked up at the ceiling and said, "I could walk out on the Hollywood Freeway at rush hour, walk against the traffic, and not even get hit. That's how cold we are. There's no sense hiding it. It's just that we can't get tracked. I think the material is okay. Like Warner Brothers . . . when you've got things going for you . . . people like to go with winners." Capitol was no longer the "hot" company. Promo men were not welcomed at radio stations by program directors eagerly awaiting the new Beatles or Beach Boys record. By 1972, Warner Brothers was the king of the mountain and Capitol was $8 million in the red. Its stock had dropped over the years from 63 to 6 points on the American Exchange. Capitol's president aptly commented: "All things must pass." The sins of Columbia and Mitch Miller were vested upon Capitol. Dick Schulenberg, then with Capitol, says: "They panicked . . . they started throwing things overboard, a lot of which they should have thrown overboard before. They may have overreacted, which once they came out of the cycle, may have put them into such a deep dive they may not be able to pull out." The roster was trimmed to 81 acts; executives were summarily dismissed. *Rolling Stone* asked, "What's Shaking at the Capitol Tower?"

The success of the Beatles and a host of other English bands found the major recording companies in the same position as in 1956, when Presley was termed a passing fancy. This time the industry understood what was happening. Billy James described the climate of the time: "There was nothing else happening in America then that anybody had capitalized on. The Spoonful were in New York at that time but hadn't quite gotten it together. The Airplane were in San Francisco, but hadn't gotten it together. Those things were happening but nobody was into them." Billy James and Terry Melcher introduced a new domestic rock group to Columbia Records, who had not experienced a "number-one" single in two years, since Steve Lawrence's "Go Away Little Girl," a middle-of-the-road ballad. Billy remembers, "So we were lucky enough, the Byrds were lucky enough to get with Columbia, to get me and Terry to appreciate what they were doing, we were lucky enough, Columbia was hungry at the time." The Byrds were joined by the Raiders and a hundred other bands aspiring to become the American "Golden" Beatles. The Electric Prunes, the Standells, the Vagrants, the Barbarians, Count Five, Shadows of the Knight, the Mojo Men and many others entered the race to record one charted single or also ran and then to disappear. Many of these bands served as training grounds for some of the acts in the post-Monterey Festival era. All of them were minus the commodity record executives call "professionalism." Critic Lenny Kaye describes what A&R confronted:

> Most of these groups (and by and large, this was an era dominated by groups) were young decidedly unprofessional, seemingly more at home practicing for a teen dance than going out on

> national tour. . . . They exemplified the berserk pleasure that comes with being on-stage outrageous, the relentless middle-finger drive and determination. . . . And as these were kids who more often than not could've lived up the street, or at least in the same town, there was no question what even localized success could mean in terms of universal attraction. Elvis had shown us the first time around that rock's greatest strength has always been as catalyst, and with a whole new generation waiting out there to be worked on, there could be little doubt that something big was about to erupt.[16]

What followed can best be described as a proliferation of product and a market deemed to be on an external escalator ride. In 1965, 3,548 albums were offered to the record-buying public. In 1967, 4,328 units were released. The same year sales crested beyond the $1 billion mark. This rise was attributed to the rock revolution. The growing affluence of American youth, the FCC edict barring the airing of similar material on both AM and FM bands and the growth of the so-called alternative culture all played a part in the rock phenomenon. The net effect was to expand the radio audience into various sectors: AM-FM, boss-free form and singles-albums. Adults and adolescents were both buying Beatles records in unprecedented numbers. Sales figures, like *Billboard* chart positions, are never completely lost on record-company executives. The Byrds, the Doors and the Grateful Dead were popularized with the help of advertising and promotion campaigns, some of which were taken from Derek Taylor, the Liverpool quartet's first press officer. Most companies' primary catalog was still in the MOR field. Eighty percent of the Warner/Reprise roster in 1969 featured Dean Martin, Bill Cosby, Frank Sinatra, Trini Lopez and the folksinging group Peter, Paul and Mary. Outside of specialty labels as Vanguard, Elektra, Chess, Takoma and a few others, little attempt was made to introduce acts outside of the normal channels of tradepaper ads, store displays and liner notes.

At the first Monterey International Pop Festival, record-company executives like Clive Davis, Jerry Moss and Mo Ostin discovered new acts for young adult audiences, which had been neglected for years. Following the festival, Columbia outbid its less affluent competitors, signing Janis Joplin for $250,000 and spending nearly as much on promotion to get it all back. Columbia began running full-page ads in *Rolling Stone* announcing, "Don't Let The Man Bust Our Music." Monterey also brought to the fore the "house hippie" or "company freak." A house hippie was usually a writer or producer who could explain the "new community" for the record company and the label to the "street." Danny Fields, one of the first exhibit A's, defined his role "a kept hippie, mediating between the turtle-necked titans of the record industry and the unpunctual, crazy monsters called musicians. The titans supply his salary and expenses, but his heart is with the musicians, which makes schizophrenia a very possible occupational hazard. . . . The company freak is someone who is supposed to provide the liaison factor between the company and its artists, and also between the company and the alternative media. No hip FM DJ will have anything to do with the promotion sharpies in shiny suits."[17] Other companies employed long hairs as a status symbol or as mere window dressing. Marty Cerf, then a writer for *Rock* magazine, was hired by Liberty Records and paid a salary of $150 per week to do nothing. "I was the long-haired Negro for the company, a token." He was told, "you don't have to come in. Sort of hang out and put your name on things." Atlantic hired Danny Fields; Columbia, Mike Ochs; Warner, Andy Wickham; Electra, Dave Anderle; Capitol, Nick Venet and Claire Brush; and A&M ran through Derek Taylor, Michael Voose, finally settling on short-haired, aerospace executive turned *Open City* writer Bob Garcia. The scene was one of organized chaos. The bands just wanted to play their music. Most company freaks, as Jon Landau would later admit, were record-business novices who took themselves very seriously. Only Billy James, who was with Columbia from 1961 through 1966, was an exception. He says, "I was their link to the street in '64; so I had three years' experience." Company executives were busily studying their rising sales figures and the proliferating number of acts. Sincere artist development began when record companies became convinced of the potential profits to be gained in the young-adult LP market, while at the same time realizing that traditional singles-oriented marketing techniques were not enough to sell albums.

ONE TOKE OVER THE LINE: THE WARNER/REPRISE TRIP

"Our philosophy," claims Joe Smith, "has always been that we would rather go down in flames with an artist like [Randy Newman] than take a shot on a singles group that has a couple of single hits and no long-term staying power in the business." While this may sound like a foolish gamble, it is not, as Stan Cornyn indicates: "We have a plateau theory that we will go from a smaller market to a bigger market, and a bigger market, trying to find a broader plateau. Randy Newman has stepped up a couple of plateaus. I think it will be a lot easier for him now to accelerate and accelerate. How far he can go nobody knows . . . we will not sign a polka band unless we think the polka band will have an appeal to the masses." The Warner/Reprise ethos is traceable to Morris Ostin and Joseph Smith who, according to those around them, understood social trends as the rock revolution before their competitors. One event is cited by Cornyn, who accompanied Mo Ostin to Haight Ashbury in 1966 where they visited the Avalon Ballroom: "It was then the whole scene started to look up for Mo and myself . . . we got into an appreciation of that point of view . . . we understood it. It didn't uptight us too much." Presumably, it is this trip that made Warner aware of the Grateful Dead, a band instrumental in the Kesey Trips Festival that also transformed Warner corporate consciousness. During the scramble for "acid-rock" bands Warner Brothers snared the Grateful Dead, a group familiar only to street people and flower children. Their songs were long drawn-out improvisational artifacts. Joseph Smith told *Rolling Stone*, "With the Grateful Dead we learned there are other ways to sell records, like sponsoring a free concert in Denver. We learned you don't have to be on Top 40 radio, that there's a whole market in underground FM. We learned that posters mean something, that billboards mean something."[18] The Dead and other groups like them opened up new vistas for the corporation. With these techniques learned from the new culture, Warner set about packaging the Monterey sensation Jimi Hendrix. With the flamboyant guitarist another lesson was learned in the Burbank executive suite: "When we saw the numbers that those records could sell in, we said 'wow,' there's something here. You'd struggle with a middle-of-the-road artist to sell maybe 300,000 albums and have a major when you could sell 2,000,000 Jimi Hendrix albums. Frank Sinatra never sold 2 million albums. Dean Martin never sold 2 million albums. I don't think there were too many artists who ever sold 2 million albums until this wave of 'involving' records." Having absorbed the economic value of the new culture, Mo Ostin proceeded to find those artists suited for the 18 to 35 market. Ron Saul, a promotion director, explains, "We went after as many acts as we possibly could that we thought would relate to this age group or this type of music." Most market surveys of buying habits indicated this age group was not attuned to singles, but albums. Warner's previous entree to this demographic unit was through Peter, Paul and Mary and the Kinks, a band they totally misunderstood. Not surprisingly, the company courted many disaffected folksingers who were fleeing Elektra, Vanguard, Apple or who had remained on the coffeehouse circuit long after the folkie revival was history. Andy Wickham found Joni Mitchell and signed her for $15,000. Joe Smith and Mo Ostin signed James Taylor from Apple, Neil Young, a refugee from the Buffalo Springfield, Gordon Lightfoot away from Liberty, David Blue formerly of Elektra and Van Morrison of London Records. They enlisted the interesting but commercially esoteric songs and voices of Van Dyke Parks and Randy Newman. Neither were or are chart busters. Newman considered calling one album *So Long Mo*, feeling he was to be dropped from the label at any moment. Unlike Tiny Tim or the Ides of March, he has not been cut out, despite their more substantial ledger contributions. The support of Newman has provided the company with an image of act building which is projected throughout the industry. Bob Regehr was quoted in *Billboard* as saying, "I have to remember I'm working for the company by working for the acts. My greatest satisfaction is seeing an act break after we plugged along behind it for years, such as Alice Cooper or Randy Newman. In a way, that's even more of a thrill than when an artist is fortunate enough to hit it right the first time and take off immediately, as America did."[19] Regehr's field personnel have a reputation with artists for providing excellent road service. "Everything from being at the airport with a limo to dope," said one competitor. The hip company image has helped Warner. Trade ads also have furthered this reputation. One announced the Van Dyke Park's album *Song Cycle* had lost $35,000. The ad read, "How we lost $35,509.50 on 'The Album of the Year' (Damnit)." The ad was both a hype for the record and the company. Repeatedly the message indicated, "it cost us $48,302," underlining the company's support for the artist. Parks was further lost when the copy stated, "We sell enough Petula and Crosby and Association, we can afford a Van Dyke Parks." *Rolling Stone* and other rock publications identified Warner Brothers with the "new" culture. Pushing the Mothers of Invention, the company told the readers of underground press, "Yes, Greater America may have Nixon, cold cream, and vacuum-packed lima beans, but we at Reprise are now allied with Frank Zappa and his Merry Pranksters." The hip corporate appearance has helped Warner considerably, attracting even more talent to its doors. Neophytes feel the company will give them a fair share at support and faith as it did for Newman and Dyke Parks. Smith acknowledges, "One artist talking to another is far more effective than royalty points, dollars and so forth." Saul adds:

> Initially everyone gets a shot. But I think that's one of the great attributes of this company, I think that's why artists love us, speaking of us as the company, because we gave them a shot, we work with them and we continue to work with them. With so many other companies, like you say, throw out the buckshot, they forget, they throw it out. Ninety percent of it is just mailed and nothing else is done other than being mailed.

Established artists wishing to back a winning horse also come to Warner/Reprise. As Andy Wickham quips, "We are an efficient machine." In 1969 with the decline of the hard-rock phenomenon due to the breakup of many of the super groups, popular music retreated to balladeers, writer-singers and novelty acts. The Ostin-Smith philosophy of blanketing the youth market worked; Warner kept a solid foot in the acoustical field. In the wake of its success the Youngbloods, the Beach Boys, John Sebastian, Donovan and Dionne Warwick signed with the company for unheard of advances and royalty terms. The reason for Warner's attractiveness, according to *Rolling Stone*, was more than just corporate image. "There's still no inducement like good old-fashioned cash, and right now Warner/Reprise is rolling in it."[20] The Beach Boys reportedly received one of the largest percentages and advances in the history of the record business. The Youngbloods, according to their manager, got "handsome and sizeable" economic rewards for signing. The company image had worked.

In late 1972 some cracks in the Warner image began to surface. A publicist said, "We're overextended." Brownsville Station, one of five acts to leave the prestigious label, is bitter. Cub Koda said, "When we went to Burbank and were playing at the Whiskey, we went down to the offices and never even got past the lobby. They didn't even know who we were. That's rough. And so you say, well what do you want to do, go around saying that you're Warner Brothers' recording artists, when it doesn't do you any good?" Mickey Lutz: "I'll give you a good example of getting buried in the shuffle.

When's the last time you heard a Dionne Warwick song since she signed with Reprise?" "Who?" answers Cub. "Exactly, now what about Moby Grape?" Ray Davies of the Kinks told writer Bill Small, "Those guys are bastards, ain't they?" He went on to say Warner was "too big," causing the Kinks to lose their identity. The Kinks, he continued, received no promotion until six months before their contract was up for renewal. Warner competitors, not unexpectedly, are all too anxious to echo these accusations. The end of a winning streak means another hot hand may be in the cards. Corb Donohue is perhaps the most articulate and if not objective analyst of the Burbank situation: "The Warner Brothers image was unimpeachable for a couple of years. What's happened is they've overextended themselves to a point where they can no longer take care of, with the same personal attention to detail, the act that they had as they were able to do originally." Donohue believes that Warner has become a captive of its own imagery:

> WB has a circuslike quality to it now. I can identify WB promotions, but I can't identify WB acts. I think they have fallen heir to that horrible thing that's always been inherent in the entertainment business [that] is believing your own press releases . . . [or] beginning to. When you've created an image with as much calculation and planning as WB, to then start falling victim to your own propaganda is deadly. And I think that's what's happened to them to a degree. They've gotten a little self-righteous, a little smug, and they've overexpanded their ability to take care of it. They've never been a great trump at breaking singles, and consequently have lost a lot of potential acts, but they've lost more then they should have because they've had more than they should have to work on. In other words, they had more things to work with. Admittedly, they broke Gordon Lightfoot, for which I will always be indebted to them; they got Gordon Lightfoot a hit. But Lorraine Ellison's "Stay With Me Baby" wasn't a hit, and it's probably the greatest R&B ballad ever done. And there are a lot of people like that. There are a lot of acts that with the same concentrated attempt and effort undiluted by previous roster of service start they could have done the kind of job they promised in the

> ads. 'I clipped out the coupon, sent it to Burbank, and you didn't make me a star.' People are still expecting that everybody that WB touches is gonna be a golden because they've done such a great job of promoting themselves. They've done almost a better job of promoting the company than they have of the individual acts, with a very few exceptions. There are a lot of good and wonderful things that have gone by the boards just because they haven't had the staff or direction that they needed basically to get it together.

Donahue concluded that another company would soon be dominant: "I think that A&M has taken advantage of all of Warner Brothers' mistakes and comes in as a much quieter, much more profound force in the industry than Warner Brothers."

A year later a Warner promotion man said, "I can't possibly handle all this product." Warner had made it in a big way and now was another CBS Records: a "laid-back" Columbia, throwing product up against the famous industry wall. Gary Buttice, the Warner promo representative in Detroit, one of the most important markets, admitted that the company was primarily concerned with buying superstars rather than raising established acts into the million sales superstar category. "They won't push new acts," Buttice said. This is not entirely true, as Warner has pushed new artists. However, their most notable successes have been with acts with previous experience on other labels. Deep Purple was lifted to superstar status by the label. Maria Muldaur, a veteran folkie, became an "overnight" pop sensation. However, the days of the Blue Velvet Band and Holy Mackerel are definitely overwith. Despite the image, the "new kid on the block" was now an established major in the industry.

A&M: THE LONELY BULLS

Herb Alpert and Jerry Moss (A&M), a wedding of trumpet player and promoter released a single titled "The Lonely

Bull" in 1962. It sold 700,000 copies and earned $25,000 in its first year. Nine years later A&M grossed 56 million dollars according to a company spokesman. On the basis of "The Lonely Bull" the company was considered a "one-shot" label. It had a gimmick. The Tijuana Brass sound dominated easy-listening charts while the Beatles controlled the *Billboard* Hot 100; in 1966 Alpert and the Brass sold 13 million LPs, surpassed only by Lennon, McCartney & Co. The philosophy of A&M is based upon the Latin-sounding band. "There was no market for Herb Alpert when he first broke; he created his own market," observes Bob Garcia, "and there's never been a waiting market for any act that we've put out." This formula was unexpectedly put successfully to the test with Sergio Mendes's Brasil '66, which earned A&M four gold albums. Until Monterey, A&M remained an MOR company appealing strictly to young adults and older people. They did have a few Top 40 acts. Tommy Boyce and Bobby Hart, who did the Monkees' instrumentals before Nesmith and Co. could play, the We Five, but nothing to compare with the performers on the pop festival stage. Only the unknown organist Lee Michaels could have qualified for the historical event. "As your traditional promo man I kept wondering why aren't there any A&M artists at this terrific event," Moss told Judy Sims.[21] Following the historical gathering he flew to England to purchase American rights to Joe Cocker, the Move, Tyrannosaurus Rex and Procol Harum, then enjoying the fruits of "Whiter Shade of Pale." Cocker educated A&M as the Dead did Warner. They discovered that pink champagne was not to be served during press parties for the underground media. Several untowardly relationships with T. Rex and the Move further disoriented executive attitude. Bob Garcia admits, "The Move was always a group that was swept under the carpet because we got the Move before A&M was into rock, very frankly. . . . My God, nobody understood that first album. That thing with the 'String in My Heart' on it, tremendous bass line. So the Move was always in the background." Another reason for dropping the act, ostensibly, was its refusal to tour. Garcia would like to see Move back with A&M. The company's experience with the Move and others reinforced the artist development ethos. The ideal label was a small one with talented artists. Jerry Moss: "We're perfectly happy hitting a lot of home runs with No. 1 artists." Bob Garcia: "We don't break an artist on the first try, neither do we go raiding other labels for artists that aren't keeping their popularity to get that popularity on our labels. We've stuck with most of our artists for 3-4-5 albums it's happened." Unlike Warner Brothers, A&M is cutting its roster instead of increasing it. "We have about 65 artists now; when we sign somebody we cut somebody, as a rule. We've never had a release bigger than ten albums; if we did we'd start getting nervous. You can't look after them. . . . We probably service artists, every artist, in a far superior way than anybody else."[22] The company recently cut its catalog from 300 to 250 titles and destroyed its close-outs to avoid competing with its new releases. The most controversial aspect of the A&M operation is its reliance upon "indie" distributors. Only Motown and A&M still do not have their own branches. Jerry Moss told *Billboard*, "We've always preferred to work with people who are working for themselves, and who make their own profits by making profits for you."[23] Some acts feel A&M's "field service" is not good. Bob Garcia answers, "Never. We'd kill ourselves. Very rarely do we have groups arriving in town and their product is not there." A&M prefers to convey a "family corporation" image and does so rather successfully, primarily because of its lack of size in both personnel, branches and product. This is what Warner attempted to do, but its own size intervened.

Following Warner Brothers, other companies echo these policies. United Artists is diligently pursuing the "quality over quantity" dictum of its competitors. ABC-Dunhill is embracing this philosophy, slowly building a roster of acts appealing to the 18 to 35 demographic group to complement their singles-oriented Top 40 artists. Columbia and Capitol are ambivalent on the subject of artist development, no doubt being influenced by the dictates of corporate overhead and uneasy stockholders.

COLUMBIA AND CAPITOL REVISITED

Columbia's pre-eminence in the popular-music field was not restored until the mid-1960s when superstars such as Simon and Garfunkel and the Byrds returned it to a place on youth market charts, and amassing the company 10 percent of the pop sales. Goddard Lieberson, then the company president, began a rebuilding process which was continued by flamboyant attorney Clive Davis. Davis signed a number of popular artists for large sums of money. He acquired Janis Joplin for a reported $250,000, followed by Laura Nyro for $2 million. Neil Diamond, Delaney and Bonnie, and Sly and the Family Stone have also received large amounts. In 1971, pop records contributed 50 percent of the company's roster, and one of every five pop records sold that year was on the red-and-yellow Columbia label. A year later Columbia led all of its competitors with a total world-wide sale of $350 million. This figure, however, included the company's entire catalog. Its popular music sales informally are estimated at $200 million. Warner Communications, with a pop-music sales figure of $180 million, claims dominance. Given the unreliability of these figures, Warner, the new kid on the block, is viewed as leading the race. Stan Cornyn quips, "Columbia's not a bad company for Number 2."

Columbia's commitment to artist development is not taken seriously by many observers, despite many company statements to the contrary. On July 29, 1972, a front-page banner in a trade magazine read, "Davis Stressing Artist Search & Development." In the article, Columbia's leader announced "We should take the point of view we are prepared to stay with an artist until he or she breaks." Davis then qualified his endorsement adding, "There are exceptional circumstances.

Members of a group can change and the essence of what you saw might be lost. They might steadfastly stick by the wrong producer and make it a condition of staying. They might, on their own accord, change musical direction."[24] It is undoubtedly true that Columbia has broken some new acts in the past few years—Firesign Theater, Doctor Hook and His Medicine Show, Looking Glass—and it sustained Poco through seven artistically sound but economically shaky albums. A large portion of the Columbia "world of rock" is comprised of defectors from other labels or spin-off groups from existing units like Mott the Hoople, Loggins and Messina, New Riders of the Purple Sage, Argent, Nils Lofgren and Grin, can attribute their parentage to the Buffalo Springfield, the Grateful Dead, the Zombies and Crazy Horse. Tom Rush, Tim Hardin, P. F. Sloane, Ian and Sylvia, Crazy Horse, Association and the unhappy John Paul Hammond established themselves prior to signing with Columbia. Certainly over the years the company has hit with Dylan, Simon and Garfunkel, Chicago, Blood, Sweat and Tears and Santana; however, this does not negate the company's throw-it-against-the-wall image. Mauri Lathower at Capitol observed, "I can't think in the past year [1971] of a group they've really broken either. They have some excellent groups, but think of someone that they've really broken."

Columbia has an industry image as a cold, removed, corporation, an image reinforced by the company's physical plants. The West Coast office is located on the fifth floor of the desert-sands colored CBS Building on Sunset Blvd.; one must pass through various armed uniformed guards to reach the record people. Most companies hire attractive receptionists to stem the flow of traffic. While this is not a major obstacle, many industry people and acts regard CBS guards as symbols of the company.

An A&M executive commented, "You walk into Columbia Records, and my God, it's like walking into General Motors or one of those places." Former employees tend to challenge this image. Mike Ochs: "I always thought Columbia was that cold, business thing, too. It turns out it isn't. They give you incredible freedom here. When I came in at first there were a lot of hassles. After I proved that I could do it, I felt complete autonomy for over two years. I listen to a record, figure out what I think needs work, and zero in on that. I worked on Firesign Theater for over two years, and it was never commercial until recently . . . in all that time, they didn't tell me stop spending money on them, or devote more time to Santana." Another refugee observes: "I think the statement that Columbia and some of the large companies sort of toss it out and if it sticks, okay, is correct only in the sense that it looks more like it is happening that way than in the smaller companies where the entire company is working for one artist, but that entire company may be 5-6 people, where in a large company you may have 20 people working the same amount of time, but it doesn't look as if as much effort is being put out." Despite these protestations, Columbia remains in the eyes of many the General Motors of the industry. The situation at the Capitol Tower two blocks away is somewhat different.

After the Beatles disbanded, a series of misfortunes and management errors beset Capitol Records. To stem the tide, the company went over to the artist-development orientation, although it still takes occasional one shots with artists. Menon said, "I must assume . . . that a lot of very powerful balls . . . get flung onto this wall, and due to a lack of an adherent fall off." The adherent, of course, is company support and development. Menon ordered a cutback on the number of acts chosen and concentration of Capitol's efforts upon promising acts, such as the Raspberries, which were believed to have star quality. Continuing the off-the-wall analogy, he says:

> I am a great believer in the concept of flinging the ball again, and flinging it again, and of trying a different groove [approach] and of throwing it by a different angle and so on. But that implies my most fundamental principle which is I have a dedicated faith in that ball. Therefore, if the first or second or third didn't happen,

> I just refuse, I am too demented, to believe my faith is about to be shattered. This is an extreme way of putting it.

Mauri Lathower, then company's director of A&R, had an unenviable position of supervising this rebuilding effort. The company wanted him to find other Glen Campbells or John Lennons. "You know," he says, "I stood on the corner of Hollywood and Vine for two days and three nights and not one Glen Campbell came by." More seriously, he added:

> When I was placed in this position about last October [1971] I simply had to focus on the new people. You're not going to have your quota busters. You're going to have to decide that you are going to have to do something with these people. There have been three people that I've been very happy with. There's a group called the Persuasions. Their first album was around 25,000 units, which is now almost 50,000. The second album is over 75,000. Or, there's Leo Kottke. He will never be a superstar, I mean that, because he doesn't create that type of excitement. . . . I'm sure he is a little unhappy because he feels his albums should be selling millions. Freddie King is excellent. You go to his performances, I mean they're standing up and screaming. But no album sales. It confuses me.

In an attempt to put the company in the black, the advertising budget was cut; consequently, selectivity in which artist the company will back is exercised. The Raspberries received an extensive advertising campaign which culminated in a long-awaited Capitol top-ten singles hit, "Go All The Way." Groups such as Flash, a spin-off act from 1972's most popular *Billboard* group Yes, Pink Floyd and several other acts with superstar potential have received similar treatment. Lathower has turned down a number of groups for this stated reason, "We are not in a position at this time to audition and seek new talent and will not be until our roster is such that we can offer new talent an honest opportunity to succeed." By 1974, Capitol had regained much of its previous stature. In LP and tape sales it had risen to the third slot among record corporations, trailing WEA and CBS.

IT'S A TRENDY BUSINESS: A BELIEF SYSTEM

Mitch Miller prophetically wrote in his *Time* magazine piece, "Only Tin Pan Alley will stay young with each new generation." Companies rise and fall. Columbia had the hot poker hand with the crooners of the early 1950s. Labels plugged into rock and roll dominated the charts well into the year of the Beatles, 1964. The Beatles gave Capitol symbolic and statistical status until 1969 when Columbia once again took over the top spot only to be nosed out by Warner/Reprise in 1971. "This is a trendy business," says Dennis Killeen, and adds:

> The old "when you're hot, you're hot, and when you're cold, you're very cold." Looking at a label like Warner's with just sort of rolling along doing absolutely nothing. Then all of a sudden because of a couple of people and lots of artist and lots of hard work, they started to grow and build and go from the everyday dealing business, in which they weren't doing very well, into somewhat taste setters, trend setters, and be labeled to be on because they were doing things over there. You sit and talk to someone about Decca and its peak and how phenomenal it was then, and what they're doing today. It's a good example of where the rubber tends to go. There's definitely a correlation between being hot and success in the marketplace. It seems to be easier to sell more, to get more played. The cycle builds up. You get one thing on one station and it happens nationally, and when you go back into that station it becomes easier to say here's something else. When that happens, naturally it becomes much easier to go in with your third thing and then you know your fourth thing, you just send it by mail and don't even have to walk in with it. Until you get to the point where things just aren't as hot and rosy as they once were. You hear artists grumbling, and it's a little bit

> more difficult to get on the air. Sales aren't quite as easy as they used to be. There's good sign to do something, to take a look, to fix it. For as much information as you get in the business day to day in the market-place, I think we react in the wrong way. There are lots of people looking at a lot of little things and the general picture seems to be ignored to the point where a company can go down very quickly. I think it's harder to go up as far as being hot than it is to go down. I think Capitol's time is coming. I think it will happen also with a change in musical direction. We've watched a tremendous flux in radio in its formats of FM stations becoming successful; so AMs are mimicking FM, and FMs are sort of picking up on AM because they can make a little more income, and all of a sudden you have this great mishmash of what's really going on out there. I think the music changes every 10 years, the Beatles were instrumental in the early 60s . . . in 1973 a new direction and a new sound.

Political observers would describe this cycle as the "circulation of elites." Italian sociologist Vilfredo Pareto argued that success itself made those in high positions oblivious to the needs of the governed. In time, the insensitive rulers are driven from power. So it is in the music industry. Success stagnates companies into adherence to formulas and sees companies expanding into their own distributorships and more field personnel. The maintenance of all of the employees and branches proliferates product and, finally, another company "closer to the street" and the "folks out there" triumphs.

Being number one is a symbolic status that has economic benefits. Radio-station personnel are more receptive to your artists and writers spend more time exposing the company's people. Being fourth or fifth in overall sales certainly is not being impoverished. Capitol Records earned $1,391,000 in profit during fiscal year 1971-72. Images are important, especially in an industry which sees each conglomerate as being a participant in a giant corporate crap game where results are tabulated by *Billboard*'s Hot 100. "The bigger you are, the more you win, the sooner you will lose," is one of the few laws that regulate the recording industry. This economic law has given rise to the great man theory of recording.

"In 1973 a new direction and a new sound," observed Killeen. Richard Schulenberg aptly articulated the great man syndrome of the industry:

> I think the whole music industry is at the place they were just before the Beatles happened in the early 1960s. It's running around in circles. But now, of course, we're aware of the Beatles, although we were aware of Elvis Presley then at that time. But everyone is aware of the fact that something new very well may appear on the scene and pick up the whole bag of marbles and go running off in a direction no one else is running off to. Everyone will make their fortune and new careers will be carved out and new corporate giants will arise.

Pausing, he added, "It's evolutionary again. Everyone is looking . . . what is the new direction everyone is going?" It is increasingly popular to compare the early 1970s with the pre-Beatles 1960s. Indeed, the against-the-wall dictum supports this philosophy. Conceivably, any new shipment of records could contain the trend-setting album. Even the artist-development ethos lends itself to this, especially when looking at the efforts of Colonel Parker and Brian Epstein in promoting their protégés. However, the demographics of popular music (see chapter 9) may well turn this viewpoint into industry mythology. The "teen-scream" idols were tied to a specific age group and managed to maintain and increase their followings with sufficient charisma and changes in style. "Heartbreak Hotel" was a long way from the semi-operatic "It's Now Or Never." "I Want to Hold Your Hand" when contrasted to "A Day in the Life" aptly illustrates that the group of 1966 had come a long way since the early Beatlemania days. Clive Davis suggests, "Contemporary rock music is being treated as serious music now and appeals to the 21-to-35 year age groups as well as teenagers."[25] Statistical evidence as well as phenomenal growth of Warner/Reprise and A&M seems to indicate that the popular-music audience is no longer the distinct property of teenage girls. At Osmond Brothers concerts six-year-olds can be seen screaming, "Donny, Donny." Their parents may well be buying Andy Williams, even Rolling Stones albums. It is, perhaps, doubtful that any one artist could capture this highly diverse audience. The success of labels like Warner Brothers, with a rainbow of pop-music acts ranging from Black Sabbath to Tom Paxton and John Fahey, seems to lend support for the changing nature of the music audience. The great man theory, however, is more in keeping with industry mystique than the cold, unexciting certainty of demographics.[26]

Majors such as Columbia, RCA, Warner Brothers and Capitol require, due to their size, an ace in the hole to pay expenses. No one denies the value of superstars, those artists nearly guaranteed to sell 2 to 5 million albums per release; artist development does not guarantee such an outcome. Leo Kottke has little chance to enter this esteemed position, nor do others like him. Consequently, companies may take the occasional pot shot regardless of their public pronouncements. Columbia and Warner/Reprise continue to issue 20 to 30 albums per month, many of which receive little attention from deejays or critics. Capitol has followed the A&M, United Artists trend, joined in varying degrees by RCA and ABC-Dunhill, which try to develop artists. RCA has mixed efforts to build artists with the contracting of Lou Reed, the Kinks, Everly Brothers and several other established artists. Other companies fall somewhere between the Columbia posture and the A&M approach, which at present appears to be working. Still, each company must keep throwing the dice. The canon of "when you're hot, you're hot" dooms those resting on their formats and superstars to failure. One never knows when a new Elvis will walk in the door.

Notes, Chapter 3

1. John Kenneth Galbraith, *The New Industrial State* (Boston: Houghton Mifflin, 1966), p. 6.

2. Joel Vance quoted in Jody Breslaw, "New Releases: Quantity and Quality in a Gambler's Market," *Rock*, July 5, 1971, p. 14.

3. Murray Ross, "The Record Business: What Makes It Run," *Record World*, July 24, 1971, p. 230.

4. Quoted in Ed McCormack, "John Paul Hammond: They All Want to Suck His Blood," *Rolling Stone* 122 (November 23, 1972): 20.

5. Quoted in Leroy Robinson, "The Responsibility of ABC's A&R Department," *Billboard*, September 12, 1970, p. ABC-12.

6. Quoted in "Money Man on Leave," *Forbes*, January 15, 1972.

7. Jay Ruby, "An Interview with Jac Holzman," *Jazz & Pop* 8 (June 1969): 18.

8. Address by Stan Cornyn Before the National Association of Record Merchandisers, Los Angeles, February 27, 1971.

9. Dean Jennings, "The Shaggy Genius of Pop Music," *Saturday Evening Post*, April 21, 1956, p. 69.

10. Quotes from Mitch Miller, "June, Moon, Swoon and Ko Ko Mo," *New York Times Magazine*, April 24, 1955, p. 19.

11. Quoted in Stuart Werbin, "Monkees Man Does A 'Fillmore on the Air,' " *Rolling Stone* 123 (December 7, 1972): 10.

12. Mike Greshman, "The Blues Once Black, Now a Shader White," *Los Angeles Times Calender*, January 19, 1969, p. 37.

13. Quoted in Ren Grevatt, "Pro's and Con's Have Their Say on Miller's K.C. Speech," *Billboard*, March 24, 1958, p. 14.

14. Quoted in "Capitol Gains," *Newsweek*, February 27, 1967, p. 57.

15. Ibid., p. 59.

16. Lenny Kaye, liner notes, *Nuggetts*, Elektra Records 7E-2006.

17. Danny Fields, "Who Bridges The Gap Between The Record Executive and the Rock Musician? I Do," in Jonathan Eisen, ed., *The Age of Rock* 2 (New York: Vintage Books, 1970), p. 153.

18. Quoted in David Felton and John Morthland, "Will Warner Bros. Corner the Market?" *Rolling Stone* 55 (April 2, 1970): 14.

19. "He Handles a Lot of Chores for Acts," *Billboard*, October 14, 1972, p. 10.

20. Felton and Morthland, "Will Warner Bros?" p. 14.

21. Quoted in Judith Sims, "Record Industry Profiles: Two Lonely Bulls and How They Grew," *Rolling Stone* 119 (October 12, 1972): 14.

22. Quoted in ibid., p. 16.

23. Quoted in Nat Freedland, "Moss Traces A&M Rise to Eminence," *Billboard*, August 26, 1972, p. 1, 84.

24. Quoted in Eliot Tiegel, "Davis Stressing Artist Search and Development," *Billboard*, July 29, 1971, p. 58.

25. Quoted in "Record Sales Led by Rock Musicians," *Los Angeles Times*, December 12, 1969, p. 32.

26. See Jon H. Rieger, "The Coming Crisis in the Youth Music Market," unpublished paper presented at the Popular Culture Association annual meetings, Milwaukee, Wisconsin, May 2, 1974.

4.

THE COP OUT: INSIDE THE RECORD COMPANY

> You cheated, you lied
> You said that you loved me.
> © *1958 Balcones Publishing Co.*

Sometime during negotiations, more likely after a contract has been signed, the act is afforded a grand tour of the record company in which it visits all of the various departments and is introduced to the people who will be working on their record. Through a maze of corridors, offices and cubicles, the hopeful is shown the innards of the "support" unit. Some facades are more lavish than others. One company has its personnel cramped in quarters across the street from the Warner Brothers movie lot. The Capitol tower, which casts its shadow over the corner of Hollywood and Vine, is spacious and seemingly well organized. Columbia is austere and fortresslike. United Artists, ABC-Dunhill and Elektra, in clean new buildings, appear stable and tranquil. Outward appearances are frequently deceiving. Still, companies need the same basic components to make and sell records.

The new artist is taken from the A&R department to meet the marketing vice-president, who tells the act of the many ploys and gimmicks they have devised to create a million-seller. The advertising and art departments make equally spectacular claims. The performer will be introduced to those in the publicity and promotion departments and will find their promises are no less heady. The tour continues to the attorneys in the legal department. The larger companies may even ferry their new acquisition out to Santa Maria or Northridge to see their pressing plants. All this is designed to impress the artist with the company's power, energy and commitment. Few companies take the artist through the accounting department or their distribution outlets, although they outweigh all of the creative divisions in wielding company power. The division heads that the artist meets on his tour essentially represent three dominant organizational entities which operate independently of each other while at the same time ideally striving for a common goal: production, promotion and publicity and distribution and sales.

Production—where the buck begins—encompasses all of the support functions necessary to give birth to a successful sound. This includes discovering an artist, getting him into the studio and then "mixing" on producing a single or an album. Having edited a tape, the other two divisions come into the picture. One attempts to create an image; the other delivers "sound" to the consumer.

Publicity and promotion (marketing) receives the mixed session tape and devises a plan to market the record. They will call upon advertising executives, market analysts, publicists, promotion people, as well as those in charge of album covers, buttons, badges and T-shirts. This division will map out an advertising and selling campaign to "hype" the record. They must consider the type of audience the record will appeal to. This is translated into "media approach," album cover, design, all of the things deemed necessary to make the total package attractive *and* commercial.

Distribution and sales is the least glamorous part of the record company. It is also the most important. Here the "bottom line" of profit and loss so feared in the industry is determined. Additionally, this division is directly concerned with manufacturing. The process begins with converting the session tape onto the clear-coated aluminum disk called a lacquer. From this disk is born a negative or reverse image of it —the grooves appear turned inside out. This negative is labeled a master. The master is used to make an impression upon another disk called the mother, which is an exact replica of the lacquer. From the mother a stamp is made which then molds both sides of the record. Side 1 is linked to side 2 by 110 tons of pressure. The result is a record. The envelope, jacket, even the plastic shrink and cover sticker are the brainchildren of publicity and promotion, but manufacturing brings these ideas to life.

A finished record is shipped to distribution centers owned either by the company or independents. Company-owned centers are called branches. Independents which stock the records from several labels are termed subdistributors and "one stops." They are wholesale houses which service record stores and jukebox operators. Some are also rack jobbers who supply department stores, supermarkets and various other outlets where their place of business is set up. Rack jobbers, much to the unhappiness of the record industry, accounts for over 60 percent of sales.

After 90 or 120 days the accounting department determines if the record is a winner or a loser. The cold figures pulled from a computer are a matter of life and death for the artist. Failures become cut-outs.

COME TOGETHER, OVER ME

Bhasker Menon describes the record-company president as occupying a position similar to a symphony conductor. With spiritual baton in hand, he must coerce and cajole disparate instruments to work together in order to have a chance at a hit record. A smooth, highly integrated company helps but does not guarantee a successful profit-earning record. Conversely, few acts get a chance at the vinyl crap table when there is internal scrabbling. Roy Silver, the agent, aptly summed up the problem saying, "Getting the *entire* record company behind you is the hardest job in the music business." The symphony direction is complicated by the number of organizational parts in a record company. Each division and department has its own specialties and values. Some unifying values exist, certainly, but others simply divide company employees. One long-standing conflict has been described as "art for art's sake" as opposed to "art for profit," or "creativity" versus "accounting." These clichés bear some semblance of truth but lack the essential economic ingredient. Records, artists and even record companies rise and fall strictly on the "bottom line" profit-loss principle. Creators may pay lip service to this dictum, but they rarely accept it. The artist's desire to use the studio for "just a few more" hours in order to create the "perfect sound" generally runs counter to the wishes of the staff producer who has another act coming in or the accounting-department executive who is totally concerned with keeping costs down. An industry observer told *Billboard*, "Bookkeepers don't understand the delicate relationship that exists between the merchandisers and the creators of the music business."[1]

This is "a traditional rivalry in all industry," says Billy James. "There are some people who say that because this is show business there is a greater degree of openness among the various departmental functions. Sometimes that's true, sometimes it's not. Often there are producers who could just as easily be making shoes as records. So the conflict does exist." Promotion people expect the A&R people to give them something that will sell. Further examples of distrust abound. The sales people at Columbia viewed Senior Producer John Hammond as "some kind of a joke." They allowed him to sign Bob Dylan and Pete Seeger to the label merely to humor him. Dylan succeeded despite the bookkeepers.

Martin R. Cerf when at United Artists, fought a long, protracted battle with the accounting department over the packaging of the Legendary Masters series, two-record sets by recording stars of the 1950s such as Eddie Cochran, Fats Domino, Jan and Dean and Ricky Nelson. Referring to the accounting department, Cerf protested, "They would rather put out super packs [economy-line records for supermarkets] than Legendary Masters series because they see a greater profit. . . . Sales people think this group of people who buy records are a group of mindless nubies, that they have no idea what they're doing. And it's not true." Legendary Masters went on to sell over 200,000 units and received critical acclaim throughout the industry. Not all of the creative people were allowed such luxuries. Billy James has kept over the years a two-line memo written to him by a Columbia Records executive reading. "We are not interested in signing Lenny Bruce. Thank you." For him, this memorandum is a perfect example of the myopia of the Columbia bookkeepers.

Dennis Killeen calls this curious organizational format the "cop out," meaning that someone else down the line is responsible. "Buck-passing" is a more common term. For Bill Graham, the villain becomes the immature performer: "Who was two years ago working in a coffeehouse, whose education is limited, who is nontrained in music. Success came so quickly, more quickly than the growth of a valid personality, that he didn't know how to handle it. He takes advantage of the audience, knowing they'll accept anything he does, whether it's good or not. A group will come on stage, tune up for 20 minutes, then do nine versions of their hit and be accepted as a god."[2] For the Byrds, producer Bob Johnston was the cause of failure. Roger McGuinn: "I let Johnston mix it because I figured, 'Look how well he did Dylan's stuff.' What I didn't find out until it was too late was that Dylan was there with him when Johnston mixed his stuff. I hate to lay a dupe man, but Johnston is an insidious dupe artist."[3] This was in response to the editing of *Dr. Byrds and Mr. Hyde*. Rod Stewart blames the Jeff Beck group's lack of success upon producer Mickey Most. "When making an album with the band laying down a tract in the studio, Mickey is always in between; it's like a big war, you can't get him to turn the knobs . . . he couldn't produce the Jeff Beck group." To this Most replies, "Rod Stewart wouldn't sing because he wasn't under contract to us. Beck didn't want us to record Stewart in case he became more popular. So what are we gonna do?" "The type of music they were playing was emptying theaters—it wasn't popular," answers Most.[4] The fear of failure, because of the great odds, permeates the record industry at nearly all levels. Artists distrust their managers and producers, while at corporate levels the A&R department may accuse promotion of laxity and not "getting behind the record" when their artist's record does not sell. At yet another level, the West Coast office of a company may be greatly at odds with the parent New York office. Record companies almost universally condemn rack jobbers—at least in private. "Our business is not corrupt," exclaimed a character in an episode of the television show "Name of the Game" dealing with the record industry, "just everybody in it." The word "unreliable" is more accurate than "corrupt."

In the everyday world of the record industry corruption is not the norm, but the divisions between departments frequently require informal arrangements to be made to accomplish internal goals. For example, a publicist had arranged for one of his artists to be interviewed for a major rock magazine. The publicist contacted field people who were in another department. Nothing happened. As the date for the interview approached, the reporter attempted to confirm it with the publicist. The long-distance call was transferred to the head of promotion when the publicist was *coincidentally* in the man's office. The promotion director was duly embarrassed and the interview was saved. Another illustration of this informal method of "pulling" in one direction is the use of a plant in the trade papers. Publicists and promotional people frequently plant anonymous items with journalists from *Variety* or the *Hollywood Reporter* that are designed to motivate others in their company to get behind a program or artist they consider important. The item, "X is considering moving to a new label," generally means someone or his publicity-promotion department wants more company support or money.

The size of a record company greatly intensifies interdepartmental cop outs. The size of corporations, where most communication is either by long-distance telephone or memoranda, adds to the structural differences. A&M and UA pride themselves on their open-door policies. Bob Garcia says:

> I've got to be able to walk into anybody's office and say, "hey, this is wrong." And they can say "you're full of shit." But if I can explain why it's wrong, then we're in agreement . . . for me to walk into a vice-president's office does not require setting up an appointment, or going through secretaries, but being brave enough to speak my mind. That's how this place seems to work. A lot of things are consummated right here in this lot [A&M]. People standing out and talking, screaming and yelling a lot, but it gets done.

Ron Saul attributes a similar approach to Warner Brothers: "Anyone, whether it's a field man or creative services can walk into the president of this company and doesn't have to go through ten people." While Brownsville Station and several other Burbank refugees hotly dispute this, it is the image Warner has attempted to cultivate, underlining the importance of free-flowing lines of communication and an open-door policy in the record industry.

The New York "home-office" phenomenon is seen by many in the industry as exacerbating the conflicts inherent within record companies. Columbia, RCA, and Elektra (at one time) had their headquarters in Manhattan. The three-hour time lag between coasts is of very real concern to RCA and Columbia, where all major decisions are made in New York while much of the action takes place in Los Angeles. Bob Garcia observes, "It's very difficult for the New York home office to understand what happens out here. Atlantic, Elektra, they're right here . . . the fact Warner Communications is here in Southern California has a great deal to do with it. . . ." In the spring of 1972 a number of West Coast Columbia executives left the company, including Heidi Robinson, Mike Ochs and Dick Schulenberg, who went into private law practice. Schulenberg outlines the problem of Columbia's New York home:

> No matter how much we use the telephone it's still 3,000 miles away. You come in here and call in the morning, and its lunch time in New York. You wait for them and they're tied up. Then you go to lunch and that's when they call you back. So you either

> adjust your eating or social habits accordingly to make sure that you get through to them when they're available because they're certainly not going to adjust their habits for us.

The time lag creates many frustrations. "Getting answers to things" was a major problem. Royalty advances in many cases had to be cleared with the home office. Responses to artists' requests were frequently delayed due to the communication lag. Delays upset temperamental artists. David Anderle, a former Elektra A&R director, comments, "The West Coast-East Coast situation is deadly." Discussing an artist he is independently producing for RCA Victor, he says: "I'll work for her. I'll definitely work with her. But I cannot do for her the things I'm doing with the other people I'm working with strictly because she's on RCA and strictly because I don't know who to go to." The key reason is the two-coast dilemma. "The power of the decisions are made in New York. They're not made on the West Coast, and [you have] the situation where you get the local head of A&R to say 'yes' to something, if it's really a major issue you go through that period of waiting again, the phones and the whole thing."

While the two-coast situation is of consequence, the bureaucracy of large corporations—getting to the right people for decisions—and the unique personalities of company heads further complicate the situation. RCA's president may be remote, but he does delegate some authority. At Columbia several employees felt that Clive Davis, prior to his dismissal, compounded the situation. "The problem is Clive," said one employee on the verge of quitting:

> What Clive really should do is he should have a counterpart on the Coast that would be able to act immediately, that would be able to make those kinds of decisions, rather than always having to go through New York for anything major. Like on a publicity thing. . . . I have to clear it through New York. It's a problem. I don't know why he doesn't do it unless it's giving up part of the power.

He adds, "At times we feel like a farm club." In many respects the West Coast office was just an outpost.

MCA executives in New York complain about a reverse situation. Mike Maitland, the company's president, conducts nearly all of the company's business on the West Coast. He makes the decisions. However, record-company business does not start, in earnest, until 11:00 A.M. West Coast time, which makes it after lunch in New York City. Reportedly, many of the conflicts that sprang up over the promotion and later production of *Jesus Christ Superstar* stemmed from this distribution of authority. The addition of Nashville offices and studios by many companies has further contributed to the time-geography split.

To dismiss the lack of company integration as solely a product of size and New York offices would be wrong. Small companies with a high level of communication and integration have many of the same problems on a departmental level. Even artists at A&M such as Gene Clark accuse the family company of lack of support. The company replies that Clark does not tour to support his records. While some accusations no doubt are more camouflage for bumbling, the structural problems become even greater when one actually begins placing sound on a record.

THE PRODUCER

The individual with whom the cop-out process begins and rarely ends is the producer. In the plant or studio the creativity and talent of an act are tested and transformed into a commodity to be bought and sold in the marketplace. In the studio, acts "sing and make noise on instruments." This "noise" is then preserved on tape, later to be broken into stereo or quadraphonic channels. Frequently neither the record company nor the act is happy with the result, but each blames the other for the undesirable outcome. "No one starts out to make a bad record" is a favorite industry statement. A Capitol Records executive said, "elements of the industry can blame their failures on the manufacturing blokes—the operations systems." This sentiment is widespread. Performers frequently blame unsuccessful albums on producers. This complaint is echoed by promotional personnel as well as the media cultural gatekeepers. Critics in *Rolling Stone*, *Zoo World*, *Phonograph Record*, *Rock* and other influential rock journals have lamented how a "producer screwed up a good artist." One veteran program director attributed the large number of stiffs to the complexity of sessions and overproduction, where a number of tempos and styles are "jammed onto one record." The producer, according to David Lawhon, is "the element between the artist and the record company." He selects the music and judges the sound. He is the most important person from the time the artist enters the studio or "plant" to the time the session tape is delivered to the pressing plant and to the marketing people. After that the success of a record is out of his control.

As with nearly all aspects of the record business, the role of the producer drastically changed during the sixties. In the hey day of Mitch Miller, the producer then called an A&R man, went through hundreds of songs selecting just the right one. A recording date was set up. Arrangements were contracted. The singer walked in the studio and left three hours after leaving behind a completed master tape. The function of the engineer was to reproduce what occurred.

Stereo, which allowed for two tracks, should have altered the role of the engineer. Les Paul and Mary Ford had already used "overdubbing" with two tracks being fed into monaural track, and the Alvin and the Chipmunks records produced by Ross Bagdasarian for Liberty used a similar technique. Rock and roll's ascendency both altered and staggered studio methods. Many professional studio men considered the new genre to be a noisy fad. They did not understand it and treated it with contempt. Using two channels they simply reproduced sound. Thus, engineers with little, if any, musical background become producers, interpreting on tape what had happened in the studio. A veteran A&R man, a studio musician during the introduction of rock music, recalls: "I was still playing at that time when Fabian and them came along. Everything was done in the key of E because that's open-string guitar. All guitar players played in the key of E because you didn't have to take any lessons because you could play three chords and that's all you had to have." One engineer when asked his opinion of a tape told the producer, "I'm sorry, man, I turn my ears off on playbacks."[5] A&M producer Creed Taylor told Gene Lees, "I once saw an engineer cutting a master [the final tape] while reading the *Wall Street Journal*. He had the sound turned so low you could hardly hear it. If anything went wrong, he wouldn't know it."[6]

John Phillip Hammond, George Goldner, Leiber and Stoller, Shadow Morton and Phil Spector were the ablest and most important producers of the pre-Beatle era. Spector, especially, transformed a fundamentally simple idiom into spectaculars rivalling those of D. W. Griffith and Cecil B. DeMille in cinema. Spector characterized his production as "little symphonies for the kids." His magnum opus, Tina Turner's "River Deep, Mountain High," cost $22,000 to make, an unheard of amount for a single in 1966. Although a critical success—one writer classified it "a 'rushing, mighty wind' the Bible talks about"—it was an economic failure. The "best record" Phil Spector ever cut was a stiff. Embittered, he withdrew from the business, only returning as the Beatles' producer of *Let It Be*. Even Spector's monumental talent could not uplift the role of the producer; most remained technicians, merely editing sound from the studio, doing little to embellish it.

The growing sophistication of recording tape and multitrack stereo equipment coupled with various combinations of over-dubbing or "mixing" signaled a breakthrough. The Beatles' clever exploitation of this equipment with the aid of EMI staffman George Martin did more than anything else to legitimate and bolster the technical status of the man behind the glass. The producer became the man who could, at John Lennon's request, hire a 41-piece orchestra and concoct a final chord with an Indian tamboura and the sound of a hand hitting the strings inside a piano to create "A Day in the Life." Richard Goldstein, the New York critic, reacted to *Sgt. Pepper* writing, "It reeks of horns and harps, harmonica quartets, assorted animal noises, and a 41-piece orchestra. . . . An obsession with production, coupled with a surprising shoddiness in composition, permeates the entire album."[7] The impact of *Sgt. Pepper* "behind the glass" was staggering. David Anderle: "It took a lot of producers many years to find out that they could not all make *Sgt. Peppers.* They all tried. God knows we had a year and a half of some of the wierdest sounds on record. Everybody trying to make *Sgt. Pepper.*" Unlike Spector, who received credit for "Lovin' Feeling," the success of George Martin was attributed to the Beatles. The artist was afforded an editorial control he had not previously enjoyed. The Beatles, not George Martin, had made *Sgt. Pepper.*

For most rock bands of the period, producers were straight technicians with little musical understanding, but immense technological knowhow. Marty Balin, then with the Jefferson Airplane, complained, "RCA's conservative. It's run by older men who really don't have anything going in rock and they were so desperate to get into it . . . when we started doing our material, they were very confused by the lyrics."[8] Nearly every Airplane LP was released only after bitter arguments between the band and the company. Jerry Garcia recalled the Grateful Dead's first Warner Brothers album: "The first record was like a regular company record done in three nights, mixed in one day. . . . So we weren't surprised when it didn't quite sound like we wanted it to."[9] The bands hired their own producers, many of whom knew little more than the performers. The record companies, sensing a new trend, dismissed a number of staff producers. One A&R vice-president explained, "Let's say for instance that you've got four staff producers working for you and you're giving them weekly salaries, and the last three acts you've signed have come in with other producers or want other producers. They don't want your people." The spiraling costs of signing, recording and promoting acts further pushed many companies away from staff production to independents who could produce or at least record an act. Beginning with Goddard Lieberson, the head of CBS Records, company executives said, "There's a parallel between records now and the movie business. Today, Hollywood finances productions by independent producers, and merely distributes the films. That's what's happening in records."[10] Jac Holzman and a score of others held the same viewpoint. The companies became Stan Cornyn's "ticket sellers," and A&R departments were transformed, in Mauri Lathower's terms, into "service organizations." Independent producers became the rage. By 1968, 60 percent of charted material was attributed to independent producers or to the performer. The self-produced act generally used a token engineer or friend as a producer. A dejected Phil Spector described that period:

> The groups said, 'well, we don't want to do anything, except make our own records. We don't want studio cats, because they can do everything we can't do, and they represent something hostile to us.' They go to the record company saying, 'Listen, we want to do our own record and that's it. . . .' The group has its own material and has its own ideas; its own thing, so the *producer has become no more than an engineer.*[11]

The Grateful Dead use a producer in this fashion. "He's an ear. He translates the band's wishes to the engineer," Jerry Garcia and "whoever cares" mix the recorded tapes into a master. Some self-produced tapes have motivated many industry people to feel the dictum "any attorney who defends himself has a fool for a client" should be posted in all recording studios. The stories of waste and misuse of studio equipment are folklore in the industry. The Beach Boys reportedly filled a studio with sand from the local seashore for effect. The Mothers of Invention made an album tripping on LSD. Many bands have spent incredibly large sums on producing an album which did not sell. Todd Rundgren, both a performer and an independent producer, feels that most performers tend to confuse their "art with their life-style" and consequently "do not know the bounds of their own act."[12] David Lawhon agrees, attributing the abuses of self-production to the lack of training inherent in rock bands, the flexibility of equipment, the absence of written musical scores and the "nonprofessional nature of contemporary performers."

One symptom of unprofessionalism cited by numerous industry people (usually off the record) is alleged excessive drug use in the studio. Andy Wickham, a staff producer at Warner Brothers, asserts that drugs distort their hearing, thus muddling the artist's ability to distinguish between illusion and reality while playing and mixing records. This accounts for the high cost of recording, he says. Wickham, once the house hippie, now labeled a "closet fascist" by some artists, does get some nods of agreement even from those who ideologically oppose him. Another producer said, "I think he's had some bad experiences first of all. If a guy has to smoke a joint to get there, fine. If another guy has to take an upper, fine. I've had incredible problems with people on acid in the studio . . . but my biggest problem is with booze. I've had more bad sessions with alcohol than any other kind of thing . . . a lot of people absolutely don't want any kind of smoking, or anything going on in their session. They're just so afraid of it themselves." This laissez-faire attitude does not apply to those inside the booth. "The engineer and the producer," cautions David Anderle, "have to watch what's going on. The engineer . . . is in front of all those machines. If somebody lays down a good take, boy it better be on that tape tomorrow. It better be exactly the same way you're hearing it. . . . Sometimes you can run into problems if the bass player's on downers and the drummer's on uppers." Self-produced groups do not have this corrective mechanism. The tempo of the Grateful Dead's first album was too fast because members of the band were on dexamyl, a diet pill with an amphetamine base.

"So we played some hyperactive music . . . the tempo was way too fast. We were all so speedy at the time. It has its sort of crude energy."[13] Sense distortion is not the only problem inherent in self-production. Ted Templeman, another Warner staffman, adds, "I was an artist [Harpers Bazaar] for a long time and I couldn't produce my own records. You can't be as objective. You need someone to say, 'okay, that's it. That's the take we want.' "

Now an executive producer, Templeman defines the role of a staff man: "He's responsible for the recording part of a performer's career. That entails money, watching the budget, submitting the budget, getting budget approval, having the right studio, being able to direct material and finding out what is the best environment for an artist to work in." The staffman's loyalty is first and foremost to the company. "I'm a firm believer in that I'm being paid by a company. I usually don't work under a situation that I live on an override from the production of an artist. I'm paid by the company a salary to do A&R as well as production." The producer is loyal to those who pay his salary. Staff producers in most cases are expected to give their fealty to the company. On the other hand the independent producer, who normally receives 5 to 10 percent of an artist's record gross, places his loyalty with the performer. While Warner does in fact attempt to combine the best of these economic arrangements, its staff people are essentially tied to the company. Ted Templeman claims he would rather take a pay cut than work anywhere besides Warner/Reprise.

Many record companies have discounted the value of loyalty for the savings of independent production. As service organizations they are now predominantly concerned with merchandising, distribution and promotion. Steve Miller, the Moody Blues, the Beach Boys and many others are now responsible for bringing in finished or master tapes. A&R then does the paper work, making sure that the record licenses are in proper shape and order, doing all the mechanical work to see that the artist gets proper payment. After that, the A&R

department ideally serves as the artist's *aide de camp.* They contact the art department, which then evolves a concept to highlight their tape. Frequently this is a problem, as art work takes longer to process than the disk. "You can make a disk overnight. Art takes weeks for color collections." Here the famous buck-passing process quickly enters the picture. "There is usually some mistake about label copy or liner notes," says Mauri Lathower, adding, "We sit through and hope that we can get and put it all together." The art department quickly answers that the hang-up is the kind of acts A&R signs, not a graphic work. A&R's shepherding a record through a company is quite a chore, for nearly every step involves a similar conflict. This has been compounded by the growing number of independent production agreements.

Depending on the artist involved, independent production deals may be treated with less vigor and enthusiasm by A&R people. However, for those in the executive suite and the accounting department, these arrangements help control excessive studio costs or unreliable and capricious artists or producers. Commenting upon the Beach Boys, considered by many to be the industry primadonnas, Joe Smith noted if they do not "deliver the record we'll keep the doors open this month." Not surprisingly most of the volatile acts are increasingly finding themselves in a pay-on-delivery basis. The Beach Boys, The Band, Steve Miller, Jefferson Airplane and many others have independent production arrangements with their record companies. A number of "name" producers also have their own companies with a stable of artists. Tom Wilson, Bones Howe, Jeff Barry, David Anderle and Wes Farrell all fall into this category. Farrell, for example, has produced the Partridge Family, the Cowsills, Brooklyn Bridge and Every Mother's Son. The advantage of such a setup is such that the independent has creative control with big company support. In recent years independent production has escalated into a host of small record labels that are distributed by a major record label. Grunt Records (launched by the

Jefferson Airplane), Capricorn, Bearsville and a number of other labels claim to have ultimate freedom over the entire record package with the advantages of large distribution systems controlled by the majors.

Artistic freedom is cited as the major bonus of independent production. Many independent producers and, indeed, record companies see CBS and RCA as a labyrinth or maze where one has to go through five executives to get a decision even on the simplest matters.

Lenny Waronker disagrees at Warner Brothers: "No one upstairs [executive level] ever forced a staff producer to work with someone he doesn't fit with. There's fantastic creative freedom, like Mo Ostin and Joe Smith have never told a producer here to delete a cut from an album. They don't dictate policy. That's the only way an A&R staff can work."[14] Nonetheless, few staff producers fare well in a dispute with a "name" performer; the higher echelons of a company almost always side with the artist. One producer said, "It's pretty much up to the artist, here at Warner Brothers, if the artist isn't happy and he has something, I think the company is going to stay with the artist." Independents, also claim staffmen, are grossly underpaid. To counter this charge, Warner Brothers has developed profit-sharing for its people. Other companies are not so generous.

Despite artistic control, independent production is a high-risk business. According to Wes Farrell there are ten independents making "big money." And, adds Tom Wilson, "any producer who doesn't score within 34 of the Top 100 in a 12 month period is in trouble." A staffman, while enjoying more security, must also know that a poor in-house chart showing can get him fired. Still, a staff position is a bit more secure, when available, than independent work.

All producers go through fairly standard procedures that are colored by their relationship to recording companies. Producers scout for new talent. They also arbitrate between the artist and the recording company.

BEHIND THE GLASS LIGHTLY

The producer's major function is to orchestrate, through the taping and mixing, the sound which will eventually become a record. Todd Rundgren defines the role of the producer as "anything you have to do to make the record meet your professional standards." This may involve arranging, engineering and even playing on a record as Phil Spector did in his glory days. The producer does everything he can to accentuate the strong points of the act in the studio. David Anderle sees himself as a mirror of the artist, "if the artist is performing and I'm not reacting, then he feels something wrong with it, so he can use me as an alter ego." Vinny Testa sees the producer as "someone for a capable artist to funnel his talent through."[15] This process—the birth of a hit record or star act—begins in the studio. The cop-out philosophy also begins both in front and behind the glass separating the control room from the musicians and singers.

Nowhere is the cost-creativity conflict more apparent than in the studio. The man in the middle is the producer. The dilemma is simple: a studio rents for $125 to $200 per hour. That is about $2.50 per minute, not including engineers' fees and the cost of hiring "sidemen." Studio musicians are paid $85 per session. Top studio men in Nashville and Los Angeles can earn from $30,000 to $80,000 per year if they can survive the inhuman pressures of four sessions a day. "Time means money," indicates producer Garry Sherman, "The more time we save and the more we accomplish in a given time period, the more money we've saved, the more we've earned."[16] The artist, although frequently unaware of it, generally pays for studio time, since record companies subtract the costs from the artist's royalty payments. Independent producers either follow suit or see their percentage of the act's earnings diminish. Tom Wilson's unsuccessful Rasputin Productions in 1967 signed a five-year $250,000 pact with ABC-Dunhill. Of this amount $100,000 to $150,000 was allocated for production and recording costs. The remainder was for promotional expenses and the producer's fee. An overrun in the former will diminish the amount available for the latter. Mike Curb, former president of MGM, admits, "One of the hazards an independent producer faces is to discover that his budgets are cut because the company has to pay high talent and production fees so the producer's promotional allowances is cut."[17]

From an accounting standpoint, the fast-paced three-hour session producing a single or even an album is ideal. This is how it was done in the days of Mitch Miller. However, the vast potential of the 16- to 24-track board and the temptation to spend extra hours, even days, in the studio becomes a seductive force. Paul Simon told Jon Landau, "A lot of times I don't do anything but sit in a studio for an hour or so. . . . I like the studio to be a home, to be comfortable, and then I think, 'I'm talking to this guy, and if I talk . . . for two hours that costs $300.' "[18] Simon has simply avoided looking at his studio expenses, which have run in the neighborhood of $50,000 to $100,000 dollars. But few performers command the stature Simon enjoys with his record company; he is a superstar in a category with the Beatles or Bob Dylan. An act that sells 60,000 albums per release cannot afford to indulge itself with lengthy stints in the studio—but many do. Brown Meggs laments Capitol's many middle-selling performers who only return studio and mixing expenses, and other record companies have performers who are viewed as exorbitant abusers of valuable time.

The producer is the time keeper and in many cases the controller. He is the policeman with one eye on the wall clock. Costs, from rents to musicians' fees, are all contingent upon the clock. Creativity, however, is not measured by this yardstick. David Anderle stakes, "The quickest way to turn an artist off is to remind him how much money he's spending at a time when he's right on the verge of creating something. . . . But at some point you have to go up and say, 'hey, man, that's it for the night, we're just wasting time, it's money down the drain.' And it is our money that somebody's putting it up. . . . There has to be discipline. An artist does need guidance, especially in a studio. Somebody has to supply that discipline. Somebody has to say, 'okay, let's go home 'cause we're wasting time and money.' " Todd Rundgren, having worked both sides of the studio glass, agrees, "People when they first get in the studio aren't aware that every hour they spend in the studio is another 140 bucks. They'll just keep going in there, and in a month the bills'll come in and they'll have spent $20,000 in studio time alone, and still not even be finished."[19] The Grateful Dead reportedly wasted over $80,000 on their early albums.

Artists, on the other hand, feel musical quality is more important than dollars. Leon Russell, Paul Simon and many others laud producers Terry Melcher and Bob Johnston for their "richman's approach" while decrying the three-hour session which produces a record regardless of the quality of the sound. Ike Turner, referring to his wife's "River Deep, Mountain High" on the *Pop Chronicles,* said "The only record I've heard that could come close to that record is a record by the Beach Boys called 'Good Vibrations.' I think these are the two records that I've heard in my life that I really like." "River Deep" and "Good Vibrations" are believed to be the two most expensive singles in recording history. The Beach Boys' song also failed to reach the *Billboard* Top 10. Worst of all, "River Deep" was the most expensive stiff ever produced in the Top 40 arena. Performers and producers firmly espouse artistic freedom over the value of record sales, but no one is sure where artistry ceases and economic irresponsibility begins. Tony Ashton says, "We get plenty of time and we should make better albums really." Too much time in the studio, some assert, simply dulls the senses, Tom Wilson told the *New York Times,* "What's good usually happens in the first 10 or 12 takes. When you go as high as 67, you lose the spontaneity and probably your mind.[20] That's a critical thing," suggests Anderle, "you're sitting there on the one side of the glass and you know that it's not quite there yet and musicians are starting to tire. The tricky decision for the producer is to force several more takes or close the session and start anew the next day." Many successful producers avoid taxing musicians because it generates tension that inhibits rather than enhances creativity. At this moment the primary role of the producer is reintroduced and his loyalties are challenged. Several takes more may capture the desired sound, but another three-hour session is expensive. The final judgment is the producer's.

In order to avoid these situations, producers have become "psychoanalysts with rhythm" using all manner of theories to understand and manipulate the "feel" of a session. Nearly all believe that some kind of psychological orchestration is necessary for a successful record. Don Gant, a producer at ABC-Dunhill, comments, "Personality is as important as ability. You have to make people feel relaxed . . . joke, laugh, and make everybody feel comfortable." Ted Templeman: "Sequence and pacing are really important." To achieve the proper "feel" Templeman employs five different engineers whose experience and temperament fit a particular act in the studio. Engineers are instructed not to comment on bad takes and not to upset the musicians. The environment for artistry must be right. Tom Wilson uses his "rap" to control a session. A constant flow of quips are a rule at one of his productions. Wilson was in the booth when Bob Dylan missed the opening line of his "115th Dream" in a fit of laughter. Dave Anderle uses a more encompassing technique. His musicians and singers are friends. He considers Rita Coolidge "like a sister." From then on it's simply a matter of making the performers reach a plateau. "I think that's why we have so much fun in our sessions. I just can't get a musician, contract him to come and play a specific part. I make him become part of the session . . . and if the drummer is unhappy or the bass player is unhappy I want to know about it. . . . He's going to have to contribute to the music."

At recording sessions manipulating the emotions of musicians is critical. The techniques vary depending on the artist. An A&M producer purposely angered one musician feeling that he played best under stress. Other artists require different tactics. "You have to get the artist relaxed so you can get a spontaneous performance." One record company, Chess-Janus, went so far as to hire a hypnotist to calm down two singers: hypnotist Damon Reinbold actually put David Teegarden and Skip "Van Winkle" Knape into a trance prior to their recording "Dancing in the Street." "I feel like I was on a gig," Van Winkle told *Time,* "I kept expecting applause." Although this was partially a publicity gimmick most observers agreed the duo had never sounded better.

Cutting a record, explains Tom Wilson, is a routine. He sits at a control panel with his engineer and separately records on one track the bass, drum, rhythm and lead guitars, piano. For balance the lead guitar may get two tracks. On a eight-track machine, a remaining track may go to the vocalists and to further supporting parts. Having achieved what he believes to be the best performance possible, taking into account costs and other factors, the producer will then mix the tapes.

There are, of course, many variations on the theme. Echo, equalizing (softening or bringing up parts) and reverberation

Exhibit 4.1

8-TRACK* CHART

1.	vocalist	6.	piano
2.	lead guitar	7.	dobro
3.	bass	8.	combination of bottom instruments (bass, drum and rhythm guitar)
4.	drums		
5.	rhythm guitar		

*Tracks appear on a continuum of left-center-right. Some parts attract one ear to the other on a stereo recording. The vocalist is usually given the center, that is, equal volume on both stereo tracks. From this figure the possibilities open to a producer are immense both in combinations and also in stress of individual parts. Sixteen- and even 24-track recording machines are now available, further complicating the possible outcomes.

are mixed into the recording. Some instruments can be further amplified. If the producer wishes he may mix in a lush violin or even a symphony orchestra. After the tracks have been executed to the satisfaction of all, the material is edited or mixed. At this point decisions are made that will help determine the fate of the recording. Here the artistry of the producer is all important but still not dominant, as many performers are given a veto power on the mixing of their tapes. Many performers, much to their later despair, have not exercised the option to participate in this crucial stage of recording. Roger McGuinn's blast at Bob Johnston would not have occurred had he participated in the mixing. The first mix is in the head of the producer or artist. Ted Templeman:

> First of all you do a basic track. You have drums on say five to six tracks, piano maybe on two, three guitar tracks . . . and you're using a lot of tracks on four instruments, but that's how you're creating the magic that is missing because maybe you can't see them. Then you go from there . . . it's got to be in your head . . . the producer does have to be a creative person. That's why a lot of engineers aren't really producers.

The Raspberries' gold record "Go All the Way" was taught to members of the group although only its writer, lead singer Eric Carmen, knew the total concept for it. "None of you guys will really know what the song's supposed to sound like until it's recorded and all mixed. Then we'll know how to play it," he said. "Nobody could really conceive of that except I would be able to hear it in my head being the writer of the song." Tom Wilson: "The producer paints on layers of technique, deciding in the process the type of echo to use, the number of tracks . . . and the choice of overdubbing and equalizing devices."[21] Volume, tempo, clearness or fuzziness of one or two tracks all are determined at this point. Other sounds are added if needed. Anderle attempts to make the song as real as possible; he will "throw in a pedal steel with a lick, or maybe a violin here or something, anything that will enhance the music and give it something that will turn people on." The artist should then have the final say. Anderle, as well as many other producers, insists that the performer accept this responsibility. "An artist has to tell me he's happy." Other producers, either due to inexperience or pressure by a company's rush to get the record out, may mix the record without consulting the artist. The consequences are predictable. The failure of the record will be laid at the feet of the producer, since he mixed the record, at least in the mechanical sense. A producer, in mixing a record, also must consider the tastes of his projected audience. A single is mixed differently than an album. The emotional impact of the single must be immediate, and the length of the song should fit AM airplay formulas. Albums can be a bit more subtle. Easy listening requires more strings. An LP cut can be used as a single. "Singles sell albums" is a cardinal tenet in the record business.

During the mix-down the realization of this economic fact begins to impact upon both the artist and the producer. If the record is a single it must have a "hook" or an infectious beginning. The producer attempts to recreate the magic Buddy Holly sound which attracted listeners' attention during the first four bars of the song. Producers are well aware that program directors and rock writers are sent enormous quantities of listening material (see chapters 5 and 6). Ron Jacobs, while the program director at the powerful Los Angeles boss radio station KHJ, would listen to only the first three or four seconds of a record before deciding if it was "hit bound." Producers of albums such such as Ted Templeman and Lenny Waronker deny pandering to the reviewing habits of program directors, however, Templeman always places the strongest song as cut one, side one on an album. "That's because the program director will hear that first. That's just common sense. It probably wasn't necessarily the best as far as the total concept, but I owe it to the artist to give him that." David Anderle and his artists, Marc Benno, Rita Coolidge and Kris Kristofferson, not to mention A&M, which distributes Willow Productions, continuously discuss the manufacturing of a hit single. "Once in a while," he admits, "we may lean to adding something, maybe we put strings on this; the AM market would have more of a chance of playing it. When we're cutting songs with Mark, we're not embarrassed to use words like 'hook' . . . it's a matter of saying here's the song, here's how we laid it out." Capitol Records laid out Bang's single "Questions" by overdubbing a heavy Kinks-like bass line introduction which was absent from the album version.

Some performers feel that there is an overemphasis on the hook. Waylon Jennings, who coproduces and writes many of his own songs said, "if a big beat compliments that song, then use it. If a kazoo compliments that song, we got just as much right to use that as anybody else. Or horns or anything. But *don't use them* just in order to make it where it will get played in certain areas." Once again, we find the conflict between artistic concerns and record sales.

Producers and A&R departments include other extraneous factors in the mix of records. The channeling of a record is determined by the idiom to which it is addressed. Mauri Lathower says, "There are times we'll mix a single differently for the radio stations than the copies we sell or marketing copy." This practice assures the company that listeners will hear the entire record. Radio stations receive monaural singles or type B monos where two stereo tracks are condensed into one. The reason for this policy is that with two channels it is possible to lose a track in transmission. The highs and lows from the rhythm section can be lost or even the vocal. To accommodate stereo broadcasters many singles sent to radio stations now have the same song in both one track and two tracks on different sides.

Time is a very important factor. Radio programming is governed by the "Drake Clock," which allots a certain amount of time for a song and no more. The producer must be aware of this policy. Many good records have failed because they disregarded the time factor. Phil Spector's "River Deep" is believed to have failed because it contained 40 seconds more music than the average Top 40 single. Another Spector production, "Lovin' Feeling" by the Righteous Brothers, almost suffered a similar fate when program directors discovered that the time listed on the record was incorrect. Although it caused Public Service Announcements (PSAs) and news stories to be cut short, "Lovin' Feeling" was Spector's biggest success. Very few other records have successfully deviated from the dictates of time scheduling. The Beatles' "Hey Jude" was the longest single to reach the *Billboard* Hot 100. Don McLean's "American Pie" was originally shortened from the album version. Only listener demand garnered the entire song air play. Most songs longer than 2:37 or 3:05 minutes have been cut down to meet the radio time requirement.

Yet another consideration facing the producer is that few bands are evenly balanced between instrumentals and vocals. The producer generally determines emphasis between the two on the basis of market. Many A&R people believe easy-listening stations prefer lush arrangement. Therefore, the listener, probably doing housework or driving to work, need not concentrate. Lyrics are incidental, the instruments provide the background noise. The same philosophy is true for so-called punk-rock bands such as Grand Funk Railroad, where energy and high volume are all-important. On the other hand, for the college youth audience, lyrics are not to be disturbed by complex arrangements that overshadow the singer. These, of course, are general rules of thumb balanced out by synthesizing both down into a single channel, orienting a song into hopefully two markets. The Moody Blues, Cat Stevens, Helen Reddy, Neil Young and several other artists have successfully appealed to both the youth and easy-listening markets, but this is tricky business and one is wiser not to stray too far from the characteristics of the audience. "It's intuition," says Tom Wilson, "knowing how to interpret demographic and sociological data, keeping one ear tuned to the music."[22] The sociological and demographic data, called Q-profiles, define what sells and to whom. Producers are specialists, labeled as being especially effective in reaching a particular taste group.

As artists, producers are categorized and self-categorized. Andy Wickham sees himself as the Roger Vadim of the industry, concentrating on producing female vocalists. He will, however, undertake "everybody but underground artists," who in his mind are mirrors of the "plastic Orwellian" state of America. Ted Templeman prefers rock music bands as Captain Beefheart, Little Feat or the Doobie Brothers because they have "a lot of quality rhythms and strong percussion." Lenny Waronker generally sticks to acoustical and folk guitarists such as Ry Cooder, Arlo Guthrie, Gordon Lightfoot and writer Randy Newman. George Goldner, in the 1950s, thrived upon acappela New York street-corner groups, as did Leiber and Stoller. Jeff Barry carried on this tradition now being called in the industry as the "maker of Top 40 hits." Steve Barri, who produces the Grass Roots, has a similar image. Phil Spector originally worked with black artists until he replaced George Martin as the Beatles' control-board operator. Bob Johnston is expert with singer-poets such as Dylan and Leonard Cohen. Bones Howe, a former engineer, has done especially well with vocal groups like the Association and Fifth Dimension, with his knack for overdubbing voices. The list goes on. Producers rise and fall with trends and fads. Indeed, some producers cannot work with certain artists either because of personality factors or because of the act's style, David Anderle who concentrates upon solo artists commented: "As a producer my biggest failure is working with a band. I have problems working with multiple personalities.

A producer can do little with some artists. For stage bands, the studio is a prison rather than a tool for creativity. Gary Duncan, of the Quicksilver Messenger Service: "Playing something in a studio means playing for two months. Playing live, a song changes in performance. In a studio you attack things intellectually; on stage it's all emotion."[23] Cub Koda, a member of Brownsville Station, further explains the difference between the studio and the stage. "There's a lot of groups that the first thing they do is they go into the studio. They don't even worry about live performance, they master the studio and sometimes they come out with good stuff. Us, man, we're dragged out of high schools, we're dragged out of basements . . . we learned everything we know on the stage." The group's lead singer adds, "Obviously you can't have all the charisma that you have in a live performance, particularly with us, because you've got the visual thing as well. You're seeing the music as well when you come to hear us play, so to speak, but you can't get that on an album. We're trying to get as close to it as possible." For many bands getting "close" has not been possible. A vinyl disk—even quad—cannot condense into one idiom the excitement of a Trips Festival or a totally orchestrated concert. The visual and sensual aspects of a performance at the Fillmore or some other auditorium are rarely captured. Records by San Francisco bands have generally disappointed critics and fans. Only the Buffalo Springfield, Crosby, Stills, Nash and Young and others have been able to recreate their "live" shows in studios. Part of the problem is no doubt technical; however, many acts simply cannot function without an audience. Jim Messina characterizes Poco as a stage band. Humble Pie, Black Oak Arkansas, James Gang and Grand Funk do their best "live." In a studio only the producer provides feedback. As a result many acts become flat on record, especially when they are asked to replay the same lines over and over again. The psychological tricks used by those behind the glass sometimes fail to generate excitement.

The art of mixing all of the ingredients which confront the producer into a salable commodity borders upon alchemy. Formulas exist but few are either foolproof or consistent. The magic that made Phil Spector a "teenage tycoon," as Tom Wolfe labeled him, an overnight millionaire, failed him after "River Deep." For the sound to be in the grooves a right number of elements must jell. Once the master tape is delivered to the A&R department it is immediately put on trial. The type of economic and psychic energy the record will receive is determined at this point. An A&R department that believes in a record will in fact try to get the rest of the company behind it. A lukewarm response will generate only a minimum of effort. It is true that most companies give everything "a shot." The kind of shot is originally determined by A&R, which hopes (and prays) the emotional contagion will carry over to marketing.

MARKETING: BUTTONS, BANNERS AND T-SHIRTS

Since Vance Packard's *Hidden Persuaders* and Milton Meyers's *Madison Avenue U.S.A.* dominated America's best-seller lists, advertising executives have come to be seen as sorcerers armed with motivational research and other magical potions with which to inveigle the average consumer into purchasing anything from toothpaste to presidents. There is considerable doubt in the record industry about the magical qualities of marketing. Murray Ross, president of Ideal Planning Associates, wrote in *Record World*: "The techniques of marketing and merchandising in the music industry are the most underdeveloped of any billion dollar industry . . .no giant industry can survive and prosper where marketing and merchandising planning is the least dynamic component of its total sales efforts."[24] An industry publicist remarked, "If a PD in the Midwest says we don't know what's going on with his people and their daily lives, I partially agree with him." Joe Smith, at Warner Brothers, feels that horse-and-buggy marketing techniques permeate the record industry: "Marketing is an industry problem. . . . It's a problem of how to get our goods out to as many places as possible . . . that's the next challenge for us. To penetrate market and get music in more homes, there's equipment to play it." Until the 1970s, penetrating the market was a relatively standardized operation. Since World War II the basic desire has been to "break the record on radio." This task has consummated a majority of industry marketing efforts. A 1966 industry-wide poll, conducted by Algin B. King, found 51 percent of resources being aimed at radio acceptance.[25] This figure has risen over the years. The difficulties of getting air time have caused many companies to look elsewhere for exposure. Neil Bogart, president of the Casablanca label explained, "Record companies simply must adjust to the times. Insofar as the radio play lists have not expanded, more and more effort is required at the development level."[26]

It is axiomatic that every album warrants "a button, a badge, a poster and maybe a T-shirt." Every marketing department in New York and Los Angeles has the memorabilia of past campaigns hanging from office ceilings, tacked on the walls and leaning in corners. These offices look like children's playrooms rather than habitats of highly paid and skilled advertising executives. Their dress is a millenium away from the gray-flannel-suited Madison Avenue men of the 1950s. They wear blue T-shirts announcing Bertha Has Balls; shirts with a multicolored skull for the Grateful Dead; or white ones with a red tongue symbolizing the Rolling Stones. Their Levis jackets bear shoulder patches depicting Quicksilver Messenger Service or Grand Funk Railroad. All of this signifies fun, creativity and commitment. Artists expect such artifacts to be part of the campaign. This is partially the answer to agent Roy Silver's daily question, "What have you done for my act today?" Buttons, badges and T-shirts are relatively inexpensive. Therefore, companies produce these devices as a matter of course. The T-shirt with the logo of the record company and the name of the act is now a cliché with minimal effectiveness. T-shirts are worn to one press party, then discarded. They are not designed for durability. After one or two washings the colors usually fade away. Deejays and critics probably have drawers full of T-shirts sent by record companies; several companies actually keep the neck sizes of important critics and programmers. While preparing a mailing of Hot Tuna gold and red shirts, in time for a local concert, an RCA secretary asked Grelun Landon, "Is J. R. Young a medium or large?" With these shirts go a plethora of toys, notebooks, gimmicks, balloons, cans, cups and shaving mugs—all designed to lend something special to an artist or his album.

Capitol Records, Warner Brothers and Mercury are perhaps the most ingenious gimmick creators. One Pink Floyd LP, *Atom Heart Mother*, was accompanied by a pink balloon shaped like a cow udder. Hurricane Smith's "has a lot of gusts" was inscribed upon a raincoat sent to deejays and critics. Tennesse Ernie Ford gave a shaving mug to the same people—with an album. *Puff 'n' Stuff*, also from Capitol, had a gigantic mobile which brightened the day for many a record gatekeeper's child. Mercury Records mails out Rod Stewart coffee cups and Uriah Heep candles. United Artists encased a harmonica in a large sealed silver can to introduce *Canned Heat 'Live'*. They sent out a rusty can for Country Gazette. A&M sent out a wristwatch to commemorate a Joe Cocker tour. The actual impact of these gimmicks is illusory; however, a well-planned gimmick, as in the case of the Raspberries' scented sticker, will bring fleeting notice to the album. After that, "it has to be in the grooves." One reviewer commented, "The gifts are fun, but really don't make a helluva lot of difference. I can't stand Hurricane Smith and a windbreaker is not going to change that. . . . But I did listen to the album," he added. For Capitol's marketing people the mission was accomplished. The writer's unfavorable response was laid at the feet of the gravel-voiced Smith. With the never-ending flow of product, new gimmicks and techniques are constantly being sought. New marketing and merchandising techniques are the key to this development. Many companies have started creative services sections which attempt to pioneer new methods of giving their record "a shot."

THE GOOD OLD DAYS

Prior to the golden year when the record industry enjoyed its first billion-dollar sales figure, marketing generally consisted of promoting air play, trade-paper advertising and store displays. These displays usually were large oil paintings of a grinning band leader with a horn or his favorite vocalist. The 78-rpm singles came in brown grocery-bag jackets with a listing of the companies' other records. Album covers either showed the toothy artist on the front or a painted portrait of a pinup girl. The appearance of the long-playing record provided more space for artistic design, a fact not immediately recognized. Columbia Records' initial LP, released in 1948, had a large marble pillar on the cover with the name of the artist and the title of the album printed within. The most prominent part of the cover was its logo with the company's name and catalog number. After this construct was used on some 200 albums, it began to prove rather unsuccessful. The LP was altering record merchandising.

The sealed LP brought a halt to the traditional practice of "listen then buy." No longer would record stores allow the patron to hear a record prior to purchase; the cellophane album skin prevented such amenities. Art departments attempted to soften the effects of the new practice by using the cover to sell the record. The easy-listening albums of Jackie Gleason or Art Van Damme left no doubt about their purpose. Couples in their mid-twenties were pictured sitting in a penthouse suite overlooking New York, with a martini glass and desirous expressions. Mood music was the sound of seduction. Albums designed for collegiates also stressed the social aspect of music. Taking a page from *Life* magazine, folksingers and pop quartets were found dating, drinking and dancing on the album cover. Surfing albums were typical, taken directly from Coca Cola ads. Following the lead of paperback novels, many album covers had little to do with the contents of the record. More typically, the artist was pictured on the front cover superimposed over some fashion photographer's backdrop with a testimonial to the record pasted on the back cover.

These marketing techniques reflected the nature of the 1950s LP audience. Adults, not teenagers, purchased most of the more expensive records. The best sellers were either from motion pictures or the Broadway stage. Soundtracks contained familiar tunes, and a pretty girl and a title were enough to make the sale. Jazz and classical records such as Columbia's Masterworks series could be pushed with a "tombstone" on the cover. These specialty items frequently contained extensive liner notes by *aficionados* like Morton Gould, Leonard Feather or Ralph J. Gleason.

Teenagers were the popular music fans. They purchased singles they had heard on the radio or perhaps in the record store booth. Many a corner record store or "mom and pop" outlet in the 1950s was an after-school hangout. The arrival of teenage rock idols Elvis Presley and Pat Boone saw record advertisers borrowing from fan magazines and placing a color photograph of the idol on the jacket. Originally this was done with LPs (extended-play 45s with four cuts) containing previously released material. Buy the record, get the picture. In time the practice was expanded to Elvis's singles. The record became an attractive item *and* it frequently advertised for Elvis Presley's latest movie—Colonel Parker rarely missed a promotional opportunity. The pop albums addressed to teenagers either lacked liner notes entirely or were synthesized statements of adulation revealing that Paul Anka, Fabian or Frankie Avalon favored certain kinds of dates, food, clothes and cars. Photos and liners were selling points, since most of these albums contained only one Top 40 hit, already mass consumed by fans, and 10 or 11 filler songs. Even the Beatles' first album was a prototype of 1950s packaging. The cover featured the four lads with a dull brownish yellow background. The backside listed the songs and announced "Introducing The Beatles" and "America's Greatest Recording Artists Are on Vee-Jay Records."

In a matter of several years the Beatles would be instrumental in altering marketing patterns. Their albums were generally a series of 10 to 12 hit songs, half of them on the singles charts. From the sheer economic standpoint, their albums appealed to a vast number of singles-buying teenagers. An album could be had for the price of four 45s. The Beatles, more than any other act, moved teenagers into the albums market.

The rise of LP sales among teenagers was also heightened by the emergence of the San Francisco Haight-Ashbury counterculture, which rejected Top 40 material as irrelevant. Many local favorites were not on singles. Rock music was, for the flower children, a total media experience—light, sound, volume and all that comprised a "trip." Records not possessing these qualities were regarded as "lame." The Jefferson Airplane's first release was highly criticized for not mirroring their stage presence. The first issue of the *Oracle* criticized Ralph J. Gleason's liner notes as a "company hype." To reach this new market, album covers for "acid" bands begin to exhibit posters from Fillmore rock concerts. The Grateful Dead's first album cover was in the language and layout of Haight-Ashbury posters.

As the 1967 Summer of Love was in progress the Beatles released *Sgt. Pepper*, which many have cited as the album that made the cover as important as the recorded material itself. The Beatles extended the theme of the album to the cover, and the "total package" idea was born. In fact, while *Sgt. Pepper* accelerated the total package syndrome, the Beatles' *Yesterday and Today* cover should be credited as the trend setter. Capitol's censorship of this cover delayed the concept for several years. The company had held back two songs from each of the Beatles' early albums, which were released in *Yesterday and Today.* As a reported act of protest, the group designed a cover depicting them in butchers' gowns in the midst of cut-up dolls and slabs of meat, meaning that Capitol had dismembered the group's previous albums. Record programmers who originally saw this cover objected and all copies of the album were recalled. Most fans never saw the cover, but they did see and like *Sgt. Pepper*. The album encouraged others to design their own covers to enhance sales potential and to make an artistic statement. Unfortunately, few other recording artists matched the Beatles' ingenuity in the graphics area.

An exception may be Roger McGuinn, who (after *Yesterday*) used the cover of the *Notorious Byrd Brothers* to express his contempt for David Crosby by showing three members of the band and a mule. The ass had replaced David Crosby in the band.

The message cover and the total package became a source of conflict between artists and their record companies. Company executives were not willing to follow psychedelic posters into the realm of sexual and political explicity. Moby Grape's first cover was changed to remove Don Stevenson's middle finger from its defiantly upward position. The MC 5's liner notes were changed to remove John Sinclair's closing comments. Nearly all album censorship fights have been won by the record company. Stars such as Jefferson Airplane, Blind Faith, Jimi Hendrix, Rolling Stones, Country Joe and the Fish and Alice Cooper all have lost to the censor. The Rolling Stones' *Beggar's Banquet* was not released for six months due to a dispute between the band and London Records. The battle was over a photograph depicting an old bathroom with inoffensive graffiti covering the walls. In time Jagger gave in, but London Records lost the war. The Rolling Stones left and formed its own production company.

Only John Lennon and Yoko Ono's first album triumphed, in part, over the censors. *Two Virgins* showed the couple standing nude on the cover. Capitol in the United States and Polydor in Canada refused to distribute it. Finally the album was distributed by Tetragrammation Records, but in a brown paper bag. The publicity generated by these cover controversies rarely have hurt sales. *Two Virgins*, an aesthetic and critical disaster, no doubt benefited from its brown cover.

The Rolling Stones' dispute with London reportedly did affect its selling power. The album was originally scheduled for late summer release. Mick Jagger's reluctance to accept a quick change delayed the release until mid-December, one week before the Beatles' long-awaited two-record set. Both albums had similar all-white jackets. Timing is important in the sphere of graphics.

The proliferation of product has heightened the quest for unique eye-catching covers and displays. Capitol's advertising director says, "In an industry where product level goes up and up and up and up, it's becoming more and more difficult, as it is for the consumer, to call attention to something you feel deserves a chance or deserves special merit." Ideally, this would entail the development of a special campaign for each act, but obviously, not all receive such treatment. Only an act regarded as potentially "hot" gets a *complete* shot.

A total media campaign involves many components. It begins by identifying the demographic group to which the artist will appeal. This is called "blue-sky" research or, more commonly, market analysis. Blue-sky research ranges from the simple-minded technique of asking girls on the lawn of Hollywood High School what is a good song to more sophisticated methods of motivation research, including galvanic skin and pupil response tests. During the days of Peter Potter's *Juke Box Jury* "is it a hit or a miss?" and Dick Clark's "American Bandstand," panels of teenagers rated songs. At this time it was not unusual for a record company to invite a group of Los Angeles teenagers into a studio to judge a record. Several companies even used high-school students to help structure a record from beginning to end. Some record companies still use students in both high school and college to render judgments upon their records. This is a most unreliable method. Students employed as consultants rapidly become critics and are no longer typical of the record-buying audience. Statisticians no doubt would also object that the sample used by some companies is not representative. Few record companies go beyond the teenage consulting level. Grelun Landon at RCA estimates that companies may budget as much as a million dollars a year on buttons, banners and T-shirts. But they will not spend more than $35,000 on market research. Most prefer to operate "by the seat of the pants."

A good deal of market research in the industry, ironically, is not directed at consumers but at other companies. Capitol's director of research proudly states, "I know our percentage of the market," adding, "I also know *their* percentage of the market," referring to Columbia, RCA and the others. Market percentage is determined in many ways. *Billboard* charts are used—but with a grain of salt. Taste preference polls are also used. "What kind of music do you like?" people are asked on the streets, in supermarkets and shopping centers. The most efficient index is the Q-profile. The Q-profile is a description of a performer's audience. Market researchers know what people like, but not what they will buy. Radio broadcasters with all of the Pulse, ARB and Hopper listings available to them do not have the same problem.

The lack of audience data on the part of the record industry is a puzzling phenomenon to outsiders. The main reason for this absence is ideological. Success in the record industry is basically believed to be a combination of luck, timing, hard work and the great man theory. Only hard work is a controllable force. Charisma and luck are magical qualities which come and go. In a discussion with Stan Gortikov, RIAA president, he suggested that a useful study might be one of the personality characteristics of industry titans as Mo Ostin, Clive Davis and several others. Ironically, successful producers and artists do have a grip on the public pulse—a very fleeting one admittedly. The use of hard demographic data is only slowly becoming quasi-respectable in the record industry.

With a good sound, an attractive record and a projected audience a record company makes certain decisions. The first involves the amount of promotion and publicity money to be spent on a specific album or act. The amount spent frequently is determined by the act's contract and also by its status in the industry. A new act is the most difficult to market, so many companies give only a marginal shot to a new act's record. If signs are good in the field then more capital and effort will be expended. Dennis Killeen explains: "With a new group you have to be *reactive.* You have to be very attuned to what's going on in DeMoines, Atlanta and Peoria. Because from there you're going to get feedback. Based upon that feedback and things growing or targeting your market you hopefully can make big things happen." For Capitol and others, some kind of movement or action must occur for the marketing push to go into high gear.

This is not so with an established act. Killeen elaborates, "You know Traffic is going to sell 700,000 albums eventually. This time you would like to sell a million. Again you make hay while the sun shines." Capitol Records spent $50,000 on Traffic in print and radio advertising, and in addition, they placed advertising through large chains in local newspapers. The retailers all benefit from a campaign of this nature. Capitol also supported a national tour in each city. With an established act such as Traffic, the Band or any other middle-range attraction, the advertising campaign is primarily supposed to bolster sales. It gives the act a feeling that it is being supported as well as making the marketing department look good in the eyes of the rest of the company.

Artists rarely feel their company is doing enough for them. A strong marketing campaign may offset this attitude. Bobby Goldsboro renewed his United Artist contract because of a biographical family album mailing sent to radio stations. An elegant album with a red cover and gold lettering enclosed pages of pictures and the performer's previous recordings. Marty Cerf recalls, "When he saw this," pointing to the record package, "all of a sudden how could he refuse to sign. This was right on the verge of going to Columbia, which has very large friends down in Nashville. Some of his closest buddies are with Columbia." While catering to the psychological needs of the artist a good campaign may generate company support. "People," says Dennis Killeen, "have to be able to see what you're doing from a retail standpoint. It's important to them, it's important to our people." The rise of the Raspberries is a classic example of the marketing of a successful popular music act.

The Raspberries is the brainchild of its lead singer Eric Carmen who talked drummer Jim Bonfanti into a collaboration. Bonfanti was previously with the Choir, a group with the hit "It's Cold Outside," as was Wally Bryson who joined next.

Raspberries was formed on the belief there exists a "teen-scream" cycle which reoccurs every eight years. After reading a *Time* magazine story the Raspberries intentionally started out to be the next Beatles. Their appearance, stage presence and even their music were linked to the English quartet. The name Raspberries was chosen by accident when the band was searching for a simple nonpsychedelic label of the 1965 era. As with all bands, one of the original members did not fit the "concept" and was removed because he "lacked charisma." David Smalley, ex-Choir member, then in the jungles of Vietnam, was invited to join the band with a letter saying "practice." Having assembled the members necessary, Eric and the others practiced nine hours a night, three days a week. Eric says: "It wasn't too hard on the fingers, but terrible on the voice." The band played anywhere they could in the Cleveland area, writing their own songs and reviving early rock-and-roll songs in the Beatles' tradition. In the process, the band signed with a New York management firm that did nothing for the group. The group fired the inactive agency after a year. As do all acts, the band made a demonstration tape of two songs, "Come Around and See Me" and "I Saw the Light." The tape was sent to many producers, including Jimmy Ienner, who hated the songs but liked the Mexican obscenities at the end of the first song. "Anyone with that much guts must be good," he reasoned. Upon seeing the band, he became the "fifth Raspberry." Ienner invited eight record companies to see the band in a small Kent, Ohio, nitery, J.B.'s, which launched the James Gang. Capitol, a company in search of a replacement for the Beatles, outbid its rivals and signed the act. A massive advertising and promotional campaign was mounted, but their first single failed to generate the desired response. The album, named after the band, was average, featuring an early Beatle-like cover pose, but with an unmistakable pungent raspberry scent sticker on the skin. Jokes about the "stinking record" only pushed the group into gatekeepers' and retailers' consciousness. Dennis Killeen explained, "A group no one's ever heard of before, like the Raspberries, you do a smelly sticker, you do something a little unique." He continued, "When a package of 10 of those albums hits any bin in any store, it's going to smell like raspberries. The consumer is going to catch on to what's going on. Reviewers are already talking about the package itself, in print, on the radio. DJs are saying 'my God, this thing smells like raspberries' on the air." Capitol also placed a trade ad with the scented sticker. All of these devices brought immediate attention to the act. At the Capitol Tower, one day in May was designated Raspberry Day. Buttons, balloons, banners and stickers were everywhere. In the afternoon raspberry ice cream was served to visitors and the staff. That evening a press party was given for the group introducing them to the media. The "day" was followed by a tour sponsored by Beechnut Gum. The Raspberries were on the same bill with the Grass Roots. For Capitol, the Raspberries were a sheer gamble. In May 1972 their advertising budget was less than $50,000. Many executives were not sure "we're going to get it back." The support given the act was contingent upon external events. An executive said, "With the Raspberries, we've taken the attitude of 'if the stations go on it we will support it.' In other words, if KHJ could go on the Raspberries record we will buy some spots and tie in with dealers to tell people it's available because you're maximizing your impact there. That, then, becomes expensive. Initially the banners you see, the ice cream, all that hoopla, is a minimal kind of thing." Making the Raspberries a well-known Top 40 act did fulfill Dennis Killeen's fear of high expenses: "Making 'Raspberries' a household word . . . it's going to cost you a lot of money." However, as Heidi Robinson, then with Capitol, added, "Raspberries are one of the more important acts on the label. . . . They have commercial potential and that's all that matters." The company reportedly has spent over $150,000 on the band. Herb Belkin, the vice-president in charge of A&R, observed, "I think light-weight rock will be it . . . anyway, I hope it does because we've got a . . . lot of money tied up in these guys."[27] "Go All the Way" described by Eric

Carmen as the "I Want To Hold Your Hand" of 1972 was certified "gold" in November of that year. The promotional campaign became more elaborate. The band donned mod white suits in the finest Beatle tradition of 1964. Capitol announced in 1972 a "Win the Raspberries Rollswagon" contest. Entrants were eligible to win a mini-custom limousine with stereo equipment and tapes. The company placed a million entry blanks in over 2,000 racks and stores. The entry forms were part of a package of displays, pictures and posters of the group and the car. The contest was announced in a tennybopper fan magazine, *Star*, to maximize the appeal to the 12-to-18 age group.

The Raspberries' initial triumphs are largely attributable to the ingenuity of the marketing department at Capitol Records. The scented sticker attracted considerable attention. The professionalism of the band as well as the timing was equally important. In 1972 the entire industry was searching for "new Beatles." The Raspberries' stated aim to follow in their exalted footsteps has helped them, but continued use of gimmicks may hurt the band. Eric Carmen observes, "Our most obvious problem is having people think we're some kind of contrived Madison Avenue project."[28] Spending too much money in fact can be as hazardous as none at all.

The story of Moby Grape is legend in the record industry, although the experience of the ill-fated San Francisco band is not unique. Moby Grape was one of the stellar Bay Area acid-rock bands. It was locally as popular as the Dead, Airplane and Big Brother, and some believed the group was superior. Enjoying the fruits of a nearly suicidal bidding war, the group signed with Columbia Records. In conjunction with the beginning of San Francisco's ill-fated Summer of Love, Columbia launched a massive promotional campaign to cash in on flower power. The Beatles' "All You Need is Love" and the Airplane's "Somebody to Love" were selling well. Scott McKenzie's invitation dominated Top 40 air play: "When you're going to San Francisco be sure to wear some flowers in your hair." The Moby Grape campaign opened with a gala press party on the East Coast and a concert for 1,500 media and "flower children" at the Avalon Ballroom. Journalists were flown in from various parts of the country to the happening. That day an unprecedented five singles and an album were simultaneously released. This was unheard of, especially for a new act. This reportedly underlined Columbia's commitment to the group, but it was also a classic example of Columbia's buckshot theory of promotion. All of the singles were so good that a disk jockey had only to air any one of them and a monster hit would result. All of the singles were on the album, accompanied by "Make It If I Want To," "Ain't No Use" and "Lazy Me." All of the trappings of Haight-Ashbury were visible. The five singles were housed in separately designed and colored sleeves. Color photos were used on the albums along with a poster inside the jacket. A special logo or insignia was prepared for the campaign. A manual for promotional people was devised. Full-page ads ran in all of the trades and teen magazines. *Billboard* announced, "Columbia Gives Moby Grape a Whale of a Buildup." At least 100,000 advance orders on the album were reported. With the exception of one single, "Omaha," which reached an unflattering 88 spot on the Hot 100, the campaign ended in economic disaster. Albums and posters were recalled because of Don Stevenson's "offensive" raised middle finger. After the Avalon concert, members of the band were charged with possession of drugs and contributing to the delinquency of two teenage girls. Neither the arrest nor the cover controversy account for the poor response to what was a critically acclaimed album. The post mortem for Moby Grape was simply that Columbia's extensive $100,000 plus advertising expenditure frightened disk jockeys and others away. One program director recalled, "Nobody could have been *that* good." Other companies relate similar tales of overfinanced advertising campaigns which failed.

The fact that a Raspberries campaign succeeded and an equally intense Moby Grape hype failed underlines the difference between advertising and hyping. A hype is simply a promotional campaign which is oversold. The line of demarcation between the two is almost totally obscure. "There are lots of mysterious elements," says Dennis Killeen. "For some artists, for some careers, it's important not to seem you're hyping it, because indeed it's the hype that you're going to turn off the people you're trying to reach which ultimately are the consumers." With an overselling job people assume "the group doesn't have any talent and this is the only way that can promote them when talent should be able to stand up by itself."

In recent years companies have gone to great lengths to emphasize their "lack of hype" or low-key advertising. Warner Brothers, under Stan Cornyn's direction, has been especially successful in this effort. Cornyn built the creative services department from two people to 30 or 35 in a space of four years. One of the concepts to emerge from their creative services was the sampler album. The sampler was not a new idea; RCA, Columbia and others had jazz, folk and classic samplers which were cheaply priced and placed in record stores. Warner samplers were originally designed by Stan Cornyn to attract the attention of both radio programmers and the public. He recalls: "There would be nothing more disenchanting than to become a program director or disk jockey and be faced with that pile of albums coming in. . . . Let's just try to hook him with one or two cuts. The same thing would go for our salesmen, if we wanted to introduce an album to them. So we made up a little promotional album, little in the sense that we didn't do many of them and they would just go out to a few people." Cornyn then compiled an album of his favorite cuts from Warner albums and the sampler was born. It rapidly reached past the deejays to the consumers. As a promotional tool the sampler has been successful in that a customer pays two dollars for hearing some songs designed to motivate him to buy the artist's entire album. The samplers have done quite well because of their overall high quality and their low cost, selling 80,000 copies on the average. The company has made money from them while at the same time promoting Warner Brothers acts, and its profits are enhanced by the low cost of production. The cuts generally included those already mixed for a previous album with a few new cuts added. The promotional nature of the set means that artist royalties do not have to be paid. All promotional activities are tax deductible. The only cost incurred were ads in the underground press and Warner record envelopes that further announced the samplers.

Warner/Reprise has also developed *Circular*, a promotional handout dealing with the company's product. Fifty-thousand copies are distributed in record stores and through press and media mailings weekly. Columbia followed suit with *Playback* in 1970 which is mailed to various consumers and media people. Consumers pay three dollars to be added to the mailing list as "consultants."

In addition to samplers and company newspapers, an increasingly popular marketing technique is the use of freebees to record shops. Record-shop owners, like disk jockeys and writers, are provided with free records to be played in the store. The philosophy behind this is that 13 percent of record sales are based upon impulse buying. Bill Roberts at United Artists commented: "If 150 people can walk into a record shop and hear one of my records being played, that's as great as if he heard it on the radio. If they hear it in the store where it's easily available, they're more apt to buy it than if they were riding down the street and listening to it on the radio. Because it's on their mind for a while then it's gone." A vast amount of product is flooding this arena. Larger stores now will play selected albums only as part of a total advertising package in which the record company is expected to buy newspaper and sometimes radio advertising announcing that *X* album is available at a specific record chain. This is called "coop" money—the amount a record company will spend on retailing advertising. Industry-bought advertising in the Sunday *New York Times* "Arts and Leisure" section can also get a record played. Smaller shops are not afforded such treatment because they only carry albums in quantities of threes and fives. Roberts explains: "They're not interested in the big newspaper ads or the getting paid to play it in the store because they can't do enough volume for you and they know no company is going to take the time to pay for getting their record played in the store." The competition for "in-store" play is intense and fraught with all of the problems of getting precious air time or newspaper review space. With record chains payola is very much the rule. One publicity director said, "If he can get paid for playing the record, he'll do it." Large record-store chains, while significant in major market cities and some college towns, comprise only 10 percent of sales in the United States. Racks and other outlets account for the rest. Consequently, creative-service departments must look even further for opportunities to expose product.

Since the demise of the variety shows, television is slowly returning as an alternative medium in which recording artists can do their thing. Performers still regularly visit Dick Clark, "Soul Train" and others on their record-hop shows to lip-synch their latest release. Talk shows are also valuable. Gerard Purcell, a publicist for RCA, said, "An appearance on the 'Tonight Show' or the shows of Merv Griffin and Mike Douglas are worth four weeks in any hotel or nightclub in the nation."[29] The rise of late-night rock concerts during the McGovern presidential campaign also added an important showcase. ABC Television's "In Concert" series doubled the regularly scheduled talk-show hosts' ratings. The first 90-minute special featuring Alice Cooper captured 19 percent of the audience as opposed to Cavett's 12 percent on the Neilson scale. NBC then created "Midnight Special" with a more Top 40ish format, which featured performers lip-synching their current single. "Midnight Special" very much followed the pattern established by "American Bandstand" only it was broadcast at 1 A.M. After a network dispute Don Kirshner, the founder of "In Concert," left ABC and syndicated his own "In Concert." Ironically Dick Clark took over ABC's version of the show. Currently, there exist two "In Concerts" and a "Midnight Special." All appear to be in good health at least in the ratings. Record companies strongly urge their performers to appear on these shows. Performers are paid scale regardless of their asking concert price. Only a few superstars like Cat Stevens and David Bowie have gotten past the "for scale only" rider. The rationale for appearing on these shows is that record sales are believed to jump 10 percent after doing "In Concert" or "Midnight Special."

Even televised Sunday afternoon pro-football games have not escaped some creative services departments. Since demographic profiles indicate an MOR audience is glued to the adventures of the NFL gladiators, half-time shows have increasingly given Andy Williams, Ernie Ford, Johnny Mathis and a score of jazz performers four to five minutes of national television exposure. The value of such exposure is questionable. Grelun Landon, RCA Victor publicity director, indicates: "The exposure is always welcome. As an instant motivation thing, I think not, particularly as opposed to the classic television show of the 1950s which broke 'Let Me Go Lover' with Joan Weber on Columbia into gigantic proportions. Subliminal motivation, sure, and maybe. There's really no way of market testing Monday morning store impact." The primary function of a marketing department is to create interest in their artist and records. Once they find some way to enter the cognitive paths of consumers, their work is done.

The final link in the chain is in the physical production and distribution section of the company. Again, coordination is the major dilemma. In 1973 there were 981 distributors in the United States, 40 record plating plants and shops, 52 sleeve manufacturers, 22 jacket printers and lithographers. Only a handful of majors have their own facilities to accomplish all of these tasks. Even those who have the facilities to print, press and ship, such as Capitol and Columbia, must deal with the amorphous entity of distribution. Shipping a box of records from a pressing plant to your local record outlet should be a simple task. It is not. Once again, the record company is faced with the problem of individualized interests and the famous cop-out.

DISTRIBUTION: THE BOTTOM LINE

Once the artist has done "his thing," the producer has delivered the tape, and marketing has developed its package, success is determined by the consumer walking into a store and saying, "do you have this record?" All of the mixing, hyping, promoting come to naught if the clerk responds, "Sorry, it hasn't come in yet." Coping with this problem has vexed record-company executives for at least two decades. With the infusion of large conglomerate assets, they are working on what may be the "final solution." Ironically, this remedy is based on the prototype of the depression years when Decca, Columbia and RCA directly distributed and wholesaled their own records to the retailer. These in turn were retailed for 35 cents. The rise in popularity of singles, which were released by an ever-increasing number of labels during the 1950s, gave birth to a new type of wholesaler: the "one-stop." the one-stop stocked all labels, allowing the juke-box operator to transact all his business in one store. The operator paid a small convenience charge of three to five cents on each record he bought, and record companies gave the one-stop a ten-percent discount for selling their singles. Many retailers later found this a quick and efficient way of obtaining records. As one retailer observed, "time is money." Originally the one-stop came between the record company and the juke-box operator, but later it evolved into a major wholesaler and middleman between the record company and retailer. Simultaneously with the emergence of the one-stops, the majors gave birth to "multiple distribution," a merchandising concept that has been the nexus of the distribution controversies of the late 1960s. Irwin Steinberg, the president of Polygram, defines this technique as "the flow of goods from manufacturer to consumer through *more than one* channel."[30] The introduction of the record club by Columbia, followed by Capitol and RCA in 1958, found majors shipping to their own branches, "one-stops" and the newly formed mail outlets.

The record clubs originally placed the majors in the role of record retailer. The clubs allowed the three majors to sell directly to the consumer thus bypassing the cost of any middle man. Retailers loudly objected to this practice. In 1962 the Federal Trade Commission responded, accusing Columbia Records of creating a monopoly by distributing only its own artists. In 1971 the clubs made available artists from other labels. This move, however, has not resolved the highly controversial practice of giving clubs favored pricing status. Many retailers believe that clubs purchase albums at less than a dollar per unit. Retailers and wholesalers must pay nearly three times that price for the same record. One retailer bitterly expressed a sentiment widely held by those who compete with record clubs: "I'm no attorney but there are some laws being broken along the line. . . . How can some of these large companies sell to dealers, sell to racks, yet still be in the record club business? . . . Some of these large corporations are wearing many hats and one of these days . . . the government is going to come and take a good look at some things that are going on." The traditional record-club audience, numbering less than 3 million members, is comprised mainly of persons over the age of 35 and their increasingly small percentage of total volume has stilled but not eliminated much retail criticism of these operations. The controversial nature of the record clubs has been overshadowed by the ascendency of the rack jobber to a place of industry prominence.

In 1952 Elliot Wexler started Music Merchants in Philadelphia. Music Merchants was the first rack jobber in the United States. The rack jobber extended to supermarkets, drug stores and variety shops the convenience of a retail record shop; people no longer had to go to a downtown record shop to buy a record. Originally racks carried budget items, in time expanding to top-selling albums. The rack jobber set up his 4½ foot Friedman rack as near as possible to the flow of shoppers in a store. Music Merchants eventually failed, but their idea was picked up by David Handleman, a health and beauty aid rack jobber in Detroit. Handleman's attempt at racking records was a smashing success. Jules Malamud, the president of the National Association of Record Merchandisers, recalls, "The rack jobber solved the mystery for the public of where to buy a record. They made it easy. When I was a kid, I was a record buff. In those days Ella Fitzgerald, the Mills Brothers, Nat Cole were popular. You'd have to walk around and go to a store that sold radios or something and try to find a record and they'd say they'd order it for you and maybe they ordered it for you and maybe they didn't. But, I wanted to hear it. When you love something and you have your girlfriend with you, you wanted to listen to a certain song. You wanted it that night. So what the rack jobber did was they really made it easy for people to buy records." Racks were convenient with ready-made buyers.

RCA Victor was the first major company to realize the importance of racks. The company produced a "60 years of greatest hits" album at a very low cost, especially for the rack. Somerset Stereo Fidelity Records produced budget records designed especially for the rack. Somerset wholesaled records at 93 cents to the rack jobbers who in turn sold them for $1.98.

The immense volume power of the rack provided the jobber with the same purchasing power as the one-stop. He was officially a subdistributor purchasing his albums from the company at a 10-percent discount. The tremendous volume of the rack provided him with yet another benefit from the record companies—a 100-percent return privilege. Prior to the rack jobber, return privilege was 10 percent of product purchased from the record company.

Rack jobbers quickly outstripped "mom and pop" retail stores. The convenience of the rack, the volume discount and the stocking of only fast-moving product gave the rack jobber a major advantage over the retailer who paid more and carried less-popular catalog items.

In volume, the bigger rack jobbers quickly became preeminent. In the early 1960s they enjoyed a third of total record sales, but by the late 1960s the racks controlled nearly 80 percent of the market. From the supermarket the rack jobbers moved into the world of discount stores such as Arlans, K-Mart or White Front, further boosting their economic power. Much to the dismay of record manufacturers, rack jobbers began to cross over into more traditional retail areas.

Department stores which had previously purchased product directly from the companies were courted by rackers, who offered to take over the responsibility of following musical tastes. No longer would the retailer be required to wrestle with the world of Top 40 radio. Many retailers found this a welcome relief.

"In a 5 & 10 cent store like Woolworths," explains Jules Malamud, "they did not know how to sell records. They didn't even have a buyer of phonograph records." He continues, "They left it up to a girl who made $25 a week. A guy would go in and buy her a box of candy or something and say 'hey, buy some records' . . . so they were constantly loading these stores with bad records. And these chains were not dumb. The manager of the store came and said 'hey, you bought these records and they didn't turn into dollars, get rid of them. They didn't pay the bills.' So the rack jobber came and said 'look, I'm an expert. Now I'm going to set up a record department for you. Give me 20 square feet or whatever amount of space he says, and I'll decide what goes in there.' The rack jobber said to the department-store owner, "We will guarantee that everything gets sold, and if it doesn't we'll replace it with salable merchandise." Jack Geldbart, of ABC Record and Tapes, recalled: "So out rode the White Knight. The rack jobber came and offered to the retailer a single source of supply, a way for the retailer to hold a single company responsible for his entire department, a way to minimize the perils of an extremely volatile and perishable product."[31]

Ironically, many rack jobbers knew little more about the record business than the beleaguered appliance manager in a department store. Ross Halamay, a veteran record salesman for Decca and RCA, as well as a rack jobber during the 1960s, comments: "Many racks gave the representative carte blanche. They gave him a figure to work with. It's up to him to turn those into dollars. He's doing a job for them that they possibly can't do for themselves."

The rack was also aided by the nature of the 1950s record market. Records stayed on the charts much longer. Audience loyalty was greater. As one rack jobber put it, "*Sound of Music* was great for a year and a half. Now this was great for the Handleman Company. They couldn't make too many mistakes there." The invasion of department stores and retailers by rack jobbers led record companies to try to coerce rackers with threats of "cutting them off" or withholding product. But by then the rack jobber had become the major merchandiser of the recording industry's product.

Ironically, the record industry gave the rack jobber his power. The 10-percent discount gave him a distinct advantage over the traditional retailer. The 100-percent return privilege allowed him to err without penalty. The rack could easily walk into a department store and make claims as described by Malamud. The 100 return underwrote the rack. He could trade off his "stiffs" or "schlock" product for top-selling artists. If the Bowling Green Full Tilt Boogie Band did not sell, the racker could exchange the album for the Rolling Stones or the Beatles.

With this cushion the rack jobber stocked entire record departments in many chains and department stores. This placed him in even more direct competition with the retail specialty shop. The White Front, K-Mart or Woolworth's record departments in many instances paralleled the specialty store. At this point the role of the rack jobber was difficult to define. Was he a wholesaler? A retailer? A distributor?

Shemel and Krasilovsky, in their industry handbook, only hint at the source of the troubles: "Although there is little argument about the functions of a distributor, which is the first link in the chain of distribution headed by manufacturers, some distributors *simultaneously* operate as rack jobbers on the side and service locations that undersell their regular dealer customers."[32] Prior to the coming of the so-called rock revolution, this rather confused mode of record merchandising was generally tolerated. The expansion of the LP market through the unorthodox avenues of "free-form" radio and the underground press created an awareness of the anomalies of the distribution and merchandising systems. The industry, according to David Lawhon, "woke up one morning to find the rack jobber in control of the market," as the decisive merchandiser of albums.

In 1965, there existed three fairly well-defined distributors and subdistributors. The record companies were the direct distributors. Decca, Columbia and RCA enjoyed close direct distribution with their branches. Subdistributors, who bought product at a 10 percent discount, were the one-stops and the rack jobbers. The rock revolution and the rise of the long-playing album had an important effect upon each of these outlets. One-stops servicing jukeboxes moved into the album field and in effect began to directly compete with rack jobbers. Rack jobbers in many cases expanded their activities to service jukebox operators. In time, rack jobbers and one-stops became indistinguishable. They performed the same functions. Rack jobbers, merged with one-stops, now service jukes, stores, supermarkets and now even own their own record chains.

In 1969 RCA Victor celebrated this wedding by classifying rack jobbers as wholesalers and lowering prices for them. Retailers and smaller jukebox-oriented one-stops were not happy because their larger competitors were getting records at cheaper rates. The one-stop servicing *only* jukebox operators had to pay more for what he purchased from the manufacturer. He would either have to absorb the cost to remain competitive of pass on the increase to the operator. Retailers were no less happy when chains, owned by racks and large one-stops, could get records at least 10 percent discounted. The record companies reasoned that racks controlled 80 percent of the market and preferential pricing would only encourage further buying and distribution. Norman Racusin, a company vice-president, explained to *Billboard*: "As part of our total approach to the record business, our objective is total balance in distribution, in selling and promotion and most of all in product. Our planned additional distribution points will give us the balance we need to maximize retail exposure."[33] With this move the terms "dual distribution" or "multiple distribution" began to dominate the trade papers. In fact racks became competitive with the companies' own franchised distributors.

Small independents and previous RCA distributors objected violently. One franchised branch perceived the action as "a strange move and a serious mistake. It takes away a distributor's customers and gives him additional competition." Another franchised branch said "We took the line several months ago and invested about $300,000. Now the racks in our market are to get the same price and have the same privileges as distributors."

Most observers labeled RCA's move as an explicit recognition of the state of the industry. Jac Holzman explained: "It is inevitable because the responsibility for promoting records has fallen increasingly on the manufacturer. The distributor has too many lines . . . when the manufacturer took over promotion the handwriting was on the wall."[34] The rise of multiple distribution underlined the problem the RCA move was aimed at. Subdistributors, prior to the mid-1960s, directed most of the "person-to-person" promotion of records, calling on program directors with the latest single. The proliferation of labels which occurred during the rise of rock and roll drastically cut subdistributors abilities to "plug" the voluminous amount of product. Even single-line franchised distributors or branches were more apt to push established artists. A "key manufacturer" observed in *Billboard*: "The independent distributors have too many lines. They cannot attend to all. They pay attention to only the hot product and much product is not getting adequate exposure in retail outlets. As a result the customer over 25 years of age becomes alienated. He finds a concentration of top hits."[35] In 1968 Henry Brief told *Forbes*,

"The distributors already have so many labels they need another like they need two heads."[36] Even one of RCA's unhappy discontinued distributors concurred with this assessment. Jim Shipley, the Cleveland distributor, said, "RCA had to do something. . . . The pure independent distributor is obsolete. . . . Nobody needs two middlemen. There has been [sic] an integration or merging of functions."[37]

Yet, selling directly to racks did not satisfy the record companies' desire to merge functions. RCA's version of "multiple distribution" treated only the distribution problem, not promotion; but the move was the death knoll for the previous modus operandi of doing business. Prophetically, Sam Sachs told *Billboard*:

> Dual distribution, if carried out fully, can lead to a marketing structure built along the same lines as the cosmetic industry, in which the manufacturer does all the advertising, promotion, and marketing, and then sells to any retailer or wholesaler who can afford to buy this product, and all at the same price.[38]

The shift to multiple distribution, while expanding the record company's retail outlets, also ignored another problem. Rack jobbers do not do across-the-board promotional work. They send few field men to radio stations and do not escort artists to meet program directors. They merely sell records in their racks and retail outlets. While the shift to multiple distribution attracted a higher volume of sales, the recording companies were left with the exclusive responsibility of breaking records. Increasingly, the trade papers carried familiar complaints from dealers, program directors and executives. A headline in *Billboard* announced: "Chaos Hits Radio on Disk Service." Claude Hall, the paper's authority on radio stations, reported, "A vast number of radio stations are asking the record industry to by-pass present distribution channels—the distributor and the rack jobbers and their local and regional promotion men—and service them directly."[39] Station managers, throughout the country accused rack jobbers and others of not "servicing" them. The operations manager at KFOR (Lincoln) said, "The distributors are extremely erratic." Bill Tanner of KACY (Ventura) urged manufacturers to "go around the racks somehow and make the product available in the market. As it is now, there's no reason to play it if they can't buy it." Several weeks later, small record companies were protesting, "It is imperative that small labels find a good distributor who can collect their company so that they can continue to promote new releases."[40]

In September 1970, 25 of the most powerful executives in the record industry rated distribution and merchandising as the industry's major problem, even above the inflation then badly cutting into sales. William Gallagher of Famous Artists accused the rack of displacing the small retailer and then failing to recognize the "responsibilities they have inherited. Too little consideration is given today to the music buyer who likes to browse and be motivated by other than the top 20 or 30 chart-busting LPs."[41] Jay Lasker at ABC-Dunhill concurred, suggesting that companies must circumvent the rack by educating the public. Jac Holzman continued the indictment, "Rack merchandisers, because they are not aware of the music on esthetic and social levels, often do not recognize a hit until it is highly placed on the charts. As a result they buy too much too late." The cost of returns was rising.

Returns are records that do not sell and are sent back to the manufacturer for account credit. Forty percent of all records released are returned. The returns procedure costs the manufacturer from 27 to 45 cents per unit of one album or five singles. The actual amount is based on the cost of shipping the product and the paper work necessary to keep the accounts in order. In 1972, rack jobbers shipped back $189,750,000 in merchandise. Record manufacturers would prefer to reduce these costs as much as possible.

It is fashionable in the record industry to blame returns totally upon the rack jobber. Jules Malamud, on the other hand, objects that returns are not solely the fault of the merchandisers. He acknowledges that in the beginning "some of the rack jobbers didn't have good personnel, knowledgeable buyers, and they bought wrong." The 100-percent return policy only covered mistakes. Malamud: "I don't think the answer is 100-percent return because in a sense there are a lot of rack jobbers that are not as good as the Heilichers and other people, and they don't buy right and what really pisses them [record industry] off is when they [racks] order things, cartons of albums and don't even open them up and put them out and then send them back, and that's been done." He cautions, "The reason that a record doesn't sell is because it doesn't really have it in the grooves. A rack jobber's not a genius. All he can really do for the companies is really expose that product."

Bob Thiele, president of the small specialty label Flying Dutchman, correctly predicted future trends: "The majors have always had good distribution. I believe it's going to be tougher than ever for the independent company to obtain proper distribution. The distribution pattern of Warner/Reprise, Atlantic and Elektra shows the way of the future." Racks and independent distributors, reasoned manufacturers, took few of the risks and gained much of the profit. "So," says Ron Saul, "the manufacturers said 'the hell with you, we're going to take over our own distributing. We'll open our branches, and we in turn will create our acts and market our acts, and promote our acts, and develop our acts through our branch system.' " A branch is simply a distributorship owned by the record company; it performs all of the functions of the independent but only for the company. According to a Warner Brothers release, "A branch works on just your own product, not on a lot of companies. . . . A branch can also hire long-haired freaky people who frequently listen to new music. A branch need not hire pudgy cigar smokers who are really into the Ink Spots."[42]

Branches were not an innovation. In the early days of the recording industry Columbia, RCA and Decca all relied exclusively upon their own company-owned distribution centers. During the 1950s, with the rise of the independent record company, "indie" distributers sprang up to perform the same functions as the branches. Decca and others believing it an economy move, dismantled their branches transferring their distribution accounts to the independents and the one-stops. Capitol and Columbia hung onto the branch system. RCA maintained both branches and independent one-line distributors. Some of RCA's branches, however, were frequently linked to appliance franchises and did not effectively sell records. Nonetheless, a 1967 *Billboard* survey found that companies with branches provided radio stations with the best service and information. Capitol, Columbia and even RCA Victor earned 59 to 58 percent excellent ratings. A&M, with the one of the most popular promotion directors in the industry, Don Graham, placed only fourth with a 47-percent excellent rating. Much of Columbia's success over the years has been attributed to its branches. Columbia executives brag that they can place a record in most record stores nationwide within a matter of days. Billy James credits the introduction of the Byrds and "Mr. Tambourine Man" partially to the branch system. He says: "Columbia's branch operation was a major factor, they wanted to get behind somebody. We were able to communicate to them that they were something they could get behind. It had nothing to do with money, it really didn't. Roy Silver, the agent, dislikes signing his acts with companies lacking branches.

The sheer magnitude of product has rendered the old system in which a distributor handled four to eight labels as basically ineffective. However, prior to the infusion of conglomerate funds and the pursuant amalgamation of companies, branches were economically out of reach of all except the majors, as a company must do 50 to 60 million dollars of volume to maintain such an operation. The Kinney Corporation (now Warner Communications) merger with Warner, Reprise, Atlantic Elektra and many smaller labels made the formation of Warner-Elektra-Atlantic Distributing Corporation (WEA) possible. Now seven national branches, close to major markets, with 30 promotion men, distribute all the

Kinney-owned labels as well as a number of smaller companies. Columbia handles Epic, Stax, Island, Bell and several others in addition to its own product. United Distribution Corporation (UDC), owned by United Artists Records, also stocks Polydor and Mercury. In 1972, RCA and MCA returned entirely to branch operations. MCA continued to carry independents as rack dealers but took over the promotional and distribution functions. ABC Records has eleven branches throughout the United States. By 1973 only two important labels still relied primarily upon independents: A&M and Motown. A&M, with a small catalog, still believes that the independent is the ideal vehicle for their records. Jerry Moss, a former promotion man, regards a self-employed distributor as much more open to the profit motive than branch managers. This is a minority view in the industry.

The rise of branches, while solving some of the record corporations' difficulties in the areas of delivery and promotion, has not diffused the power of the rack jobber. A West Coast rack manager commented, "What can they do to us? They need the outlets as much as we need product." Pausing he emphasized, "Maybe more."

CUTOUTS: THE GAMES PEOPLE PLAY

An important part of the rack jobber's role results from the high number of unsuccessful records. Only a very small percentage of albums or singles reach the charts. In 1970, only 242 of 5,685 singles climbed onto the *Billboard* Hot 100. Three years later Ron Jacobs, a pioneering program director, estimated the odds for a boss radio hit were 33 in 1,400. The industry gives its mistakes to the rack jobber to bury.

"You know what he is?" asks Malamud. "He's an undertaker. It's a necessary evil. Nobody likes undertakers but you need them because when people die somebody has to . . . and that's really terrible work to do . . . but you need an undertaker and they make a lot of money. A schlock dealer or a cutout company really is not the kind of company that has real love for the music or feel. They'll sell anything. They'll sell dirty old socks or anything. They sell whatever the market will take."

The expenses of manufacturing a record are rarely discussed by industry spokesmen; however, Arhoolie Records provided a brief glimpse into this secretive sphere. According to the company's president Chris Stachwitz, the minimum expenditure circa 1971 involved:

Production	
artist's fee	$2,000
studio for recording	500
tape for recording	130
mastering seven dubdowns	300
tape for mastering	30
master acetate disk	80
metal parts	60
cover art	200
type	100
negatives	100
TOTAL	$3,500

Costs per 1,000 disks	
labels	$20
printing of covers	50
printing backs	10
assemble jackets	70
1,000 LP disks	350
TOTAL	$500

These costs reflect production, expenses, the cost of the object placed in a retailer's store. As the volume of sales increases the cost per unit diminishes. According to Arhoolie, the original 1,000 albums cost $1.10 each. After the album has sold over 2,000 units, the cost goes down to 80 cents per album. Larger record companies, have lower manufacturing costs. Joe Smith told Jann Wenner, "It does not cost 50¢ to manufacture, it costs maybe 30¢ to 38¢."[43] Subtracted from $6.98, the manufacturer should make a considerable profit. Or so it would seem. Record-company executives claim that the average profit margin on an album is less than one dollar. Retailers usually take 30 cents, wholesalers deduct 60–70 cents, publishing royalties 24 cents, the American Federation of Musicians earns 6.6 cents and the artist makes 30 cents on each of the first 100,000 units sold, 50 cents thereafter. This, of course, does not include shipping and other expenses, not to mention some of the other costs of doing business, such as promotion. The point at which a record company actually breaks even on a record is difficult to assess. "I'd say you have to sell $60,000–70,000 [worth of albums] to get your money back [and] in an industry where 20 percent of the albums do not get that far," Smith estimated in 1972. At the 60,000–70,000 figure, Warner Brothers would earn about 76 to 60 cents an album, and would have its investment back when it had sold 20,000 copies of the album. The company would then be off the hook. Promotional costs are standard expenses and are not retrievable. The ads in the trades and rock magazines do not immediately bring in enough money to cover their costs. In fact, costs have risen astronomically: in 1968, according to RIAA figures, a pop album had to sell only 7,800 copies to break even. When a pop record fails to break even," said Harry Brief, "it usually is a total loss."[44]

The number of records that pay for themselves is quite small. During the banner years of the late 1960s, over 60 percent of the pop albums were losses. In the early 1970s the attrition rate rose even higher. Joe Smith, "I'd say between 25–30 percent of all albums get their money back." Even Warner Brothers in the midst of its meteoric rise, had 40 percent of its releases in "the red." Recouping these losses is an important object of record manufacturing.

The cutout allows the company to regain part of its loss. Merrill Rose, a wholesaler and major retailer, alleges, "I know a label dumped 4 million, and maybe they were able to salvage 1 million to 1.5 million of their investment. . . . A large proportion of releases are instant cutouts. There is no reason to destroy them. The manufacturers are entitled to realize some return on their mistakes."[45] Cutouts are records which are discontinued in the company's catalog. A notice is sent to retailers and wholesalers announcing the recall. They are allowed a stated period of time in which to return these items.

These records are then wholesaled to rack jobbers. The return to the company is usually less than a dollar. Lenny Goldberg, once a buyer for Ampex, a New York rack, declares, "LPs are made available at prices like 50 cents to a dollar each and are resold on $1.00, $1.25 and $1.50 lists."[46] If the rack cannot get that price he will lower his sights. "You gotta keep going down the level with these cutouts until you get some dollars out of it. Before it is a zero." Ross Halamay maintains, "You can always get rid of something at 57 cents or 99 cents." Racks are ideal for this mode of operation. Stocking only the "quick movers," the jobber does not have a more specialized catalog stock to compete with. He also can keep shifting these "bargains" from one chain to another, lowering prices on slow movers as he goes. A similar rationale is at work in stocking and selling so-called budget records of ten cuts from $1.39 to $1.99.

The practice of deleting albums from the catalog is not entirely beneficial. For the artist, the cutout bares the stigma of failure. Warner/Reprise announced one cutout order with the apt title "96 on Death Row!" "This death sentence for 96 has its humane side," said *Circular*. "No one has accused Warner/Reprise of producing a classic every time at bat; many of the bombs were schlock the day were born."[47] It wasn't in the grooves.

Cutouts are the product of disillusionment. "When we think we've taken our best shots and haven't had encouragement to go on with it," states Joe Smith. "When there's a kind of apathy, none of our promo men say 'hey, they're great,' no radio stations, the group doesn't shake up anybody in their personal appearances." He adds, "I don't think we've turned out many artists with less than two shots, or an album and a few singles. Just to see if we can stir up some interest. At Capitol, a similar philosophy exists. Mauri Lathower: "Their appearances aren't making it. It's an attitude, when you just don't think you can do anything more with it." Capitol will not cut out "*unless* the first album and everything falls apart . . . because there are energies [psychic and economic] that went into promoting it and we [A&R] have told our force that this is a good group."

The retail impact of cutouts is a matter of concern. A&M has accused its competitors of dumping cutouts which compete with $5.98 albums. Rick Frio, MCA vice-president of sales, acknowledged. "Many retail record shops, in order to compete with the record stores selling cutouts, are now trying to buy cutouts themselves to sell, which takes away from the space devoted to selling new product."[48] Ira Moss, president of the budget line Pickwick label, attacked manufacturers for creating a marketplace of "deep confusion and instability." He told *Billboard*, "These manufacturers see only the quick buck . . . and hurt the industry as a whole." His concern was generated by Pickwick's competitive stance with cutouts. His records usually sold for $1.49 or more. Some cutouts, found in the same rack, cost less. Moss, however, has no easy solution. "Tighter A&R control perhaps," he said.[49]

In 1972, an independent record distributing company offered albums originating at Atco, Bell, Buddah, Decca, Kapp, Dot, Paramount, Liberty, Motown, Roulette, RCA, Sun, UNI and Warner Brothers for one dollar. Albums from Cotillion and Elektra were available at slightly higher prices. Name acts such as Sonny and Cher, Lovin' Spoonful, Vogues and the Temptations, were available for 50 cents wholesale. Such cutouts, retailers believe, unfairly compete with their merchandise not only in pricing, but availability. A record-store owner complained. "There's an album called *Gracious*,

Capitol Records has just cut this out. It's a very fine album. If I could get my hands on 50 to 100 of it, I would buy it . . . because this is an item that we could make so many people happy with, but I can find five or ten. I guarantee that if some push around college markets were put on this album, Capitol would put it in the catalog again, because it's a great album and it has great appeal." The editorial pages of specialty rock magazines—fanzines—abound with similar denunciations. Epic Records has received many condemnations for its treatment of old Yardbirds albums. MGM cut out much of its early rock music catalog including the Velvet Underground material, but due to consumer demand this material was reissued. Many collectors spend hundreds of hours annually searching through racks for those oldies manufacturers felt were worthless. Record-shop owners prefer they spend this time in their place of business.

Cutouts also involve a considerable bookkeeping problem for retailers. Termination notices are sent to record stores with a notice of six to eight weeks to return the cutout records. The dealer must then receive an authorization to ship back the items in order to receive exchange credit. Some companies mail these notices with the hope of sticking the dealer: "I've seen . . . X put out a cutout list and on the date of the letter they'll have January 15 and when you receive it it's already January 27. And they've given you 30 days to get it back. Some companies do this deliberately so they go on the books saying they've given you the satisfaction of a date and you must move very fast if you have a sizeable amount of this product."

The fall of 1972 found artists, retailers and fans, joined by music publishers, attacking cutouts. Manufacturers, they charged, were avoiding payment of mechanical royalties. Music publishers' percentages, charged Al Berman of the Harry Fox publishing agency, were decreased by the sale of discontinued merchandise. Rack jobbers countered, blaming artists for excessive royalty fees and urging the continuance of cutouts.

Many record companies maintained a loud silence during the debate. A&M sided with critics, since the company has consistently ground their failures into ecological black dust. Only MCA publicly acceded to the critics' claims. Acknowledging that cutouts do earn a company a fast dollar, Mike Maitland announced, "The publishers and the musicians' union and the artists are the ones who suffer from cutouts, because even those companies who're honest—MCA, Columbia, Warner Bros., and a few others—usually pay lower royalties on cutouts . . . future cutouts from MCA Records will probably be nil."[50] Several competitors privately mused that MCA had just dumped several million dollars of merchandise and was engaged in a promotional stunt to improve its image with small retailers. Despite attacks upon racks and independent distributors, record companies still find most of the retail action in the hands of the rack. Cutouts remain very much a part of the industry, and so does the rack jobber. Eighty-four percent of the members of the NARM sell over a million dollars in records and tapes annually.

Grelun Landon at RCA calls rack jobbers "cherry pickers." They only carry what is a proven success. Yet as Ron Saul indicates, "Remember! The name of the game is breaking an act." This is a mammoth obstacle for record companies, especially in areas where radio stations are equally governed by "getting behind" *Billboard*'s weekly ratings. Bill Roberts says:

> United Artist doesn't depend on the jobber to expose our new product. It's impossible for him to do it. He buys just the hit recordings. The ones that are in the top 50 of *Billboard.* The big problems we run into are the secondary markets which are the means we use to break a new product, usually. Where it's racked, there's no way possible that you can get your recordings into that market. Because the rack is the only one who can expose them into the shops. What you have to do is basically forget about that market.

There is no successful way that record companies can impel rackers to introduce new product. Bhasker Menon explains,

"Because the rack jobber says when you get it on the charts then I'll stock your record." There is economic security in the *Billboard* charts. It is only wise business to go with a winner. Rackers live by the dictum of "I'm in this business to make money. Period!" There is an equally compelling reason for the racker's reliance upon *Billboard.* Most rack jobbers are not of the current generation. They may wear mod clothing, but their musical tastes are of another era. Joe Smith at Warner Brothers states, "They're so remote from it. They're still waiting for the next Sinatra album, because that they understand. They don't know who Black Sabbath is or who they represent. Black Sabbath represents a certain kind of music. As does Van Dyke Parks and Randy Newman. . . . They're no help with that for us. . . . They're a problem." Ron Douglas, Epic's Detroit promotion man, concurs: "They don't know how to buy. We need exposure and they won't touch it." Regardless of the disdain record companies have for rack jobbers, they can't afford to ignore them. In order to pry the racker away from his *Billboard* chart, record executives have tried numerous techniques ranging from incantations to futile coercion. A Capitol executive believes rackers do not solely buy off charts. Consequently, an effective salesman can move a racker. "It may mean a few extra advertising dollars. It may mean asking a favor. It may mean *whatever* it means in the business." The most obvious "whatever" has been to entice the swing generation business man to appreciate the "new sounds."

"Act your age," Stan Cornyn told a gathering of the National Association of Record Merchandisers (NARM). "Talk to the rock generation, without fear or prejudice. Try being curious, not know-it-all. Act your age by *listening.*" Invitations such as this occur semi-annually at NARM gatherings as well as numerous meetings sponsored by record companies. Jack Gelding advised "know your product. What you are selling and where. The long-haired kids have made us all a lot of money. Take the time to understand the music you sell and more importantly, know your demographics. . . . Know the market, not old philosophies."[51] This advice has largely gone unheeded. Many rackers got up and left as a rock band began to play at the 1969 NARM meetings. This lack of appreciation is a major problem; companies sorely need the merchandiser to do more than just stock records. Atlantic President Ahmet Ertegun says, "There is a great challenge to the NARM to expose new artists because the 'now sound' may not be . . . tomorrow. It's very important to be aware of changing musical tastes. It is our responsibility to keep aware of what the public wants."[52]

As might be expected, NARM President Jules Malamud takes issue with this indictment. "Smith and Menon and all those guys," he says, "they're not completely wrong but they're not completely right. . . . It's a dual blame. There are rack jobbers who are bad buyers and there are manufacturers who have very bad policies. And the combination of the two creates the problem. Every week Warner Brothers and Capitol have to go out and sell the records, and they got to sell them to the same people. It behooves them to make better buyers out of some of the companies that are not too good."

Rack jobbers feel they know what the public wants. Their income is derived from providing the public with what it wants. One prominent racker told *Billboard,* "Businesses last longer than acts."[53] They, like radio programmers, are not in the business to expose new artists from Capitol, Columbia or Warner Communications. Indeed, the larger rack jobbers, such as Amos Heilicher, may have *more* accurate figures of consumer preferences than the RIAA or *Billboard.* Heilicher uses a computerized daily sales report of the records that have actually walked out of his stores with the consumer. Record-company statistics are originally based upon the number of records *shipped,* not sold.

The RIAA certifies a record as gold or even platinum on shipping figures. Only after a minimum six-month period, when returns and promotional materials are deducted from the amount shipped, can an accurate figure be reached. Corb Donohue notes, "It's based in speculation more than facts." Rack jobbers, of course, are aware of this and are consequently quite skeptical of record-company statements about an act being "hot" unless *Billboard* supports this claim. Many observers also question the accuracy of trade charts. However, not all of the rack jobbers are wedded to the charts. Ross Halamay maintains that 76 percent of the racks are tied into only "key product." Others, especially those in the discount stores, must be necessity carry large amounts of catalog. Those servicing smaller retail outlets have a similar demand. Where persuasion fails, other less high-minded techniques have been used, generally with little if any success. Rack jobbers have been approached with discounts of "buy a hundred and get six free," knowing that the rack will only take a certain number of so-called key records and that a few new acts may receive some exposure. The use of advertising as an inducement is helpful. Companies are known to offer to pay from 3 to 8 percent of the purchase order for ads which plug both their records and the store. This amount varies depending on distributor or region.

The record companies' most potent weapon is the "hold." Every 90 days distributors and retailers receive bills from the manufacturer. It is in the companies' advantage to have quick payment. It is not in the interest of the retailer or racker to comply. A retailer or racker may easily have much of his cash locked up in stock, and may be unable to pay at the time requested. The record companies motivate the jobber to pay through a "hold." Hold refers to refusing to ship a retailer or racker newly released records until he pays his bill. A Capitol executive stressed the positive aspect of hold. "Big sellers bring in outstanding accounts from retailers," he said. The Beatles, Carly Simon and Carole King keep bookkeepers happy.

From the retailers' perspective, hold is a bothersome and generally ineffective method of soliciting payment. A racker who services a major California chain of discount stores explained, "You must pay in 90 days or be placed on hold, but this puts the record company in a bind, because no product moves at all." This hurts both the record company and the merchandiser. Hold, in fact, does not accomplish this end. Rather, as one retailer outlined, it only makes him buy the record somewhere else. "If you have the bucks to pay," he observed, "the product is always available." He continued, "Let's say tomorrow Carly Simon comes out with a new album. Now what do you do if you're on hold. So you've got to get that product some way, don't you? Now you might not be able to come up with $2,500 to pay yourself off 'hold' the following morning so it's important to have sources and resources so if you can't get it here, you can get it elsewhere." The elsewhere is either from other racks or one-stops. Since alternate sources of product are available from other racks or retailers, the hold system is relatively ineffective. The withholding of product is further compounded by the shadier areas of record distribution. While certainly not as glamorous as payola, considerable wheeling and dealing occurs under the distribution and merchandising table. Not all of it can be pinned on rack jobbers, whose ethics are constantly questioned by the more "respectable" corporation record executives. Record salesmen have quotas to fill, so in order to make their ratios they make various arrangements with rack jobbers. For example, they may persuade him to buy a stated quantity and then return the goods after the deadline has passed. This is a rather prevalent practice, as Malamud indicates: "They will wine and dine the rack jobbers, romance the pants off of him, and build a relationship with the guy and say 'hey, you gotta do me a favor. If I don't make the quota it's my ass and they're gonna fire me or I'm gonna be low man on the totem pole' and the guy feels bad, and I think it's stupid business, but it goes on. And so what happens is first thing you know the guy says, 'if it doesn't sell I'll give you a return authorization.' "

A former rack jobber described a company which used advertising in a more subrosa fashion. A major company had a sales quota. By the 25th of each month one of its sales people would come in and tell the racker, "If you do this, I'll give you this (amount of money) in advertising." The racker recalled,

"One large manufacturer came in right on the 23rd, the deadline date came in about the 25th and we bought some budget albums and he gave me a full-page ad and I didn't even have to run the thing. He just told me to send him a charge back . . . but I didn't have to mail in tear sheets."

In many parts of the country, other company representatives, who have considerable access to product, have been known to sell unmarked "freebee" records at a discount to retailers, pocketing the proceeds of the sale. The discarding of promotional records by media people (see chapter 6) is paled in contrast to the "rep's" operations. In all, as Joe Smith, Bhasker Menon and many other company executives admit, distribution and merchandising remain the chief barriers to the introduction of new artists and their music.

Much to the delight of Joe Smith, William Gallagher and many other company presidents, the nature of the large rack jobber began undergoing some changes in 1973. Many have gone into the retail business. North American Music, for example, has over ten stores in shopping malls. Amos Heilicher is retailing his own stores. Russ Solomon has a million-dollar-a-year chain store operation with Tower Records. Shelby Singleton of SSS Records appears to have been correct when he told *Billboard*, "The mass users of product—the rack jobbers—are great. But the day may come when, if these head shops continue to grow, they may do a total business larger than the racks."[54] This has not yet happened. The 4½-foot wire rack is still the dominant retail outlet in America. However, so-called free-standing stores, using the volume principle of the early rack jobbers, are on the rise. Even major record companies have moved into the retailing end of the business. Columbia owns one of the largest chains in the United States, Discount Records—again to the displeasure of small retailers. Many observers, off the record, feel the movement of a manufacturer into the retail sphere may well be against the provisions of antitrust laws.

Distribution and retailing constitute a major barrier to the success of a record. Only the radio-station program director is a greater obstacle. If this decision-maker airs a record long enough in the proper market, it will make the *Billboard* charts and the racker will have no choice but to stock it. After all, he is only "in the business to make money. Period!" Repeated air play is the most effective method of introducing a new act; however, it is also the most difficult.

Notes, Chapter 4

1. Quoted in Mike Gross, "Music Rumbles—Wall St. Tumbles," *Billboard*, December 6, 1969, p. 8.
2. Remarks by Bill Graham from Second International Pop Music Festival, Monterey.
3. Quoted in Bud Scoppa, *The Byrds* (New York: Scholastic Book Services, 1971), p. 114.
4. Quoted From Harold Bronson, "Call Mickie Most 'The Hitmaker,'" *Rolling Stone* 124 (December 21, 1972): 12.
5. Gerry Sherman, "Mixing the Right Ingredients," *Billboard*, December 9, 1967, p. 37.
6. Quoted in Gene Lees, "Music Business Maverick," *Hi Fi*, May 1969, p. 116.
7. Richard Goldstein, *Goldstein's Greatest Hits* (New York: Prentice-Hall, 1970), p. 148.
8. Quoted in Ralph J. Gleason, *The Jefferson Airplane and the San Francisco Sound* (New York: Ballantine Books, 1969), p. 84.
9. Quoted in Charles Reich and Jann Wenner, "Jerry Garcia: The Rolling Stone Interview, Part Two," *Rolling Stone* 101 (February 3, 1972): 30.
10. Quoted in "He Makes Music Pay at CBS," *Business Week*, October 7, 1967, p. 107.
11. Jay Rudy, "Phil Spector Interview," *Jazz and Pop* 8 (January 1969): 26–27.
12. Quoted in George Uhlman, "Record Producers: The Lure of Independence," *Rock*, August 14, 1972, p. 31.
13. Reich and Wenner, "Jerry Garcia," p. 30.
14. Quoted in "Lenny Waronker and the Burbank Sound," *Circular* 3 (June 14, 1971): 3–4.
15. Quoted in Uhlman, "Record Producers," p. 31.

16. "Sherman Spins Time Saving Tips," *Billboard*, December 23, 1967, p. 16.

17. Mike Curb remarks at 2nd Annual International Music Industry Conference.

18. Jon Landau, "The Rolling Stone Interview: Paul Simon," *Rolling Stone* 113 (July 20, 1972): 38.

19. Uhlman, "Record Producers," p. 31.

20. Quoted in Ann Geracimos, "A Record Producer is a Psychoanalyst with Rhythm," *New York Times Magazine*, September 29, 1968, p. 60.

21. Ibid., p. 58.

22. Ibid., p. 60.

23. Goldstein, *Greatest Hits*, p. 118.

24. Murray Ross, "The Record Business: What Makes It Run," *Record World*, July 24, 1971, p. 230.

25. Algin Brady King, "The Marketing of Phonograph Records in the United States: An Industry Study." Ph.D. diss., Ohio State University, 1966, p. 173.

26. Quoted in "Buddah Group In Banner Quarter," *Billboard*, October 21, 1972, p. 6.

27. Quoted in Michael Jaye, "They're Lightweight Title Contenders," *Rolling Stone* 126 (January 18, 1973): 16.

28. Ibid., p. 16.

29. Quoted in Claude Hall, "Disc Co's Seen Role as Distributor Only," *Billboard*, April 15, 1969, p. 4.

30. "Individual Approach to Market Counts," *Billboard*, May 23, 1970, p. 20.

31. Jack Gelding, "Survival Tools for the 70's," *Billboard*, May 23, 1970, p. 21.

32. Sidney Shemel and M. William Krasilovsky, *This Business of Music*, rev. ed. (New York: Billboard Publications, 1971), p. 103.

33. Quoted from Paul Ackerman, "RCA's Dual Distribution Draws Uptight Responses," *Billboard*, September 6, 1969, pp. 1, 112.

34. Quoted in Paul Ackerman, "Key 'Indie' Record Firms Split on Dual Distribution," *Billboard*, September 13, 1969, p. 1.

35. Ibid., p. 8.

36. Quoted in "$2 Billion Worth of Noise," *Forbes*, July 15, 1968, p. 24.

37. "Mainline: Indie Faces Oblivion," *Billboard*, September 13, 1969, p. 1.

38. "Dual Distribution Posing Promotional Puzzler: Sachs," *Billboard*, October 11, 1969, p. 1.
39. Claude Hall, "Chaos Hits Radio on Disc Service," *Billboard*, August 1, 1970, pp. 1, 34.
40. Quoted in Eliot Tiegel, "Small Label Co-Op Urged to Fight Distribution Danger," *Billboard*, August 29, 1970, p. 1.
41. All executive quotes from Lee Zhito, "Execs High on Rest of '70—Distribution Top Problem," *Billboard*, September 5, 1970, pp. 1, 12.
42. "The Transmogrification of Joel Melvin Friedman," *Circular* , July 12, 1971, p. 2.
43. "What's Involved in Making Arhoolie LP's *Arhoolie Occasional* 1 (1971): 1.
44. Quoted in "$2 Billion," p. 26.
45. Quoted in Earl Raige, "Retailer Defends Cut Out as Halt to Bootlegging," *Billboard*, September 16, 1972, p. 55.
46. Lenny Goldberg, "Inside Record Distribution," *Rock*, March 1, 1971, p. 21.
47. "96 on Death Row," *Circular* 3 (March 22, 1971), p. 2.
48. Quoted in Claude Hall, "MCA Brass Sally to Halt Cutouts," *Billboard*, October 28, 1972, p. 15.
49. Quoted in Robert Sobel, "Pickwick's Ira Moss Hits Manufacturers On Cutout Dumping," *Billboard*, September 9, 1972, p. 1.
50. Hall, "MCA Brass," pp. 1, 15.
51. Gelding, "Survival Tools," p. 21.
52. Quoted in "Challenge Thrown to Racks Expose More 'Now' Acts," *Billboard*, March 15, 1969. p. 2.
53. Quoted in Mike Gross, "ABC's $100 Million Rack Jobbing Wing," *Billboard*, May 10, 1969, p. 1.
54. Claude Hall, "Head Shops Gain As Album Sellers," *Billboard*, October 24, 1970, p. 1.

5.

THE GATEKEEPERS OF RADIO

> Oh I'm a teenager just like you
> Please won't you help me, here's what you do
> Write to your Deejay, send a request
> Say that my record is the one you like the best.
>
> © *1958 Monument Music. Inc.*

The "cultural gatekeeper" determines what information is transmitted. Social scientists have come to look for gatekeepers in the media and its reporting of the news, and to a lesser extent in the dissemination of cultural artifacts.[1] David Manning White, for one, found a midwestern newspaper editor who did not use 90 percent of the stories on the national wire service because he felt they were unsuitable for his community. Investigations of radio and television news broadcasts have reported similar censorship. Gatekeepers have been troublesome for many, in light of the American credo of "an informed electorate." But those who determine what the electorate shall know are not confined to the newsrooms of America. They are also prominent in drama, literature, film and music. Negative reviews in the *New York Times* and its competitors have closed many a Broadway production after one night. In the area of literature and music, the gatekeeper's power is less manifest, in that here the question is one of entry rather than disapproval; the *Times* reviews less than 10 percent of the books published each year. In popular music there exist two primary types of gatekeepers: the radio programmer and the record reviewer in the rock press.

Martin Block, considered by many to be the prototype disk jockey, as early as 1942 expressed the notion that the standard of musical excellence was being "left to the good judgment of the man who plays the records."[2] This esthetic judgment in time became all important. Few in the music industry would openly challenge the opinion of a Florida record-store owner. "We can get in a pretty good record, but if it isn't played on the radio, it won't sell."[3] Sociologist Howard Jolly, a quarter of a century after Block's remark, commented, "Disk jockeys, above all others have the almost unique characteristic of participating in promotion and the 'sifting' process through which all records go." He continued to argue that the radio audience is "an electorate, *in its own way*, which is to say that it is in the limited way that a disk jockey is a gatekeeper."[4] Another sociologist, Paul Hirsch, points to deejays as "institutional regulators" of hit records since "record companies are dependent on radio air play as the only effective vehicle of exposure for new pop records."[5]

The record reviewer, or Donald Weller's "roll critic," is a gatekeeper because he, too, influences the exposure a record will receive. His status is complementary to that of the radio program director (PD). He can bring to public attention those records rejected by the dictates of formula radio, FCC regulations and the desire of advertisers to reach as large an audience as possible. Furthermore, the printed page can facilitate much greater and wider coverage than the broadcast media. Turning McLuhan, *camera obscura*, on his head, the printed page can accomplish in a few short minutes of reading time what a three-quarters of an hour air play may fail to do. Writers for *Rolling Stone* and the other rock publications do not have to contend with government and commercial restraints imposed upon the public use of airways. *Rolling Stone* can, with impunity, publish the lyrics of John Lennon's "Working Class Hero" with the "word" and all, while even the most progressive underground stations were forced to blip out the "offensive" Anglo-Saxonism. Not surprisingly the Mothers of Invention, the Fugs, the New York Dolls, Country Joe and Kinky Friedman are more familiar to rock magazine subscribers than the consumers of boss radio. Record reviewers, as the "letters to the editor" section of

Rolling Stone and other magazines aptly illustrate, lack the persuasiveness of a song played on the air. But a record ignored by both the press and the audio medium is almost certainly doomed to a rapid trip to the cutout record bins at discount stores.

Gatekeepers in the music industry are the Berlin Wall between the manufacturer and the audience. The foundations of this barrier are multiplex in that each medium has its own unique set of value systems which color the perception of the gatekeeper. The projected demands and responses of an audience or taste culture as well as fear of possible failures all contribute to the makeup of the wall. Program directors know better than to offend their youthful listeners with Pat Boone records, yet they must avoid the FCC. "One Toke Over the Line" may appeal to the values of Top 40 listeners, while provoking the ire of the FCC. On the other hand, as *Creem* discovered, the championing of a teenybop or "bubblegum" act can produce considerable reader displeasure. The glorification of Grand Funk Railroad generated one of many letters which said: "You are trying to alienate you (sic) readers toward most pre-Grand Funk musicians. Why? It's a shame that you write for *Creem*."[6] While the actual power of cultural gatekeepers in popular music has been brought into question, their control over records and their exposure is undeniable. Block's statement "programs help popularize tunes" is a commandment engraven in concrete in the music business. "Roll critics" may not possess equal prowess, but in the rags to riches world of popular music, it is believed foolish to ignore any avenue which may lead to the gold record or stardom.

THE DISK JOCKEY: INDIVIDUAL VS. COLLECTIVE GATEKEEPING

The American Federation of Television and Radio Artists (AFTRA) says the number of disk jockeys can be estimated by "multiplying the number of AM and FM stations by an average of four." According to this formula, at least 25,000 persons were employed as disk jockeys in 1972, a 400-percent increase from 1957 when *Time* discovered 5,000 deejays pontificating over the airwaves. Not only has the number of record spinners changed over this time span, but also the role of the disk jockey.

The term disk jockey is believed to have been coined in a *Variety* cover story of Jack Kapp, where the pioneer Decca executive wrote "record jockey." As Arnold Passman was later to observe, the label came to connote "jockeying or riding a record toward success."[7] A more typical definition is the art of announcing records on a program featuring only phonograph records.

A series of conflicting claims notwithstanding, the evolution of the disk jockey can be traced to the inception of radio broadcasting, where announcers played gramophone records and chatted informally with their unseen audience. The practice of broadcasting records was attractive, especially to smaller stations, considering the minimal investment necessary to fill air time. The opposition of sheet music publishers and a number of performers such as Fred Waring and Bing Crosby at the outset hampered the broadcasting of gramophone records, but did not end it. As Judge Learned Hand was to rule, copyright control ended with the sale of the record. Radio stations, therefore, "could not be restrained from using records in broadcasts." This interpretation of the 1909 copyright law, coupled with the publishers' realization that radio could provide a forum for their songs, uplifted the status of radio as the central avenue for public recognition of a songwriter's product. The bandleaders of the swing era were quick to recognize the value of having their songs on the air.

Radio announcers prior to the arrival of Al Jarvis to KFWB, Los Angeles, were aptly described. "The same staff spieler who read poetry announced each disk solemnly, impersonally, and formally enough to qualify as an adept funeral director." Jarvis personalized the announcer's role with the addition of a conversational and friendly microphone style. The approach, perfected by Arthur Godfrey on the East Coast, elevated the announcer from a mere stylized reciter of poetry, ads and record introductions into a "personality" who commanded the attention of his listeners, thus adapting an equal, if not superior, status to the music he played. Jarvis also pioneered a format within which his "liberated" radio personality could function with success—"The Make Believe Ballroom." The program format was simply to play dance tunes and simulate an atmosphere of a marathon ballroom with real or contrived conversation with the performers and dancers. Martin Block, a library assistant at KFWB, seeing the success of the Jarvis vehicle, moved it to WNEW in New York. Block, a former pitchman, parlayed this framework into a medium-wide phenomenon which in time would spawn "Your Hit Parade" and "Lucky Lager Dance Time," programmed by Bill Gavin who later became the publisher of an influential record tip sheet.

Arthur Godfrey's approach to his audience was similar to Block's but confined to the early morning hours where he used "earthiness, independence, enthusiasm" and irreverence to announce disks and a growing list of profit-hungry, but masochistic, sponsors awaiting his barbs. By the late 1930s, it was clear the record-playing radio personality was a force to be reckoned with. Benny Goodman, in 1937, in anticipation of things to come, reportedly paid Al Jarvis $500 to play his latest recordings. In turn, "Ballroom" listeners increasingly insisted that the bandleader's public appearances be exactly as on record. For the road band, this meant playing the same trademark arrangements identically night after night. Swing historian George Simon described the role of the disk jockey in the big band era:

> Some [bandleaders] romanced disk jockeys with intense and sometimes nauseating ardor. Some jocks reacted in kind . . . many disk jockeys actually sought out records by new, upcoming bands

and promoting . . . such discovering remained a labor of love for many a big band disk jockey.[8]

The success of the Jarvis-Block format induced the American Tobacco Company to nationally sponsor "The Lucky Strike Hit Parade," adding the dimension of ranking records as to their popularity. In the early 1940s, Martin Block was to write, "If the platter is a good one, the most effective type of direct marketing has taken place. And sales are sure to reflect the airing of the disk."[9] After nearly 20 years of sporadic attempts to contravene radio, few singers, musicians, record companies or sheet music publishers would dispute the merit of this claim.

In the early "Ballroom" days, Jarvis and Block were forced to purchase the records they aired. However, the wartime rationing of shellac, as well as the growing recognition of radio impact upon music taste, found selected programmers receiving, *gratis*, personalized sample records. Glenn E. Wallichs, a cofounder of Capitol Records, recalled: "We typed special labels with their [top 50 deejays] names on both sides, pressed them on expensive lightweight, unbreakable vinylite compound and then had our limited employee force drive around and distribute each sample personally. It was a service that created a sensation. *We made the jock a Big Man*, an Important Guy, VIP in the industry,"[10] Capitol not only formally recognized the importance of the deejays but also introduced the freebee "exclusive record," which was a precursor of the payola of the 1950s. The "exclusive" was a form of reward to important deejays in the industry. As Norman Prescott noted in his congressional testimony:

> It was more important for a jockey at that time to get an exclusive record and be able to shout, 'I have got it,' where nobody else had it on the one or two other stations, than money. . . . As the disk jockey grew into a businessman, he realized his power. At that time, he did not know what his image was, because he was just starting in a relatively new business. So he went into the areas of

> personnel management, publishing, putting his name on songs, and whatever it is.[11]

The advent of the "exclusive" and the "freebee" underlined the industry's recognition that a new institution, with power, had been created. A cultural gatekeeper stood in the path of a record's success. The Blocks, Jarvises and Godfreys were not mere announcers who filled up air time with the handiest record around. The sponsoring of records by bandleaders and "exclusives" were the opening scenes of what was to become the cost of doing business.

The importance of the disk jockey was even further enhanced by the diversification and proliferation of the record and sheet music industries. The rise of Broadcast Music, Inc. (BMI), to successfully challenge the all-powerful American Society of Composers, Authors and Publishers (ASCAP), and the ensuant emergence of independent or "indie" record companies made air time, or exposure, all the more precious and difficult to obtain. The disk jockey reigned over air time and became the arbitor of economic success and failure for recording companies and songwriters. A *Newsweek* correspondent in 1947 cynically chided deejays: "With all the power in their programs, and no directors to ride herd on them, some are unrestrained in swiping ideas from anyone. They mercilessly play the records that will do *them the most good. . . .*"[12] Dexter attributes even greater influence to the triumphant jock, "His ever-rising power turned the jukes from hit makers to meek little machines that . . . only the music the local jockey ordains. Not even television . . . can affect the nation's music tastes."[13]

Despite occasional disclaimers by deejays that they merely reflect public taste, there is little question that broadcast exposure remains the key to a record's success.[14] One record store owner exclaimed, "If they don't know about a record, they sure as hell are not going to buy it." A program director adds, "People don't know what they like, they like what they know." This is especially true for "name" disk jockeys in key market areas of the country since these regions greatly determined which songs placed upon the *Billboard* Hot 100. Other stations then follow. Consequently, only a handful of jocks in key market cities can determine the fate of a record. The concentration of power in the 1950s made payola even more attractive to the donor (especially smaller or independent companies), since it could assure airplay. Payola became a trade euphemism for an honorarium for special consideration or what *Billboard* termed "play for pay."

The significance of the payola scandals of the late 1950s does not lie in the morality of the practice nor in the feet-of-clay posture of Dick Clark and Alan Freed. Rather, payola was the industry's abortive attempt to control its market in a manner similar to its nonentertainment counterparts listed on the New York and American Stock Exchanges.

PAYOLA: GATEKEEPERS FOR SALE

Norman Prescott, the opening witness before Representative Oren Harris's subcommittee investigating "deceptive practices in the broadcasting field," in 1960 aptly described the reason and function of payola. He explained:

> The tremendous output of records, and the fierce competition that exists within the industry, it is a matter of who can play what, when there is limited amount of play on the air . . . payola has become the prime function of this business to get the record on the air at any cost and dispose of it, because if you do not . . . you cannot get individual income [profit].[15]

Prescott, a former deejay in a top market area, elaborated on this statement, observing that his four-hour popular music show aired 50 to 52 records per day, many of which remained on play lists for four to six weeks. Meanwhile, the industry overproduced some 200 new singles per week, all in the hope of breaking into the magic circle of *Billboard*'s top 40. To further compound the situation, deejays in cities such as New York, Boston, Cleveland, Detroit or Los Angeles were aware of their power. The pressure, as Prescott indicates, was tremendous. Payola was supposed to buy the manufacturer control over his product, making access to the folks in "radio land" a bit more promising.

Payola, as it existed prior to the scandal, evidenced two dominant forms: "play for pay" and "consulting." "Play for pay" was simply "how many dead presidents [$20 bills] are there for me?" This mode of payola was direct payment from the industry to the gatekeeper for air time.

The most spectacular practitioner was "American Bandstand" host Dick Clark. The "breaking" or introduction of "Get A Job" and "All American Boy" aptly illustrate how "play for pay" worked on the Clark program. The Silhouettes' "Get a Job" was originally produced by Philadelphia disk jockey Kay Williams on his Junior label. The disk was purchased by Ember Records. During the transition, the song copyright was transferred to the Wildcat Music Co., which was controlled by "Bandstand" producer Tony Mammerella. Then the national television show "broke" the record. "All American Boy," written by Orville Lunsford, was a talking blues number about the rise to fame by Elvis Presley. Lunsford took his song to Fraternity Records and was urged to have the song processed by Mallard Pressing Co., owned by Dick Clark. As soon as 50,000 disks were ordered, the song received extensive air play on "American Bandstand." Although the song was actually recorded by Bobby Bare, the nonsinging Billy Parsons was provided with appearances on the Dick Clark show to promote the record. The money he was paid for the appearances was charged against his royalties at Fraternity as "promotional expenses."[16] Overall, 50.4 percent of the records available through the companies in which Clark had an interest were played on "American Bandstand." Of these, 65.4 percent were played before they had appeared on a *Billboard* chart listing. Quite simply, Clark "broke"

MAURI LATHOWER (courtesy of Capitol Records)

MO OSTIN (courtesy of Warner Brothers)

JULES MALAMUD (courtesy of National Association of Record Merchandisers)

ALAN FREED (courtesy of BMI)

MARTY CERF AND BILL ROBERTS (courtesy of United Artists)

"YOUR HIT PARADE"—*from left to right:* Russell Arms, Gisele MacKenzie, Dorothy Collins and Snooky Lanson (courtesy of NBC-TV)

TOM DONAHUE (courtesy of KSAN-FM)

JANN WENNER (courtesy of *The Rolling Stone*/Anne Leibovitz)

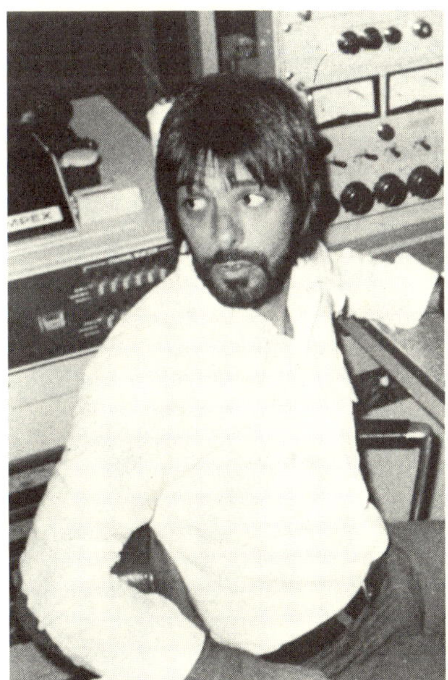

TERRY KNIGHT (courtesy of Capitol Records)

JOHN SINCLAIR (courtesy *Exit*/John Rockwood)

VELVET UNDERGROUND (courtesy Roy Beaumont)

BOB LARSON (courtesy of Bob Larson Ministries)

MC 5 (courtesy of Elektra Records)

ALICE COOPER (courtesy of Warner Brothers)

DAVID CASSIDY (*right*) and BOBBY SHERMAN (*left*) (courtesy ABC-TV)

GRAND FUNK RAILROAD (courtesy of Capitol Records)

records on his network dance show for personal gain, banking on the exposure power of "American Bandstand." "When I recorded 'Venus'," Frankie Avalon observed, "Dick got behind it and it sold 1.5 million copies. He's the greatest." Many congressmen disagreed. In the concluding moments of Clark's testimony, chairman Harris told the beleaguered television personality, "You are a product of that system, not responsible for it. You took advantage of a unique opportunity to control too many elements . . . in the popular music field, through exposure of records to a vast teenage audience."[17] This overt type of payola was unique in that few disk jockeys commanded the kind of power possessed by Dick Clark or Alan Freed. "Play for pay" was generally found in large market areas and was not widespread. More common was the subtle and covert practice of consulting.

William B. Williams told *Life*, "If a disk jockey had to listen to all these records, he'd go to the kookie house." A fellow jock added, "No broadcasting company expects its men to listen to each and every record." It is just a physical impossibility."[18] The problem, as Paul Ackerman, the music editor of *Billboard*, correctly observed was "the abundance of product." Too many records were being released each week. Consequently, as the *Billboard* editor told the probers, "Competition for exposure is extreme, for without wide public exposure, the potential buyer would never hear most of these records. This is true not only at the broadcast level, where payola enters into play, but also at the retail level."[19] To circumvent the sheer number of releases, the music industry, through its local distributors, in fact hired "name" deejays to listen to their product. The jock was listed in ledger sheets as a "consultant." A 1959 sample of 23 major cities found that a total of $263,244.00 was paid to deejays for consulting and other services. Some distributors and recipients of these fees interpreted them as bribes and acted accordingly; however, many viewed these payments as earnings for reviewing records on "one's own time." One "consultant," Charles Young, said, "One of their problems was on labeled records by unknown artists . . . he [distributor] would send these records to my house, and he would call me and ask me what I thought of these records. . . . It did not influence me in one way or another."[20] The distributor's perception of this exchange was similar. Donald Dumont explained consultants' fees were partially for "equal consideration in listening to my new releases." Another distributor said, "We made payments . . . for these people who gave us their time and attention in listening and helping us evaluate our new releases."[21] "Play for pay" predicted an outcome, while consulting provided preferential treatment. Obviously a record familiar to a jock had a better chance than one he had not heard, especially where new artists were concerned.

After nearly a year of exposures, the Congress passed a bill making payola a crime punishable by a fine up to $10,000. Both the industry and the disk jockey were somewhat dismayed by the entire episode. An "indie" record manufacturer told *Billboard*, "Today, it's more difficult to tell if you're actually getting anything for your money. There's absolutely no guarantee your record will be played." Disk jockeys added, "There are still too many records. . . . Payola still flourishes. . . . Payola is practiced in practically every business I know of. The biggest example and most glaring example I can think of is 'lobbying' in Washington."[22] Since the Harris investigation, payola has continued in an altered form, but the perceived autonomy of the individual deejay has been altered.

The payola scandals provide an important glimpse into the mechanics of music marketing and the function of gatekeepers. In order to reach the public, the manufacturer has to go through the radio station, the central vehicle for product exposure. In the case of "play for pay," nearly all risk was removed by purchasing exposure time, in effect aborting the gatekeeper role. Consulting—being paid to listen to records—provided less risk in the quest for precious air time, but it did not insure it. The disk jockey in this instance maintained his discretionary powers as gatekeeper. The payola hearings greatly curtailed the "play for pay" system and shifted the gatekeeper role from the individual to the collective of station management.

With the diminution of direct payola, the industry representative or promo man was restored to a position of importance. His task was to gain exposure for his acts. In part, this restored the majors to a place of competitive advantage over the indies since many of the smaller companies, having relied heavily upon payola, did not have a promotional apparatus of any magnitude. Nor could they afford to develop one.[23] The scandals also indirectly hastened job standardization, particularly in the major market areas. The freedom of the jock had already been severely limited in the midwestern and southern states due to the injection of Top 40 radio into the region in the middle 1950s.

In 1955, Todd Storz introduced the concept of Top 40 radio at WTIX, New Orleans, and applied it throughout an entire chain operated by a southern pharmaceutical company. The formula was based upon the method traditionally employed by jukebox operators. Demand determined staying power. Storz used local record stores' sales to establish popularity. He discovered that the average number of well-selling singles was 40. His fascination with this figure was further reinforced by the fact that most jukeboxes at the time had 40 plays. These "top" 40 records were repeatedly aired on the Storz station. The repetition pattern, as radio lore has it, was based on Storz's experience in an Omaha bar where patrons played certain songs over and over again. Later, the *Billboard* chart took over the primary function of providing material for popular music stations. Interspersed with these continuous hits were jingles and patter in what can best be described as a carnival or medicine show atmosphere. The philosophy underlying this concept was that the airing of material from the *Billboard* chart, then containing a mix of country and western and rhythm and blues material, would attract the largest audience, then the index of success in radio. For Storz and his imitators, the formula worked. In the beginning, deejays in the Storz chain were controlled not by policy but by the mechanics of the format. As one former Storz employee noted, "An announcer was required to cue six turntables with ETs [transcribed commercials and newscasts], records, give time and temperature." He had time to do little else. In time, what he did say was monitored by the home office. One executive order was to avoid "excessive talking" thus the rapidity of delivery. As comedian George Carlin, once a jock, recalled, the policy was "shut up and play the music." The home office of the Storz chain automatically built the play list behind the established charts. For this reason, Storz's personnel missed out on the payola given their big-city counterparts. Bribing a Storz jock would be a waste of money since he had no control over the songs he played. The payola scandals introduced similar controls into the cities such as Cleveland, Boston, New York and Detroit where the practice of payola had been rampant. Bill Drake streamlined many of Storz's gimmicks into a rigid format—the ultimate in play-list control. The introduction of demographics in polling further tightened up what the jock could play or say, since he had to be concerned not with large numbers of listeners but with a specific limited and affluent segment of the audience. Other stations merely shifted the responsibility of compiling a play list to support personnel such as the program director or the music director. In most cases, the result was the same: the era of free-willed deejays was rapidly drawing to a close. The idiosyncratic mike styles of the Niagras, Millers, Carneys, Hancocks, Biondis and Russ Knights would be synthesized into one: the boss jock. The "wild and screaming" jock now "does nothing but announce the records, he does this in a hysterical style with fast talk and pitched sell."[24]

The wide acceptance of the Storz "50,000 watt jukebox of the air" had a profound impact upon both the record and broadcasting industries. The highly individualized personality jock had little place within the framework of Top 40 radio. He was merely the arm and voice of the prearranged play list. As Top 40 became more refined, Storz expanded his operation into many other cities. Storz ran the entire operation from a home office. It was not a network operation or even syndication, but simply a formula, which was adapted in various southern and midwestern cities. In time, Bill Drake, the Bartlett chain, ABC radio and Metromedia developed similar formats and imposed them on their stations. This all but totally relegated the deejay into an interchangeable part of a large machine. This seemingly dehumanizing trend prevailed for the simple reason that the Top 40 formula *worked*. Top 40 stations consistently beat their competitors in the Hooper and ARB rating battles. At WINS New York, Alan Freed consistently topped Martin Block's WABC ratings. Indeed, not until "Cousin Brucie" Morrow took over at WABC New York in the early 1960s did the station become a popular music power. "Cousin Brucie" was a Top 40 prototype. A competitor said, "there was no personality because you never know what kind of a guy Bruce Morrow is. You don't know whether the guy's got a family, if he went to the ball game. He never says anything. I don't think there is a Cousin Brucie."[25]

Top 40 radio was largely responsible for pushing so-called rhythm and blues stations back to servicing the black ghetto. Alan Freed in Cleveland began enticing white youngsters into listening to "race" music, and the feat was repeated in countless large American cities. Small rhythm and blues stations found themselves playing Muddy Waters, Ruth Brown, the Clovers, the Drifters and a legion of other artists for a totally new and highly appreciative audience. But Top 40 radio stole the economic heart out of those stations. The rhythm and blues hits were originally covered by white artists. When that failed the original records were incorporated into Top 40 play lists. This action brought many young white record fans to the Storz chain. Rock historians and nostalgia buffs rarely remind us that the appreciation of black music in the 1950s was highly selective: Fats Domino, Little Richard, Chuck Berry and a legion of acapella quartets gained white popularity, but the majority of black artists did not. "Down home" music did not fit the *zeitgeist* of the Eisenhower era, so rhythm and blues stations, the birthplaces of rock music, were permitted to evolve on their own. Their evolution, as we shall see, has come to fascinate and perplex the entire pop-music industry.

COLLECTIVIZED GATEKEEPING: BOSS RADIO VS. THE UNDERGROUND

Al Jarvis and Martin Block originated formula radio with their "Make-Believe Ballroom" shows. "Your Hit Parade," sponsored by a cigarette company, added the next ingredient of ranking songs as to popularity. Top 40 and boss sound radio were the end products of a synthesis of record ranking, microphone technique developed by Block and structured time use perfected into an art by Bill Drake and Ron Jacobs at KHJ in Los Angeles. Boss radio was a highly slick structure into which all of these pieces fit. Nothing was left to chance. Deejays, songs, even commercials and news ("20–20 News Time") were designed to fit the rigid mold; if they did not, they were not aired.

And the Hits Keep on Comin' . . .

Boss radio first appeared in the Los Angeles area on May 5, 1965, two weeks prior to the opening scheduled by Bill Drake and Ron Jacobs. The catalyst for this unanticipated event was a dejected KHJ newsman. Dick Spangler, in search of another position, approached KFWB, a competitor, and told them, "I know what they're going to be doing at KHJ." On the morning of May 5, deejay Robert W. Morgan hurried up to the KHJ program director, Ron Jacobs, and announced, "Turn on KFWB, they're calling themselves Boss Radio and they have 20–20 News and the disk jockeys are called the Boss Jocks." In order to save the emerging KHJ identity, Don Steele previewed the new format the same afternoon. KFWB retreated, leaving the Boss Sound to the Drake station. The unexpected introduction of the Boss Sound was symbolic of what came before. One of its founders, Ron Jacobs, indicates, "Most of that stuff was ad lib or created out of necessity." It was not, as some would have it, a cool, calculated and restricted format, at least in the beginning. The generic title itself was adopted as a convenience, KHJ's original slogan in the 1920s was "Kindness, Happiness, and Joy." This slogan gave way to an unsuccessful attempt to program rock during the early 1960s which was overshadowed by "Color Radio" at KFWB. In order to differentiate the KHJ of the sixties from its predecessor, the management searched vainly for a new supporting slogan. One of many suggestions was "Boss Radio KHJ." "Boss" at that time was considered an old-fashioned term. Not able to find another catchword the adjective was affixed on billboards and in newspaper and trade ads, but not on the air. Three and a half hours after KHJ was forced on the air by its competition, the station aired an identification jingle followed by the deejay's name and the time. Ron Jacobs recalls, "So we had the jingle, 'KHJ, Los Angeles' and the guy comes in and says, 'It's 6:30 in Los Angeles.' I was standing there in the booth and said 'That's redundant. We just said Los Angeles,' so I said try saying 'Boss Angeles' so he did it the next time, and thereafter, we did it every half hour, 168 hours a week, forever." Other refinements were brought in by this haphazard manner. The first year's play list was borrowed from a rival station. The famous formula was drawn up on a cocktail napkin in a Los Angeles bar by Bill Drake, Ron Jacobs, Gary Mack and Les Turpin. The format consisted of airing 33 current records. These 33 songs were taken from established charts. The KRLA chart was the model for the first year, then the *Billboard* Hot 100 and local store reports became the guideline. Three singles were picked by the program director as "hit bounds." Intermixed with these records were approximately 400 oldies which were termed "goldens." On weekends, especially during rating sampling periods, "goldens" predominated. Each hour operated on what has come to be called the Drake Clock. The first single was aired at the top of the hour. Three minutes later a commercial or air check would follow, then seven minutes after the hour something else would happen and then another slot until the 20–20 news. The numerical sequence for spots was "3–7–11–16–20 . . . 30–33–37.. . ." The deejay patter was highly stylized and in time predictable: "Boss Radio . . . handing you the heavy hits, around the clock . . . where the hits always happen first . . . the hits just keep on coming!" With the exception of the rapid-fire and structured deejay delivery, boss radio was an extension of the Top 40 format developed in the 1950s as Jacobs is quick to observe:

> KHJ was just a refinement. If it had the appearance of going faster . . . it was because we were just starting out like crazy with less of the extraneous stuff. . . . There had been a tendency with people like McClendon and Storz, when they got successful, not to protect the amount of music they could play. They would get successful and if somebody could sell another spot to a used car dealer, they would put on another spot.

The station kept its rigid commercial limit, which would only allow about 12 minutes per hour of commercial fare. The station also strictly enforced its policy of minimizing the chatter by its disk jockeys. Jocks were told "Brian Wilson has just spent nine months of his life wrestling with this thing that takes two minutes and forty seconds. So unless you got something really terrific to say, for your eight seconds, shut up." The better deejays at KHJ such as "Humble Harv" Miller, the "Real" Don Steele and Robert W. Morgan complemented the format. Steele, for example, possessed the ability to provide a continuity within the contrasts in the Drake format. According to Jacobs, "He was very loud, and he can rise above all the production things that are engineered, the elements that surround him. That's quality . . . [he] really understands this parade of sounds, and that it is a contextual series of contrasts." However, Miller, Steele, and Morgan were exceptional radio personalities within that format. Others were merely imitators captive in a formula which dominated the AM music idiom. While KHJ never resorted to buzzers that went off after eight seconds other stations may have, thus generating the belief that in boss radio a jock is little more than an appendage to a Top 40 chart. The programming power at KHJ was in the hands of the program director and the music librarian, Betty Breneman, who assisted him.

A majority of songs aired at KHJ were charted, that is, were currently on the *Billboard* list or had been, as with the "goldens." The opportunity to break a new record at the station was statistically very small. Open programming slots in a given week ranged from one to five. At least 50 or more singles competed for these slots. Songs were picked on the basis of "pacing, the tempo of the record, the category of the record as to musical configuration, emotional mood at the time, what people are going for, who's happening in television . . . the criteria is what the hell sounds good." In other words, a song was chosen if it possessed a number of qualities and met several conditions, one of which transcended the intrinsic quality of the "in the grooves" doctrine so widely quoted in the record industry. Drake and Jacobs considered "momentum" the key. Momentum meant that an act or record was visibly on the ascent or was, in industry argot, "hot." Sonny and Cher, the Supremes and the Beatles in the mid-1960s all possessed momentum. A song by an established performer following a previous success more often than not was made a "hit bound" on KHJ. The value of exposure for a proven group was really quite minimal. Ron Jacobs, the recipient of numerous golden records thanking him for making a record a hit, considers many of these awards superfluous since "some of them would have been a hit regardless because the group was so big."

Even momentum, however, did not guarantee KHJ air play. Timing or "pacing" was equally important. Two records of similar style, volume, sex of singer, etc., would not be played one after another. As a result the injection of a new record in the field of 33 changed the entire complexion of the play list.

Jacobs would not put three rhythm and blues songs on his play list in a given week regardless of the quality of the record or the momentum of the performer. He recalls, "There would never be a week that we would put on Wilson Pickett and the Temptations and Otis Redding no matter if all three had made their greatest record." In this sense a group with a sound similar to another with a chart item was doomed to failure. Why play Zager and Evans when Simon and Garfunkle have something going? Only in rare instances does imitation or similarity help a new performer. America's "Horse With No Name" in 1972 was an instantaneous hit in part because the trio's music was identical to that of the supergroup Crosby, Stills, Nash and Young, which had not made a record in over a year. It is widely believed that had "Horse" been released at the same time as a Crosby, Stills, Nash and Young record the group would have remained an obscure trio. Timing, therefore, is an important variable in a record's ability to break into a boss sound play list. While timing can help a group, the clock frequently works against it as well. The time of a program director is valuable. Consequently, the screening of records at KHJ worked against most performers. Ron Jacobs was able to review up to a 100 singles in a half-hour simply by listening to the first bar or opening four seconds of a song. If the opening was not infectious or did not meet the immediate needs of the format it was rejected. "I can afford to disqualify anything that's going on my station if it doesn't make it in context, and if it makes it in context, it has to come on strong in the beginning." Many record producers, being aware of this review policy, would stress strong bass runs as in "Smoke on the Water," "Green Onions," "Sunshine of Your Love" or "You Really Got Me" for an opening, thus providing the "hook" or attention-getting sound. This rather cavalier technique is a product of the excessive volume of product that the program director was faced with. Citing the statistic that a new album appears every 90 minutes in America, Jacobs explains that he "don't have the real time capability to listen to all the songs."

The importance of KHJ lays considerably beyond its immediate market area, since the *Billboard* chart, as well as the Bill Gavin, Bob Hamilton and Kal Rudman *Friday Morning Quarterback* tip sheets, are based upon the air play afforded records in major market areas. Los Angeles is the most important of these areas. Songs not introduced in these areas rarely are played in the so-called secondary markets, since their play lists are based upon what is popular in the major markets. The Catch 22 aspect of this is most distressing to promotional people, who have devised numerous channels to get around program directors such as Ron Jacobs. While acknowledging the power of a gatekeeper at KHJ, Jacobs does mildly dissent from the importance of getting a record played on boss radio: "I'm sure I could give you an example of ten incredible records that were played routinely as hit bounds for 2–3–4 weeks—nothing happened to them, absolutely nothing." In fact, he could not cite any and added, "There are *very few* that we stuck our neck out just because we liked it, that were totally unknown. I think *those probably comprise the ones that we got burned on*." In other words, KHJ basically programmed records with momentum, that is, those by name artists. In recent years, KHJ has utilized its smaller sister stations in the RKO chain to air-test singles that are believed to have potential, thus eliminating the risk factor in the major market area. Still, getting a record on the KHJ play list is a crowning achievement for any promotion man. Jay Lasker, the flamboyant president of ABC-Dunhill, has erected a large oriental gong in the executive hallway to be rung by promotional personnel when one of their acts breaks on a major market AM station. A dull buzz is used to announce secondary breakouts. KHJ, no doubt, gets two hits on the gong.

Free-Form Radio

Underground, progressive or free-form radio was born in the still of the San Francisco night. Russ "The Moose" Syracuse, who held forth on the number-one Top 40 station, KYA, during the midnight to dawn shift, played material never aired during the daytime "ratings" hours. "All Night Flight" was a staged space voyage with music, exotic characters and satire. In conducting this simulated "air trip" the deejay tapped a reservoir of musical material ignored by the formula stations: the long-playing album. Devotees of the *Billboard* Hot 100 and other charts in 1965 were oblivious to Bob Dylan, Joan Baez and the many other artists who had never had a hit single. In San Francisco, especially, many local favorites had

Exhibit 5.1

FIRST KHJ PLAY LIST

The Boss 30 Records in Southern California! *

Last Week	This Week	Title	Artist	Label	Weeks on Survey
(1)	1	Satisfaction	The Rolling Stones	London	5
(2)	2	Hold Me, Thrill Me, Kiss Me	Mel Carter	Imperial	5
(3)	3	All I Really Want to Do	Cher	Imperial	3
(2)	4	I Can't Help Myself	Four Tops	Motown	9
(5)	5	I Got You Babe	Sonny & Cher	Atco	3
(6)	6	Yes, I'm Ready	Barbara Mason	Arctic	5
(7)	6	I'm Henry VIII, I Am	Herman's Hermits	MGM	3
(8)	7	What's New Pussycat?	Tom Jones	Parrot	4
(7)	8	What the World Needs Now Is Love	Jackie deShannon	Imperial	9
(16)	9	I'm a Fool	Dino, Desi & Billy	Reprise	4
(10)	10	This Little Bird	Marianne Faithful	London	6
(9)	11	Laurie	Dickey Lee	TCF	6
(11)	12	Oo Wee Baby, I Love You	Fred Hughes	VJ	4
(12)	13	Crying in the Chapel	Elvis Presley	RCA Victor	9
(13)	14	Whittier Blvd.	Three Midnighters	Chattahoochee	5
(19)	15	Seventh Son	Johnny Rivers	Imperial	7
(14)	16	Cara Mia	Jay & The Americans	United Artists	4

(23)	17	Save Your Heart For Me	Gary Lewis	Liberty	2
(15)	18	Wonderful World	Herman's Hermits	MGM	7
(22)	19	Sunshine, Lollipops and Rainbows	Leslie Gore	Mercury	2
(20)	20	You'd Better Come Home	Petula Clark	Warner Bros.	1
(17)	21	Mr. Tambourine Man	The Byrds	Columbia	10
(25)	22	I'll Feel a Whole Lot Better	The Byrds	Columbia	2
(21)	23	Wooly Bully	Sam The Sham & the Pharoahs	MGM	10
(26)	24	Hung on You/ Unchained Melody	The Righteous Brothers	Philles	1
(30)	25	Papa's Got a Brand New Bag	James Brown	King	1
(27)	26	Let Her Dance	Bobby Fuller Four	Mustang	2
(HB)	27	Baby, I'm Yours	Barbara Lewis	Atlantic	--
(28)	28	Easy Question	Elvis Presley	RCA Victor	1
(HB)	29	One Dyin' and a Buryin'	Roger Miller	Smash	–
(29)	30	Theme From "A Summer Place"	The Lettermen	Capitol	1

* Courtesy of Ron Jacobs.

not yet signed a recording contract. During the daylight hours there was little incentive to change the KYA format; Tom "Big Daddy" Donahue and the other boss jocks were leading the Drake-managed KFRC in the ratings race. In the wee hours of the morning Syracuse violated nearly all the canons of boss radio. He did not "shut up and play the music." Much of the music he did air was generally not found on any chart. He played tapes of the Grateful Dead, the Great Society, Wildflower, Big Brother and the Jefferson Airplane. During the day, as Airplane bassist Jack Cassady observed, "KYA refused to play our RCA single." Due to his unique time slot, "The Moose" avoided most station-management interference. He was able to demonstrate the fact that albums were no longer just a one-hit single with 11 fillers. Each of the Beatles' albums was a total package that frequently outsold hot "hit" singles. Big Daddy Donahue explained his disaffection with the AM format as partially attributable to the fact that "the Byrds' LP or the new Bob Dylan album was outselling the single records on their play lists, in most cases Top 40 programmers chose to ignore them rather than attempting to determine cuts." In 1966, few Top 40 program directors deluged with 7,086 singles had the time or inclination to plow through some 3,752 albums containing 12 cuts each. Syracuse could and did review material during his six-hour air stunt, literally "bombing" those he did not like. The new format worked with college students and street people, indicating that a youth audience existed which preferred musical fare other than the normal AM material. This fact was not lost upon advertisers increasingly concerned with demographics.

Demographics became important in radio industry early in the 1960s when some radio stations either unable or unwilling to compete with Top 40 acceded "numbers" to stations as KHJ and KYA. The Top 40 philosophy was: "If we had the kids listening, we figure we could be Number One because the stations in L.A. before them had gotten to be Number One by making the kids listen . . . demographics are absolutely silly for programmers to consider." But, as the demographic profiles indicate, the major consumers of singles and Top 40 radio in the mid-1960s were in the lower age brackets ranging from 9 to 18 with an emphasis on bubblegummers and teenyboppers. Although they were avid consumers of blemish cream and American International films, this age group did not purchase many products bought by their older brothers and sisters, the major consumers of albums. Top 40 radio centered upon the 9 to 18 audience, while so-called middle-of-the-road (MOR) stations concentrated upon those 35 to 49, thus leaving the highest consumption demographic of 18 to 34 unattended. This economic fact alone lent indirect legitimacy to the Syracuse format. A large speciality audience in a major city is not to be ignored, especially when that taste group buys most of the autos, appliances and stereos in the United States. The identification of this alternative audience lent considerable support to formats other than Top 40, especially because *Time*'s "man of the year" was the "under-25 youth." As if to underline the existence of an alternative taste public, the Federal Communications Commission in 1966 ruled that AM and FM stations under common ownership separate their programming formats as of January 1, 1967. The rise of the LP, more sophisticated sampling techniques and industry awareness of a youth culture all provided the soil in which underground radio was to flourish.

KMPX-FM in San Francisco was a foreign-language speciality station on the verge of bankruptcy. The station listed "vanity" ethnic shows where the announcer was also the sponsor. For a time, the station held an "announcing school" where part of the training was conducted on the air. Only Roy Trumbull's Sunday evening folk-music show featuring Dylan, Paxton, Ochs, Baez and others had any youth appeal. Trumbull, who also broadcast on the Pacifica station KPFA, chatted informally and played requests, usually from university students. This was KMPX's first exposure to the emerging "new community" in the city. A Detroit deejay, Larry Miller, came to do an all-night rock program. It was the only one on the station. The show was to become the "style setter" of the underground radio format. The management originally knew nothing about rock music; their forte was the "Portuguese Hour" or "Italian Hour." Consequently, Miller was afforded considerable leeway. He chose records, asked for requests, introduced songs with the precision of a jazz announcer detailing group personnel. The jargon was "street rap" without any of the vocal acrobatics of boss jocks, in part due to the lateness of the hour. Students crammed for exams with KPMX in the background; others smoked dope. The play list was huge in comparison to the boss radio's 33 selections. Miller used 200 to 300 records by "Frisco" bands, bluesmen, folksingers, poets and whatever else seemed appropriate. The show was a success. A year after the initiation of the Miller show, Tom Donahue joined KMPX as the program director of the first FM "free-form" station. The programming format embraced rock 'n' roll, folk traditional, and city blues, raga, electronic music, and some jazz and classical selections. "I believe music should not be treated as a group of objects to be sorted out like eggs with each category kept apart from the others, and it is exciting to discover that there is a large audience that shares that premise."[26] Donahue hired a number of his ex-KYA people who compiled their own play lists. An engineering staff of women was employed. Advertising revenues rose from $3,000 a month to $25,000. In the late 1960s Donahue's evening show became the top-rated program in the Bay Area, appealing to the magic demographic 18-to-34 group. An FM show had done the impossible, getting bigger "numbers" than its AM counterparts. The success of KMPX spawned a vast number of so-called free-form stations. In 1973 there were an estimated 400 nationally.

For the record industry the success of underground radio was like a breath of fresh air. An entire new avenue for the exposure and marketing of product had opened. A hit single, while still the most effective catalyst for fame, was no longer the *only* way to break an act. The success of Warner/Reprise in the late 1960s is attributed by many of its executives as being directly connected to the rise of "free-form" radio. Warner/Reprise originally was an easy-listening album label with nearly 80 percent of its catalog represented by Dean Martin, Frank Sinatra, Petula Clark, Trini Lopez and Peter, Paul and Mary. These artists rarely broke into the exhaulted *Billboard* winner's circle. When Warner/Reprise moved into the youth-music sphere its reliance on albums did not change. Singles were taken from albums rather than the other way around. Consequently, as an album label the company greatly benefited from "free form," which stressed the specialty album as opposed to the Top 40 single. Indeed, the alternate media established the Warner Communications Corporation as the company with the "hot hand" in the late 1960s. Other companies were equally delighted with the shift away from the dominant singles emphasis of AM radio. A Columbia Records executive added:

> Thank God for underground FM stations because that's given an outlet for the artist who wouldn't be played on Top 40 or might not get broken on Top 40. One saving light on the horizon. But again, the Top 40 stations are in the position the buyer is in. If they've got, in the case of KHJ, 300 singles to choose from in one weeks, obviously if they're only gonna be able to add 3–4 singles to their play list that week, and there's a new Santana or a new Bob Dylan or new Chicago, those are the ones that are going to be the first shot.

While underground radio has in fact liberalized and opened up play lists and allowed deejays to get away from the Drake Clock, the "freedom" of this idiom has been an issue since the advent of KMPX.

On March 18, 1968, Tom Donahue and Milan Melvin resigned from KMPX, beginning a long strike and facilitating the emergence of KSAN as a major "free-form" station. A major issue, besides money, was artistic freedom. The strikers accused the Crosby-Pacific Broadcasting Corporation, which had taken over ownership of the station, of interference. Melvin claimed he had been asked to cut his shoulder-length hair if he wished to be station manager. He chose to strike. A deejay was told not to play classical cuts longer than five minutes in order to maintain program balance. Other complaints centered upon the banning of some songs from air play, such as "The Pusher" by Steppenwolf and "Parchment Farm" by Blue Cheer.

Meanwhile, in New York, Murray "The K" was fired from his "free-form" show on WOR-FM. The reason was the takeover of the station by the Drake Syndicate. In leaving Murray claimed, "The music's back in the hands of the people who don't care. There's no personality on the air and the station is developing a routine and a format."[27] Drake's interjection did, indeed, raise WOR's ratings, a fact many AM 40 program directors quote any time liberalization of play lists is hinted at. The assertion that the progressive format has taken on the same rigidity as boss radio has some merit. Some FM stations have replicated to the last decibel the original KMPX and KSAN sound. After purchase of KSAN by Metromedia, a large conglomerate and communications network, its philosophy was employed in Philadelphia, New York, and other major cities.

A 1972 *New York Times* survey indicated that a considerable standardization of the progressive format had taken place. In some cases the stations had reverted to boss radio. The major catalyst for the decline of "free form" was the so called Love network on the ABC-FM Chain. Stations on the Love chain were supplied with tapes and radio spots produced in New York. The show for the affiliates was anchored by Brother John, who read poetry and introduced records, certified by trade magazines, over a 24-hour period. All seven FM affiliates instituted this policy and program directors dictated the play lists and the time that certain records were to be played. A network vice-president commented, "We feel that in the last year [1971] there has been a major shift among young people away from radicalism and esotericism."[28] A record-company executive sadly noted, "The free-form stations are nonexistent with the exception of two or three: KMET here [Los Angeles], WBCN in Boston. There are not very many others that I can think of that are either profitable or visible. So it isn't going to change." Pete Fornatale, an FM jock in New York, wrote: "Progressive commercial radio in the United States is a myth. As long as broadcasting remains wed to financial concerns, the idea of a totally committed radio . . . is absurd."[29] The "free-form" policies of the latter half of the 1960s, outside of campus stations, were rapidly disappearing.

Allen Shaw, president of ABC-FM, after a brief flying at free form, introduced his version of the Drake Clock. The Shaw formula was to create a play list of preselected songs taken from charts, oldies and cuts from successful albums. These are then inserted into a timetable like the Clock. The deejays are tightly controlled and monitored. They are told to say, "Hi, this is. . . ." Shaw explained, "It's good radio principles: little DJ talk, careful spot placement, call-letter frequency, weather. . . . The jingles are not a limitation." The selection of the play list of ABC-FM is quite similar to the boss radio formula:

> We operate on two premises: certain recording artists are more popular than others. Two, a station can choose to present the new, less popular music to a segment of an audience or present only the more popular—without reproducing Top 40. We've been accused of turning into an FM Top 40. What's wrong with it? If that's what people want, then there should be one station in town to do that.[30]

This formula has been described as the "Chinese Menu"; that is, a song is chosen from an album, another from the Top 40 chart, another from the oldies list and so on. For the record company attempting to break an artist, the move away from free form is greatly inhibiting.

At the present time some independent FM stations still adhere to free form. The Metromedia chain still allows its deejays some editorial control. WPLJ in New York is one example, although it is consistently beaten in the ratings by the Drake-controlled WOR-FM. Don Morehouse at KMET in Los Angeles runs a "free-form" station where deejays still pick what they will play. WABX-FM in Detroit also leaves much of the programming discretion in the hands of its announcers. Dennis Fawley, a WABX jock, comments, "You have to be aware of everything that's coming out and decide whether or not to put it on the air. Each person here on this staff is aiming at a different audience depending on his *own tastes and personality*."[31] Such discretion is becoming increasingly restricted, even on FM radio.

FM radio increasingly is moving into a modified version of "free-form" broadcasting. Many progressive stations use what is called a "pie chart," which slices up time periods into musical categories. For example, 3 to 6 P.M. is "heavy metal hour." Deejays are then permitted a certain degree of freedom in selecting which Black Sabbath or Deep Purple cut they will play. Some pie charts have more rigidity, again restricting the freedom of the deejay.

AM radio has been affected by the rise of the progressive stations and by the move away from "free-form." A rather typical reaction by AM programmers has been to dismiss the progressive format. George Wilson of the Bartell broadcasting chain, which had number-one rated stations in Milwaukee and San Diego until Ron Jacobs came to town, reacted this way. Wilson refused to play album cuts on his Top 40 stations, arguing that LP cuts "lose ratings for you." "People," he insists, "who're into album cuts . . . aren't into Top 40 radio."[32] Furthermore, Wilson cites the statistic that only the 18-to-24-year-old age group listens to progressive. Consequently, he feels Top 40 commands a greater market. A vast majority of AM popular-music program directors probably concur with Wilson's sentiments. Don Armstrong, a veteran southern broadcaster, totally supports this notion. Having worked in the southern, midwestern and Canadian markets, Armstrong feels the audience is "unhip" and desires familiar material. He says, "You can't keep an audience with new material unless they're locked in a building. People don't know what they like, they like what they know. They know those songs that you can hum, sing, whistle, tap your foot to, preferably all four."

THE JACOBS CONVEYER BELT

In order to cope with the advent of FM programming, many stations in major markets have begun to play a limited number of cuts from successful albums. The degree of album infiltration into play lists varies and is difficult to ascertain. Even Bill Drake has incorporated some LP material as long as it has been successful on other stations. The most elaborate attempt is underway at KGB-AM and FM in San Diego, where Ron Jacobs is program director.

Unlike George Wilson, Ron Jacobs contends that Top 40 stations are increasingly getting a smaller share of the radio audience. To verify this contention Jacobs commissioned a survey of over 3,000 interviews with a representative sample of local residents as to musical tastes, radio listening hours and station preference. In turn, Jacobs and the KGB staff applied this demographic data to a music system in which records circulate around a sequence. According to the sample, "Bridge Over Troubled Water" can be played with equal acceptance at any time, because it appeals to all listeners. Some categories of songs are played at various times of the day. Tempo, length of record, age of song all are correlated with a projected audience. For example, a 6-minute or longer track of down-tempo rock by Black Sabbath can be programmed in the late-night hours when the dominant listeners are high-school and college students.

KGB started playing 1,400 titles and in December 1972 was up to approximately 3,000. These songs are played on the criteria of a time-style–audience correlation. The mathematical possibilities are immense when compared to the 33 songs that originally were the foundation of the Drake play list at KHJ. Jacobs observed, "In May 1972 we've put 300 [songs] on since we started and I don't know where we're going to end up. All I know is we have the capacity for 10,000 titles in there." In 1974, when playing all of the shortest cuts—2.5 to 3 minutes—KGB broadcast 2,700 songs a week. Jacobs adds, the station is as "free form as a roulette wheel." The formula basically consists of the organization of time and music. Because of the flexibility of the format, Jacobs made two major alterations after several months of broadcasting, again departing from tradition. After evaluating listener feedback, he decided that "fifties rock singles" in many instances could not be handled compatibly with more contemporary material. Disregarding the sanctity of golden oldies, KGB eliminated a large portion of the oldies from the play lists in order to focus on "progressive oldies." The sacred repetition of current favorites also was changed, limiting the frequency of air play for Top 40 material. The belt shifted to older familiar album cuts mixed with current fare. The play list retains the 2,000 plus items. Jacobs's belt is a new concept which feeds upon, as well as violates, established broadcasting edicts. The all-pervasive "they like what they know" is scientifically documented in a computer storage bank. All tastes can be accommodated, while appealing to the most desirable groups. In fact, the demographic conveyer belt is a sophisticated extrapolation of the Top 40 system *minus* many of the shortcomings of laid-back FM or relaxed FM programming. The rich panorama of the system, encompassing the 18 through 34 age brackets and older, does increase the quantity and quality of the play list. Hypothetically, the audience can be increased by expanding the time parameters. The cut-off point at present is measured by the early 1950s when rock and roll was born.

The potentialities of the Jacobs belt for radio programming are revolutionary, but record-company promotion directors, who hated Jacobs for his tight play list at KHJ, may view this innovation with mixed emotions. The opening up of any AM play list would appear to be a welcome development. However, Jacobs has really successfully pushed categories into the background. He plays music, not charted singles. The acceptance of this blueprint, in an industry as trend-oriented as radio broadcasting, could well challenge the sacrosanct notions of chart security as well as the future of the single. The elimination of the single would shatter the "singles make stars" dictum, one of the few cardinal tenets of faith in the industry. On December 13, 1972, the first ARB figures appeared since the conveyer belt began to roll. Jacobs won the ratings battle over Wilson's Top 40 singles approach. In radio, being number one is the name of the game. Jacobs writes: "KGB really scored in the exact areas we've been shooting for! So right on it's scary! . . . ten months of doing something 'weird' that nobody outside our trip believed." "It works," he exclaimed. The impact of KGB's ratings climb has yet to be felt, however, the December ARB reports on the San

Diego market will not be dismissed easily at future sessions of the annual Gavin, Hamilton and *Billboard* broadcasters conference.

The diminishing idiom of free-form radio continues to be the record companies' favorite outlet. Bill Roberts, who broke "American Pie," explains: "At progressive stations you can go in the studio and sit down with the deejay and rap to him while he's on the air in between records, and sometimes you can hand him a record. And if he has enough trust in you as a music expert, he'll put it on immediately and you tell him what cut you want played and he'll play it." On Top 40, he maintains, the situation if different: "All they give you is 15 minutes to promote maybe 20 singles and 15 albums. If you don't talk fast your chances of getting a record on are not too great."

GETTING THE NEEDLE ON THE RECORD

In a survey of Florida high-school students, George Allen Booker found that 54 percent of his respondents listed the disk jockey as the most important influence in the development of their musical tastes.[33] Despite the artists' dues paying and record-company mixing and hype, it all comes down to getting a deejay to play that record so a sufficient number of people can hear it. Some of these listeners hopefully will like it well enough to buy it. The more people who hear a record the greater its chances for success. This relatively simple process is complicated by the sheer volume of product. AM Top 40 stations are deluged by dozens of record companies with at least 7,000 singles each year, 2,000 more than in the payola years. AM and FM stations receive that many singles plus approximately 4,000 LPs, a thousand more than in the late 1950s. Since the average album has 12 cuts, the program director has a hypothetical choice of 48,000 cuts and 7,000 single selections from which to choose. Obviously, all 55,000

Exhibit 5.2

COMPARISON OF PREVIOUS SAN DIEGO MARCH/APRIL ARB SHARES WITH OCTOBER/NOVEMBER RESULTS IN MAJOR TIME PERIODS*

	Men 18–34		Women 18–34		Adults 18–34	
6 A.M.–Midnight, Mon-Sun						
KCBQ	(20.1)	9.9	(18.0)	11.5	(19.2)	10.5
KDEO	(17.2)	6.0	(6.0)	6.3	(12.5)	6.1
KGB	(9.3)	13.0	(6.0)	8.4	(7.9)	11.0
KPRI	(7.7)	9.9	(4.9)	2.1	(6.5)	6.5
6–10 A.M., Mon-Fri						
KCBQ	(18.7)	10.3	(21.6)	12.4	(20.0)	11.2
KDEO	(21.0)	3.4	(9.2)	9.6	(15.8)	6.2
KGB	(7.5)	14.7	(5.8)	8.6	(6.8)	12.0
KPRI	(5.5)	4.4	(1.8)	1.6	(3.9)	2.9
10 A.M.–3 P.M., Mon-Fri						
KCBQ	(19.1)	12.7	(15.3)	7.2	(17.4)	10.3
KDEO	(24.8)	7.9	(6.3)	3.2	(16.5)	5.8
KGB	(9.0)	8.8	(5.5)	8.7	(7.4)	8.7
KPRI	(7.5)	9.2	(3.4)	1.6	(5.7)	5.8
3–7 P.M., Mon-Fri						
KCBQ	(21.4)	10.3	(16.4)	12.8	(19.5)	11.4
KDEO	(16.1)	5.2	(5.7)	7.8	(12.1)	6.3
KGB	(11.3)	17.5	(6.4)	10.6	(9.4)	14.4
KPRI	(8.2)	11.8	(6.0)	1.9	(7.3)	7.4
7 P.M.–Midnight, Mon-Fri						
KCBQ	(26.6)	5.2	(21.7)	13.3	(24.9)	8.5
KDEO	(14.8)	9.6	(4.3)	3.6	(11.2)	7.2
KGB	(5.3)	12.8	(5.8)	4.2	(5.5)	9.4
KPRI	(11.4)	13.7	(13.8)	3.6	(12.2)	9.4

* Figures are average quarter-hour shared; April/May figures in parentheses.

songs are not going to receive air play. Even Ron Jacobs's very liberal conveyer belt only housed 2,000 cuts, spanning nearly two decades. The question therefore becomes which new product is going to get exposure. The answer in many instances is quite simple. Charted material gets air play because it is on the charts. If this sounds like Catch 22, it is. Many record programmers will only "get behind a record" on material which has already proven itself successful. A typical midwestern program director proudly announced that his station had *never* broken or introduced a new record to his audience. He played only songs listed in the Top 30 slots on the *Billboard* or *Cashbox* ratings. Others augment the safety of trade charts with the "bibles" or tip sheets.

The most widely read of the "bibles" are the *Gavin Report*, Ted Randal's *Tip Sheet*, the *Hamilton Report* and Kal Rudman's *Friday Morning Quarterback*. Bill Gavin, Bob Hamilton and the others were once deejays. Subscribers pay $150 and more annually for the mimeographed four to eight pages of selections by these knowledgeable gentlemen. Four hundred stations pay $144 for the *Gavin Report* and in turn receive four sheets of blue paper containing a "smash of the week" and four other songs labeled as "hot shots" or "sleepers to watch," as well as a recommended play list. Gavin also provides a list of his top 20 and an equal number of "hit bounds" compiled from 200 national correspondents who are mostly record people. The *Gavin Report* is *the* sheet by tradition, due to the editor's reputation for honesty. Gavin will not accept promotional material for his sheet. Neither does Bob Hamilton, but he has the disadvantage of following Gavin on the scene and possessing a flashy image. *Friday Morning Quarterback* rivals Gavin for dominance in the tip-sheet market. It includes on its front page a "Bill Drake Report" and hit picks similar to the others. Many programmers, while subscribers, have some doubts about Kal Rudman's dual roles of chart picker and record promoter. There are obvious conflicts of interest. Rudman accepts paid promotional material for *Quarterback*, Gavin does not. One business agent told a reporter,

"It puts some people off."[34] Rudman is perhaps no less honest than Gavin or Hamilton, but his credibilitity is somewhat tarnished in some quarters. An anonymous record-company executive told *Rock* magazine, "Gavin is untouchable. Rudman can be bought."[35] Gavin's high sense of ethics has got him in some trouble. Bob Hamilton feels Gavin is too conservative. Undgerground media especially decry Gavin's editorials on drug lyrics and sexually liberated songs like "Acapulco Gold" and "Honky Tonk Woman." Others disagree with some of his business sentiments. "You can be a good record man," he feels, "and have a good radio station without necessarily showing up number one. . . . There are other things to be proud of."[36] In a business where jobs depend on being first, this sentiment explains why many PDs prefer Rudman's "money music" style. To the record company, the PD clutching a *Billboard* chart in one hand and a tip sheet in the other is nearly a lost cause. But they must continue to court him, for the trades and tip sheets rarely do justice to their voluminous output of product. Gavin's five front-page picks constitute less than 1 percent of the week's new singles. Consequently, the promotion director must aim his product and efforts to those program directors and deejays who might be receptive to new product. When all is said and done, the interaction between the promotion and publicity departments of the recording company and the keeper of the play list makes or destroys a record or an artistic career.

A majority of program directors feel that record companies do not appreciate their business. A West Cost PD said, "The record people don't understand that the competitiveness in the radio business is such that people cannot listen to two radio stations at one time. I can go and buy a Columbia album and an Atlantic album, but I can't . . . listen to more than one radio station at a time." In radio there is an "either-or" or "zero-sum" situation. Only one radio station is on top in the ratings. Promotion directors, with different degrees of empathy, are aware of this situation. "They want to be sure they're playing the right music," says Ron Saul at Warner/Reprise.

"One bad rating and usually the program director or music director is out of a job. And that's the terrible thing about it. If the industry was a little more secure in terms of positions held and the ratings were not so important—which again, it's the life of that industry—then I'm sure there would be a little more room to play a little more than we have." At United Artists, Saul's counterpart Bill Roberts echoes this interpretation: "It's difficult to walk into a major station in a major city and ask the music director to go on an unknown record by a group . . . his job may be at stake if he makes the wrong decisions too many times. When he puts on a record, it's usually because it has started to break in another area." For security, most PDs attempt to get "behind a record" rather than "get in front of it." The record company obviously wants to move the station in front.

The fundamental problem for acts is that the perceived interests of radio-station program directors are antagonistic to those of the record company. Especially in the major markets, radio is a tremendously competitive business. The competition historically has been for higher "numbers" as measured in the Pulse, Hooper and American Research Bureau (ARB) ratings polls. On the basis of these numbers advertising contracts are awarded and withheld and profits and losses result. In recent years large numbers alone have not been sufficient, as advertisers have become more sophisticated and concerned with the social characteristics of audiences. For example, an advertiser with blemish cream account will be most concerned with the 9- through 18-year-old audience rather than the 18 through 34 group, which is most attractive to beer, appliance and automotive manufacturers. As in television, failure to achieve the proper numbers results in the cancellation of advertising and consequently formats and radio personalities. Any well-trodden avenues to higher ratings are welcomed. If a youth demographic is the targeted audience, safety is the Top 40 format and MOR when the 24-to-49 age group is being courted. There are, of course, many variations depending on markets. Markets are compiled on the basis of size and income. Most record companies, according to Dennis Killeen, consider the highest ten as majors: New York, Los Angeles, Chicago, Philadelphia, Detroit, Boston, San Francisco, Oakland, Washington, D.C., Pittsburgh and St. Louis (population). But the last two are replaced by Newark and Cleveland on buying ratings. Stations in major markets can be more esoteric since a sufficient number of people may be attracted to any specialty stations. Progressive FMers traditionally pull the 18- to 24-year-olds, much to the delight of stereo manufacturers and other advertisers seeking to exploit the college–young-adult set. In smaller secondary market cities, the large numbers philosophy is hooked to demographics. The case of WOHO in Toledo provided an illustration.

The Toledo market comprises about 100,000 people. The local AM competition is primarily between WSPD and WOHO. The Canadian 50,000-watt boss radio station CKLW-AM also is prominent in the area. CKLW successfully services a segment of the 9-to-18 age level with the remainder going to WOHO and WIOT, an FM rock station. However, WOHO and WSPD are in direct competition for advertising accounts geared for those adults between the age levels of 24 to 49. WSPD is primarily an MOR or middle-media station. In spring 1972, to compete with WSPD, Don Armstrong, then of WOHO, devised an elaborate play list designed to lure the desired demographed audience. This approach is a variation on a very popular theme in many nonmajor markets.

The play list is based entirely upon charted material. Current hits are gleaned from the *Billboard* Hot 100 and the easy-listening charts. Mixed into this are Top 40 and middle-media selections from the Bob Hamilton sheet. The tip sheet, for which the station pays a $160 fee, complements the three trades with charts, thus adding more safety in compiling play lists. To these lists the program director adds local record sales figures, scant as they may be. He then adds up places on each chart for songs. The lowest figure receives the greatest amount as the most popular song and so forth. For example, the week of November 25, 1971, found the "Theme From

Shaft" placing number 2 on the Hamilton hit chart. It was number 1 on the Hot 100, placed 6 on the *Billboard* "Easy-Listening" chart and 2 on Hamilton's "MOR" listing and gained a 32 in the local area. The added total was 43. Armstrong adds to his play list extras usually taken from oldies and designed either to appeal to a specific age or sex group.

The rationale for this complex list is that by playing oldies which go back to 1950 regularly, those past current Top 40 material will be attracted. To avoid offending this audience, Armstrong avoided youthful punk-rock material which might present an irritation or "turn-off factor." However, he did play a sufficient amount of current Top 40 material to maintain listener loyalty in the 18-to-25 bracket. In this way, WOHO runs neck and neck with WSPD. There can only be one top station in Toledo. A program director in a similarly sized city responded that the percentage of the market he wanted was ".01 percent over his competition." To accomplish this feat the program director programs the safest, most acceptable material. As Bill Drake indicates, "Picking records will be determined by what occurs . . . the criteria will be the same to find out what records *please the most people*."[37] The record companies' goal is to get *their* records played on the station. The station in turn only wants to air records that are established hits. Program directors customarily tell promotion men, "We're not in the businesss to sell your records. We're in the business to entertain, to get listeners, not to sell your product," or "When it's on the charts we'll play it," or "I'll take all the Beatle records you got." In view of this attitude, it is safe to say that more recording careers die in a program director's office than anywhere else. The task of converting the PD is getting around these cop-outs and is left to the promotion director and his field representatives.

UNDER-ASSISTANT PROMO MAN

The promotion department is not particularly popular with recording artists or producers, given its failure rate with records. The Rolling Stones early in their career wrote, "Under-Assistant West Coast Promo Man" with the line, "Sitting here and thinking just how sharp I am, I'm a necessary talent for every rock and roll band." Richard Robinson, author, deejay and producer, portrayed the promo man as "a breed apart, resembling human beings, but living lives based on plastic being the true essence of good. To say, therefore, that the promotion man is, of necessity, jive is simply to state a sad fact of life."[38] Despite the disapprobation hurled upon the promo man by Robinson and the Rolling Stones, to the company he is the pulse of the people. He is closest to the street. His sole function is to get precious air time for his records. This is no simple feat, given the amount of product available. Promotion departments use standard techniques of selling: visits, calls, artist biographies and an adequate supply of sample copies. Occasionally, the promotion man is assigned to escort a touring act from station to station. Beyond this is the shady area of "goodwill." One Detroit program director defined goodwill: "The game of the promoter is to get you obliged, be it through exclusives, dinner, theater tickets, or what have you."[39] The "what have you" is a sticky subject. Various favors are frequently exchanged in some markets and none in others. Some underground stations consider plastic bags containing "grass" or pills inserted in an album jacket a token of goodwill. At the easy-listening station a bottle of Chivas Regal or J&B is still welcome. The soul-music market, which is nearly identical to the Top 40 milieu of the late 1950s, is the most susceptible to under-the-table promotion.

Small black companies vie with the Hollywood giants for air time. Payola is an important promotional technique with soul radio stations. Because of this situation many industry executives do not accept soul charts as accurate. Kal Rudman refuses to have a soul section in his tip sheet. He says, "I started the whole R&B thing, and I want no part of it."[40] Most professionals consider themselves corporate executives and consequently frown upon activities which are openly beyond the FCC or other legally prohibited rules of the game. However, there is a fine gray area in which goodwill abounds in junkets, gifts of drugs and alcohol and practices which are also seen in the dealings of nonentertainment corporations, all designed to promote air play for the company. Many program directors view this continuous attention as an occupational hazard. Some AM stations allocate one afternoon a week for promo men, who are given a quarter of an hour to present their current product. Others have quota systems that balance product from the various companies. More rigid stations demand that product be mailed to their library for review. Most of these copies are never played. Ken Robbie, a Midwest music librarian, has a huge cabinet full of singles which are kept for a six-month period and then donated to a local university library. He never plays any of the records unless they are charted, despite calls from promo people "who come on like long-lost friends." This approach he resents, preferring the more objective fact sheets mailed by ABC-Dunhill. Most program directors interviewed regard promotional literature as useless. Each record company has similar promotional ploys, but they also differ in their approaches, depending on the emphasis of the company. Singles companies vary from album companies, but their goals are still "getting the needle on the record."

The singles company has a distinct advantage in exposing its product, for nearly all radio media will play singles. Album cuts are more selectively treated; PDs do not have time to listen to hundreds of album cuts just to find a few that might please their audiences. As Bill Roberts commented, "If he listened to every record that came in he [the PD] would go mad." Album companies therefore are at a disadvantage in exposing their material through the AM channels. A singles company with a proven track record can command considerable respect with program directors. ABC-Dunhill is quite popular with Top 40 programmers, whereas Buddah is considered erratic and unpredictable. Jay Lasker, Dunhill's president, has a long history of successful singles beginning with "Eve of Destruction" through the lastest Three Dog Night or

Grass Roots hit. ABC's promo people have little difficulty in airing their material. As Billy James observes, "They do it on the basis of relationships that are developed and relationships that are based on *trust*." People believe that Lasker produces hit singles. Consequently, programmers play his material thus assuring more successful records. Sociologists call this a "self-fulfilling prophecy."

Lasker's philosophy is, "You've got the product and you've got good promotion then you've got a successful company. Without one or the other you're dead." Corb Donohue, creative services director at Dunhill, indicates that their small 12-person promotional staff is very important because it cultivates the trust of programmers:

> Lasker has a phenomenal promotion staff that has spent a lot of years and a lot of energy in cultivating and both knowing what major programmers like: Drake people and Bob Hamilton what their tastes are, what they like; what they listen for; and [they] have built a credibility about their own product and about themselves so that when they go in with a piece of product and say "I really believe in this product," they're going to get a listen. They're not newcomers and they're not shuck-and-jive guys, by the traditional sense.

Unlike his competitors, Lasker does not attempt to convince his promotional people of the quality of product. Much of the ABC-Dunhill singles catalogue is bubblegum and teenybop material, and would be difficult to persuade grown people of its esthetic quality. As a result, Lasker tells his staff, "I don't want any philosophy. I don't want to know what you think about records. These are the records, take them out and get them played." Lasker's approach is predicated partially upon personality, but it is also a function of the type of company he has. Until recently, ABC-Dunhill almost exclusively focused on the singles market and did so with considerable success.

Album companies are faced with greater obstacles to overcome. In 1971 the premier album company was Warner/Reprise. "We as a record company," says Ron Saul, "realize that dollars are in albums not in singles." To this end the company has been forced to develop various techniques by which to either circumvent or entice the traditional singles-oriented program director. The company has aimed its appeal directly at the new alternative media. Stan Cornyn explains:

> We've had to work harder. We've also had a lot of artists who are not about to have single successes. The basic folk artist ain't going to go pounding through on the Top 40 radio. Therefore, at a time when FM was just a glimmer, I personally and several of this company rushed in and said, "hey, where have you been, and this is neat and we love you." I remember someone would rumor that an FM station would be cropping up in St. Louis and I would try and find that station and give them advertising money for the time that they were on the air because we needed them so much.

Warner did in fact fill the coffers of underground media, both radio and press.

In addition to going around the traditional radio gatekeeper, Ron Saul has been innovating various means to hook the program director. His promotional philosophy is to collaborate with the radio stations. In approaching the Drake chain and other Top 40 outlets he attempts to complement their play lists: "Say they've added four records that were up records. Most likely, they would be looking in terms of programming balance for a downer record, and if you happen to have a downer record as opposed to an upper record, both equal in terms of priority, you better be pushing the 'downer' record first and talking about the 'downer' saying, 'hey, you added three "up" records, I'm sure you're looking for a "downer" record.' Then right away, they are more receptive."

Another technique to get to the program director is through the use of advertising. Saul explains:

> We will give our promotion people the monies necessary to be able to walk into a station and advertise a product. So that . . . they

> not only talk to a music director or program director about what kind of music he should be programming, but they can walk down the hall, up to a sales manager or the general manager of the station, talk to him about fixing an advertising program, and then go back to the program director and incorporate these two things. This makes them much more professional and vital to the total successful operation of the radio station and not just a delivery boy.

The buying of advertising has increasingly become a promotional tool. Spots provide the record company a minute in which to expose their acts before Top 40 audiences without having to go through the program director's screening process. Theoretically, with enough advertising revenue a company can break an act in this manner. Spots feature one or more cuts on an album followed by an announcement of the title and the closing "on Warner Brothers Records." There is sufficient precedent to believe that spots are going to accelerate both on radio and television. Warner Brothers has been experimenting, especially in England, with television advertisements for Deep Purple. Company executives are extremely high on this possibility. The validity of spots, perhaps, has best been illustrated by the popularization of two commercials as popular songs. "It's Only Just Begun" was originally a theme for a California savings and loan firm. The song earned the Carpenters a gold record. The New Seekers followed this success with "I'd Like to Teach the World to Sing in Perfect Harmony"—a Coca-Cola commercial. Spots, according to Dennis Killeen, Capitol advertising director, do not always work. Shelter Records's Freddie King did a spot with minimal results, while J. J. Cale's radio ad was a success. The reason for this differentiation was probably due to the infectious guitar opening to Cale's "Pretty Women." Warner/Reprise, as Stan Cornyn is quick to observe, will try any method available to solve the problem of getting the sound to the "folks out there."

A&M, considered by many to be "*the* hot company of the 1970s," concentrates a large segment of its public-relations effort on its 40 promo people out in the field. Bob Garcia, of creative services, states, "Our prime emphasis is on informing the promo men and the lot people [company] first and media people second. Our promo men are us. A promo man is the publicity department. He's a sales promotion department. He's everything out there. So we have to have him get the ball first, and he's got to know everything and then let the media know." In keeping with their "family" concept, the communications between the field and the "lot" are very close. A&M publishes a mimeographed weekly magazine called *Fluff*, which unlike Warner's *Circular* is addressed directly to its employees. It contains a review and summary of all product forthcoming during the month. It also contains media reviews and chart positions of product and in-house chatter. At A&M the promo man is the front line and company success is seen as being closely related to his activities. Like ABC-Dunhill, Garcia sends out a straight fact sheet to program directors which is receiving closer scrutiny since the "monster hits" by Cat Stevens, the Carpenters, Carole King and Humble Pie. The following notes are illustrative of the A&M style.

Hello:

Here is the first single by A&M's singer/composer Michael Murphey who also happens to be the first solo artist that Bob Johnston has produced since Dylan, Cash and Cohen.

A-side is GERONIMO'S CADILLAC, with music by Murphey, and lyrics by Charles John Quarto, while flip is BLACKSLIDERS WINE, another Murphey original.

Both cuts were recorded and produced in Nashville by Johnston, and are from Murphey's first solo album for the label, GERONIMO'S CADILLAC.

Sincerely,

Director of Publicity
A&M Records

Hello:

Fast on the heels of their second smash single, HOT N' NASTY, comes Humble Pie's 30 DAYS IN THE HOLE b/w SWEET PEACE AND TIME, from their Gold Album SMOKIN.

Both cuts are originals and were written by Steve Marriott and the group, with production by Humble Pie.

Enjoy,

Director of Publicity
A&M Records

A&M and Warner/Reprise are album companies while ABC-Dunhill still is primarily a singles company. The orientations of these companies are quite different. Lasker is concerned with AM air play; Warner and A&M welcome AM air time but realistically attempt to reach the audiences through other channels. Both companies stress the college market and intelligent advertising. A&M has 36 paid representatives canvassing seven to eight college and university radio stations in a particular area. Warner has a department addressed to the campus with promotional personnel visiting them. They also service college newspapers with review records. It is only in the area of media that Warner and A&M sharply differ with the latter placing more emphasis upon their promotional people. Cornyn and Saul believe that reaching opinion-makers in the media is the most important task of the company, whereas Garcia feels that press coverage is relatively ineffective. Companies like ABC-Dunhill, Warner/Reprise and A&M, with established track records or "hot hands," have an added advantage over their competitors. Company images are very important (see chapter 3), an image of success frequently generates further triumphs. In a 1967 *Billboard* poll of record stations Capitol and Columbia were voted the best suppliers of material to program directors. Capitol Records squeaked by Columbia, not surprisingly, since 1967 was the year of the Beatles, the Beach Boys, Bob Dylan, Janis Joplin and numerous other superstars from the two companies. In the early 1970s, Dunhill's ever-growing list of golden singles by Three Dog Night and the Grass Roots guarantees a return for the apprehensive program director with one eye on the Pulse or ARB ratings. Warner and A&M can also invoke this ethos or they can bargain with "exclusives." "Exclusives" involve package deals. That is, Capitol Records, when the Beatles were recording, could approach a program director with their hot-off-the-press recording and another single that the company wanted played. Warner/Reprise would make the pitch with James Taylor's latest single, while A&M could use Cat Stevens or the Carpenters for breaking new groups.

Some labels will provide records by big-name artists, prior to release date, to favored stations, in exchange for a spot on a play list for other acts. This latter approach can be quite hazardous; slighted PDs from other stations may retaliate. However, the exclusives practice does take place, especially in major markets. KHJ in Los Angeles historically has received product "hot off the press" many hours and even days before their competitors. Record companies justify this practice saying, "If 'HJ gets on it everyone else will anyway."

Companies lacking a hot hand are forced to work harder to break their acts. Perhaps the most spectacular example of this has been the media campaigns undertaken by Bill Roberts and Martin R. Cerf at United Artists to break acts. "American Pie" by Don McLean was the biggest record of 1971. While Roberts and Cerf give McLean all credit for its success, their promotion of the record had a good deal to do with it. As Roberts indicates, "American Pie" had it in the grooves. "Without a doubt it stood out in everyone's mind . . . it was just one of those songs that stands out." In preparation, Marty Cerf wrote a letter to the rock press announcing its impending release, advising that recipients should not trade it in at Aaron's or Goody's prior to listening to the title song. This is an unusual message; the trade-in practice is openly engaged in but rarely discussed, especially in promotion copy. The dramatic effect was accomplished. At the same time a McLean recording of the song was being aired in the New York area as a public service announcement, hopefully creating a "built-in market." Tapes of the album were sent to progressive FM stations in areas where McLean was known either through his college concerts or his stint on Pete Seeger's ecology boat the *Clearwater*. His acceptance on FM radio, particularly in the Chicago area where the singer was appearing at the Quiet Night club, hastened the issuance of the album. Roberts and Cerf envisioned "American Pie" as a hit single on AM radio. There were two major barriers: the AM program director and the artist himself. "American Pie" is 8½ minutes in duration, violating the 2:37 or 3:05 minute length so popular with AM programming. The second problem was McLean's anti-record company attitude. A veteran of the *Broadside* (NYC) New York folk-protest scene. McLean was anti-establishment and Top 40 radio is, as free enterprise, as "dog-eat-dog" as any of John D. Rockefeller's early oil companies. Bill Roberts, in time, convinced Don to "go around to the radio stations and meet some people with [him]." He was never able to get McLean to explain the message of "American Pie." This problem was minor in contrast to breaking an 8 ½ minute folk song on AM radio. According to Marty Cerf, United Artists ignored many of the traditional avenues. At first they went *around* the Top 40 PD to the progressive stations, this being done with a two-week national tour of FM stations and a mailing. Also, "we didn't buy one ad. We didn't buy one T-shirt. We didn't buy one button. We went after it as straight AM product. It was a lot of money." UA allotted the largest album expenditure on "American Pie" in its history, at least $100,000. Cerf recalls, "It was the greatest success this company ever had, but had it not been it would have been the greatest expenditure in a flop we ever had." Nearly all of the money was spent on AM radio spots, again going around the program director to the people. This was all prior to releasing the shortened single version. Mike Stewart, UA president, personally ordered the field men to break it in best Jay Lasker style. "Mike would have looked bad if it bombed," said one UA employee. College radio play was arranged. All this was done *prior* to issuing the single. "It was," says Marty Cerf, "a totally planned committed promotion . . . we totally committed ourselves. We tried to develop it and sincerely tried to bring it in." Both the album and the single have sold nearly five million copies.

United Artists's media relations staff uses an interesting mix of techniques introduced at other companies as well as their own original innovations. UA's approach to program directors includes the traditional "people-to-people" game with goodwill, and Bill Roberts's attempts to indoctrinate his some 25 field people on the aesthetics of UA product. He says, "We have to turn them on to our product or they're ineffective. They're really ineffective because they'll go in and promote something else they like." As with A&M, the emphasis is first placed upon energizing the field people. If this fails, Roberts and Cerf would frequently go directly to the program or music directors, as they did with "American Pie." UA also places considerably more emphasis on the significance of media.

In the summer of 1971 United Artists introduced 7-inch scale miniatures of the 33 ⅓ album with a full-color deluxe design down to the printed dust cover. United Artists announced the miniature album saying, "It's something the radio stations have been demanding for some time . . . with new acts . . . we must find as many areas as possible to promote the groups, for PDs and DJs just simply don't have time to dredge through 45 minutes with every new act that crosses their desk." The United Artists experiment with the mini-album was fundamentally an attempt to get around the barrier of getting people into the albums. These mini-albums contain four cuts from the parent album which the United Artists staff feels are the most salable. Another technique developed by Cerf and Roberts consists of direct promotional mailings to record-store personnel, not just the dealers. Coupled with their innovations was *Phonograph Record* magazine, which unlike *Circular* and *Fluff* was a full-scale *Rolling Stone* size rock paper. All of these devices were used to reach consumers if the gatekeepers were uncooperative.

As the number of stiffs produced yearly painfully illustrates, most records fail. Not unexpectedly, much of the blame for this is placed squarely at the feet of the radio industry. Joe Smith says, "Most disk jockeys today, even program directors, they talk the same lengths, they're all doing Drake, you go across the country with very few exceptions. They're all doing 'the good guys,' boss radio. How many stations tape KHJ in this town . . . they tape them and copy them exactly." Bob Hamilton argues, "If you do not get a record on KHJ in Los Angeles, then you're sunk in the entire area."[41] Smith goes on to stress that PDs are guided strictly by charts. On promotional records, he says, "They don't play their records." Sixty-eight percent of the stations queried by *Billboard* in 1967 replied that they listened to "every record sent to them." There is little evidence to support this figure. Bill Roberts feels most stations do not review all new material. Program directors, he says, will use "any cop-out that he can use to tell you that he's not going to play the record until you break it nationally." With a gleam in his eye, Roberts tells the story of the music director who says, "That is the worst record I've ever heard," and then proceeds to throw it in the waste basket, exclaiming, "That will never be played on this radio station!" Six months later, the same record is number one nationally. This doesn't happen very often. With few exceptions, radio programmers are viewed as ranging from formula puppets to tin-eared idiots capable only of reading the Monday-morning issue of *Billboard*. Program directors frequently reply that if the record companies manufactured "decent" (hit) songs they would play them. Since the demise of "play for pay," the record companies have virtually no control over programming, but they can blame their field men for not working hard enough on product. Many home-office executives privately lament the shortcomings of the branches and their promotional staffs in the field. Some of this is buck-passing, to smooth over domestic office problems, but some charges have some validity. Interviews with touring acts frequently are messed up, as are other dealings with local press and broadcasters. A Detroit branch of a company renowned for its promotional staff frequently fouls up media relations. Primarily these difficulties stem from so-called communication breakdowns. Some blame, nonetheless, can justly be placed upon the shortcomings of individual field people.

Social distance partially accounts for the promotion representatives' vulnerability. It is easy to blame the faceless ones in the field for failures. On one occasion Jay Lasker told a promotional meeting: "Thirteen people walked in and bought *X* records in Salem, Oregon. Why isn't it getting spread?" Several promotion people, almost in one voice, have said, "You can't sell a piece of shit. You may once, but after that your reputation has had it." Certainly trust is a major factor for the promotion man's ability to deal with PDs; most of these statements are termed cop-outs, but all are based on an element of truth.

The confrontation between promotion and program director is complicated by the variable of geography. That is, *X* number of promotion people have to "turn on" *Y* number of program directors. This process of "spreading" further reverses the odds against the recording company. As one record-company executive noted, "So we turn on a PD in one station in Phoenix. It's not enough." For a record to be a hit, a sufficient number of radio stations throughout the country must get on a record. Ideally, several stations in major markets can break a record. The tremendous power of KHJ is built on the simple fact that it is a prototype for hundreds of others. Furthermore, *Billboard*'s Hot 100 is "based" upon air play in major markets. Even now heavy air play on a handful of stations will chart a record. Kal Rudman identified CKLW (Detroit), WCFL (Chicago), KJR (Seattle), WIXY (Cleveland), WTIX (New Orleans), KHJ (Los Angeles), WRKO (Boston), WPGC (Washington) and WFIL (Philadelphia) as the outlets for a successful record. Bob Hamilton feels, "Forty-two radio stations in the country sell all the records."[42] At these stations promotional people are falling all over themselves. But in this type of market each company is usually allotted 15 minutes a week to present its new product. Consequently, some companies, especially United Artists and Columbia, have taken to "surrounding" major markets by focusing upon secondary outlets. For example, to make an impact upon the Cleveland market, a record company will push a record in Cincinnati, Dayton, Columbus and other cities in the area. Columbus is especially important because many advertisers use Ohio's capital as the prototype American city. Success in Columbus is a strong promotional selling point. To succeed in spreading, a coordinated promotional drive of equal magnitude must be mounted. Each field man must accomplish his individual mission. The odds against good fortune are tremendous, especially when nonprimary cities are emphasized. Two break-outs in 25 major markets is a formidable task. Five or ten advances nationally just to move these two stations in large cities is even more unlikely, considering that secondary markets are usually guided totally by charts. The life of the under-assistant promo man is not an easy one.

Breaking a record through radio involves certain factors. Singles companies, with a lower production cost ($2,000) can afford to send more product to a larger number of radio outlets than the album companies. Albums cost more money ($15,000 to $75,000) and appeal to a much smaller number of radio-station programmers. Motivating a program director to listen to an entire album compounds the task. The only certainty for the recording company is a single or album by a superstar; however, only a handful of artists can guarantee air play; the Beatles, Beach Boys, Bob Dylan and Crosby, Stills, Nash and Young are a rarity. Consequently, the promotion departments of record companies must try to "hook" program directors with their product. The volume of records and the competition between companies renders this a difficult, if not impossible, task. The number of stiffs in the industry is a reflection of this interaction. Ideally, the superstar with a single is the best bet for success. But, as Ron Saul indicates, "albums is where the dollars are." More people spend *more* money on LPs than singles. An album by a successful rock group usually sells in the desirous neighborhood of three to five million copies. Multiply that by $5.98 or $6.98 and one can readily understand why the most profitable companies are album oriented. However, they do experience more problems than their singles competitors. Warner, rather than issuing *Gold Rush* or *Harvest*, could release 12 Neil Young singles, but Young's constituency is in the LP rather than singles market. The same is true of James Taylor, Carole King and many others. Given the difficulties of dealing with formula radio, especially the AM variety, the recording companies have attempted to open up other avenues. Warner economically assisted the growth of FM progressive radio. "Spots," *Billboard* ads and packaging innovations have all been efforts to go through or around the program director to the potential consumer. After all, the number of the game is record sales, and record companies, as Stan Cornyn told us, are the ticket sellers. Since 1965 recording companies have extended their operations to reach the public. One method appeared to be a partial return to payola, popularly called "drugola."

PAYOLA CIRCA 1973—DRUGOLA?

Paul Ackerman, testifying before the Harris subcommittee, attributed payola to "the abundance of product." By 1972, product had nearly tripled since the Clarkola days. Competition was intense. Giant conglomerates were pitted against one another in the mighty battle for a "pick" slot on a major market station. Getting "next to" the program director became increasingly difficult. Joe Smith told a 1973 *Billboard* forum "If there have been excesses [in the promotion of records] it is because this is the only way to get records played today." And in 1973 the specter of another payola scandal cast its shadow.

In 1971 Roger Karshner, a former Capitol Records vice-president, published *The Music Machine*. The 196-page book purported to tell what "really goes on" in the record industry. It received little attention. People at Capitol dismissed Karshner's portrait of the "world of payola, loyola, flyola, hype, phony charts, phony billings, and phonies" as merely a slap at the company which fired him. Other readers felt Karshner took unusual events of a seamy nature and presented them as the norm. A year later many of Karshner's charges reached a wider audience.

In his March 31, 1972, column, Washington journalist Jack Anderson announced "Payola Returns to Record Industry." Anderson charged, "We have uncovered evidence of a new payola scandal in the billion-dollar record industry. Disk jockeys and program directors across the country are provided with free vacations, prostitutes, cash, and cars as payoffs for song plugging."[43] He did not provide any specific details, except to point to the soul-music market as prime example. Record-company executives, while irritated with the columnist, shrugged off the article.

It was an open secret that soul-market conditions were identical to those of AM popular music broadcasting in the late 1950s. Small companies were pitted against the majors for air play and "play for pay" was not unheard of. The payoffs were now distributed in product rather than cash. Unmarked LPs were very easy to convert to cash; almost any record store will be happy to pay $2.00 for a top-selling album which wholesales for $3.40. Some black deejays eliminated the middleman and ran their own retail outlets, all in return for air play.

Several weeks later Anderson renewed his charge. He claimed promotion men were "buying" air play with $20 lots of marijuana. Artists were passing on pills to rock writers in return for good reviews. He concluded. "We have learned that drug-for-play promotion men buy dope in broker's lots, charging off the cost to 'routine promotion expenses.' They deal mainly in marijuana although insiders have repeatedly told us cocaine is the 'with it' drug this year in show biz."[44]

The drugola charges were not taken very seriously by industry people. One executive quipped, "We sell dope not records here." He was only half-joking. The record industry does have a tradition of drug use and abuse. Country and western singers who traveled from town to hamlet in the rural South found that pep pills made their ardous schedules more bearable. Touring swing bands reached a similar conclusion. Heroin made its way into the industry through jazz and later rhythm and blues. While not encouraged, drug use was tolerated as long as business was not affected. A burned-out artist was considered stupid, not morally weak.

The industry's identification with the youth movement of the 1960s found pot as common as booze. Many an executive could be found partaking of his rock band's lid. Pot and later other drugs became very much a part of the industry life-style. Pot, in particular, was as popular with record-company people as alcohol is at General Motors. Some underground radio programmers shared this outlook; and not uncommonly a promotion man in search of air play might offer a PD a joint or a bag. If a progressive jock was "short" a company rep might give or sell the broadcaster some "dope." A minority of people in the record industry have expanded the sociability aspect of dope sharing into an avocation. Some rock bands in Los Angeles, during a layover, may moonlight by dealing.

In typical fashion, Anderson broke the drugola story. However, his attention was distracted by charges of corruption in the Nixon administration and the Thomas Eagleton affair during the 1972 presidential election. On the heels of Anderson's revelations the Federal Communications Commission began an investigation of drugola. The Federal Bureau of Investigation and the Bureau of Narcotics were also called into the case. The FCC, bitten by the "drug lyrics" controversy (see chapter 8), was more than anxious to prove that drug use was a broadcast-industry problem.

But in spring 1973, the Watergate break-in and its subsequent White House coverup began to dominate the nation's news media. Headlines and televised hearings daily revealed new misdeeds in the executive branch of government. The

Washington Post, *New York Times* and the televised "CBS News" took the lead in exposing various aspects of the scandal. Anderson's drugola charges were all but forgotten, so it seemed.

The last week of May was dominated by stories about the firing of CBS Records's president Clive Davis. The "street rap" (the industry grapevine) had Davis behind bars for "dope dealing." On May 30, the *New York Times* confirmed the dismissal. No mention of any drug involvement was made, but CBS Records charged Davis with illegally spending $94,000.[45] The funds allegedly were spent decorating Davis's New York apartment, renting a Beverly Hills mansion and on his son's bar mitzvah. The company filed suit against its former president.

The announcement was greeted with industry-wide disbelief. One executive told *Newsweek*, "CBS doesn't sue a Clive Davis just for $90,000. They're trying to get out of something fast."[46] Similar statements abounded. A Warner Brothers spokesman said, "A company like CBS is idiotic to bust a president of one of the major profit-making divisions for a mere hundred G. They're affecting their stock, and the entire record business."[47] In *Billboard*, the newly appointed Columbia president Goddard Lieberson denied the firing had anything to do with a drug scandal.

Investigative reporters and industry insiders were not convinced. David Wynshaw, a vice-president for artist relations, was fired before Davis. Wynshaw was responsible for "getting close to people"; some called him "Dr. Feelgood." Wynshaw was summoned before the Federal Strike Force Against Organized Crime and reportedly told investigators of various payoffs to radio stations. He indicated CBS had become involved in payola about the time CBS entered the soul market two years previously with Philadelphia International Records. He also implicated Kal Rudman before the body, alleging the tipster accepted cash for reviews in his weekly paper.[48]

The *New York Times*, *Newsweek* and *New York* magazine, all highly regarded "investigatory" publications, carried running accounts of the unfolding scandal. Rona Barrett, the televised

Hollywood gossip columnist, nightly made sensational charges without much substance. Nearly all of the material was based on the unproven theory that CBS fired Davis for payola and for supplying artists and broadcasters with drugs. *Billboard* editorialized that "care" be taken as "it is still too early to ascertain how seriously the current charges of payola and other evils impugn the total industry."[49]

As during previous scandals, many record-company people, usually anonymously, took advantage of the situation to fingerpoint. David Clayton-Thomas, who had left Columbia after a contract dispute, repeated the charge that Davis was a sovereign over the company. He complained to the *Times*, "If the word went out from his office that you're on the blacklist, suddenly no one answers your phone calls. It affects your concerts, which the record company is responsible for promoting; you find yourself playing to empty houses. My royalty checks stopped coming in."[50] Others gave Davis mixed praise. He was "egocentric" but fair; he carried the company around in his back pocket. *Rolling Stone* said, "Columbia was *his* label more than he was its president." Nat Weiss, manager of a Columbia group, summed it up, "Clive had created a one-man company with press releases being written about him, and I don't think that was the best situation. But listen: We're all saddened when this kind of thing happens to any human being."[51]

The RIAA formed a committee to investigate the situation. Stories about industry links to mobsters, and more payoffs, appeared in print. Still, the main question remained unresolved: Why was Clive Davis really fired? A popular interpretation was that the record industry was a pawn in a political game. Corporate corruption could be used to draw attention away from the Watergate hearings. CBS was especially vulnerable, since the television network and the record division were under the same conglomerate logo. As such "CBS was very concerned about being involved in a scandal," said one employee.[52] It would not do to have a network that was instrumental in exposing the "White House horrors," as former

Attorney General John Mitchell called them, linked with a drug or payola scandal. Hence, the firing of Clive Davis. In light of the original comments and Davis's success, this view possessed considerable appeal. It was reinforced in a column by Nixon partisan William Safire:

> I'd like to hear Dan Rather cross examine an official of the Bureau of Narcotics and Dangerous Drugs about what is known so far, and to watch Dan Schorr on the steps of the courthouse in Newark reporting the lastest leaks from the grand jury room on the penetration of the record industry by Mafia drug peddlers.
>
> Let the journalists of CBS News cover the story of the CBS Records in depth, Mr. Paley—and after they have finished, you can take a few minutes of your own for "instant analysis."[53]

All of the references in the column were to reporters who were considered hostile to the White House. The following day the Justice Department intensified its probe of CBS Records. CBS News announced its own investigation of the drugola story. The conservative senator from New York, James Buckley, also charged that CBS may be involved in a "massive coverup." Senator John McClellan announced another probe by the staff of the Senate Copyrights Subcommittee into payola.[54]

Some six months after the firing of Clive Davis and the excessive media coverage of drugola the issue was quietly laid to rest. Senator Buckley read into the *Congressional Record* a paper titled "The Record Industry and the Drug Epidemic" which restated many old right-wing charges concerning drug songs (see chapter 8). Buckley charged that record companies were not meeting their public responsibilities by releasing such songs and allowing their artists to use drugs.

The McClellan probe did not find any evidence of widespread drugola or payola.[55] The McClellan findings, however, are not the most reassuring. The conclusions of the Senate Copyrights Subcommittee were reached on the basis of some 300 questionaires sent to record companies. Nonetheless, the drugola and payola scandal of 1973 did not blossom into the epic proportions of 1959. This result certainly adds credibility to the arguments that Watergate may have inspired the federal investigation into CBS Records.

The relationship between radio and recording will not change so long as the volume of product continues. There are simply too many records being released to receive exposure, and as a result, any "hook" is used to get close to the program director. Many of these attempts do not go beyond any common business relationship. In some gray areas "favors" occur, ranging from an album for your cousin's birthday to a hooker at a Miami broadcasters' convention. However, as most deejays *sadly* report the lavishly warm attentions of prostitutes have not yet been bestowed upon them by any record company.

With radio remaining imponderable, the record industry has emerged since 1968 in a strong relationship with a medium of its own creation: the rock press.

Notes, Chapter 5

1. See David Manning White, "The 'Gatekeeper': A Case Study in the Selection of News," *Journalism Quarterly* 27 (Fall 1950): 383–90. Walter Gieber, "How the 'Gatekeepers' View Local Civil Liberties News," *Journalism Quarterly* 37 (Spring 1960): 199–205.
2. Martin Block, "The Case for the Disk Jockey," *Billboard Band Year Book*, September 26, 1942, p. 46.
3. Quoted in George Allen Booker, "Disk Jockey and His Impact on Teenage Musical Taste as Reflected Through a Study in Three North Florida Cities," unpublished Ph.D. thesis, Florida State University, 1968, p. 48.
4. Howard Jolly, "Popular Music: A Study in Collective Behavior," unpublished Ph.D. thesis, Stanford University, 1967, pp. 11, 25.
5. Paul M. Hirsch, "Processing Fads and Fashions: An Organization Set Analysis of Cultural Industry Systems," *American Journal of Sociology* 77 (January 1972), p. 656.

6. Julian Ravine, "Mail," *Creem* 3 (March 1972): 65.

7. Arnold Passman, *The Deejays* (New York: The Macmillan Company, 1971), p. 64.

8. George Simon, *The Big Bands* (New York: The Macmillan Company, 1967), p. 56.

9. Block, "Case for the Disk Jockey," p. 45.

10. Wallichs quoted in David Dexter, "1930–1945, Disk Jockey: Origin of the Species," *Billboard Annual Supplement*, December 27, 1969, p. 58.

11. Testimony of Norman Prescott, *Responsibilities of Broadcasting Licenses and Station Personnel*, part I. House of Representatives, 86th Congress, 1960, p. 39.

12. "A Jockey's Life," *Newsweek*, December 16, 1946, p. 72.

13. Dexter's position, while generally valid, does ignore a spate of songs popularized through the medium of television. The most noteworthy is Joan Weber's "Let Me Go Lover" featured on a *Studio One* play. Themes from several shows also reached the number one spot on the Hot 100 such as "Davy Crockett."

14. Nearly all of the press reports before and after the payola hearings stress the "mirror" thesis. Howard Miller told *Time*, "I play the things they want to hear. Unless I do, I don't have an audience, and, therefore, I have denied my station, my second integrity, an audience. And the station loses the account of my advertiser, my third integrity." "What Makes Howard Spin," *Time*, April 29, 1957, p. 50.

15. Prescott, *Responsibilities*, p. 39.

16. Testimony of Billy Parsons, part II, *Responsibilities*, pp. 1083–95.

17. Quoted in Mildred Hall, "Clark Winds Up Testimony with Stout Payola Denials," *Billboard*, May 9, 1960, p. 3.

18. "Gimme, Gimme on the Old PAYOLA," *Life*, November 23, 1959, p. 45; and testimony of Joseph Finan, part I, p. 145.

19. Testimony of Paul Ackerman, part II, *Responsibilities*, p. 904.

20. Testimony of Charles Young, part I, *Responsibilities*, pp. 203, 205.

21. Testimony of Donald Dumont, part I, *Responsibilities*, p. 532; and testimony of Harold Dinesten, *Responsibilities*, pp. 355–56.

22. June Bundy, "Payola NOT Dead Now Underground," *Billboard*, August 29, 1960, p. 1; and "Deejays Taboo Payola Probe as Bootless Political Football," *Billboard*, December 19, 1960, pp. 1, 4.

23. Bob Rolontz, "Promotion Man Back in Saddle as Payola Tide Ebbs," *Billboard*, August 8, 1960, pp. 1, 33.

24. A. Bester, "New Age of Radio," *Holiday* 33 (June 1963): 56.

25. Quoted in George S. Trow, "Money Music," *New Yorker*, December 23, 1972, p. 43.

26. Tom Donahue, "A Rotting Corpse, Stinking Up the Airways" *Rolling Stone* 2 (November 23, 1967):15.

27. Bob McClay, "Murray the K on WOR-FM (They Screwed It Up)" *Rolling Stone* 1 (November 9, 1967): 10.

28. "New Trends Alter Underground Radio," *New York Times*, January 10, 1972, p. 46.

29. Pete Fornatale, "Radio and Mediacy: A DJ Spells It Out!" *Rock*, August 28, 1972, p. 25.

30. Shaw quoted in Ben Fong-Torres, "Radio: Ups and Down in the FM Ozone," *Rolling Stone* 112 (July 6, 1972): 22, 24.

31. Patti Johnson, "WABX-FM," *Phonograph Record*, June 1971.

32. "George Wilson Propounds His Potent Programming Technique," *Billboard*, August 12, 1972, p. 20.

33. Booker, "DJ and Teenage Musical Taste," p. 79. Also see Algin Braddy King, "The Marketing of Phonograph Records In the United States: An Industry Study," Ph.D. thesis, Ohio State University, School of Business Administration, 1966, p. 172.

34. Trow, "Money Music," p. 32.

35. Quoted in Steve Reiner, "Would You Buy a Used Tip-Sheet From This Man?" *Rock*, June 7, 1972, p. 21.

36. Quoted in Ben Fong-Torres, "Bill Gavin on Top of the Pops," *Rolling Stone* 123 (December 7, 1972): 16. Several PDs are especially critical of Gavin's conferences "to better the industry." They feel all they are doing is giving away their "own broadcasting secrets to those who may one day be their competitors."

37. "Bill Drake Interview: His Early Experience and Radio's Future," *Billboard*, June 3, 1972, p. 18.

38. Richard Robinson, "The Record Company," *Crawdaddy*, August, 1972, p. 28.

39. Quoted in Paul Hirsch, *The Structure of the Popular Music Industry*, mimeographed, Ann Arbor: Survey Research Center Institute for Social Research, University of Michigan, 1970, p. 58.

40. Quoted in Trow, "Money Music," p. 43.

41. Quoted in Reiner, "Buy a Used Tip-Sheet?" p. 2.

42. Ibid., p. 21.

43. Jack Anderson, "Payola Returns to Record Industry," *New York Post*, March 31, 1972.

44. Jack Anderson, "Spinning Out A Scandal," *New York Post*, April 21, 1972.

45. Fred Ferretti, "C.B.S. Ousts an Executive and Sues Him for $94,000." *New York Times*, May 30, 1973, p. 62.

46. "The Specter of Payola '73." *Newsweek*, June 11, 973, p. 79.

47. Quoted in Ben Fong-Torres, "Clive Davis Ousted; Payola Coverup Charged," *Rolling Stone* 138 (July 5, 1973): 32.

48. Grace Lichtenstein, "Mob-Linked Conducts Get Subpoenas in Payola Case," *New York Times*, June 8, 1973, p. 23.

49. "Editorial: Care and Action." *Billboard*, June 16, 1973.

50. Quoted in Grace Lichtenstein, "Pop-Music Scandal Laid to Pursuit of Fast Money," *New York Times*, June 11, 1973, p. 63.

51. Quoted in Fong-Torres, "Bill Gavin," p. 34.

52. Ibid., p. 34.

53. William Safire, "The Drugola Scandal," *New York Times*, June 21, 1973, p. 39.

54. Fred Ferretti, "Buckley Wants Record Industry Investigated by Four U.S. Agencies," *New York Times*, June 26, 1973, pp. 1, 13.

55. Mildred Hall, "Record Cos. Deny Payola In McClellan Promotion Quiz," *Billboard*, November 3, 1973, pp. 1, 10; and Mildred Hall, "Payola Replies Show Promo $ Hike," *Billboard*, November 10, 1973, pp. 3, 14.

6.

PROZINES AND FANZINES

> Wanna see my smiling face
> On the cover of the *Rolling Stone*
> © *Eve Music, Inc.*,

> Don't follow leaders
> Watch the parking meter
> © *M. Witmark and Sons* (ASCAP)

While the promotion director of a record company is trying to get air time for his act, the publicity director competes for print space. The task of the publicity director is somewhat simpler, for packaging an entire act or even an album is easier than selling a single. Print media are much more available, although making the cover of *Rolling Stone* is considerably more difficult than getting into a mimeographed fanzine from New Haven. Indeed, the sheer volume of rock publications has raised serious questions as to their influence and the efficacy of supporting them.

The value of the rock press is a highly controversial subject among industry publicists and promotion directors. Ron Saul views it as "insurance" because "anything and everything to *expose* our product is of value." Harvey Marshak of *Rock* magazine says, "Record reviews are as important as film reviews in influencing the sale of a particular record." Tim Ferris of *Rolling Stone* believes reviews have a "strong effect on the sale of records"[1] Yet many publicists and writers do not agree with Saul's conservative insurance policy. Mike Ochs, a *Crawdaddy* writer and publicist, says, "The only thing that really sells records is radio. They're not going to go in and read a review in *Rolling Stone* and go out and buy it. They're not going to buy it blind, which is what a review is." Bob Garcia agrees: "The so-called working rock press is invalid unless it has a lot of other things going along with it . . . Nobody reads rock critics anymore except industry people, and . . . industry people don't buy records." Corb Donohue believes that most of the rock press is irresponsible and unprofessional. "They are obligated to their readers, not to the elitist group of close writer friends, to turn in reviews that are informative even if they are devastating to the act, but not to do cute reviews, not to do the sort of reviews of the lead guitar player's outfit, not to do reviews on how drunk they got." Since few writers can ever live on the income derived from their writing the rock press offers opportunities to exploit the record industry. Lew Segal tells of a Los Angeles rock writer who earned $800 in one year; the rest of his maintenance was provided by the recording companies. Chet Flippo refers to several of his colleagues who manage on $1,200. Mike Ochs explains:

> With the fringe benefits, like for all the press parties you get free food, you get free records, and so you get like 500 records in the mail. Say you're going to sell 450 of them, so you've got money coming in. There's just a lot of freebees that keep you going. The average mediocre writer just cannot make it. There's no way you can make a living off of it, because the papers don't pay that much.

The cost of servicing the rock press is a bone of contention with record-company executives. One said, "It's not the record companies' responsibility to support free-lance writers any more than it is the free-lance writer's obligation to return a good review for a free drink." Furthermore ". . . a lot of kids who turn four reviews for the [L.A.] *Free Press* suddenly feel that it is the obligation of the record industry to indulge them and entertain them. I look at it as investment and return." Bob Garcia: "I will honor a request from a kid that can't buy a Humble Pie album in Cleveland, Ohio, before I will for a second-string writer . . . because I know the kid's going to get more fun out of that record than that critic. And the critic isn't gonna do the record any good anyway." Despite these feelings many record companies do service a large number of writers with everything from free food to press parties to publicity material and, of course, review records. Capitol Records, for example, has a mailing list of nearly 600 people who receive some product. The reason for supporting writers and publications is simple: product exposure. The rock press, like progressive radio, provides an alternative medium to Top 40 programming, one more avenue to the "folks out there." Product distribution for a writer is generally, but not always, linked to the status of his publication. Lew Segal, then publicity director at Capitol, determined the amount of review material a publication is allotted on the basis of its circulation, the number of reviews per issue and the influence of the publication. *Rolling Stone*, of course, would rank high on all three criteria. *Who Put the Bomp* would qualify on the basis of influence. Regular staff people generally receive more than free-lancers but not always, for some nonaffiliated writers have more prestige than staff people. The rock press, while lacking the immediacy and experiential appeal of the audio medium, has also evolved into an important vehicle for advertising record albums. Here the cultural gatekeeper is the record reviewer, who writes analyses of long-playing records for specialty and underground publications such as *Crawdaddy*, *Rolling Stone*, *Creem*, *Phonograph Record*, *Fusion* and a legion of other smaller publications.

Record reviewing is not a new occupation. Writers in magazines addressed to the arts or to specific musical tastes such as jazz, classical, folk or polka have always pontificated on the relative merits of performances, festivals and records. During the first ten years of its existence, rock music lacked the intellectual respectability afforded these other genres. Outside of lengthy analyses of the sociocultural implications of rhythm and blues groups and rock-a-billy, most rock writing prior to the Beatles was confined to pulp fan magazines primarily concerned with the dating habits and romances of various singers and teenage idols.

THE FANZINES

Rock criticism, or what Patricia Kennedy of *Jazz and Pop* terms "musical cum-politico/socio/cultural commentary," was born in the Ivy League grid of Massachusetts in 1964 largely through the efforts of an 18-year-old Swarthmore College student, Paul Williams, who founded *Crawdaddy: The Magazine of Rock*. It was the first fanzine. A fanzine, according to Greg Shaw, is "usually the product of one person, published at his own expense and in his own house, for little or no reward above the pleasure of self-expression and writing about something he loves that is ignored in the larger press. They are read by people with the same interest. . . ."[2]

The first four issues were crudely stapled mimeographed multicolored pages distributed in the Cambridge area. Within two years *Crawdaddy* grew from these modest beginnings to a nationally distributed color slick selling 20,000 copies per issue. Most of these were over-the-counter and newsstand sales along the East Coast college circuit. The magazine boasted a modest 2,000 mail subscriptions. Record criticism in the journal was typified by a flowing literary experiential stream of consciousness. *Crawdaddy* was, as Williams once wrote, "our letter to you." The editor's reviewing style raced from a Joycian stream of consciousness to historical reporting:

> Earth Opera/Joni Mitchell are an aspect of experience, as well as the product of same; what we are today and soon is shaped by what we hear of them. And we are you and me. Our understanding of the world is daily added to, crossed out, erased, struck over, pasted together by various cyclones and breezes that blow through.[3]

Another contributor, R. Meltzer, adopted a quasi-academic style, using song titles and lyrics as footnotes in a teutonic effort to find philosophical import in the most banal subjects:

> The unit of rock significance is the whole of rock-'n'-roll, and this is not merely the result of the failure of reduction, as Hegel's unit of historical significance as all of history seems to be. Just as permissible, anyway, is Jamies' position in 'Summertime, Summertime,' which resembles Hegel's end of history, 'No studying' history.'[4]

Jon Landau and Robert Somma, on the other hand, employed more conventional journalistic and analytic techniques which predominate in record-review sections during the 1970s. Landau and Somma placed albums and performers into historical niches reminiscent of the *auteur* school of film criticism. The review would usually begin by placing the performer into some tradition, with a mention of the higher points and performers in that genre. The record under consideration would then be compared to the entire field and rated accordingly. Somma especially labeled some performers as indicative of social trends in America, thus allying himself in part with the *verte* material of Richard Goldstein.

After 19 issues the magazine was sold to Chester Anderson, formerly an editor of the San Francisco *Oracle*, and ceased to be a rock journal. The subtitle was changed to "a magazine of roll." Unlike the French *auteur* school of film criticism or the Socialist *Masses* of the 1910s, *Crawdaddy* did not develop a standard technique. Instead, it set a precedent and provided a model, but not a direction, for other publications. Meanwhile on the West Coast a "new" community in San Francisco was slowly beginning to develop a critical awareness of its music.

In 1966 Greg Shaw and David Harris founded *Mojo Navigator Rock and Roll News*. The first 12 issues were mimeographed and generally confined to the Bay Area. The magazine, with a top circulation of 1,000, ran feature articles and reviews during its short-lived two-year span. *Mojo Navigator* was the second fanzine in the United States. Landau would call this "cultism," in which passion and emotional involvement are the basic motivation for reviewing or publishing. Other fanzines are devoted to the esoterica of rock and roll, such as the history or discography of countless one-hit groups. There have been literally dozens of them with such exotic names as *King Harvest Review*, *Zoot*, *Flash*, *Tuesday After Lunch*, *IFF*, *Who Put the Bomp*, *Rockpile*, *Let's Rock and Roll*, *Stormy Weather* and *Blue Flame*. The structure of *Blue Flame*, a Chicago-based magazine, was fairly typical:

> BLUE FLAME is published by students, ages 14 through 21. That's quite a range, but we've managed to put out seventeen big issues. We find, now, however, that time is becoming scarcer, prices for printing and supplies are rising, and that we're really becoming TOO big. Letters pile in each day, and we have so little time to answer them all. We've been breaking our original promise of keeping in touch with all of our readers. Every spare moment, however, is spent behind this typewriter, or at the Chicago, Wilmette, or Evanston post offices weighing, paying, and filling out bullshit forms. Also, there's zero space left for more issues in our spacious ¼-of-a-bedroom office at 2701 Birchwood Avenue. We're bursting at the seams.[5]

Many fanzines published writers who also contributed to commercial magazines. Some featured industry advertising. Greg Shaw's *Who Put the Bomp*, although reportedly not an economic success, did have many pages of ads from record companies. *Blues Limited*, an English fanzine, also carried industry advertising due to its large subscription list. Most fanzines subsist on the basis of their meager subscription lists and the economic resources of the publisher. *Blue Flame* folded after 17 issues. Its editor, Gary Baker explained: "I made this decision after losing quite a bit of money and after two years of being tied down to a typewriter and a post office." Tom Bingham of the New York based IFF wrote a similar post mortum. "IFF died early this week," he observed:

> I'd put months and months of hard work into it, before I decided I was killing myself, both financially and physically, over the whole thing, and I finally convinced myself that it just wasn't worth it. My health hasn't been good for quite some time, but it's not any wonder, working on an MA (in math no less), teaching as a grad assistant, writing reviews and articles for close to a dozen magazines . . . and trying to put out a 50 page fanzine. Something had to go, and not wanting to put out a zine at all if it couldn't be the zine I wanted it to be, well it was either IFF or me. I really feel miserable about it, it was pretty much my life.

Bingham's remarks aptly capture the love for the music nearly all fanzine writers express. However, publishing is an expensive and time-consuming business. This fact alone accounts for the high mortality rate among fanzines.

Fanzines possess the spark and enthusiasm of writers whose love for music prompted their endless analyses and reams of prose. Prozines entered journalism with the aim of making money by applying the traditional tools of magazine editing to the popular-music field.

THE PROZINES

Richard Goldstein was the first of the prozine writers. His *Village Voice* column "Popeye" treated many artists and concerts in a descriptive *verte* fashion. But Goldstein was really a chronicler of the music scene as it existed in New York.

Cheetah, a monthly, was written for young people rather than by them. It was a well-produced slick. Articles such as Tom Nolan's "Groupies: A Story of Our Time" and Harry Shearer's "Captain Pimple Creems Fiendish Plot" dotted its pages. The articles addressed the more bizarre and sensational aspects of rock, leading one *Crawdaddy* partisan to write. "Everything read very well, but you never remember anything when you finished reading it."[6]

Following the lead of the *Voice*, other underground papers included pop-music criticism and articles in their back pages.

The first issue of the *Oracle*, then titled *P.O. Frisco*, contained a review of the Beatles' *Revolver* and the Jefferson Airplane's maiden album *Takes Off*. The unsigned reviewer praised both albums while chiding Ralph J. Gleason's handling of the Airplane's liner notes as "unfortunately little more than a Madison Avenue tooth paste commercial." After an editorial change to a totally psychedelic format the *Oracle* rarely carried record reviews except when it recommended some albums as proper for "inner space flights."

The *Los Angeles Free Press* and *Open City* ran occasional record reviews by writers such as Liza Williams, Bob Garcia, Clair Brush, Pete Senoff and Michael Ochs. All of these critics have subsequently gone on to publicity departments of major record companies. Only the *Free Press*'s spirited John Carpenter did not retire into the industry scene.

The *Berkeley Barb* featured a weekly column by Ed Denson, manager of Takoma Records and later Country Joe's road manager, dealing with weekly happenings at the Fillmore and the Jabberwock, a folk-music club. Denson, a folkie by heritage, devoted much of his column to this genre. While with Country Joe, Denson wrote a chronolog of their tours and encounters with fans, other bands and the police.

For the Bay Area music buff, Ralph J. Gleason was the only above-ground, regularly printed critic. Gleason's musical credentials were rooted in the world of jazz where he spent many years as a critic for *Downbeat* as well as the San Francisco daily. The increasing fragmentation of jazz into esoteric subgenres, the closing of the Blackhawk night club and the decline of the big bands left Gleason with only the folk music revival to fill his "On the Town" columns in the *Chronicle*. He began covering night-club appearances of pop and folk singers at the Hungry i and the Purple Onion, with occasional treatments of "Fatha" Hines and visiting jazzmen.

The pro-civil rights thrust in folk music in 1963 and 1964 found a natural ally in the former jazz critic. Gleason devoted a number of his columns and Sunday features to the Weavers, Joan Baez and especially Bob Dylan. Dylan's first West Coast appearance at the Monterey Folk Festival converted Gleason. Glowing headlines such as "Dylan Places Poetry in the Hands of Youth," "The Voice of the New Generation" and "Bob Dylan, Poet of the '60s" typified Gleason's approach to the singer. When Dylan fled the folk genre he took many followers into the rock scene. Gleason was among them. Unlike the East Coast Greenwich Village setting where white blues interpreters reigned supreme, San Francisco provided the writer with an endemic rock milieu composed in part of people who had made a similar musical transformation. The Jefferson Airplane gleaned its name from bluesman Blind Lemon Jefferson. Many local groups such as Wildflower, Quicksilver Messenger Service, Big Brother and the Holding Co. and the Warlocks, later called the Grateful Dead, specialized in folk-rock and blues. Gleason became friend, counselor, promoter and critic of the entire commercial San Francisco rock scene. In the "This World" section of the *Chronicle*, Gleason frequently did album reviews in a style reminiscent of his *Downbeat* days, pointing to the brilliant guitar work of Jerry Garcia or the improved bass playing of Phil Lesh.

By 1967 certain clear paths of popular music journalism were on the horizon. *Cheetah* and *Eye* were prozines. They were profit oriented. Some of the material consisted of play-by-play descriptive coverage. They directed the reader's attention but did not excite him. Jon Landau labeled writers for these publications as "careerists" who lacked imagination and passion for their subject matter. Indeed, he claims the cultists in time became careerists: "growing professionalism begins to contain their emotional involvement with the subject, ultimately bleeding it dry. Their inspiration recedes, the ambition expands, and we are left with another critic whose career outlasts his commitment."[7]

Crawdaddy appeared as a labor of love, flounting convention, missing publication dates, skipping issues. It was in fact an informal "open letter." Most of its early contributors were students and music freaks long before the term was popularized. Only the most dedicated fan could read through its free associational prose and science fiction without a sense of bewilderment. Neither *Crawdaddy* nor *Cheetah* fulfilled their goals, but the posture exemplified in the two journals became recurrent themes. Terms such as "fanzine" and "cultist" would be applied to *Crawdaddy*-like critics and magazines, while "prozine" and "careerist" would be indicative of the *Cheetah* approach. Somewhere between these two approaches lay the ideal emotionally motivated, technically good music criticism.

ROLLING STONE: PROZINE AND FANZINE?

Rolling Stone attempted to merge the excitement of a fanzine with good professional writing. The idea originated with Jann Wenner, a former University of California student. While at the university he wrote a rock-music column for the *Daily Californian* and went on to a brief stint as entertainment editor for *Sunday Ramparts*. In the summer of 1967 the unemployed journalist approached *Ramparts* colleague Ralph Gleason with his plan for a rock paper. Wenner recalled, "I knew we could do it right. We'd have something that was clearly needed and nobody else was doing."[8] With an investment of $7,500 and a part-time volunteer staff, *Rolling Stone* appeared in November 1967. The first run of 45,000 copies earned $1,000 from four pages of records ads. The 16-page magazine sold 6,000. The paper introduced itself to a few curious readers saying:

> You're probably wondering what we are trying to do. It's hard to say: sort of a magazine and sort of a newspaper. The name of it is ROLLING STONE, which comes from an old saying: 'A rolling stone gathers no moss.' Muddy Waters used the name for a song he wrote; The Rolling Stones' took their name from Muddy's songs, and 'Like A Rolling Stone' was the title of Bob Dylan's first rock and roll record.

> We have begun a new publication reflecting what we see are the changes in rock and roll and the changes related to rock and roll. Because the trade papers have become so inaccurate and irrelevant, and because fan magazines are an anachronism, fashioned in the mold of myth and nonsense, we hope that we have something here for the artists and the industry, and every person who 'believes in the magic that can set you free.'
>
> ROLLING STONE is not just about music, but also about the things and attitudes that the music embraces. We've been working quite hard on it and we hope you will dig it. To describe it any further would be difficult without sounding like bullshit, and bullshit is like gathering moss.

The paper was an unusual mix of the *London Times* Roman typeset and the underground press format. The opening section included news stories; feature articles on music, drugs and politics; an interview section; and finally book and record reviews. Early issues urged readers to submit articles and reviews. The *Stone*, as Wenner is quick to point out, was not an underground newspaper. It was, instead, a hybrid encompassing some of the fervor of fanzines, since some of the early contributors did come from this tradition, with a distinct leaning toward professional journalism absent in some fanzines and segments of the underground press. *Rolling Stone* did not adhere strictly to rock music; it also focused on segments of the "new culture."

Articles appeared on custom cars, the roller derby, political gatherings and films, prompting *Newsweek* to characterize its fare as "executed with news sense, style, intelligence and fervor by a young staff for whom rock is a way of life." Wenner's business tactics and philosophy that "capitalism is what allows us the incredible indulgence of this music" evoked considerable criticism.[9] Abbie Hoffman, for one, in a letter to *Rolling Stone* (October 28, 1971), accused the paper of being controlled by the Xerox Corporation. Wenner's placement of an expensive full-page ad in the *New York Times*, which concluded, "If you are a corporate executive trying to understand what is happening to youth today, you cannot be without *Rolling Stone*. . . ." and various promotional gimmicks such as free books and records with subscriptions all raised eyebrows in the "new community." The *Stone*'s relationship to the music industry and politics has inspired even more polemics. Mike Lydon, a free-lance writer, has been a vociferous critic of the music industry. In a *Newsweek* interview he charged that *Rolling Stone* had "lost the battle to be a newspaper independent . . . they're part of the industry. They're still a trade magazine."[10] This description was not without some merit in the early years when much of the publication's income was derived from music-industry advertising. By late 1970 this dependence was considerably reduced since newsstand sales, estimated at around $60,000 per month, matched the advertising revenue of the paper. Subscriptions were an added plus for the paper. With a circulation of 400,000 per issue and a "book value" $7.5 million operation, Wenner prides himself on the fact, "We've never missed a payroll, that is just being a smart businessman." The fact that Wenner is a self-admitted high-salaried executive has not endeared him or the paper to segments of the counterculture.

Wenner and *Rolling Stone* have been frequently attacked for lack of political commitment. Frank Kofsky, writer for *Jazz & Pop*, charged, "*Rolling* is the ideal vehicle for corporate-liberal ideology . . . because it is striving manfully to reduce the revolution in youth consciousness to nothing more than a handful of novel consumer tastes."[11] Closer to home, Greil Marcus, former record review editor for the *Stone*, told one journalist the paper had neglected the significant issue of the times such as the shootings of college protesters and Black Panthers. He said, "I didn't find that Jann was really interested." Wenner denies this charge, pointing to numerous stories dealing with street and campus confrontations.

John Burks, a former editor, took a more cautious stance, observing "Kent State and Cambodia have concerned more of us . . . than the latest news on Paul McCartney." This, he continued, was "the trivialization of *Rolling Stone*." To these charges Alan Rinzler, the head of *Rolling Stone*'s Straight Arrow book publishing line replies, "There's no rhetoric in *Rolling Stone*, no doctrinaire position. I know a lot of people have accused the paper of making millions off the movement, but that's just nonsense because . . . it's never made a dime. It's just out there, and it isn't exploiting anyone."[12]

For music-industry executives, *Rolling Stone* was "out there" as a barometer. Record makers in mod clothing read it as closely as *Billboard*, *Cashbox* or the *Wall Street Journal*. Texas blues guitarist Johnny Winter reportedly received a $300,000 contract from Columbia Records on the basis of an audition made possible by a story in *Rolling Stone*. A Columbia executive claims it was the curiosity factor—"who's worth that much?"—and not the praise that resulted in the signing. Quotations from laudatory reviews frequently are used in record ads. Indeed, many industry people feel that good reviews are valid only for future advertisements. Ruthann Ponnech, a former Epic Records publicist, recalled, "Their main function is to clip out for advertising. And it's through advertising and getting a record played on the radio that you really get it sold"[13]

This was especially true after the spring of 1972 when *Rolling Stone* began to withdraw from the rock music as its major staple. The presidential campaign of George McGovern further reduced an already skimpy record-review section. Jann Wenner decided that the publication should become "the *Time* magazine of youth." *Rolling Stone* began to stress the abortive McGovern run for the White House, the California Marijuana Initiative, the activities of narcotic-control agencies, Jane Fonda and some "news briefs." "It doesn't take me *as* long to read it" was a frequent comment from subscribers. The magazine was longer, but the fare was no longer geared primarily to the music fan. *Creem* began to advertise itself as "America's only rock 'n' roll magazine." The *Stone*'s Los Angeles editor, Bob Chorush, resigned in protest and was replaced by Judy Sims, a Warner Brothers publicist. The music stories began to shift to the more bizarre or to artists like

David Cassidy and Grand Funk, previously considered beneath the tastes of *Rolling Stone* readers. David Bowie, Alice Cooper and Black Sabbath received extensive coverage. In August Jon Landau mailed out his first impersonal Xeroxed letter to reviewers announcing his move to New York. Stephen Davis, a friend from Cambridge and a virtual unknown to most West Coast critics, took over as review editor. Davis maintained the writers of the Landau regime. In the August 3, 1972, issue the review format changed, presenting longer, more in-depth reviews of established artists. Only 22.5 percent of the 151 reviews printed in 1972 under Davis's editorship were of new artists. Many of these were either on blues reissues series or on jazz artists generally foreign to rock-music fans. Seventy-seven percent treated known performers. Even some "greatest hits" albums got space. In 1973 Landau returned to the record review section.

Following the Nixon landslide victory, subscribers to *Rolling Stone* received a letter announcing: "Evil, mysterious elements of our society are trying to put us out of business. Our costs have skyrocketed because of these friends." The friends turned out to be the forces of inflation plaguing the entire American press. "They charge us more for paper, for printing, for postage. Yes, postage too. To continue putting out 26 great issues a year and deliver them to your eager fingertips is costing us an arm, a leg, and possibly a few other vital organs." The reader was asked to renew prior to the expiration of his subscription. At the same time, *Life* magazine announced its dissolution. *Rolling Stone* does not appear destined to a similar fate. However, the *Stone* is no longer predominantly a music magazine. Ben Fong-Torres, one of the few original staffmen with the paper, says, "Many of us turning 30 are less enthralled with the teeny-bopper approach to music and are therefore more interested in other cultural events."[14] By the mid-1970s, *Rolling Stone*'s claim to being a music magazine was questionable. Record-industry privately grumbled about this changeover. One publicist said, "Jon Landau's doing a good job with the review section, but the rest of it." A *Stone* staffman adds privately that even the music covered is now totally conservative and tied to the *Billboard* charts. The change in emphasis certainly is not going to help the record industry's ability to reach people in secondary markets.

WE TRY HARDER

The unprecedented success of *Rolling Stone* spawned a large number of other rock magazines, many of which received industry encouragement if not actual economic support. *Crawdaddy*, under new ownership was revived in tabloid form. Many other papers such as *Circus*, *Rag*, *Rock*, *Creem*, *Phonograph Record* and *Zoo World* appeared on the scene. Nearly all fall somewhere on the continuum between the fanzine and the overt professionalism of *Rolling Stone*.

Creem is unique since it began as a platform for the Detroit John Sinclair's punk-rock. This school saw rock music as a revolutionary force; rock generated "energy," which was then transformed into sociopolitical action. Groups such as the MC 5 were presented as "killer bands" that produced loud music with exaggerated stage performances. Subtle, long-lauded "in" folk-rock and Beatles material was considered too intellectual and bourgeois. Some of the assumptions of the Sinclair school would in time reemerge in the reviewers' debate over the esthetic quality of Grand Funk Railroad, a group from the Ann Arbor-Detroit grid.

Phonograph Record magazine was originally owned by United Artists Records and uses name reviewers. The magazine was a successor to the *Liberty Record*, a promotional magazine circulated during the early 1960s. It was described as being "published in the interest of Liberty loving people," which it was, featuring ads and many "in-house" communications as sales figures, gold record presentations and a great deal of hype. Norman Winter, who later made Elton John into a star, was the *Liberty Record* editor. *Phonograph Record* is staffed by many *Rolling Stone* and *Creem* reviewers. The magazine has a circulation of over 100,000 and is distributed through radio stations in major markets such as Cleveland, St. Louis, Detroit, Los Angeles and Chicago. *Phonograph Record* editor Martin Cerf claims, "It is not a UA hype sheet. The way it helps United Artist is that we have advertising in there—exclusive advertising except for usually half a page we give to a record company we editorially feel needs exploitation and isn't getting that chance to have their product where it's seen." The only United Artists acts that receive exposure in *Phonograph Record* according to Cerf, are those that are discussed in other publications: "We get percentage of product covered in our publication that would get into any publication because when it comes time for us to have something meaningful in there then people believe it." Cerf readily admits that *Phonograph Record* was designed to get around the usual gatekeeper. With this magazine United Artists was in a position to reach both media and customer. United Artists considered it a good investment until mid-1973, when Cerf departed. *Phonograph Record* now solicits ads from all record companies. The distribution to radio stations remains the same, and the magazine's status appears secure.[15]

Music magazines are finding it increasingly difficult to turn on readers and maintain a unique identity. Nearly all of the music publications are tied to the same cover stories, tours, concerts and record reviewers. Style of presentation and quality of writing vary from paper to paper; however, in the mid-1970s content remains remarkably similar.

THE CULTURAL COMMENTATORS: THE REVIEWERS

The precise role of the record reviewer vis-à-vis the industry and readership is unclear. Robert Christgau, a *Village Voice* and *Creem* writer, sees reviewing as a "consumer convenience." An anonymous introduction to a collection of *Rolling Stone* reviews defines the reviewer as standing "between the listeners and the incredible mass of phonograph records cast forth by the music industry every month. Compared to the burdens and responsibilities of the reviewer, the work of Nader's Raiders is mere child's play . . ."[16] A record once purchased remains with the consumer, at least when the defects are esthetic rather than mechanical.

This is a highly romanticized view of the reviewer. As the prolific Lester Bangs noted, "Rock writers are absolutely expendable, unnecessary slots filled for reasons of tradition and capitalist publishing ventures." Another critic said a review in *Fusion* or *Changes* might possibly yield "37 album purchases in either a direct or indirect manner."[17] As Lester Bangs suggests, many industry people feel that reviewers "know something they don't." This is a highly dubious proposition, since a large number of "name" reviewers are in fact employed by recording companies in their publicity departments. The critic-publicist route is a well-traveled one.

The main function of record reviewers for both the industry and the audience is to expose. A review by Jon Landau motivated one reader to purchase the records and then write: "I'd heard some of those LPs he recommended before, ran out and got all the ones he cited that I hadn't heard, and he was fucking right. They are all excellent." With a few well-chosen paragraphs a reviewer can convey, at least in part, a message that would take at least 45 minutes of air play. Moreover, a review section can accommodate 20 to 30 reviews depending on the space. For the industry the review is properly another avenue by which the potential consumer can be reached, since it is earnestly believed, as Mike Gormley of Mercury Records indicates, "Once they hear him, all is well."

TO: ALL REVIEWERS

FROM: Mike Gormley
Director of Public Relations

> The fact that Paul Carney is Art Carney's son may get people interested in this artist. It may even get them to open the album to find out what a comedian's son is doing in music. But Paul's heritage is not what's going to make people keep putting "Threshold" back on the turntable again and again. His talent will do that. There's a great range to the Paul Carney LP. "Threshold" consists of many soft-rock tunes, but a couple of them even hit the middle of the road stream. He's an interesting artist with an interesting talent. "Threshold" will not be difficult to get into. Once they hear him, all is well.

To accomplish this end, record companies employ a number of gimmicks ranging from a myriad of press releases to West Coast junkets with all expenses paid. Loraine Alterman, a contributor to *Rolling Stone* estimated that in a three-week period she received 65 pieces of mail from 22 record companies and assorted flacks. "That," she noted, "makes a three-inch pile." Many reviewers are mailed anywhere from 25 to 30 albums a week. These freebees appear to serve as the main magnet attracting many writers into the reviewers' role. Marty Cerf says he is in the business "to get records." Mike Ochs hosted a late-night jazz show while at Ohio State in order to secure free records. Another writer, who preferred anonymity: "The promo stuff corrupted me in college. I have to keep writing to receive the ever-increasing number of LPs. I would go broke buying them." Some prominent critics, such as Greg Shaw, Chet Flippo, Mike Ochs and Lester Bangs, are avid collectors. In addition to these freebees, critics are gifted with numerous colored posters, and knicknacks. Stan Staaph of *Rock* magazine has received a Joe Cocker watch, harmonicas, maracas, a Jeremy Steig flute and numerous T-shirts. The overall reaction to these goodies appears to vary from recipient to recipient. Loraine Alterman considers much of her mail to be "garbage." Conversely, Staaph, Bangs and others appear delighted to be bestowed with all this material. One critic stated, "one of the nicest aspects of doing this is that it's Christmas every weekday morning. You never know what goodies the mailman may bring." Established "name" reviewers are occasionally flown out to the West Coast for a weekend convention by some company or for a gala evening being given by an act such as Hot Tuna, Three Dog Night or Creedence Clearwater Revival.

The effectiveness of all of this press agentry and gift giving is difficult to assess. Nearly all of the larger record companies participate in the ritual, negating any advantage one company might derive over another. One industry executive indicated that some reviewers will accept gratuities in exchange for a good review. This may be true, but there is precious little reported evidence. (In my nine years of music writing and reviewing I have yet to see or hear about the exchange of cash for a review.) Other corrupting influences may be more significant. The personal contact between writer and artist may in some cases influence a review. Bruce Harris, of *Cashbox*, told *Rock*, "As soon as you hear a rock critic say he hangs out a lot with so-and-so, run. The guy is not to be trusted."[18] Reviewers employed by record companies, while generally objective, can be placed in a questionable position. Geoffrey Stokes in the *Village Voice* compared the industry-reviewer relationship to a "corrupt political machine." He wrote: "Record companies hire rock writers as publicists; the same writers then publish favorable articles about their clients. And you and I, the poor slobs who buy records have no way of knowing who's on the take."[19] The dual role is rather commonplace. On the West Coast Pete Senoff, Sue Clark, Judith Sims, Mike Ochs, Claire Brush and Coleman Andrews all are or have been publicity directors at various record companies. In New York Toby Goldstein, Toby Mamis, Howard Bloom and Andy McKaie wear two hats. Most of the rock press is not terribly concerned about this conflict of interest. Toby Mamis: Some of us write about it, some of us talk others into writing about it, and some of us do both. But we're all doing the same thing. There's no conflict of interest there." A *Zoo World* writer: "It's something I keep meaning to think about, but I just haven't."[20] These dual vocations, in some instances avocations, do not appear to have major affect upon esthetic judgments, but friendships do appear to have some considerable influence in getting a reviewer's attention. Attention does not always insure a positive review of the publicist's act. Several people take the position that in many cases it is an act of kindness not to write about an album. *Rolling Stone* avoids running critical reviews, especially of a new act: "It's better simply to ignore a record like that," says Tim Ferris.[21] Friendship does work in a publicist's favor when he is aware of the tastes of various writers. "Knowing that a critic is really into an act is a great help," said one publicist. One RCA executive observed that friendships do impact upon what appears in print. "Critics write for each other," he observed, "Kind of Freudian-Skinnerian reinforcement or whatever." In all, the bias in record reviewing appears to be more structural than consciously induced.

Jon Landau believes that cultists become careerists because of the freebees: "The music critic is oppressed by records. He is surrounded by them. In fact, he may be receiving as many as a hundred in a week, all free, and all crying out for his time, energy, and interest. Whether he realizes it or not they become merchandise . . . he searches through stacks looking for something interesting, something he can love, something he can hate, something he can respond to. Because of the limited time and the unlimited volume of what lies before him, three plays of an album is a lot."[22] Another critic echoes this statement, "Say you hear a thousand records in a year, the odds are you aren't going to like very many of them because you get to know what is derivative and what isn't. The kid on the street gets off on Grand Funk. The writer just passes saying there isn't one original lick there . . . the kid gets off on it. He doesn't care." Both points are well taken. Reviewers are inundated with records and free concerts, thus minimizing their emotional involvement. In this manner cultists become careerists.

Realising this a number of review editors and, indeed, publicists appeal to the prejudices of contributors. For example, a writer known to be a strong supporter of a particular act will be given an advance copy of a record. A review editor will assign the same album or story to the writer. The odds of a bad or mechanical review in such a case is negated. "Off the record," said one nationally known writer, "X knows I'm into a performer. So he assigns me his new album. Ain't *no* way the review will be a turkey." This practice eliminates much of the careerist aspect of journalism. While certainly not the most objective forms of journalism, this assignment procedure does provide generally well-written and researched reviews. Record companies resort to other techniques to reach the music writer.

MCA Records sent out a press release in 1971 with the albums bearing the slogan "damn it, this is important, read it." MCA, then under the direction of Michelle De Garzia, released albums in staggered amounts. One press release informed the critic:

> In keeping with our policy, unofficially known as DOTP (Don't Overload the Press), PART ONE of our "FUNKY FALL" release consists of a mere hot half dozen new albums offered for your delight and delectation. PART TWO will include some equally exciting releases and you should be receiving them within a few weeks. In the meantime, it is hoped you'll *set aside a few quiet hours to allow yourself* a chance to get into the goodies comprising PART ONE.

This request, under normal conditions, would not be unreasonable. However, when one multiplies the number of competing companies making less polite demands for time, the result is predictable. Of the six albums in this mailing only John Entwistle's *Smash Your Head Against The Wall* received any critical attention. Entwistle, of course, is the bass player with The Who, a super group. Many companies such as RCA, Vanguard and Polydor expect critics to request the albums they want when they are released. Warner/Reprise, after several years of sending out 12 to 20 albums at once planned to convert its system to the check-off technique. Billie Wellington, then Warner's publicity chief, noted, "And we won't be offended if you don't request the San Sebastian Strings." Independent or "one-stop" distributors and some branches frequently circumvent company safeguards by delivering albums directly to critics. A "one-stop" I am familiar with has a bin of over 100 albums per week from which a writer can choose.

As with beleaguered program directors, the record critic is exposed to a phenomenal amount of product, making it almost impossible to give new acts a hearing. Many critics use Ron Jacobs's yardstick: if the opening cut on side one does not have a "hook," the listener forgets it. The net result is that most new acts find their records, one week after release, in Sam Goody's or Emmanuel Aaron's used record bins where they are traded or sold for "known winners." As one critic put it. "You're not gonna wanna *keep* every album by the Putnam Sisters, are you? Or even play all the cuts." Martin Cerf, announcing the release of *American Pie*, wrote, "So before you put it in your Goody's or Aaron's Record Store pile, I suggest if you don't have an opportunity to hear it, you at least hold on to it . . .' Cerf's advice in this instance was valid in that *American Pie* was one of the most esthetically successful albums of the year. A year later Capitol Records attempted a similar maneuver, sending reviewers one Bloodrock album for trading and the other (minus the jacket) for listening. Copies without the jackets were still sent on to Aaron's and Bloodrock did not receive the critical acclaim its record company desired. The explanation for this may be simply that *American Pie* would have sold regardless of the Cerf letter. However, as one UA spokesman indicated, "But then it may not have. You never know."

The number of "good" acts which escape recognition is almost impossible to estimate considering the relativity of critical judgment. One contributor to *Rolling Stone* quipped, "The number of really high-quality albums which don't get in the *Stone* is small. I can't think of but a half dozen! Over a three-year span that's not bad. Folk stuff has taken a beating. Phil Ochs may be right when he claims his stuff never gets in."

Not all observers of the *Rolling Stone* record review section would agree with this analysis, most notably Terry Knight, former manager of Grand Funk Railroad.

LET THE PEOPLE SPEAK

Early rock writing and reviewing was directed at a small group of music lovers. Their tastes were relatively similar, since most listened to the Beatles, the Rolling Stones, the Zombies and the Byrds. By 1967, bands had proliferated, and many different hyphen-rock bands existed. Critics no longer spoke for a monolithic body of fans as they had during the days of Beatlemania. Monkees fans outnumbered the older rock-music buyers, but rock critics ignored so-called teeny-bop bands like Blue Cheer and the Strawberry Alarm Clock. Any comparison of a band reviewed in *Rolling Stone* to the Monkees was a distinct "put down." Led Zeppelin, a spin-off band from the Yardbirds, muddled the distinction between the teenyboppers and the more avid Cream fans. Led Zeppelin was loud, flashy and "raunchy" in the eyes of most critics. They were seen as "heavy" in the most negative respect possible. Critical judgment notwithstanding, Zeppelin was an enormous commercial success. *Rolling Stone* readers attacked John Mendelsohn's reviews of the group. One replied the analysis "was a 100% lie. Pure bullshit." A Boston broadcaster added, "If I used your record reviews as a guide to my personal record purchases, I would have the worst pile of garbage in the history of record collecting." The band itself while in Los Angeles tried to find the critic. Led Zeppelin more than any other group, introduced the distinction between popularity and quality. Other performers and fans, seeing their favorite acts ignored or panned, joined in the chorus., "What do we need critics for?" At first, much of this dissent was labeled sour grapes and ignored. The continuing fragmentation of the rock-music scene in the late sixties and the disbanding of many of the quality bands revived the issue of popular—prozine, careerist—as opposed to esthetic—fanzine, cultist—as the criteria of quality.

Terry Knight made Grand Funk the principle pawn in the controversy. Prominently displayed on a Grand Funk poster is the following newspaper clipping:

> *On Time*, Grand Funk Railroad (Capitol St–307). One of the most simplistic, talentless, one-dimensional unmusical groups of the year. The drumming guaranteed to send you up the wall. Absolutely unbelievable.

The review is from *Rolling Stone.* Another from Mike Jahn, formerly of the *New York Times*, termed the group "hideous." Also included on the poster were fan letters printed in crayon. The letters and the negative reviews clearly outlined the adolescent public to which Grand Funk appealed. Most of the rock press, until the summer of 1971, ignored the trio as best they could. Private conversations at times raised the issue of their popularity and the taste of the record-buying public. Jahn's comment that "Mussolini was popular, too" found a sympathetic hearing, but Terry Knight's success was not to be denied. After the Beatles' dissolution, Grand Funk became Capitol Records's major property, selling upwards of 10 million records. Knight's explanation for their success was "noise. Pure undiluted, ear-splitting, brain-numbing noise." Knight added. "The reviews just don't matter. Take *Rolling Stone*, for instance. Its importance is a myth. Word of mouth travels faster than their presses. . . . *Rolling Stone* means nothing to the success or failure of a record or a concert."[23]

The only prozine to follow Knight's lead and raise the touchy careerist/cultist dichotomy was *Creem*, no stranger to loud bands. Detroit, after all, was the embryo of punk-rock. Knight and his protégés were products of the area. In the June 1971 issue of *Creem*, Greil Marcus, ex-*Rolling Stone* review editor, presented a lengthy analysis of rock writing and ideology. Music is the possession of teenagers who want something of their own, he wrote, "the fact that what they've got is scorned by critics and the people they speak for can do nothing but heighten the sense of delight in being separate and self-contained, bound together by a sense of common and exclusive experience."[24] Marcus singled out Grand Funk Railroad, echoing Terry Knight's charge, "only *the* people like the group." The act, he continued, had sold ten million records in 1970 and was the "biggest group in the world" despite the fact that their material was not aired on FM or AM radio. Their records were panned or ignored by the rock press, and many older rock fans were either unaware or contemptuous of them. Marcus went on to challenge the sociopolitical assumptions of rock, arguing that the music essentially is "noise, fun and sound." Much of the article was a repeat of Knight's charges, but the speaker was a highly respected member of the rock fraternity and could not be easily ignored, especially since his departure left *Rolling Stone* with numerous internal conflicts, personnel changes and "commercial excesses." In *Creem* Marcus found a sympathetic audience, which saw *Rolling Stone* as establishmentarian and Detroit as more "energized" and grass roots than other cities. One *Cream* reviewer, Richard Pinkston IV, saw this article as vindication: "How come when I said all the things that Greil Marcus said . . . everybody laughed and called me a punk kid?"[25] Donny Osmond of the Osmond Brothers, a bubblegum group, entered the fray in a letter to the *Village Voice*. Osmond contended that the time had come "for old rock critics to quit knocking the music people my age [14] like." In a defense of Black Sabbath, a group quite similar to Grand Funk Railroad, Osmond charged that critic Bob Christgau was of another generation and did not understand the new sounds.

> Your column probably started long before I was ever a teenager. The Kennedys, the Movement, hippies, San Francisco, and so on —a lot of hopeful myths turned sour were all dismal failures by the time I was old enough to get stoned and buy records. . . . Watch out, Bob, admit you don't understand our music and con-

> centrate on yours. Otherwise you'll sound like those old '50s jazz writers who used to try to analyze the Beatles.[26]

Creem, unlike the Stone, still requested submissions and reviews from readers urging, "Nobody who writes for this rag's got anything you ain't got." David Marsh, the editor of *Creem*, concurred by suggesting the magazine had ignored "people who are really significant" since there was a "whole new audience and the rock 'n' roll writer suddenly finds that he's the one freezin'." Furthermore, "TEENAGE would seem to me to be one definition of rock'n' roll, in the first place."[27] The essay outlined the position taken by Woody Guthrie, "you can't write about a whorehouse unless you been in one."

Patricia Kennedy lamented this trend. Writing in *Rock* magazine, she entitled her article "The Decline and Fall of Intelligent Rock Journalism." In the dissent she took note of the esthetic debate: "The criticism fell off to the point where today [c. 1971] rock writers (there are probably no real critics anymore) find themselves justifying a horror like Grand Funk Railroad for the sole reason that if so many kids like Grand Funk there must be something there. Pigswill."[28] Jon Landau, several months later, acknowledged the critic was being polluted by his role because he doesn't "live with the record; he only plays it." The role of critic has built-in elements of careerism. However, Landau contends that these conditions can be overcome if the writer is commited to music. "Commitment is the prerequisite of all valuable criticism," he says. *Honolulu Star Bulletin* critic Don Weller, in part, takes issue with the Landau formulation of the rock reviewer as careerist. He writes, "Critics of course cannot do their job and remain a 'cultist.' That's because whether they realize it (or desire it) or not, they are by occupational definition, an elite." He continues, "The critic is a neurotic antenna, not an enthusiastic fan. He discriminates more than the fan. He thinks more. He knows more. He feels differently about music. And, there is nothing wrong about that, nothing to put the critic down for. Because the critic, as a member of a special elite, has special functions attached to his job." Weller's point is not without support. Many critics do, in fact, feel, as does much of the press, that their knowledge is objectively superior to that of the everyday music fan. However, there is a good deal of dissent as to whether this accumulated expertise is careerism or transcendental vision. "I get turned on by one in fifty albums," wrote another critic, "but that's the one I write about. But then record reviewing is an avocation not my profession."

The tone of this discussion underlines the nebulous nature of the role of the record reviewer. He is expected to be a cultist representative of a specific taste public, yet Terry Knight accuses all reviewers of being insensitive to Grand Funk Railroad. In one interview Knight acknowledged that his complaints regarding critics were publicity-getting devices: "We've baited the press, and I'll be the first to admit it." Now that this group had reached the stardom he added, "We don't need the press today to make Grand Funk more popular." The assumption that one group popular with adolescents personified all of pop in a given genre in the 1970s is difficult to accept considering the varieties of hyphen-rock available. Knight's charges, however, do have merit, a point Landau by implication concedes. Grand Funk is a totally experiential unit with few, if any, pretentions. Minus its symbolism as targets of an establishment elitist press, Grand Funk, would probably not have surpassed Knight's first group, the Pack, which failed dismally. Knight admitted that *Rolling Stone*'s antipathy "made them rebels. If Grand Funk could overcome it all, they [adolescents] could, too. It offered the kids a hope and an escape." The difficulty lies in the fact that most critics are no longer 16-year-olds in need of escape and rebellion. Reviewing practices are greatly influenced by the taste preferences of reviewers as well as the mechanics of putting together a review section.

WHAT GETS REVIEWED

In 1971 *Rolling Stone* covered 410 albums in its review section. Twenty-four writers with six or more reviews accounted

Exhibit 6.1

ROLLING STONE AND CREEM REVIEWS—1971

	Rolling Stone	*Creem*
No. of reviews	410	175
Reviews of established artists	295 (71.9 %)	128 (73.1 %)
Reviews of new and esoteric acts	115	47
Regular or "house" reviews	322 (78.8 %)	130 (74.3%)

for 78.8 percent of the section; five writers did 31.2 percent of the anaysis. *Creem*, which evokes an image of being closer to their readers by requesting submissions from them, has 18 regular reviewers who write up 74.3 percent of the albums. When occasional contributors to *Rolling Stone*, who also appear in *Creem*, are added to this list, then 82.3 percent of the LPs are covered by professional reviewers, musicians, students, teachers, street people, academics or record-company publicists. Record reviewers make only a small part of their living from the craft of writing; each *Rolling Stone* review is worth only around $15 to the free-lance writer. Frequent appearances in the "Records" section do reap him other rewards such as junketing to the West Coast and employment opportunities in the industry. Volume is especially important for the less-established writers. One might expect that the high number of reviews would give more new acts exposure. But 1971 record reviews in *Rolling Stone* and *Creem* indicate this is not the case: over 70 percent of the published LP reviews in both papers concerned established artists, except when the unit was a spin-off from a previous name unit such as Nils Lofgren, a former member of Crazy Horse. *Creem* relies even more on established units than does *Rolling Stone*. A canon for reviewers is, "lesser acts are the first to go when space is a problem."

As in radio, the editors of rock publications are faced with the constant barrage of product as well as reviews. With the tight economic situation facing the rock and underground press, competition for space has intensified. Marty Cerf, the editor of *Phonograph Record*, receives approximaty 100 performance and record reviews a month, of which less than 20 percent are actually published. Inclusion hinges on four variables, "not necessarily in order of importance." The first consideration is the writer. Lester Bangs or John Mendelsohn take precedence over most other writers. Record label becomes another criterion; company with a large amount of product cannot hope to have it all reviewed, even if it is of exceptional quality. This obviously works against Warner and Columbia, which release 20 to 30 albums per month. Geography and the performer being reviewed are also important. Balance in print, like pacing in radio, are built-in hurdles over which the critic has little or no control. The editor knows that a large number of reviews is obviously less important than advertising or feature articles which have newsstand appeal. Given the time pressure for reviews, the elimination of one due to space considerations does not auger well for its future inclusion. Because writers want to get their material published, the pressure is toward the safer, more salable topics. A writer without a regular list of publications may well find himself off the record companies' "freebee" list. As one publicist indicated: "You're only important as long as you have a byline and soon as you lose it you're off my 'A' list and we'll still be friends, but you're no longer important."

For the rock writer, the editor of his magazine is the chief gatekeeper who determines his fate in the profession. Despite the safety of doing "name" acts, established critics are most likely to give exposure to newcomers than are amateur writers. This is undoubtedly due to the faith editors have in their contributors. Despite the credo of "letting the people speak," then, regular reviewers are more inclined to write up new acts. (30.7 percent in *Rolling Stone*), than are amateur or occasional contributors (18.1 percent). In 28.7 percent of *Creem* reviews new acts were written up by regulars as opposed to

22.2 percent for "one-shot" reviewers. This, of course, negates the recording-industry executive's desire to expose his developing products.

The contraction of review space, and the exhaustion of so-called superstars and those with long, easily salable history, will no doubt make a published review all the more important until other avenues of exposure are found. As one Canadian Warner/Reprise field man quipped, observing the flamboyant Tiny Tim in 1968, "We'll be here long after he's gone." In the short run, he was quite correct. Nonetheless, a lack of good material will in time do considerable harm to the rock press. In 1973, the financial health of this medium was not good. Martin Cerf observed that "America's monthly rock rags are all hanging' on by the skin of their teeth." The so-called dog days also find a segment of the industry re-evaluating the value of the rock press as an exposure medium. Michael Ochs, who has been on both sides, observes, "You can't prove that a good article will sell more records or won't. I maintain that publicity is really not valid anymore. It used to be a joke that if you got a good review in *Rolling Stone* that was bad news because that meant it would't sell." Ochs continues, "The record-buying public hates the critics because the critics are trying to play rock star. They're trying to say, I am equal to them. And when you're a writer, you do express yourself. You do use your own ego over who you're supposed to be doing. That always happens. The critics have become so sticky." Only a small specialty label, Arhoolie, has actually taken to minimizing its assault upon critics. On January 25, 1973, Chris Strachwitz informed reviewers and deejays: "This drastic measure of dropping many names from our active mailing list has been made necessary by the fact our sales in the U.S. dropped this past year despite the fact we sent out an unprecedented number of promotional copies on all our new releases in 1972. So apparently promo copies really don't do much good! But perhaps more accurately stated, they only do good in the *right* hands and so we shall try to cut our mailing list to just the *right* people who apparently do enjoy more ethnic music and will give us help in promoting Arhoolie Records." Other record companies in late 1973 followed Arhoolie's lead in cutting their review lists. These actions were prompted by the so-called vinyl crisis. ABC-Dunhill, MCA and several others severely trimmed their reviewers lists. CBS, Atlantic and RCA resorted to the "by request only" system. Despite these problems, as long as the marketing of popular music remains, in the industry view, one of alchemy and rabbit feet, any beacon is better than none. The overall effectiveness of record reviewers, outside of their entertainment function, is perhaps best summed up by one practitioner: "As long as promo people get their tear sheets [clippings of reviews] everybody is happy, *except* for those who make the record that is not reviewed." Or as Barbara DeWitt at United Artist states, "Tear sheets . . . are after all the lifeblood of any reviewer's service."

ROCK WRITERS OF THE WORLD: FAN, JOURNALIST OR UNIONIST?

The confused role of the rock writer in 1973 was best highlighted by a very ambitious event billed prematurely as the First Annual National Association of Rock Writers Convention, held in Memphis.[29]

During the first week of May, nearly 200 popular music writers received invitations to attend a convention in Memphis during the Memorial Day weekend. Writers were selected from the United States and England. The announced purpose of the gathering was to create "an organization to provide improved communications with an increased cooperation among writers and all other segments of the music industry, as well as to enhance the professional standing of the rock journalist." The letter was signed by John S. King.

The plan for such a convention was born in a cradle of self-interest, which in time fragmented in a number of directions. John S. King, a kindly publicist for Stax Records, attempted to promote an English band, Skin Alley, under contract to his label. Other organizers—such as Greg Shaw of

Phonograph Record and Jon Tiven, a 17-year-old Yale underclassman and fanzine publisher—wished to have an organization that would enhance the income and status of rock writers. Most of the other writers, being more skeptical, came to meet people and have a good time. A handful of labels sent representatives and opened hospitality suites to entice wandering writers to have a beer, listen to a record or just get on the product mailing lists. None of these facts was known until after the 140 writers arrived in Memphis.

On May 24 rock journalists boarded jets to junket to Memphis. They were greeted at the half-constructed Memphis airport by Jon Tiven and several other people, Stax employees, who had erected a card table near the baggage counter.

A chauffer-driven black Cadillac limousine was provided to drive the journalist VIPs to the Rivermont. Writers with experience at the ABC-Dunhill, Grunt and Warner junkets no doubt became suspicious. At the hotel, the writer was greeted by a long table commanded by three hostesses who registered the participant and handed the newly arrived journalist a parcel of passes to the scheduled events and the usual promo albums and sample copies of various music magazines. Most of the review material came from local southern labels. John S. King was quick to admit that Stax was sponsoring the meeting "for this year only." Toby Goldstein of *Rock* magazine estimated the affair had cost Stax approximately $40,000. Greg Shaw later observed that this was correct and really quite reasonable in light of the famous Grunt label one-nighter that cost a reported $100,000.

The opening-night cocktail party found writers floating from group to group comparing interviews and bylines. Nearly everyone had spent an evening with Jerry Lee Lewis. There was more "hype" of individual publications than records. *Creem* distributed T-shirts. Esoteric fanzines such as *Nix and Pix*, *Easy Access*, *Punk* and others were circulated. Discussion generally turned to the health report of a given publication or record company. New fanzine publishers repeatedly asked, "How do you get on their list?" "Who do you know at . . .?" What emerged from these informal discussions was a definite mood of hostility between writer and industry and in several cases critic and magazine. Many complaints were lodged against the publishing giant, *Rolling Stone*, which did not consider the meeting worthy of its attention. Only Chet Flippo attended, and he was covering the meetings for the journalism magazine *More*. The indictment against *Rolling Stone* was both long and passionate. "You sent them a piece" and they return it in six months. "You can't sell it to them" was a repeated complaint. "He (referring to Stephen Davis) accepts a review and then doesn't publish it." The believed domination of the review section by Boston writers also evoked considerable comment, all of it negative. Jann Wenner was frequently pictured as a "rip-off." One reviewer noted, "With a subscription list of 300,000 and $3,000 a page advertising he could pay more than $20.00 for a review."

The industry's attitude toward the writers was not one of awe. A representative of Polydor Records said, "We weren't quite sure how to handle this." Another publicist said his attendance was a "last-minute decision." "Some of the others were coming," he said, "so we figured we'd better." Only a handful of companies actively courted the writers. MCA, Blue Thumb, Polydor, London and, of course, Stax had formal suites. Columbia, Motown, Mercury and A&M sent representatives. Marty Cerf and Greg Shaw, both of United Artists, emphasized, "We're here to represent *Phonograph Record*." Cerf and United Artists were in the process of parting company. Capitol, ABC-Dunhill and Warner/Reprise, a company that stresses its media relations, ignored the conference.

The evening cocktail hour was an auger of things to come. It ran beyond its alloted 60 minutes. A 1965 rock film, *Tami*, with the Rolling Stones, Jan and Dean and James Brown played through a tinny sound system. Following the poor showing, some writers aimlessly moved from floor to floor in search of open hospitality suites. Their major concern was finding a publicist or "industry person" who would supply the next day's free breakfast.

John S. King opened the morning (and only officially scheduled) business meeting. "Our hype," he said, was to expose Stax acts on Saturday night. He continued, "it is your meeting." The purpose of meetings was to free the writers because they "wouldn't have to be dependent on the industry." This last sentence was a call to arms which resounded during the entire hour-long meeting. Jon Tiven followed, issuing a series of proposals. "Some form of organization," he pleaded, "should be formed as soon as possible." This body would guarantee participants "more money and status." The organization would publish a directory of writers which would be financed by selling ads to the record companies. Both King and Tiven stressed the "strength in unity" theme, presenting the giant conglomerates as being very susceptible to organized pressure. Richard Meltzer, from the floor, indicted the companies on two themes. "Magazines," he said, "do not pay the writers." The record companies were no less culpable for they "drop you from their lists." Meltzer, a veteran writer, was very bitter about the treatment he received from *Rolling Stone* and Atlantic Records over a Jackson Browne article. As a result of the piece, reportedly, Meltzer was dropped from several promotion lists.

A number of writers supported these universal complaints. Many regional rock papers do not, in fact, pay contributors. *Fusion* was frequently mentioned in this context. The promotion lists, a source of income for most writers, are in fact capricious, dependent upon personnel changes and other seemingly inexplicable factors. The feeling of rock journalists against both record companies and their immediate employers was not without merit. Favorable reviews of an artist or album—called money reviews—are quoted in trade and popular ads. The writer of the review rarely receives any "bucks" or compensation for the reprints. The magazine and company, of course, benefit. Other writers felt considerable unhappiness over the 200-to 500-word (dollar a word) liner note fees paid to "prominent" deejays for nonreviews. Meltzer's plight was a reminder. At this point the desire of those at the meeting was to establish a union or guild strong enough to influence record companies and publishers.

Greg Shaw, a talented writer, underlined the plight of the individual rock writers. "Record companies don't believe in the rock press anymore," he said, "We are all parasites of the record companies . . . we exist off of them." Discussing magazines (Greg is a co-editor of *Phonograph Record*) he added, "publishers rip you off." The solution was to organize.

Meltzer, apparently half-joking, suggested that record companies should pay for record reviews—more for good ones. "Payola or salary—it's all money." A surprising aspect of both Tiven and Meltzer's arguments was the notion that the record companies act as the agents of the writers against the rock magazines. For some, this was worse than a company union. It was asking the president of General Motors to represent the auto workers against the foremen and his own company.

The suggestion is not quite as naive as it sounds. Few reporters have the power to intimidate any editor or newspaper owner. The rock press is powerless without the advertising dollar of the recording companies. Rock writers feel they have power over the advertisers. It was over this issue that the debate was drawn. Various speakers rose to speak pro or con. Those in favor of Meltzer's argument generally urged that an organization be formed that would have the power to strike and boycott publisher, record company and any other wrongdoers. Dissenters argued that writers even in an organization were powerless against *Rolling Stone* or the majors. Vince Aletti discounted the strike as a weapon. "They can always get someone else." Connie Heckter, the owner of a successful Minneapolis entertainment magazine, *Insider*, scolded the assembled writers for not being "valid" to the industry because of the type of writing being done. Anyone, he claimed, could "sit on their ass and do a record review." With justification, critics were visibly upset and angry. Because of his rhetoric, Heckter's point was totally missed or not accepted. "We are very necessary to companies," shouted Tiven.

Ironically, Greg Shaw, in attempting to clam the discussion, only underlined the Minneapolis publisher's statement. "I'm a fan not a writer," he said. Shaw went on to urge a step back. He advocated a loose organization with undefined goals. Such an amorphous organization was quickly approved by those in attendance. The fan-journalist debate resumed.

Al Levy, then of *Record World*, a trade magazine, who also had experience as a Polydor publicist, presented a strong rebuttal. "Publicity departments," he said, "get yelled at no matter what they do. Writers do not make or break acts. That's absurd. Civilians—the people—make acts, not us. We are children of affluence. The record companies have us by the balls." He went on, "We perform a service. A kind of luxury service." Pointing at John S. King, Levy finished, "He paid for this whole thing." Few denied this last point. Stax was bankrolling the entire affair. Food and drink were being supplied by several companies. Even the writing pads issued for the meeting bore the inscription, COMPLIMENTS OF MCA RECORDS, INC. The T-shirts worn by most of the participants were publicity freebees. Greg Shaw closed the gathering announcing the tour to the Schlitz brewery was about to leave, but urged that another be held at 4:00 that afternoon after the Stax Record barbecue. Ironically, the afternoon meeting did not take place because Shaw did not appear. One stood-up writer, walking to the MCA hospitality suite, said, "It's going to be a party."

That evening, while cruising upon the Mississippi in a riverboat, the writers were informed of a new business meeting to be held again at 10:00 A.M. The tone of the second gathering was less optimistic. Levy's points and, especially, the no-show "4:00 meeting" took their toll. Shaw, realizing the mood, scolded the audience for the general apathy of the participants. He no longer felt as confident and echoed the feelings of many in attendance. Indeed, Shaw became the subject of considerable discussion. "What is UA getting out of this?" queried one writer. Others mused about Shaw's dual affiliation with the record company, a paying rock paper and his sponsorship of the organization. During the nominations for a governing board this concern was made evident by Chet Flippo, who made a highly applauded motion, "No record-company employees could sit on the board."

The organization now was seen as a very loose pressure group or "united front against those screwing us." Shaw requested that people volunteer to run for a five-member governing body. Less than one-fifth of those attending volunteered. Writers were then elected on the basis of region: New York, Los Angeles and London were to have two representatives; Boston, Florida and Detroit got one. Another committee was set up to advise the board; this committee, again based on volunteers, found seven hearty souls willing to serve. Tiven and Shaw were among them. With all this business completed, one task remained—choosing a name. Karen Berg offered Rock Writers of the World (RWW), which was accepted. "It's our trip," mused one correspondent. By this point the credibility of the entire affair was strained to the breaking point. Jon Tiven's suggestion that rock bands—including his—be recruited to give benefit concerts for the rock press struck many writers as silly. "He's never paid for anything in his life," remarked a New York critic.

After the meeting, journalists scattered to free luncheons and record-searching expeditions. The Stax hype of the evening was appreciated, but not terribly exciting. One writer was heard to say, "I wanted to like them for King's sake. He really tried."

The first annual Rivermont convention of the Rock Writers of the World emphasized the nebulous relationship of the rock press to the recording companies. The record companies, while denying the validity of the press, nonetheless continue to provide much of its substance. Writers were housed and fed for four days to the tune of $40,000. The press is very much aware of this. Their conglomerate suitors do in fact court and pamper them. All the while, publicity directors decry the ineffectiveness of the same press. Perhaps they are a "corporate luxury," as Al Levy suggested. Nonetheless, as long as the "crapshooting" philosophy of the industry persists there will no doubt be a second Rock Writers of the World convention.

Record reviewing in the rock genre began as a cultist or fanzine operation. The legitimation and success of the rock press, as exemplified by *Rolling Stone*, has transformed this function into a specialized skill. In the transformation the review procedure as well as the end product have been changed. The values of observers, however, have in some cases remained the same. Greil Marcus aptly summed it: "Rock should be fun." Record reviewing does contain some of this euphoria, but it is also part of a capitalist enterprise, again underlining the fine thin line between art and finance.

This line has always existed in the record business, but never was it as pronounced as during the last years of the 1960s. Rock became symbolic of generational conflict and what was then believed the birth of a new culture, one in opposition to corporate America. Popular music, especially rock music, became a pawn in this battle. Record companies attempted to identify with the "new culture," much to the dismay of those who saw Columbia and Capitol Records as little more than "rip-off" artists. The conflict between the "street" and the industry, while short-lived, aptly illustrates the record company's inability to control its markets and consumers.

Notes, Chapter 6

1. Marshak and Ferris, quoted in Tom Seligson, "The Media: From Groups to Groupies," *Crawdaddy*, August 1972, p. 38.

2. Greg Shaw, "The Real Rock 'n' Roll Underground—Fanzines," *Creem* 3 (June 1971): 24.

3. Paul Williams, "The Way We Are Today: Earth Opera and Joni Mitchell," *Crawdaddy*, August 17, 1968, p. 26.

4. Richard Meltzer, "Aesthetics of Rock," J. Eisen, ed., *Age of Rock*, vol. 1 (New York: Vintage Press, 1969), pp. 224–53.

5. "Deflamation," *Blue Flame* 17–18: 3.

6. Jon Landau, "Rock and Roll Music," *Rolling Stone* 77 (March 4, 1971): 50.

7. Jon Landau, "Performance," *Rolling Stone* 94 (October 28, 1971): 56.

8. Quoted in "Rocking the News," *Newsweek*, April 28, 1969, p. 90

9. Quoted in "Rolling Stone Rock World," *Time*, April 25, 1969, p. 78.

10. Quoted in "Rocking the News" p. 90.

11. Frank Kofsky, "The Scene," *Jazz and Pop* 8 (June 1969): 31.

12. Quoted from Jane Wilson, "Communicating Via Arrow," *Los Angeles Times West* (Magazine section), November 22, 1970, pp. 37–45.

13. Quoted in Seligson, "The Media," p. 38.

14. Quoted in "Gathering No Moss," *Newsweek*, March 18, 1974, p. 68.

15. On magazine distribution see "*Zoo World* Locked To 70 Radio Stations," *Billboard*, March 23, 1974, pp. F–37.

16. *Rolling Stone Record Reviews* (New York: Pocket Books, 1971), pp. 3–4.

17. "Sam Swanson" (pseudonym), "A Sam Goody's Discography," *Who Put The Bomp* 7 (Summer 1971): 23–26. Also, see Lester Bangs, "Free Form Music in San Francisco," *Phonograph Record*, November 1971.

18. Quoted in Patricia Kennedy, "The Decline and Fall of Intelligent Rock Journalism," *Rock*, December 20, 1971, p. 28.

19. Geoffrey Stokes, "Nothing But the 'Nice Truth', " *Village Voice*, January 24, 1974, p. 67.

20. Quotes from Ibid.

21. Quoted in Seligson, "The Media," p. 38.

22. Jon Landau, "Performance," p. 56.

23. W. Stewart Pinkerton, Jr., "Grand Funk Railroad is No Penn Central: It Makes Noise, Money," *Wall Street Journal*, June 15, 1971, p. 1 and Robert Hilburn, "Grand Funk Rock's Newest Phenomenon," *Los Angeles Times* (Calender Section), February 21, 1971, p. 1.

24. Greil Marcus, "Rock A-Hula Clarified," *Creem* 3 (June 1971): 42.

25. Richard Pinkston IV, "Mail," *Creem* 3 (September 1971): 4.
26. Donald Osmond, "Letter to the Editor," *Village Voice*, December 14, 1971, p. 22.
27. David Marsh, "Looney Tunes," *Creem* 3 (October 1971): 24–25.
28. Kennedy, "Decline and Fall," p. 13.
29. For a similar but more detailed account see Chester W. Flippo, "Rock Journalism and *Rolling Stone*" M.A. thesis, University of Texas at Austin, May 1974.

7.

"THE STREET," JOHN SINCLAIR AND THE INDUSTRY

> And the words of the prophets
> Are written on the subway walls
> © *Eclectic Music Co., BMI*

Popular music is subjected to a plethora of interpretations placed upon it by a myriad of taste publics, each marching to the beat of a different drum. A. J. Weberman's original claim that Dylan's later poems were in fact admissions of heroin addiction or David A. Noebel's perception of the Beatles as Communist agents are but two overt manifestations. Beauty, deviance and musical worth do, in fact, exist in the eye of the beholder. Each social group applies its particular brand of common sense upon reality. They may, however disagree with each other. Some visions of social reality are more widespread than others. The belief that music is primarily for pleasure and entertainment is dominant, but some people interpret music through eyeglasses colored by political and cultural assumptions. For the latter groups and publics the influence and impact of music are paramount.

Music may be a "cry for justice" in the Marxist sense. Writers in John Birch Society publications find that popular music "corrupts" the young. Other pamphleteers and social observers may see popular music as the social glue of a new culture based on Consciousness III or Trans-Love Energy. Yet others, such as art historian Carl Belz, may view popular music as emergent form of high art. All of these points of view bring to popular music new dimensions and interpretations. In the early days of the MC 5, then managed by John Sinclair, Grande Ballroom concerts were designed to transmit energy and encourage audience-performer interaction. The affairs did, indeed, produce some of the desired effects considering the mutual expectations, but for the uncommited, what transpired at the ballroom was just an unusually loud rock concert. The impact of political ideology upon popular music has generally been confined to the pages of the radical press. During the 1930s, the *Daily Worker* presented Tin Pan Alley as the purveyor of "false class consciousness," charges which found little support among people not on the subscription list of the *Worker*. Activists generally ignored popular music as either "kid stuff" or background noise until the 1960s, and for several years thereafter a debate raged over popular music and its role in society. Slogans such as "rock revolution" rang out. The industry unsuccessfully attempted, at least in print, to identify with this sentiment. Columbia's infamous "Don't Let the Man Bust *Our* Music" is but one example of this manipulation of imagery. Street people and political activists were not convinced, and a series of skirmishes between the industry and the alternative culture occurred. These encounters explicated the fundamental cleavage between the "bottom line" interests of the companies and those of their consumers.

THE STREET PEOPLE

The 1950s have been portrayed as the decade wherein ideology ended and a generation of students became silent. The following decade was its antithesis. John F. Kennedy was elected to the presidency on the slogan of "a new frontier." While a political cliché for many people, especially the young and minority group members, it held a germ of possibility. The fact that Kennedy was never able to actualize his new frontier only enhanced his memory. The 1960s witnessed a dedication to a search for many new vistas and horizons, few of which were found. Many prophets appeared to suggest new avenues to political equality, justice, self-consciousness and changing one's lifestyle.

There is little point in reviewing the political-ideological turmoils of the early 1960s. Few readers will be unfamiliar with the freedom rides and sit-ins by blacks and whites in the black belt of the South, or with the rise of Black Power in 1966. With Berkeley's Free Speech movement and the San Francisco hippie phenomenon emerged a *zeitgeist* of the turbulent decade. Part of this *zeitgeist* employed traditional political ideologies, particularly those associated with the utopian Socialists and other communitarian movements. Predictably, the upholders of tradition reacted with their usual arguments against the advocates of social change. In the midst of all of this social confusion, popular music began to attract considerable attention (and controversy) as a catalyst of change. Heated exchanges about popular music began to appear in print, all of which hinged upon similar assumptions, regardless of ideological coloration.

Both the radical right and segments of the New Left portrayed rock music as a useful tool for revolutionary activity. John Sinclair of the White Panther party and right-wing lecturer Dr. Joseph Crowe found themselves echoing each other, both arguing rock has psychopolitical effects upon the unconscious minds of youthful audiences. Only their evaluation of the desirability of the outcomes separate them. Because of the loose and spontaneous nature of much writing on the sociopolitical impact of music during the 1960s, it is difficult to present a nice, neat, clear-cut typology or continuum of ideological perceptions.

The "street" is the alternative life-style so widely publicized during the late 1960s. Theodore Roszak characterized this life-style as a counterculture in opposition to the dominant one. This group was young, white, middle class, Protestant or Jewish. Charles Reich described carriers of Consciousness III who for a few years will "pulse to music, know beaches and the sea, value what is raunchy, wear clothes that express their bodies, flare against authority, seek new experience, know how to play, laugh, and feel, and cherish one another."[1] To which he might have added "smoke" and in some cases "take dope." Both chroniclers of the new life-style made popular music its focus. Academician Theodore Roszak's approach to popular music was not overly enthusiastic. He acknowledged the vital role it played in the lives of young people; he found its potential for molding a counterculture questionable. He admitted: "I find this music difficult to take. . . . I fear I tend to find much of it too brutally loud and/or electronically gimmicked up . . . the pop music scene lends itself to a great deal of commercial sensationalizing: the heated search for startling new tricks and shocks."[2] This is in the traditional "opiate of the masses" posture taken by those who opposed the advent of folk-rock and, indeed, criticized the Beatles as political opportunists. Phil Ochs, once a major proponent of protest songs, had outlined a similar sentiment in the liner notes for a Jim and Jean album some four years earlier: "Many grew their hair down to their wallets and jumped on the Beatle bandwagon in true hands-across-the-sea spirit. Palms upward as usual . . . discotheques spread like fungus. Many were moved to proclaim a new era of culture for the masses."[3] Prior to his metamorphosis in Hollywood, Ochs violently opposed the "overwhelming blare of drugged speakers." The Left's position on rock music was not totally negative. John Sinclair interpreted rock music as the *geist* (life force) for its achievement.

Until John Lennon championed his cause, John Sinclair meant little outside the Detroit area. Abbie Hoffman, in *The Woodstock Nation*, discussed him as a *cause célèbre*, but Sinclair never became a household word. In the Detroit-Ann Arbor area, home of the University of Michigan, John Sinclair was both political guru and martyr. He was a prime catalyst in the Ann Arbor underground scene, one of the founders of the Detroit-based White Panther party and a self-styled rock promoter and manager. He served part of a ten-year sentence in a Michigan penitentiary for the possession of two marijuana cigarettes. In the music world he is best known for his early tutelage of MC 5. Sinclair, like his philosophical contemporary, Timothy Leary, is a verbose pamphleteer who has treated many subjects in rambling essays. One of his favorite themes is the political significance of rock and roll. As with most political manifestos Sinclair's tracts touch upon many metaphysical levels and can be appreciated by the most anti-intellectual, while possessing some attraction for the academically inclined. At the simplistic level, Sinclair's world view is predicated upon the belief that a combination of rock music and drugs has created a new "energy force" which is both humanitarian and political. This force in turn is communicated by liberated rock and roll bands to "the people" who respond to the acts by creating even greater degrees of cosmic force, which in time will destroy the dominant or existent "death" culture. Rock music is that force. At a higher plain, Sinclair, as did the German dialectians, assumes that an independent force, rock music, has inherently "political" effects at every level of consciousness. In the Sinclair model, rock and roll is the advanced or vanguard power that creates consciousness. In one long autobiographical paper he recites his conversion to the "new music" at the screening of *Blackboard Jungle*, which he saw seven times.[4] The purity of "Rock Around the Clock," he claims, was corrupted to the point that the music transmitted false consciousness. Only the advent of mind-expanding drugs altered this course. "We started gobbling all that good LSD," he writes, "and got turned on to the rest of the world, and at the same time we started hearing and feeling an incredible new music in the air."[5] While rock music remained an overall microcosm of the contradictions of the "death culture," it was being liberated by Dylan, the Beatles and the Stones. These performers, by their music, added to the sensate power of drugs and helped create a "new people's culture" or "a wholly organic expression of a people's life-style" antithetical to the values of "Amerika."

> While we were off our feet lying on the floor trying to get our heads together, the greedheads and vultures of the death culture moved in on us and ripped us off for our music and the pure force

> of our energy and love and started using them against us, and we didn't realize it until the rip-off was almost complete. And then we said . . . we might as well go along with this, it isn't what we wanted but it's what's happening now and we might as well flow with it until it runs itself out, because it's too big and too powerful for us to fight it and besides this is all we've got, if we don't take this, *shit*, we might not get *anything* we want.[6]

Organic power, according to this view, was terminated or temporarily side-tracked by the overt repression of the "new community." In defense the alternative culture must band together and mobilize against the oppressors. Music and the rock concert, at the Grande, would once again be the consciousness-expanding weapons. In an earlier manifesto Sinclair described the interaction between audience and the performer as central to his thesis. Star quality and profit were negations of this posture in that a star or a profiteer was above the new people's culture. Stars and entrepreneurs, he contends, are the minions of the rulers of the death culture:

> These fucking PIGS! They've made our music and our celebrations into cheap consumer products, they've destroyed the use-value of our culture and converted it all into dollars and cents, anti-feeling and anti-sense, all in the name of profit and greed, and most of our people don't even know what they're missing because the pigs did this so fast that it's the only thing most of us have ever known—concerts where you sit down in a seat all night and watch the S*T*A*R*S. . . .[7]

The solution to this problem in part was to return to the simple communal "happening" where energy blared from giant speakers to the audience, who responded with even greater force. In "A Letter From Prison" Sinclair outlined the "energy transmission" of the communal rock-and-roll concert:

> The stage show grew directly out of the music, all of the dope we were smoking, and out of our culture and our collective history.

> As the music got more frantic the stage show got farther out, and the people responded wildly and it got more and more wild. It was a beautiful demonstration of the principles of high energy performance. The performer puts out more, the energy level of the audience is raised, and they give back more energy to the performers, who are moved to the audience and sent back, etc. until everything is total frenzy.
>
> This process changes in the people's bodies that are molecular and cellular and which transform them irrevocably just as LSD . . . does. The transformation may last only as long as the performance, but with repeated exposure the transformation becomes *permanent, and you can never bring those people back down* to television consciousness again.[8]

Implicit in this argument is the assumption that participants must be of the same communal group or culture. Sinclair argues that the "capitalists" and "imperialists" are attempting to exploit the new community.

> If the people of the rock and roll culture, the people of Woodstock Nation, continue to consume and support everything the pigs hand them, the capitalists and rock and roll imperialists will determine the future of our culture just as they have determined its recent past. If, on the other hand, the people of the rock and roll culture start to get themselves together and work out solutions to their problems and unite with their bands and workers and diggers and start implementing these new solutions, the people will be able to recapture the control of their own culture and move for righteous revolutionary change.[9]

The manifesto went on to urge bands and performers to play more benefits, more "free gigs for the people." The funds derived from these benefits should be used to further expand the institutions of the alternative culture. One of the alternative structures would be a People's Record Cooperative which would record, produce, package and market records by local bands. However, bands might, he argued, begin with established recording companies in order to make themselves known to the people as well as building up capital for the new culture. Coupled with the recording company would be a People's Booking Agency, which would serve to contract jobs for those artists in the cooperative. Sinclair's program, in essence, is a reformulation of the Roszak approach in that both see popular music as exploitive. Roszak objects to the sensate qualities of the music while Sinclair dissents from the political implications. Roszak, no doubt, would find Detroit concerts and bands loud and extravagantly gimmicked, with overtly dramatic postures such as on MC 5 *Kick Out the Jams* or Mitch Ryder and the Detroit Wheels; Amboy Dukes or Iggy and the Stooges. Followers of John Sinclair, on the other hand, claim that it is all a manifestation of high energy transmission. Rob Ryner of MC 5 explained the loudness of their early performances: "Pure sound energizes. The more energy in the sound, the bigger the sound that gets to you, the more intense the experience is . . . the more intense your reality is."[10] What many critics of the Detroit sound consider noisy stage gimmickry is in fact viewed as nonverbal sensate propaganda. The imprisonment of John Sinclair somewhat modified the trust of rock music in Detroit. The overt political aspect has been downgraded, with many of the local groups either disbanding or changing esthetic directions. MC 5 no longer presents itself as a "killer revolutionary" band. Nor does *Creem* magazine, once a major forum for Sinclair's ideas, totally support them. Dave Marsh's review of MC 5 in late 1971 was illustrative: "The question becomes, how much politics can rock and roll carry? I haven't the answer to that, but it seems explicit politics might tend to over-burden the medium, which after all is extremely simplistic at its root. Rock and roll is never going to carry the burden of defining our ideology for us . . . but it is always going to point some things out . . . there are going to be some things in it that will inspire us to *think* and act in certain manners."[11] Even Sinclair has retreated somewhat from his manifestos. In June 1974, he indicated that "energy" spurts occurred every ten years or so and had limited impact upon society. The reason for this was the coopting of the musicians by the record companies. He still feels rock music is a powerful force, but he is much more cautious about its ultimate influence upon the culture. Despite this switch in emphasis, Detroit stills appears as the capital of loud working-class bands which specialize in glorifying and replicating the early sounds of rock and roll. The Detroit image of rock and roll was not universally shared outside of the Michigan area. Many rock fans looked upon acts from this region as oddities, an attitude which several bands (Iggy and the Stooges and Alice Cooper) capitalized upon.

Segments of Sinclair's world view were in fact shared by many of the street people. Music was presented as a form of generational conflict and the dawning of a new consciousness or culture by segments of the student protest movement and other youth enclaves. This belief thrust the street community into direct confrontation with the popular-music industry.

RITES: FOR LOVE OR PROFIT

The generational-political polarization commonly held to have been characteristic of the 1960s has been employed as a form of unique ideology. The late Jim Morrison of the Doors in "The End," proclaimed, "Father?" "Yes, son?" "I want to kill you." "Mother, I want to. . . ." The Freudian connotations aside, this stanza is a clear statement of generational conflict as portrayed in some of the writings of Jerry Rubin and Abbie Hoffman. Jerry Rubin, in discussing the role of the urban guerilla, indicated that they must be willing to "murder" their parents. Neither Morrison nor Rubin were advocating patricide, but they were pointing to the nature of the struggle as they saw it. The struggle is defined, in terminology originally used by the early Catholic theologians, by the tactics. The ends justified the means. Abbie Hoffman wrote *Steal This Book.* The Jefferson Airplane intoned, "All your private property is target for your enemy/and the enemy is We." Regardless of the ideology of separation or cultural dissociation such as the "greening" return-to-nature theme, the deployment is the same: "Them" against "us." One of the major arenas of conflict has been in the sphere of rock music, where youth constitutes a forceful percentage of the consuming audience.

The music industry is part of corporate America. All of the majors are owned by giant conglomerates. Whatever risks the industry takes, it is a profitable venture. Its primary consumers are the very young people, viewed by Roszak and Reich as the "new" historical vessels of change. In almost pure dialectical terminology, a number of writers have posited the historically significant struggle between the "street" and the "industry." As one partisan observed: " 'New Rock,' as it began to be called, was inextricably bound—one basic fact has been consistently ignored: rock is a product created, distributed and controlled for the profit of American (and international) business."[12] Another critic further outlined this position:

> We 'freaks' rap a lot about the growing momentum of our groovy 'alternative' subculture. The fact remains, nevertheless, that its driving force continues to be dampened by a fundamental conflict: the attempt to develop a truly human, revolutionary lifestyle within the confines of an exploitative commercial system. Profit motive is robbing us of our thing, especially our music, which doesn't get better just because somebody makes money from it.[13]

This argument is not terribly innovative or unique. The editorials in *Sing Out!* magazine railed at the economic excesses at folk festivals during the hootenanny craze. However, rock critics added a new dimension to the "music is meant to be dug for its own sake; not traded and sold as a market commodity that's no good if it doesn't sell" posture. The new dimension is that of a new culture partially based upon rock emerging in opposition to the dominant social order. T. Proctor Lippincott wrote:

> The content of rock may have revolutionary implications, however, money factors consistently work against this tendency. The calculated hype and image that enshroud an artist's real self . . . not only set him or her apart as something super, thus virtually forestalling the possibility of human relationships between performer and spectator (a dehumanizing situation for both parties) but it establishes a false basis for exchange of any kind.[14]

This statement is a classic definition of alienation. Capitalism has deprived man of creativity, thus reducing him to a commodity. As such he is separated from himself and humanity. A central assumption in this conception is the exchange process. Paul Kantner, of the Jefferson Airplane, once remarked, "The record companies sell rock and roll records like refrigerators." Craig Karpel, in "Das Hip Kapital," elaborated the cultural damage incurred due to industry exploitation: "If hip capitalists were simply taking something from freaks and selling it back to them at a profit, members of the counter-culture might end up with less cash on hand, but at least they'd be getting their culture back in one piece. They aren't. Only property can be stolen. The countercultural value of community is the polar opposite of property. Hip capitalism is pernicious not because it 'steals the people's culture' but because it has lulled 'the people' into thinking that culture is *their property* susceptible to larceny, rather than their community, which is inalienable."[15] The process outlined by Karpel is popularly called the "rip-off." The term originally was confined to drug dealers and client transactions on the streets, but has taken a more general meaning. Rip-off is a euphemism for stealing, however, within it lies a cultural-political rationale. The rationale, harkening back to the "ends-means" idea, is that the dominant sociopolitical order is exploiting or ripping off the people or the "new community." Recall John Sinclair's notion that "all the money goes out of our community and into the pigs' bank . . . to be used again to keep us deeper in our . . . [concert] . . . seats." The two units, unlike Sinclair's usage, are not always the same since *the people* is customarily a political slogan as opposed to the communitarian ideal which stressed a disaffiliation life-style. The underground and rock presses over the years have painstakingly documented the abuses of the people and the counterculture by the power structure in political misdeeds ranging from the Berkeley People's Park to the Chicago Convention of 1968 to Kent State. *Rolling Stone* for a time devoted a full-page section devoted to confrontations between the police and drug "freaks." Establishment interference in the music of the counterculture has also received considerable attention ranging from FCC warnings about the content of songs to the arrests of Janis Joplin and Jim Morrison during their concerts for alleged threats to the public morality. Records have been a prime focus of attention both esthetically and economically. Greil Marcus concluded a review of *The Who On Tour/Magic Bus* writing, "The Who are the spirit of rock and roll—and because of that even Decca's clap-trap collection is worth buying for 'Magic Bus' and 'Pictures of Lily' and 'Disguises.' But maybe we all ought to be writing angry letters—The Who deserve better, and so do we."[16] On other occasions record buyers and even stores have rebelled against pricing policies. In Berkeley, Leopold's, a student-owned cooperative, refused to stock the Beatles greatest hits album, *Hey Jude*. The store manager, Jason Grevich, explained the boycott: "We're trying to make it clear that the boycott is not against the Beatles themselves but against Capitol Records in specific and other labels in general for their outrageous record prices. . . . This is just a greatest hits album —there's no production on it at all except to put some already existing songs on it in a different order. It should be cheaper than most records. . . ." Greatest hits records in the industry are considered "clean ups" usually issued as a "free ride" for both company and performer, that is, the only work required is to promote the album. In recent years greatest hits albums have frequently appeared after an artist leaves a given label or a group disbands. The so-called live album also serves this function, with an artist singing his hits plus a few fillers before a concert or night-club audience. Grevich went on to indict the quality of the records as well: "We ended up taking boxes of the Band album back to our distributor because they were returned to us with excessive surface noise, or because they skipped or were so thin you couldn't put two records on your record player."[17] Several weeks later, Capitol's national merchandise manager announced that the price of the album was being reduced a dollar. In his statement Rocky Catena aptly illustrated the basic cleavage between business and the counterculture. He said: "Look, the record business is no different than any other business. You charge what the market will bear. We sold four million *Abbey Road* albums at $6.98, but apparently a lot of people felt the price was immaterial. . . . If people are willing to pay for it, it's not a wrong price."[18] Announcements of price hikes in *Rolling Stone*, *Creem*, *Rock* and other idiom publications usually go through a similar scenario with industry spokesmen confronting advocates of the Woodstock Nation.

BE-IN OR PAY-IN: THE CONCERT-FESTIVAL TRIP

The role of ritual in any community or culture is integral. As the late French sociologist Emile Durkheim observed, through rite "the group periodically renews the sentiment which it has of itself and of its unity . . . [while] . . . at the same time individuals are strengthened in their social natures."[19] Religious rites, for example, reinforce and perpetuate the individuals' commitment both to the faith and to the existing social order, as in Marx's dictum that religion is the "opiate of the masses." Groups in opposition to the status quo such as sects, cults, political movements and even criminal organizations such as the Mafia have also relied upon the ritual to attract and maintain members. The Methodist revivalists, the Abolitionists, Klansmen, Populists, Socialists and Communists all expanded upon the tradition of camp meetings and encampments where the faithful would travel many miles to sing, work and visit with like-minded people. Political aliens in a politically hostile urban world were no less happy to find comrades and friends who reaffirmed their faith. The counterculture has retraced this time-worn path with an elaborate and at times medieval appreciation of pageantry which has been absorbed from a number of disparate sources beginning with the first hallucinogenic multimedia performances in New York and San Francisco, the Great Be-In in Golden Gate Park —the high point of the hippie phenomenon—and finally the serendipitous three-day Woodstock "festival of love."

The original multimedia "happenings" such as Andy Warhol's Exploding Plastic Inevitable were intellectually avant-garde. The Plastic Inevitable was an "assemblage that actually vibrates with menace, cynicism, and perversion for the wealthy." Richard Goldstein described the house band, the Velvet Underground, named after a novel by Delmore Schwartz, as producing "a savage series of atonal thrusts and electronic feedback. Their lyrics combine sadomasochistic frenzy with free association imagery. The whole thing seems to be the product of a secret marriage between Bob Dylan and the Marquis de Sade."[20]

The San Francisco bands, who also claim title to originating the multimedia concert, expressed optimism and joyfulness absent in the music of the Velvet Underground or the symbols used by Warhol. The Trips Festivals staged by author Ken Kesey and the Merry Pranksters focused upon the semireligious rites of primitive or feudal communities. Marty Balin, a founder of the Jefferson Airplane, elaborated the "message" of the early days, "All the material we do is about love, a love affair, or loving people."

In New York, "I'm Waiting for the Man" and "Heroin," both depicting the plight of the narcotics addict, were representative songs, while on the West Coast "Get Together" was emerging as the song typical of the community. In time Warhol's interest shifted to other media, and radical-chic intellectuals discovered other more political distractions. The San Francisco scene continued to pioneer part of the ethos now labeled "the street." The original Trips Festivals were produced by Ken Kesey in an attempt to "get people on the bus," a metaphor for an experience beyond the mental asylum Kesey considered society. In support of McLuhan, he contended it was impossible to communicate, via the printed page, the mechanics of the Trips Festivals. Consequently, the following journalistic accounts will have to serve as poor second-hand narratives. Paul Krassner, editor of the *Realist*, described the first event as:

> A ballroom surrealistically seething with a couple of thousand bodies stoned out of their ever-lovin bruces in crazy costumes and obscene makeup with a raucous rock 'n' roll band and balloons and heads and streamers and electronic equipment and the back of a guy's coat proclaiming *Please don't believe in magic* [a paraphrase of the Lovin Spoonful song] to a girl dancing with 4-inch eye lashes so that even the . . . Pinkerton Guards were contact high.[21]

The festivals were multimedia affairs. Movie screens were hung covering the ballroom walls upon which were flashed old movies, slides and other light mixes. Loudspeakers surrounded the hall. Additional speakers were placed near doorways and balconies. Local rock-and-roll bands were featured —Quicksilver Messenger Service, Wildflower, the Great Society, Big Brother and the Holding Company, the Airplane and the Grateful Dead. In front of the bandstand, dancers whirled and jumped. The scene was from a De Mille characterization of Nero's last grand party. All of the senses were assaulted with light, sound and visions frequently encouraged by alcohol or drugs. The Trips Festivals were the model of rock concerts to follow. The light show, the intermingling between performers and audience and most importantly the sacramental artifact drug. The Trips Festivals were celebrations of the hallucinogenic drug LSD. Originally, LSD was given as a gift or placed in the fruit punch, Kool Aid or any other public drinking convenience. Giving or sharing was the ethic at the Trip Festivals. The performances in many respects paralleled the ideals of the early Christians and resembled a sort of electronic camp meeting.

The religious and ceremonial connotations of these events has not escaped attention. Richard Robinson noted, "Rock concerts are religious experiences and today's rock musicians and audiences view the church in the regalness of their robes and mystical trappings." Richard Goldstein has compared the rock musician to the shaman of the primitive tribe, who transcends the group and then describes the mental journey to the rest of the village. Mike Settle, former New Christy Minstrel and First Edition member, told me that the rock concerts held in San Francisco were really spiritual rites with a nonverbal sensate mode of communication: "There's something in the sound of all this music that the words of the songs cannot explain that brings together everyone who sees it, like a kind of church." This, of course, was a paraphrase of his composition "Church Without a Name." As quasi-religious rites the pioneer acid-rock concerts transcended the basic audience-performer dyad that focuses upon the appreciation of the intellectual-spectator aspect.

There was no space for entrepreneurs on the Kesey bus. The audiences at the Longshoreman's Hall at the Fillmore at first comprised a strange mixture of relocated beatniks, college students, intellectuals and motorcycle gang members who wore clothing best characterized as "early Goodwill." For a very reasonable price one could see the Jefferson Airplane, Big Brother and the Great Society. At the Matrix with luck they could be enjoyed for less than a dollar on a Monday night. The Grateful Dead and other rock groups performed gratis at the now famous Page Street address where musicians could find food and shelter when they were broke, which was generally the case. At the outset of their career Country Joe and the Fish earned a magnificent sum of $25.00 per week, most of which was invested in amplification equipment. Chet Helms, reportedly, was the first to suggest charging admission for rock shows ostensibly to keep the crowds at a manageable size. Helms in short time developed the Family Dog, an underground production company, which continued the Trips Festival ethos—with an admission price. At the Avalon Ballroom the slogan "May the Baby Jesus Shut Your Mouth and Open Your Mind" was prominently displayed. Burton Wolfe, one of the many chroniclers of the Haight-Ashbury, characterizes the typical family Dog concert as involving:

> Continuously changing light projections of liquid colors and protoplastic forms bathe the dancers. Their luminescent, striped, and dotted clothes glow eerily amid the flashing lights. Symbols, concentric circles, and pictures of Indians and Oriental priests are beamed onto the walls.
>
> Suddenly, the fast, screaming music dies down to a soft love song and then gives way to mournful Indian dirge. The light show changes. On one wall there is a picture of Buddha and on another a picture of Christ on the cross. Several hundred of the youngsters on the dance floor join hands. They sway back and forth in a trance-like state. They keep it up until the lights begin blipping all over the cavernous dance hall. Once again, the Avalon is a sea of maddening motion and deafening sound.[22]

The action of the ballroom floor notwithstanding, the weekend rock concerts advertised by the psychedelic posters, tacked to telephone polls, became profit-making operations. Concert promoters were no longer the sacrament-giving altruistic priests, but rather businessmen in search of profit. The short-haired Jewish actor and merchant Bill Graham became producer *par excellence* at the Fillmore, a dance hall in the heart of San Francisco's black ghetto. Many a Pacifica Radio talk fest, KPFA in Berkeley, was devoted to his villainy; Graham's expensive car, his Marin County country home and his profit margin. In the context of the music industry he was a remarkably ethical man. He booked the best acts possible at the lowest admission fee his not unsubstantial profit margin allowed. His prices were moderate for a three-act bill, in contrast to other similarly sized urban areas. Graham began charging $2.50 and climbed to $3.50 over a three-year span. Other cities charged $4.50 to $6.00 for similar or shorter performances. Graham continuously has attempted to explain the rationale for his admission fees. Prices, he maintains, simply mirror his costs. In 1969 he told Ralph Gleason:

> Whereas the budget a year ago was $5,000, it is now $10,000 for the weekend. All I know is that two years ago we went from $2.50 to $3.00 which is a 20 percent markup on our original price. In that same amount of time, the overall operating budget has gone up 250 percent. . . . The light show when we started . . . 18 guys for $3.00! Now a light show costs a couple of hundred dollars a night. . . .[23]

The San Francisco rock concert including its unique staging devices and utilization of new sensory stimuli was economically rather conventional. The patron paid the admission price and saw a show. Neither the Fillmore nor the Family Dog were nonprofit enterprises, at least in the box office. Indeed, had the Fillmore and the Avalon remained the prototype for the "new community," the issue of cultural exploitation may have remained in the foreground confined to traditional Marxist interpretations. Two rather serendipitous events with remarkable similarity made the even "reasonably priced" rock concert suspect and a cultural battleground: the Human Be-In and Woodstock.

John Sinclair has labeled the Human Be-In or Have-In "our first mass public venture." While it is quite possible to suggest that the Beatles' or Rolling Stones' first American tour was the opening manifestation of the new culture, there is little doubt that the January 14, 1967, gathering of some 20,000 people at the Polo Grounds in Golden Gate Park was the event that sparked national recognition for the hippie phenomenon. The affair was billed in the underground paper *The Oracle* as a "gathering of the Tribes" and "The Human Be-In." It was advertised primarily by word of mouth throughout Haight-Ashbury and complemented by a brief notice in Ralph J. Gleason's column in the *San Francisco Chronicle.* The Human Be-In featured nearly all of the major rock bands—the Airplane, the Dead, Big Brother—and gurus including Allen Ginsberg, Timothy Leary and Gary Snyder. The Merry Pranksters and the Hell's Angels motorcycle band—"security forces"—were also in evidence. The free event was peaceful and a model of a harmonious culture. Not even Jerry Rubin's poorly received attempt to bridge the gap between old politics and new life-styles could not ruin it; his pitch to free a fallen comrade was greeted by a sea of indifference and a few boos. The modern-day encampment began at one o'clock Saturday afternoon and lasted into the fog-filled evening. Even marijuana cigarettes or "joints" were passed freely to strangers dressed like the extras of many different epic films. The air of the gathering was medieval, and flowing robes and costumes were the rule: "The costumes were a designer's dream, a wild polyglot mixture of Mod, Paladin, Ringling Brothers, Cochise and Hell's Angels, Formal. . . . Small parties of medievalists raised banners, gorgeous flowing sheets of color, on the green as though knights were assembling on the Camelot plain."[24] The cutting of amplification cables, a sky diver's attempts at publicity and Jerry Rubin's effort to merge the Berkeley political world with San Francisco's "astronauts of inner space" all went virtually unnoticed. The event was a public statement of the dawning of a new movement in a manner the Broadway show *Hair* could only superficially suggest. Many journalistic accounts of the conclave were printed, Gleason's conclusion, perhaps, was the most apt: "The first of the great gatherings. No fights. No drunks. No troubles. Two policemen on horseback and 20,000 people. The perfect sunshine, the beautiful birds in the air, the parachutist descending as the Grateful Dead ended a song." The wholesale police ticketing and harassment of patrons after the Human Be-In did not mitigate the basic nostalgic ingredients of the contemporary camp meeting. It was free, entertaining, communal and, as Gleason noted, the "gathering was an affirmation, not a protest. A statement of life, not of death, and a promise of good," or according to *Newsweek*, "There was little pushing or elbowing—people twirled around a Maypole, clapped, laughed, embraced and danced to the music."[25]

The Be-In began a series of similar events which, while street oriented, were very much commercial ventures. The first was the Magic Mountain Music Festival staged across the bay from San Francisco. It was held at the beginning of the Summer of Love. Associated with the Fantasy Faire, a local artists' exhibition, the festival featured the Byrds, the Doors, Jefferson Airplane, Country Joe and the Fish and many others. Tickets were sold for $2.00. Several thousand youths were turned away because of lack of space. Proceeds were contributed to the black community.

The Monterey Pop Festival, which opened the eyes of legions of record-company executives to the new culture, was a continuation of the Be-In and Magic Mountain. The Monterey atmosphere was one of "love." Girls gave flowers to policemen. The earnings, again, were destined for charity and the esthetic development of the rock scene. Performers at Monterey were courted and offered enormous contracts by executives anxious to capitalize on the new youth market. Janis Joplin and Jimi Hendrix were introduced to the world and furious bidding took place over their talents, capped by Warner and Columbia. The commercial potential of festivals was not lost upon many industry people or concert promoters.

Woodstock was the culmination of the Trips Festivals, the Golden Gate Park gathering and Monterey wedded to a blend of "free rock and roll in the parks, dynamite acid flowing in the streets and through the veins and cells of the people and a whole new world to be explored."

The importance of Woodstock in any examination of popular music cannot be overestimated since, as *Time* correctly observed, "The spontaneous community of youth that was created at Bethel was the stuff of which legends are made; the substance of the event contains both a revelation and a sobering lesson."[26] Woodstock generated an ethos, a mythology, which lent support to the most ardent proponants of the dawning of a new community as well as to its many opponents. The Woodstock Music and Art Fair was almost a spontaneous unplanned event. It was originally scheduled to be held some 15 miles from Woodstock, in the hamlet of Wallkill, whose main claim to fame was the residence of Bob Dylan. The aroused residents of Wallkill banded together into a Concerned Citizens Committee to keep the "dope-smoking hippie hordes" away. They were successful in their efforts and there was some question as to whether the three-day event would be held at all. The concerned citizens of Wallkill were not alone in their opposition to the festival. Mark Kramer, correspondent for Liberation News Service, the underground version of the Associated Press, filed a story titled "The Rock Imperialists" which condemned Mike Lang and Artie Kornfeld of Woodstock Ventures as rock investors who "look hip and talk hip," but were in effect exploiting the youth culture and the "revolutionary energy of rock." "So the rock imperialists," he wrote, "deliver the goods. When you want a banana, United Fruit sells a good banana. And when you want a rock festival, Woodstock Music and Art Fair, Inc., sells a good rock festival—at $7 a day."[27] After some five weeks of haggling, the festival was moved to Bethel and billed as an Aquarian Exposition—three days of peace and music in White Lake, New York: August 15, 16, 17. Handbills distributed in New York City announced "To Insure Three Days of Peace & Music We've Left Wallkill and Are Now at White Lake." The handout went on to thank "the people of Bethel for receiving the news of our arrival so enthusiastically." This was a slight exaggeration of the situation. The citizens of Bethel were no less happy about the location of the affair than those of Wallkill. Their protests, however, were not as effective. A judge refused to grant an injunction after the promoters pointed out that only 60,000 people were expected and then promised to deal with all security, sanitation and traffic problems. Given the incorrect crowd estimate and other unforeseen events, nearly all of these assurances would not be kept. New York City off-duty policemen scheduled to provide security were refused permission to "moonlight." A hundred members of the Hog Farm, a New Mexico commune, led by Hugh Romney (Wavy Gravy), were enlisted to deal with health, sanitation and other problems. On the night before August 15, half of the expected 60,000 were already camped on the grounds, and many more were on the way. The early arrivals were the vanguard of the street community. They, as press accounts reiterated, were very much into the "oppositional life-style." Those that came after were in search of an experience, a happening. The next day a crowd of 200,000 people was milling about on Max Yasgur's thousand acres, which he had rented for the weekend for the reported amount of $50,000. Another 50,000 to 200,000 persons, depending on which crowd tally is used, soon joined them. From the beginning the affair was serendipitous. Not even the most optimistic promoter could imagine an estimated million people clogging up the highways trying to reach the festival. Because 186,000 tickets has been sold, Woodstock Associates expected 200,000 people, maximum. As *Rolling Stone* commented, "No one was prepared for what happened and no one could have been."[28] Lines of cars stretched for 20 miles from the fair; the fences surrounding the Yasgur farm collapsed, allowing thousands of gate crashers to mingle with those who had paid their $18 for the three days. One promoter labeled it a "financial disaster." The sanitation facilities, 600 portable toilets, were overtaxed and in many instances ceased to function. The water supply proved inadequate, a situation made more desperate by heavy rainstorms and various illnesses, 300 of which were believed to be related to adverse drug reactions. By the night of August 15, as journalists and spectators duly noted, Woodstock was the third largest city in the state of New York, minus any formal organization. All the while, the parade of entertainers, ranging from folksingers to the high-energy theatrics of Jimi Hendrix and The Who, continued, interrupted only by Chip Monck, the unofficial master of ceremonies. It was Monck who best outlined the situation at Bethel the first day. To the assembled throng he said: "We're turning a little of the responsibility back onto you. We have the ability to gather this many people here and now it's also our responsibility to take care of ourselves in the midst of a phenomenon. And it's a responsibility no one ever had." He continued, "There are a hell of a lot of us here. If we are going to make it, you had better remember that guy next to you is your brother." Jerry Hopkins as well as other journalists have repeatedly reported this *gemeinschaft* or communal aspect of the gathering. "Everywhere there was a sense of 'family,' a sharing, a forthright mutual concern."[29] Woodstock was the antithesis of individual enterpreneurship and exploitation. One does not make a profit from his brother or sister.

On August 16, Chip Monck announced to the crowd that Woodstock Ventures had ceased selling tickets. Woodstock was now entirely in the unsuspecting hands of the celebrants, not the management. In this announcement much of the "love-in" festival ideology was born. Festivals from that point on were to be gatherings of the people united by joy and music. As many participants assert, this image was more a contrivance of the media than a reality. The first day's rain drove off a considerable number of people that night, and mud and the lack of sanitation forced others to leave. Many were *not able* to withdraw. Still, Woodstock transcended the most far-fetched dreams of nineteenth-century utopian-anarchist writers who saw salvation in the death of God and the state, who believed that once the masses are free, they will create a new culture. At Woodstock this appeared to happen, despite the structural anomie. By its apparent success, Woodstock became the model for future festivals, as well as the

1960s version of Rousseau's ideal state of nature. As the *Life* editorial concluded, "Everybody remembered. Woodstock made it."[30] Woodstock, in the vernacular, "blew a lot of minds." Only the radical Right, with its usual distaste for anything associated with drugs or sex, and the New Left objected to the festival.

The Left was not happy with Peter Townshend pushing Abbie Hoffman off the stage while he was trying to make a "free John Sinclair" speech. A *Rolling Stone* correspondent would later remark, "That's the relationship of rock to politics."[31] Hoffman left the affair to write *Woodstock Nation* in five days, applauding the political potential of youth while denouncing the rock stars and promoters. A more typical reaction is provided by Joseph Sia:

> The big thing was being there and taking part in a festival where everyone shared what he'd had. In any crowd this large you expect some misfortune. There were three deaths and two births over the weekend—far below the usual statistics for a city of half a million people. . . . Where was the violence that was supposed to accompany any large gathering of young people? What the straight world failed to understand was that these young people, wet, tired, hungry, simply were not interested in fighting. They had come to a remote, peaceful setting to get together and rap, and to listen to the supersounds of their favorite superstar rock groups.[32]

Sia's argument echoed most of the press and media reports from Woodstock. The wanton savagery predicted by the media had not occurred. Indeed, many newspapers, including the august *New York Times*, took highly positive editorial positions after August 18, although they had originally opposed the affair.

Analyses of Woodstock generally centered around the peaceful nature of the gathering and the theme of youth as a new social force. Psychologist Rollo May portrayed it as "a symptomatic event of our time that showed the tremendous hunger, need and yearning for community." Paul Williams, founder of *Crawdaddy*, in a promotional blurb for Warner Brothers, noted, "Old world crumbling, new world being born, Woodstock a festival of getting together, celebration of birth, not the first and scarcely the last but every time you're born it feels like a whole new life. . . . Peace be with you brother till we meet again." Ellen Sanders, contributor to *Saturday Review* and the Los Angeles *Free Press*, saw it as "a three-day live-in where food, shelter and joy were shared. Authority was missing in action, hundreds of thousands of young people suddenly realized they could have it any way they wanted. A choice was made; genuine peace, love and humanity prevailed. It worked. Joyously, profoundly, we were all touched by one another en masse for the duration of a festival after which nothing could ever be the same." Greil Marcus of *Rolling Stone* indicated it was a "foundling of something new, something our world must now find a way to deal with. The limits have changed now . . . the priorities have been rearranged, and new 'impractical' ideas must be taken seriously . . . this is just the beginning—or the end—and we must now sit down and figure out how to make it work." *Life*, a mirror of middle-class values, reported "Woodstock had been a total experience, a phenomenon, a happening, a high adventure, a near disaster and in a small way, a struggle for survival."

Not all voices were affirmative. Barry Farrell, in a review for *Life*'s special issue on the festival, cautioned that while the fair was "a victory for music and peace," it was also "a display of the authority of drugs. . . . It was groovy, as the speaker kept saying, but I fear it will grow groovier in memory, when the market in madness leads on to shows we'd rather not see."[33] To this, Abbie Hoffman added, "It never ceased to amaze me how groups, instead of imitating our . . . [political] model and trying to rip-off Woodstock Ventures again or the Fillmore or Columbia Records, tried instead to devour us."[34] Woodstock was all of these things and more. It became a standard of comparison no less utopian than Rousseau's world of the noble savage. It was the prototype, as Greil Marcus urged, for future events. The festival also created a form of generational consciousness that implied a superiority of purpose absent in other sectors of society. Most importantly, Woodstock, while deemed a financial disaster by its promoters, suggested to many other entrepreneurs that, with the proper precautions and financial outlays a great deal of money might be made in staging rock festivals, conclusion which was totally at odds with the "new community" aspect of the gathering. The notions of family, sharing, love and community which permeated the descriptions of the event in the underground and rock press all pointed to the lack of commercialism and acts of individual altruism. The thundering ovation given the announcement that the festival heretofore was "free" was but one evidence of this. Promoters Roberts, Lang and Kornfeld grossed approximately $1.3 million dollars in ticket sales and still ended up in the red, at least prior to the release of the festival albums and the film, which returned a huge profit.

Later promoters hoped to avoid the same mistakes, but they consolidated some of the less-glamorous economic practices of the festival. The alleged losses incurred by Woodstock Ventures could partially be attributed to the fact that only one customer in ten actually paid his way, and to the phenomenal fees and services rendered to entertainers. There is considerable controversy over the expenditures at Woodstock. The promoters claim they paid eight helicopters $500 an hour to ferry performers and medicine to and from the festival area. They further claim that the talent was paid $250,000 dollars, although the actual tally is closer to $150,000.

Many of the participants never worked again for less than $10,000 to $20,000. Escalating costs became a major catalyst in the struggle between the street people and the concert promoter; once again, Bill Graham was in the center of much of the controversy. Prior to his cessation of his operations in San Francisco and New York, Graham explained the situation: "When a group asks $5,000 for a concert, you can charge $3

Exhibit 7.1

COST OF TALENT PER "NAME" UNIT AT WOODSTOCK	
Jimi Hendrix Experience	$18,000
Blood, Sweat and Tears	$15,000
Creedence Clearwater Revival	$10,000
Joan Baez	$10,000
The Band	$ 7,500
Jefferson Airplane	$ 7,500
Janis Joplin and Big Brother	$ 7,500
Sly and the Family Stone	$ 7,000
Canned Heat	$ 6,500
The Who	$ 6,250
Richie Havens	$ 6,000
Arlo Guthrie	$ 5,000
Crosby, Stills, Nash and Young	$ 5,000
Ravi Shankar	$ 4,500
Johnny Winter	$ 4,500
Ten Years After	$ 3,250
Country Joe and the Fish	$ 2,500
The Greatful Dead	$ 2,500

to $4 for a ticket, but when they demand $20,000, $30,000 or $40,000, you have no choice but to raise the ticket price. Then, the ticket-buyers get mad at me! I've been called a filthy capitalist pig. But then it's easier to attack me than it is to attack their idols. My prices are based on the artist's demands."[35] These demands began to escalate with the advent of rock festivals. Several groups at Woodstock made over $7,000 for a 45-minute set. Other groups, such as the Jefferson Airplane, earned a similar amount for a four-hour performance. The more expensive groups became all the more expensive for any weekend (two sets a night) gig at the Fillmore. Grand Funk Railroad began their career in 1969, playing for *free* as an opening act at the First Annual Atlanta Pop Festival. Two years later, the trio averaged $50,000 per concert and appeared at least six times per week. Their July 9, 1971, concert at Shea Stadium in New York grossed $306,000 —or approximately $3,400 per minute. The Who, in a 1971 tour, played only 17 performances and grossed $1.1 million. John Fogerty, leader and spokesman for Creedence Clearwater Revival, a Bay Area band which started out at the Fillmore, discussed the escalation in act prices: "When we started out, you have to take a flat fee, then as your reputation grows you demand a percentage of the gate. Maybe you take 60 percent or more. For a three-night stay at the Fillmore East back in 1968, we got a flat fee $500. Now, our take is an excess of $30,0000 to $40,000 for one night on a percentage basis."[36] In 1972, the James Gang played 147 concerts, grossing $3,674,368 in ticket sales.

The apparent commercialization of what was originally considered a gathering and celebration of the new community brought it into conflict with concert promoters. In San Francisco, the communal tradition was bifurcated between the presentation of the Family Dog and Graham's Fillmore as opposed to the free weekly Sunday afternoon open-air concerts staged in Golden Gate Park at which the Grateful Dead and numerous other bands appeared. A Sunday afternoon gig in the Park became a step to future successes, just as third-place billing on a psychedelic Fillmore poster once was. Bill Graham on occasion made the Fillmore available to radical and other groups for benefits and other events. Graham was never loved, however; he was tolerated. After the "hippie community" declined as a San Francisco tourist attraction, Bill Graham took the brunt of criticism as a rip-off artist.

Graham was predominantly a businessman operating in a milieu which on the surface was totally antagonistic to the values of the marketplace. He provided a product. However, to his customers, music was much more than a commodity to be bought and sold, and Graham was an exploiter and marketer of the people's culture. The notion by this community that they had some moral claim on him was antithetical. In a heated confrontation with the striking underground light-show guild, Graham shouted: "I will *never* share my profit with anyone in the community. . . . As long as I control the show, no one will ever tell me how to run it or what to do with my money. I have a house in Pacific Heights and an $8,000 Mercedes-Benz and it's mine, I *earned* it." The communal be-in ethic of free concerts and benefits for the oppressed originally helped Graham to maintain a shaky relationship with various San Francisco interest groups. Woodstock altered his position. As *San Francisco Chronicle* critic John Wasserman noted, when Graham was "only making $1,000 a night, he could afford to give one away, but now he's making $6,000, so he can't."[37] The days of $10 a night light shows and the Airplane and Quicksilver for the grand total of $1,000 were over. Despite occasional criticisms by the underground press, Graham's West Coast operation was relatively carefree, compared to his Fillmore East venture in New York City. The difference between the Fillmore East and its western counterpart was similar to that of the Warhol shows with the Velvet Underground and Ken Kesey's sacramental Trips Festivals of "love and giving." Moreover, the glad tidings and optimism of 1965 has given to the violence, pessimism and despair of the post-Chicago Democratic Convention years. In New York Graham encountered the "revolutionary" segments of the East Village scene, led by a group with the unprintable name of the Motherfuckers. In October 1968 the group made its first demands to "liberate" the Fillmore. The group wanted to take over the hall on Wednesday nights for 'free food, music, dancing, smoke, tumbling, nude dancing, and a flock of meetings, a free exchange of goods and energy."[38] After a series of confrontations, Graham instituted Wednesday free nights, which only partially satisfied the parties concerned. The shaky détente was dissolved when the police charged that free nights in fact did conform with demands for dope smoking and threatened to revoke the Fillmore's license. On December 23, 1968, the promoter issued an open letter announcing the termination of the free nights. Three days later, Elektra Records rented the Fillmore East to stage a promotional concert featuring the MC 5. During the affair, Graham was attacked, hit with a chain and sustained a broken nose, an usher's arm was broken, equipment was destroyed or stolen, seats were slashed and the MC 5, once the prototype of "revolutionary killer" band, was harassed by street people and their confederate "outlaw" bike gang. Several days after this prophetic incident, Graham wisely offered to help put together a "constructive, realistic, and lawful program," which would aid the East Village community. After considerable haggling, the offer was accepted and the quid pro quo was temporarily a success. Several years later, Graham finally retired, pointing to the astronomical costs of operating a continuing rock concert series. In a press release Graham charged that the rock music scene had become intolerable for him. "In 1965 when we began the original Fillmore, I associated with the employed 'musicians.' Now, more often than not, it's with 'officers and stockholders' in large corporations —only they happen to have long hair and play guitars." Graham pleaded he could not fill his auditorium with new acts. The established performers, however, were either too expensive or part of a package deal. "The agents have created a new rock game called 'packaging'; which means simply that if the Fillmore wants a major headliner, then we are often forced to take the second and/or third act that the agent or manager insists upon." At his press conference Graham decried the high prices of headliners using the example of a group which had started at the Fillmore years ago, that refused to play the auditorium for $50,000 a week. "Woodstock," he said, "was the beginning of the end."

In contrast to some promoters, the San Francisco entrepreneurs were relatively above board in their dealings. In the Midwest, various acts have impersonated the genuine product. One rotund drummer performed as Buddy Miles prior to being discovered. Delta Promotions, a Bay City, Michigan, organization, booked the defunct Animals, Zombies and Archies of "Sugar, Sugar" fame into a series of small towns. Eric Burdon, head of the original Animals, referred to this practice as the creation of "bogus groups" and threatened to take a baseball bat to the promoters. Ticket holders no doubt shared this sentiment. Similar consumer deceptions, not all intentional, have also plagued rock festivals, where money has been collected and the event canceled without refunds, or where various acts have been billed which have not in fact been contracted. The most dramatic and most widely reported rip-off was the so-called free concert presented at Altamont in California by the Rolling Stones.

Rolling Stone, in the December issue of 1969, ran a banner headline proclaiming FREE ROLLING STONES: IT'S GOING TO HAPPEN! After a series of planning mishaps the event took place on a dusty auto race track near Livermore where 300,000 people attended. During the chaotic afternoon, a young black man, Meredith Hunter, was stabbed to death by one of the Hell's Angels, who were hired to keep order at the affair as they had done at the Be-In. In all, four persons died, one more than Woodstock, and a number of injuries and discomforts were endured. Even a performer, Marty Balin of the Jefferson Airplane, was felled by a Hell's Angel. A good deal of Consciousness III was contradicted that day, when it became clear that the entire event had been staged to allow the Rolling Stones' management to film a *Woodstock*-like movie. The film, *Gimme Shelter*, including the murder scene, was released a year later. The headline of the underground San Francisco paper, *Good Times*, summed up the general reaction to Altamount: "Mick Jagger Used Us For Dupes," a quote attributed to a member of the Hell's Angels.

It could have been said by any of those who went to Altamount in search of another Woodstock weekend of love.

Supporters of the alternative culture have put forth a plethora of schemes to curb what they considered promotional rip-offs, ranging from boycotts to assaults upon the personnel at the Filmore East. Some boycotts have been temporarily effective. A coalition of Seattle, Washington, high-school students, calling themselves the Eagles Liberation Front, forced local promoter Boyd Frafmyre to reduce his prices as well as his codes against "making out" and "smoking." Their ideological thrust was summarized in a street leaflet which said:

> Rock music began in the alternative community, our community. Rock expresses the ethos of our community, its force is filled by our struggle. But over the years the established entertainment industry—promoters, agents, record companies, media, and every name group—has gradually transformed our music into an increasingly expensive commodity. They have stolen our music.
>
> We are taking it back.

The result of the two-week boycott was a 50-cent reduction in price for advanced tickets and the promise of future benefit shows charging a dollar admission fee. The booker also promised to arrange meetings between the Front and passing rock musicians to discuss mutual problems. *The Great Speckled Bird* noted that ELF set a "good example of what can be done in Atlanta, specifically concerning the pop festival. The promoters of the festival are now in the process of choosing the bands. If the people could get together, demands could be raised concerning the exorbitant prices of pop festivals and the lack of relationship to the community which fosters and provides the best audience for rock music. Bands can be induced to lower their fees and promoters can be forced to stop ripping-off profits from the community."[39]

Crosby, Stills, Nash and Young were the target of another such action in the St. Paul, Minnesota, area. The act was booked into the Metropolitan Sports Center with prices ranging from $5 to $10. A boycott was organized primarily by McAllister College students. Their goals were to reduce the prices and to hopefully stage a free or minimum-cost concert. They directed their attack to the quartet's records and the concert itself. As with Leopold's record store, which refused to stock Beatle albums, the boycotters maintained that "we're not against Crosby, Stills, Nash and Young. We just don't want promoter rip-offs in this area."[40] The result of the boycott was the lowering of some $5 to $2 and the reduction of premium seats to $7. Eliot Roberts, the band's manager, while labeling $10 as "outrageous," defended the $25,000 guarantee and the 60 percent of the gate that the group was to receive. The boycotters' "victory" at best was a hollow one.

Several artists, notably Steve Miller and Joan Baez, have responded to consumers' indignation by refusing to play halls where the top price was more than $3.75 per ticket, but they are glaring exceptions. United Artists held a Hollywood Bowl afternoon concert for the admission price of 99 cents. In the fall of 1971, Capitol organized a tour called The Joy Wagon featuring guitarist Leo Kottke, Joy of Cooking and Joyous Noise. Elektra put together a short-lived tour of the Alabama State Troupers which featured the Muscle Shoal sound with Don Nix, Jeanie Greene and Lonnie Mack at a top price per show of $1.50. The admission costs were uniquely low, primarily because the recording companies considered the tour a promotional item. The Grateful Dead, which started with Kesey's Merry Pranksters as the Warlocks, has long been considered a "people's band." They were stalwarts at the Sunday afternoon concerts in Golden Gate Park. In an interview in 1970 they were asked to lower their concert prices. Phil Lesh replied, "We can't afford to play for less money, for one thing. We would like to but can't. Unless we start to sell millions of records, which hasn't happened yet. We support 50 people for one thing. . . ." Pigpen of the Dead once said, "Rock and roll owes me a living."[41]

Grace Slick, of the Jefferson Airplane, comments, "Musicians can be incredibly lame about carrying on business affairs. They get together and say, 'Oh, sure'd be neat to have a whatever-it-is,' but it takes a little more than an 'it'd sure be neat.' It doesn't hold up unless you get someone who can do that stuff, who wants to do that stuff."

Repeated criticism in the rock and underground presses has not appreciably harmed the concert tour. It continues to be a very lucrative aspect of the music business. Consumers, values notwithstanding, are frequently left with the unpleasant choice of gate crashing, a practice which has become an art in many cities, or paying the entrance fee. Many grumble while paying their $9.50 at the door. The concert, like Woodstock, continues to be popular if the act is worthwhile. Ironically, the very festival which has been acclaimed as the evidence of the new community is the very event which has done it the most harm. As Bill Graham noted in his farewell news conference, Woodstock set the precedent for high-priced acts, the costs of which were passed on to the concert-goer. Conversely, the same festival created the expectation of the "free communal happening of peace and love," which was divorced from economic reality and in conflict with it.

Street people have been more successful in their skirmishes with the recording industry. The phonograph record or tape is a product independent of the artist's control and open to duplication. Record companies can be combatted with a tape recorder, access to a pressing plant, willing consumers and a small amount of capital.

THE RECORD LIBERATION FRONT: BOOTLEGGING

One of the key artifacts on the street in the later 1960s was the bootleg record. The practice of pirating recorded sound is as old as the piano roll and the early Edison phonograph disk. As early as 1905 the Victor Talking Machine Co. urged Congress to enact a law to end unauthorized copying of its products. Because of a lack of interest by publishing companies and the then questionable constitutionality of such a bill, recorded sound was left unprotected. The question of the copyrighting of recorded performances was left in an unclear and chaotic state until litigation in 1955 when the decision in the *Capitol Records Inc.* v. *Mercury Records Corporation* case indicated that recorded performances were potentially copyrightable, although not under the 1909 statute. The support of radio broadcasters finally motivated segments of the music industry to secure legislation to protect their recorded products. Senate Bill 5.646 was passed in the fall of 1971 and signed by President Nixon. The law stipulates that any commercial rerecording of an original record, for public distribution or sale, made without the manufacturer's permission, violates federal law. It will henceforth be illegal to duplicate a record or to knowingly sell such a record whether or not royalties have been paid on the copyrighted music. A major catalyst for the passage of this bill, it appears, was the countercultural practice of ripping off record companies and their artists.

The practice of nonlegitimate record duplication is a complex one with considerable ideological shading. There is, on the one hand, the aberrent counterfeiter or pirate who copies established artists and hits and sells them as the original. He may even present his product as bonafide. He profits because he does not pay any promotional costs or copyright fees; his only expense is to manufacture the records, which costs less than a quarter per unit for a long-playing record. His product is an exact replica of the original label and cover. It is a quick way to make money, and prior to the passage of the McClellan antipiracy bill, carried minor legal penalties.

On the other hand, record bootleggers produce albums and tapes of material which is not otherwise available through legitimate channels. During the 1950s this activity was customarily limited to jazz and country collectors and enthusiasts who would put together anthologies of old recordings originally found on the Bluebird, Okeh and other labels and issue them under the Jolly Roger or Swaggie label or with no identification at all. Due to the esoteric nature of this subrosa activity and the vagueness of the law, copyright holders rarely went beyond threatening with legal action these scholarly music bandits who believed esthetic values transcend legislative ones. Many of the transgressors paid royalties to the artists whose work they reproduced. Blues singer Memphis Minnie and other artists occasionally received checks from unknown sources for "services rendered." Early King Oliver, Bessie Smith and Louis Armstrong cuts believed buried in the Columbia Record vaults frequently surfaced on the Jolly Roger or other labels. Collectors would pool their resources and make up a record. The poor quality of many of these bootlegs reflected the originals. The folk-music revival stimulated wider activities. Several smaller but well-known labels issued collections of country-music records made during the 1920s and 1930s. Again, the major companies chose to overlook this activity. While there is no evidence to support this, one might argue that the legal reissues of Carter Family, Jimmie Rodgers and other country greats during the 1960s may have in part been linked to the folkie bootleggers. The advent of low-cost tape-recording equipment negated the need for this type of bootleg. Students and other folkniks during the 1960s taped and retaped unavailable records such as the Almanac Singers' controversial *Songs for John Doe* and *Dear Mister President* albums, which were legend in the East Coast folk-music scene. The rise of the tape recorder also allowed people to pool their funds and build up their music collections. On the college campuses as well as Haight-Ashbury, one record purchase might well spawn 10 to 20 tapes.

On June 22, 1968, *Rolling Stone* ran a front-page review of an informal musical session in the basement of a house in Woodstock, New York. The article was titled "Dylan's Basement Tape Should Be Released." The participants in that gathering included Robbie Robertson, Richard Manuel, Garth Hudson and Rich Danko—later known as the Band—and Bob Dylan. The songs recorded were designed for Dylan's Dwarf Music portfolio. Acetate copies of the session were sent to the Byrds, Manfred Mann and a number of other acts. The result of this famous session was the "basement tape." Originally the tape was circulated subrosa throughout the inner circles of the New York and Hollywood music community and finally it drifted out onto the campuses. The tape was transposed to record and announced in *Rolling Stone* and other papers in the fall of 1969. The album title was *Great White Wonder*. Most of the songs of Dylan with the Band had already been covered and were known by other artists, notably Joan Baez, the Band and the Byrds. The album's main asset was Bob Dylan. Greil Marcus best outlined the significance of his bootlegged records:

> The fans could not bear to be without him and musicians could not afford to ignore him. . . . Some search these out because they want to listen, some because they want to hold them in their hands, some because they provide The Key. For whatever reason, it becomes clear quite quickly that far more material remains unreleased than has ever appeared in Columbia LP's.[42]

Despite this lack of interest in the designation, Bob Dylan was for millions the symbol of the youth culture of the 1960s. He was originally believed to be the successor to "people's artist" Woody Guthrie. For many outside and inside the folk music scene, he, more than the Beatles, was the spokesman of a generation. A mystique surrounded Dylan, part of which suggested that Columbia Records and his manager Albert Grossman were overmanaging and supressing Dylan's better, more humanitarian efforts. As with all myths, there was a grain of truth. Columbia Records had in fact taken all of the controversial songs out of his first album. They recalled the original version of *Free Wheelin'* and removed "Talking John Birch Society Blues" prior to its reissuance after the CBS television network had refused permission for him to sing the antirightist song on "The Ed Sullivan Show." Moreover, a goodly number of Dylan's songs remained in the Columbia Records vaults unreleased. The reason offered to explain this artist manipulation ranged from the alleged "one album a year" policy set forth by Albert Grossman to the singer's own defection from politically oriented material. Many of his followers believed that Dylan was a pawn controlled by a large conglomerate or a poet coopted by the trappings of wealth and fame. Beginning with folk-music magazines such as *Sing Out!* and *Broadside* (NYC) (and later, the New Leaf press) the one-time successor to Woody Guthrie was labeled as an "opportunist" and worse. Perhaps the most persistent, informed spokesman of the anticommercialization forces was A. J. Weberman, the founder of the Dylan Liberation Front. In his Greenwich Village loft Weberman amassed the most complete library of Dylanology, as he terms it, to date. He writes highly exegetical pieces, dealing with the singer's latest album, for the underground press. For a time his income was mainly derived from the selling of bootleg Xeroxed copies of *Tarantula*, a Dylan volume not published until Weberman became somewhat of a celebrity in his own right, garnering articles in *Rolling Stone*, *Newsweek* and many local newspapers. On one occasion, Weberman led a group of New School students and street people to Dylan's home and chanted the slogan: "Free Bob Dylan! End rock rip-off! Free Bob Dylan!" or "Hey, Hey, Hey, Bob Dylan—Time to give away your million! . . . Hey, Hey—Bobby D., the revolution is in need of thee!" Finally, in a rather bizarre confrontation with his idol, Weberman summed up the view of Dylan held by many Consciousness III people:

> No, Bob, I wanna talk! You see . . . like people are saying you've turned into a capitalist pig, that your wealth has corrupted you. You once said that the more stake you have in the system, the more conservative you become. You know . . . 'relationships of ownership, they whisper in the wind' . . . and all that. And man, you *used* the struggle of black people to get yourself ahead. . . . You ripped-off their music! *You owe them quite a bit!*[43]

Dylan replied, "could be." The validity of Weberman's charges is best left to future historians.

Activists such as Weberman feel they are trying to liberate Dylan from forces of evil which cause him to rip off the very people he is supposed to represent. Indeed, few consumers of his album *Great White Wonder* interpreted the simply packaged set as anything more than a cultural breakthrough. *Rolling Stone*'s coverage of the album in its normal review space only further legitimated it. The first copy of the underground bootleg album appeared in Los Angeles in the late smoggy months of the summer of 1969. The original run was reportedly 2,300 albums. Although demand was created by five local radio stations that played the album, supply was haphazard and impromptu. One of the bootleggers commented. "We don't have a car of our own. We have to borrow cars to take the records around." Given the nature of the operation, names and addresses could be left with record-store operators. The record was wholesaled for $4.50, or $4.25 for orders over 50. The response to the record was greater than the bootleggers' wildest expectations. In an interview with Jerry Hopkins, they indicated that other Dylan tapes were being offered to them "by persons unknown." One of the procurers, calling himself Patrick, said, "Bob Dylan is a heavy talent and he's got all those songs nobody's ever heard. We thought we'd take it upon ourselves to make this music available."[44] "Patrick," and Vladimir" (a/k/a "Merlin") pressed 8,000 copies of the set and then fled to Canada with their profits.

Great White Wonder was very similar in packaging to the Beatle's album released the previous Christmas season. The two record set appeared in a plain white jacket, minus any labels or identifying marks, and with no listing of songs or notes. Most of the songs on the album were taken from the "basement tape" and from another tape made in a Minneapolis hotel in 1961. One further song was added from the first Johnny Cash television show broadcast. Songs on the album were "Candy Man," "Rambling Around," "Hazekiah Jones," "Ain't Got No Home in this World Anymore," "Emmett Till," "Ole Lazarus," "East Orange, New Jersey," "I'm a Man of Constant Sorrow," "New Orleans Rag," "If You Gotta Go," "Only a Hobo," "Killing Me Alive," "The Mighty Quinn," "This Wheel's on Fire," "I Shall Be Released," "Open the Door, Richard," "Too Much of Nothing," "Nothing Was Delivered," "Tears of Rage" and "Living the Blues." The set sold anywhere from $5.50 to $20.00, with prices higher as one moved further from the West Coast. Leopold's Berkeley coop sold the record for approximately the usual price of their two-album sets. In Chicago, the record sold for $9.95 and at the House of Oldies in New York it was $20.00. The mechanics of merchandising were simple. Emanuel Aron of Aron's Records in Los Angeles described part of the operation: "It's bargaining thing . . . they ask whatever they think they can get. It's always cash and carry away." According to Columbia Records investigators, two Los Angeles record-store owners, Norton Beckman and Ben Goldman, copied an original *Great White Wonder* disk to produce their own second-hand version in September 1969. Their copy was engineered in a home near downtown Los Angeles. Here a "master" pressing was made at a cost of $161.76, and then taken to the James Lee Record Processing Co. for processing, where three more "mothers" and "stampers" were made. S&L Record Manufacturers produced the finished bootleg records. In the interim, attorneys for Columbia Records, Bob Dylan and Dwarf Music obtained a restraining order from the Los Angeles U.S. District Court and asked for $20,000 in damages, "the smallest amount that could be figured against loss of income and good will." According to the brief filed against Beckman and Goldman, the plaintiffs alleged that they had engaged in "a simple case of piracy of Dylan's private musical performances for defendants' profit, and a brazen disregard of the Copyright Act provisions respecting recording licenses, copyright royalties, and elementary fair play." Most reactions to the bootleg album were not as negative. The *Rolling Stone* record-review editor noted, "Whether or not this ought to be called 'unreleased' is up to the reader." A record-store owner, until being approached by Columbia Records personnel, sold the album because, "like, all I could think about was, now, it's Dylan, and I really don't think about the moral question."[45] *Great White Wonder* spawned a number of other countercultural bootlegs. *LIVEr Than You'll Ever Be* combined the live performances of the Rolling Stones at the Los Angeles Forum and the Oakland Coliseum, nearly a year prior to the release of *Get Yer Ya Ya's Out* by London Records. *LIVEr* was the prototype of another major aspect of the underground bootleg, one which in time has to be its ultimate undoing. *LIVEr* established that "any kid can take his tape recorder to a Rolling Stones performance and become a millionaire."[46]

After the Dylan tapes had been exhausted the "live" or concert facsimile became the standard. In December 1969, two major Dylan "bootlegs" appeared. One appropriately titled *Stealin'* and *John Birch Society Blues*. Both were reviewed along with *LIVEr* and *Live Peace*, a bootleg attempt to compete with Apples *Live Peace in Toronto* by John Lennon and the Plastic Ono Band. Greil Marcus, one of the most prestigious of rock journalists, clearly outlined the ideological and cultural implications of the bootleg in his introduction. The *Rolling Stone* editor began by observing that one or two disks a year from "the Big Three of rock and roll"—Dylan, the Beatles and the Stones—were not enough. He argued that despite the mediocre fidelity of many of the records, an objection raised by some segments of the underground radio and press, they were in many cases esthetically superior to the material being released by the legitimate record companies. Marcus echoed a sentiment frequently raised by Consciousness III proponents that the record conglomerates were not sympathetic to the needs of the people or the "new community":

> In a way, the bootleg phenomena may well force artists to respond to what the public wants—or lose a lot of bread. One

> obvious way to squelch the *Great White Wonder* album, without arousing any bad feelings, would have been to issue the basement tape; the way to kill the new live Stones' album would be to release a similar LP that was even better.
>
> There are at least two reasons why this isn't happening. First of all, an artist is supposed to be able to select what he wants to release to the public, regardless of what his record company, or the public, thinks it wants; and secondly, it's never too good an idea to flood the market with too much good stuff. Or is it?
>
> The bootleggers might well force more albums out of the Stones and Dylan, in particular.[47]

Marcus, also, cautioned that the excessive number of bootlegs might in fact inhibit performers from giving concerts, but he did conclude with a glowing endorsement of all of the bootleg albums under consideration: "They aren't going to be around for very long, and simply on the basis of their musical quality, they should be bought right now. None of these albums is a mere 'collector's item' like the *Great White Wonder* stuff—all of them are listenable and exciting on their own terms." Few of the actual bootleggers have come forth to present their viewpoints. In a rare interview, one of the producers of *Stealin'* told the Los Angeles *Free Press* that his product was superior to that of Columbia Records: "Some of these songs are better than the shit Columbia has released. They just keep sitting on them so you might say in a sense, we're just liberating the records and bringing them to all the people, not just the chosen few."[48]

Quality Records, a mail-order bootleg operation that catalogued six Dylan albums, *LIVEr* by the Stones, concerts by Donovan, the Beatles, Frank Zappa, Led Zeppelin, Jethro Tull and the Jefferson Airplane advertised:

> WE PRIDE OURSELVES IN MAKING AVAILABLE THESE ORIGINAL PRODUCTIONS OF WORTHWHILE ART, THEY ARE NOT COPIES OF PREVIOUS ALBUMS. GREAT CARE

> HAS BEEN TAKEN TO PRESERVE THE DIGNITY AND SOUND QUALITY OF THE MATERIAL INVOLVED AS MUCH AS POSSIBLE. LOOK FOR THE "TRADEMARK" OF QUALITY LABEL, WHEN PURCHASING THESE COLLECTOR'S ITEMS, IT'S YOUR GUARANTEE.

The rock press, while rarely questioning the ethics of the bootleg itself, did object to the alleged inferior quality of the records. One of the first to raise this issue was Dave Marsh of the Detroit-based *Creem* magazine. Marsh saw bootlegs basically as rip-offs:

> It's a completely underground operation: the purchaser meets a middle-man, who sells him the records, money in front, flies the discs in from the coast and splits. No guarantees—half the discs could be blank. The analogy between wholesale dope dealing and wholesale bootleg records is near complete.[49]

Kaleidoscope, a Madison, Wisconsin, underground paper, also took note of the rash of bootlegs appearing in the community, condemned "gigantic profits" but then went on to say: "Now . . . some of us who feel that freak-rock belongs to the people from where it came have liberated Dylan and Beatles' tapes and returned the music to the people."[50] The reporter went on to describe how community members had taped parts of the Beatles *Get Back* and Dylan's Isle of Wight appearance and had pressed 1,000 bootleg records with a picture of John Sinclair on the cover which would be sold for $3.00. The money earned would be "returned to the community," in the form of contribution to the "bail fund." The article ended proclaiming: "This album is a step toward reclaiming the people's music from filthy capitalist record companies." The different emphases may be explained by the fact that both *Creem* and *Kaleidoscope* were influenced by the Sinclair rock *qua* politics ethos as opposed to *Rolling Stone*, which interpreted its role more in the Consciousness III or alternative culture framework. Despite the reservations about the high prices and poor quality of album rip-offs the rock press continued to announce the issuance of new bootlegs. On March 7, 1971, *Rolling Stone* printed an article entitled "Sons of 'Great White Wonder'," which alerted its readers to the availability of Dylan's *1000 Miles Behind*, *Great White Wonder Vol. II* in the Bay Area, as well as *This Way In and That Way Out*, a midwestern version of *LIVEr*, and *Come Back*, a bootleg of the Beatles' *Let It Be* on the East Coast. The next issue reported the appearance of *Great White Wonder* in the United Kingdom. The quality of bootleg records by spring 1970 has risen. *Wooden Nickel*, a two-record set of a Crosby, Stills, Nash and Young concert at the Pauley Pavilion in Los Angeles, was partially of good sound quality. It was released on the Canyon "label" with a cover photo and included the timing of several cuts such as "Down by the River" and "Suite: Judy Blue Eyes." The side with electronic music was described by David Crosby as "just shit probably taped right off the PA."[51] In July, *Rolling Stone* analyzed the Beatles' *Live*, a bootleg of their 1965 Shea Stadium appearance in the regular record review section. Ed Ward's assessment was quite negative; however, he did conclude with the familiar statement that these inferior products would have to do until Capitol or Apple saw "fit to release the nostalgic reminders."[52] In the interim, bootlegs of the concert tours of most of the "name" bands continued to appear. Critics by and large treated them as any other record they received. Bootleggers by now had also amassed promotional lists to match those of the major record companies. A few record critics went so far as to suggest topics for bootlegs, if the majors weren't interested.

The street bootleg was an artifact of the alternative lifestyle. It was originated, whatever the motivation, to furnish a service which the major record companies had not provided. Critics thought many of the Dylan bootleg albums were superior to his later efforts on Columbia Records. Early Dylan was in fact competing with the "new" Dylan of *Nashville Skyline* and *Self-Portrait* for consumer dollars. It is difficult to measure the exact value of the bootlegs since they were confined to the larger urban areas and to university and college towns. However, Bob Johnston, producer of several of Dylan's Columbia albums, told one reporter that he had been offered $200,000 for the unreleased "out takes" he had in his possession.[53] Record companies at first were relatively reluctant to respond, as witnessed in their dealings with *Great White Wonder*.

The record companies' reaction to bootleg originally was more of disbelief than moral outrage. According to a former Columbia executive the attitude was, "if we ignore it perhaps it will just go away." Many Columbia executives tended to see *Great White Wonder* as merely a collector's item similar to the jazz bootlegs of the previous decades; others considered it a unique event. Only Michael Ochs appreciated its significance. Ochs recalls that most Columbia executives refused to believe that it would sell anywhere near the estimated 50,000 to 100,000 copies it did. Freaks supposedly just "weren't that enterprising." Columbia's original outcry was that the bootleggers were producing inferior material, thus presenting the artist in an unflattering light and harming his image. Albert Grossman and Dwarf Music objected that they were not receiving royalty payments from the album. Richard Schulenberg, then a Columbia attorney, observed: "We were worried not that we were being ripped off so much, but that this service was being foisted off on the public because the quality of the records was not that good . . . Dylan and the music publishers were not getting paid . . . these people were not doing us a public service even as they said they were, because they were taking money themselves for it." When bootleggers were no longer content to issue buried vault material and "out takes" they began to compete directly with legitimate product. A Columbia executive confidentially noted that *Great White Wonder* had in fact rekindled interest in early Dylan material and had increased their sales. *LIVEr*, on the other hand, was not merely historical tapes appealing to political folkies and counterculture types, but direct competition. The 1969 Rolling Stones American tour was a well-orchestrated and arranged affair up to its tragic climax at Altamont. A tour album was planned from the outset. Consequently, the bootleg, which was cheaply produced with a surprisingly high quality of reproduction, hurt the group as well as its recording company, although the estimated $100 million record and tape counterfeiters made the bootleggers appear small in contrast. "Then," says Schulenberg, "they decided that perhaps there was moral indignation on top of economic indignation." Joe Smith at Warner Brothers recalls. "The first one was Dylan, and then they did somebody else, and then they hit us." Smith expresses considerable displeasure with the attitudes of the street and rock press concerning the bootlegs:

> What disturbed me most was this great cavalier attitude the press took about that, and the rock community. . . . Wow, here's this Robin Hood coming along. Ain't that good, look what he's doing. Bullshit, they're not paying anybody . . . I really was incensed with this rob from the rich and give to the poor attitude. Because they were robbing from the rich and weren't giving to anybody. They were getting rich from robbing the rich.
>
> I called Jann Wenner of *Rolling Stone* and said 'I cannot understand how you could even talk about those things,' at which point he stopped. Not because of me alone, but I think because it dawned on him what total absolute robbery and bullshit that whole operation was. Ralph Gleason tore into Jann because it was dishonest.

In a stern and fatherly editorial, Ralph J. Gleason warned that counterfeiters such as Rubber Dubber and bootleggers were "simply thieves." Gleason went on to accuse the music industry—artist and company—of being responsible for the bootlegger since they charged "inflated prices." This rip-off of the counterculture produced a spate of "quack Robin Hoods" who posed as public benefactors—"giving the public a chance to get some more of what they wanted when the artists themselves (and companies) were unable or unwilling to supply the demand." He went on to reiterate the argument originally posed by Greil Marcus that most of the Dylan bootlegs could have been curtailed if Columbia had released the "basement tape." Having said this, Gleason continued to list the individuals that were being harmed by bootleggers—the composer, members of the band, the public and the record companies. On the latter, he qualified his statement acknowledging they are cheated, "but it is fashionable these days not to worry about corporate entities in this way, a dangerous fad as time will show."[54]

Gleason lashed out at the "public service" aspect of bootlegging, comparing it to procuring or pimping: "after all, we are performing a public service. So is bullshit." The editorial closed on a note previously not heard in the rock and underground press:

> The artist has a true right to work at his art and to make it come as close as possible to what he envisions for it. In the instance of making phonograph records, this includes the right to reject performances in favor of other performances and he should not have to suffer the indignity of hearing his rejects on some underground radio station just because the public is insatiable in its lust for him.

While qualifying his argument with the statement that record companies, perhaps, were charging too much and unresponsive to public tastes, Gleason was one of the first to assert the validity of the notion of individual artist control over his product.

In Michigan, New York and Arizona, raids were staged and records, tapes and equipment seized. In nearly all of the cases, raids were directed at counterfeiters rather than bootleggers. The industry's tact in regard to bootlegged records is probably consequence of their dependence on field men, radio-station managers and record-store owners to get their products before the public. While these groups share some common interest in seeing records succeed, they do not necessarily champion the concerns of record conglomerates. The control that the conglomerates exercise, while increasing, remains unreliable. They may sanction an errant field representative or deejay; the punished may respond with equal force. Hypothetically, a company may, in rage, writhdraw its advertising portfolio from *Rolling Stone* or a radio station in response to negative reviews or treatment of its product. This action may cut the sanctioned's immediate revenue, but the exposure of the company's products would be greatly curtailed by such an action. Record-store owners, while more dependent upon the company than cultural gatekeepers, have similar powers. Consequently, aggrieved companies generally employed gentle persuasion in their efforts to stop the sale of *Great White Wonder*. The bootleggers were found (no easy task), were sued and restraining orders obtained. However, the bootleg remained a very touchy subject. One record-company executive told me that it was not in their interest to alienate business associates just to find a few "hippie" kids selling Dylan tapes. The incursion of bootleggers into direct competition with the conglomerate appears to have altered this posture. Originally, record-store owners were tactfully approached and warned of poorer service if they handled counterfeits or bootlegs. In 1971, owners were specifically told that they would no longer receive any promotional or advertising money from Warner Brothers or Columbia Records. One owner told *Rolling Stone*: "I was also instructed by the Warner-Elektra-Atlantic group that if I carried a single bootleg, they wouldn't sell me any more records. They were unwilling to put this in writing."[55] Ed Ward, then with *Rolling Stone*, recalled: "the record companies had turned the heat on. Small record stores that sold bootlegs began to get threats and visits from large men who claimed to represent one label or another. Several of Bud's [Rubber Dubber] salesmen were shot at in the streets. Jack Apache was attacked while servicing an account. Some record stores were told that the distributors would stop selling them records if they continued to stock Rubber Dubber's but, since this was clearly illegal, Bud sent out a flyer offering legal assistance to any store able to prove it had been threatened. The threats stopped."[56] Sam Goody, one of the major independents in New York, was sued for selling bootleg records. A jury found him not guilty, but the decision was later reversed.

This lack of immediate success apparently temporarily forced the industry to shift its efforts to the halls of Congress, where the McClennan antipirate bill was lobbied through the House and Senate. Just prior to the passage of the antipirate bill, Ode Records, a subsidiary of A&M, sued Emanuel Aron for $1.5 million for damages and punitive costs. Aron was selling a bootleg of Carole King's Los Angeles concert. The passage of the McClennan amendment extending copyright to recorded material appears to have greatly strengthened the hand of the industry.

This legislation as well as the general decline of the Consciousness III ideology has curtailed bootlegging. However, there remain companies like Godzilla which still provide collectors with bootleg tapes and records. Actually, the major industry problem is the pirates who steal from already released hit records. In this area, the record industry has launched a vigorous state by state lobbying attempt. They have been successful in at least half of the states as of 1975.

Frederick Engels, in a critique of utopian Socialists, once observed that social change is to be sought "not in the philosophy, but in the economics of each particular epoch." The 1960s equivalent of this position is that revolution is a product of political action, not of cultural endeavors. Marxist Gil Green aptly summed up the political interpretation of counterculturites: "Unable to build utopian islands on earth, they began to build them in heaven. Religious superstitution was the opiate that made the hell of earth more endurable, just as Zen Buddhism, rock music and pot have become the opiate that enable many youth today to escape to the new found heaven and heaven of 'Woodstock Nation'."[56] Conversely, proponents of Consciousness II advocate that "a revolution that expects you to sacrifice yourself for it is one of daddy's revolutions" or "to serve the cause would be to subvert the cause." Events have brought the antagonists into common cause in opposition to the Establishment, but beyond a shared hatred of police, the American presence in Vietnam and legislative injustice, the two philosophical groups are at sword's point. The politically oriented ask cultural leaders and rock stars, "Would you finance the revolution if somebody gave you $500,000?" This is a sentiment widely held by record-company executives. Replying to critics Stan Cornyn exclaimed, "It's not exactly slavery that we're talking about. Artists have record companies by the balls. They dictate their packaging, they really dictate how long they're going to record, how long it's going to take them and how much it will cost. Blank check in terms of recording studio time. Who is benefiting by this revolution? I don't find an awful lot of recording artists who say 'Sinclair you're right. Warner Brothers is screwing us.' Or any record company." Joe Smith and Bhasker Menon hold similar opinions: "As soon as a rock artist makes ten cents," says Smith, "they move to their home with a swimming pool and they want the things that other people want. They realize that some kind of business establishment world must intrude on that. The companies aren't ripping them off." Brownsville Station does not share this view. But they are equally critical of the Grande Ballroom and what they see as "political bullshit." Mike Lutz says: "During the whole duration of the Grande, the kids liked us but because of the political aspect and everything the promoters and the top rock people they couldn't stand us . . . we were adamant about the fact we weren't gonna be political bullshit, no dope bullshit, no bullshit at all. Let's just get up there and have a good time, and no one understood that at all. It was crazy."

Dylan has cautioned, "don't follow leaders, watch the parking meters." The cool reception of Jerry Rubin at the Be-In and Abbie Hoffman's unceremonious ejection from the Woodstock stage are but two encounters between the politically oriented and those urging a withdrawal from participation in the "death culture." One school, perhaps best represented by the folks at *Broadside* (NYC), emphasizes protest in lyrics and artists' social action. The other sees music as a force independent of intellect—and action—which will "change the heads of its listeners." The idea that rock is in itself revolutionary negates the need for manning the barricades. Many street people, while merging with the "greening" movement, have joined with Theodore Roszak in identifying their actions with William Blake, Allen Ginsberg and Bob Dylan rather than Marx, Lenin or Mao. Several writers, notably Reich and Sinclair, have attempted to transcend this cleavage, which dates back to the Marx-Feuerbach polemic. Both have failed, since their paradigm argues that culture changes the polity, and that political men who ignore the cultural preferences of their potential converts fall by the wayside. Still, their perceptions have added new and exciting dimensions to what is called popular music.

By 1972 the "battle of the street" was generally over. Bootleg records emanating from countercultural groups diminished in the wake of numerous prosecutions made possible by the 1971 Copyright Revision. Bootlegging, it appears, has returned to nonideological profiteers. Yet the notions of people's music and the rock revolution remain a pressing and burning issue for some Americans, especially those in what is termed the radical Right.

Notes, Chapter 7

1. Charles Reich, *Greening of America* (New York: Random House, 1970), pp. 169–70.
2. Theodore Roszak, *The Making of a Counter-Culture: Reflections of the Technocratic Society and Its Youthful Opposition* (Garden City: Doubleday and Co., Inc., 1969), p. 291.
3. Phil Ochs, liner notes, Jim and Jean, *Changes*. Verve Folkways FT.3001.
4. John Sinclair, "A Letter From Prison," *Creem* 2 (no date provided) also see John Sinclair, *Guitar Army* (New York: Douglas Book Corporation, 1972).
5. John Sinclair, "Liberation Music," *Creem* 2: 19.

6. Ibid., p. 20.
7. Ibid.
8. Sinclair, "Letter."
9. Sinclair, "Liberation Music," p. 21.
10. David Walley, 'MC5 Interview," in Johnathan Eisen, ed., *Age of Rock*, vol. 2 (New York: Vintage Press, 1970), p. 272.
11. Dave Marsh, "MC5: Back On Shakin Street," *Creem* 3 (October 1971): 45.
12. Mike Lydon, "Rock For Sale," in *Divided We Stand* (San Francisco: Canfield Press, 1969), p. 153.
13. T. Procter Lippincott, "The Culture Vultures," in Johnathan Eisen, ed., *Age of Rock*, vol. 2, p. 124.
14. Ibid., p. 125.
15. Craig Karpel, "Das Hip Kapital," *Creem* 3 (March 1971): 32.
16. Greil Marcus review of *Magic Bus*, *Rolling Stone* 21 (November 9, 1968): 21.
17. "Beatles LP Boycott: Outrageous Price," *Rolling Stone* 51 (February 7, 1970): 13.
18. " 'Beatles Again'—You Figure It," *Rolling Stone* 54 (March 7, 1970): 8; and "Capitol Says $6.98 Is A Fair Price," *Rolling Stone* 53 (March 7, 1970): 8.
19. Emile Durkheim, *Elementary Forms of Religious Life*, trans. Joseph Ward Swain (New York: Free Press, 1968), p. 375.
20. Richard Goldstein, *Velvet Underground and Nico*, Verve V-5008 liner notes.
21. Quoted in Tom Wolfe, *The Electric Kool-Aid Acid Test* (New York: Bantam Books, 1969), p. 225.
22. Burton H. Wolfe, *The Hippies* (New York: A Signet Book, 1968), p. 42.
23. Quoted in Gleason, *The Jefferson Airplane and the San Francisco Sound*. (New York: Ballantine Books, 1969), p. 296.
24. Ibid., p. 41.
25. "Dropouts With a Mission," *Newsweek*, February 6, 1967, pp. 92–95.
26. "The Message of History's Biggest Happening," *Time*, August 29, 1969, p. 32.
27. Mark Kramer, "The Rock Imperialists," *The Fifth Estate*, Fall 1969, p. 7.
28. Greil Marcus, "The Woodstock Festival," *Rolling Stone* 42 (September 20, 1969): 17.

29. Jerry Hopkins, *Festival! The Book of American Music Celebrations* (New York: Collier Books, 1970), p. 140.

30. "The Great Woodstock Rock Trip," *Life*, special edition, 1969, p. 4.

31. "It Was Like Balling For the First Time," *Rolling Stone* 42 (September 20, 1969): 24.

32. Joseph J. Sia, *Woodstock 69: Summer Pop Festivals* (New York: Scholastic Book Services, 1970).

33. Barry Farrell, "Gloria! Donald! Countermiracle at the Great Stones Rock Show," *Life*, special edition, 1969.

34. Abbie Hoffman, *The Woodstock Nation* (New York: Vintage Books, 1969): p. 130.

35. Jan Hodenfield, "After Woodstock: Money and Smiles," *Rolling Stone* 43 (October 4, 1969): 1, 6 and "Global Replays of Woodstock Fest Parlay Rock, Fun, Drugs and Peace," *Variety*, September 3, 1969, p. 56.

36. Quoted in Ernest Dunbar, "Music Is Where the Money Is," *Look*, August 25, 1971, p. 17.

37. Quoted in "Shooting Up a Rock Bonanza," in *Divided We Stand* (San Francisco: Canfield Press, 1970), p. 159. The Beatles' song "Revolution" in Part echoed this sentiment.

38. "Motherfuckers Hit the Fillmore East," *Rolling Stone* 26 (February 1, 1960): 4.

39. Quoted in Mitchell Goodman, ed., *The Movement Toward a New America* (Philadelphia: Pilgrim Press, 1970), p. 384.

40. "They Just Don't Want Rip-Offs," *Rolling Stone* 59 (May 28, 1970): 10.

41. "CREEM Interview With Grateful Dead," *Creem* 2 (December 1970): 20.

42. Greil Marcus, "Records," *Rolling Stone* 47 (November 29, 1969): 44.

43. Quoted in Claudia Dreifus, "The Alan J. Weberman Story," *Rolling Stone* 77 (March 4, 1971): 44.

44. Quoted in Jerry Hopkins, " 'New' Dylan Album Bootlegged in LA," *Rolling Stone* 42 (September 20, 1969): 6.

45. Quoted in John Morthland and Jerry Hopkins, "Bootleg: The Rock and Roll Liberation Front?" *Rolling Stone* 51 (February 7, 1970): 6.

46. "Revolutionary War," *Time*, June 28, 1971, p. 72.

47. Greil Marcus, "The Bootleg LPs" in "Records," *Rolling Stone* 51 (February 7, 1970): 36.

48. Quoted in John Carpenter, "Bootleggers Hustle New Dylan Album," *Los Angeles Free Press*, December 19, 1969, p. 52.

49. Dave Marsh, "Rock and Roll Bootleggers and Other Strange People," *Creem* 2 (November 15, 1969): 13.

50. "Bootleg Records," *Kaleidoscope*, March 18, 1970.

51. Quoted in "They Just Don't Want Rip-Offs," *Rolling Stone* 59 (May 28, 1970): 10.

52. Ed Ward, "Beatles Live," *Rolling Stone* 62 (July 9, 1970): 39.

53. Quoted in "Bob Johnston Remembers," *Rolling Stone* 87 (July 22, 1971): 19. Also see Joshua P. Fitzroy, "Melvin Potter Interview: Pirate A Record, Make $8,000," *Los Angeles Free Press*, April 10, 1970.

54. Ralph J. Gleason, "Perspectives: All the Quack Robin Hoods," *Rolling Stone* 93 (October 14, 1971): 30.

55. Quoted in Bob Chorush, "Feds Are Leaning on Bootleggers," *Rolling Stone* 93 (October 14, 1971): 10.

56. Ed Ward, "The Bootleg Blues: The Rise and Fall of Rubber Dubber Records," *Harpers*, January 1974, p. 38.

57. G. I. Green, *The New Radicalism: Anarchist or Marxist* (New York: International Publishers, 1971), p. 23.

8.

THE RADICAL RIGHT AND THE FCC

We need a lot more Jesus
and a lot less rock and roll
© *Oleta Starday, 1966*

Once a record has survived the many hurdles placed in its path and actually attracted the attention of gatekeepers and distributors, it is still not guaranteed success. In a small number of cases a "hit-bound" record or even a charted song may be subject to the interference of ideological groups and the imposition of legal sanctions. Some of these groups see popular music as a "social evil," antithetical to their peculiar values. Many adults regard pop music as an esthetic disaster area, but some impute to it more sinister connotations.

With these assumptions flying high, campaigns have been launched to suppress those portions of popular music—songs and artists—deemed harmful to Top 40 and progressive listeners. Petitions have been aimed at broadcasters and their sponsors, urging the removal of Beatle records from the stations' play lists. Record stores in some communities have been boycotted for stocking "offensive" records. Citizens committees have approached the Federal Communications Commission (FCC) to complain that local broadcasters have not carried out their responsibilities to the "public interest" due to the playing of certain songs. Several successful artists, Jerry Lee Lewis and Chuck Berry in the late 1950s, were blacklisted from AM radio for alleged "immoral behavior." Chuck Berry was placed in a federal penitentiary. The organization most responsible for these assaults since the early 1950s has been the radical Right.

THE RADICAL RIGHT AND POPULAR MUSIC

Surrounded by the splendor of a Las Vegas gambling casino, former Vice-President Spiro Agnew told a crowd of assembled reporters, "We should listen more carefully to popular music, because at its best it is worthy of more serious appreciation, and at its worst it is blatant drug-culture propaganda." Nearly all of the media carried Agnew's statement that some rock music was harmful to America's young. Pop music had become yet another target of Agnew's 1970 congressional campaign effort. For the radical Right this was absolution. Finally, at long last, a ranking government official had validated their contention: that rock was corrupting American youth. For them this was no mere Agnewism but the high-water mark of a 20-year effort to rid popular music of "subversive" elements.

In the public mind the radical Right is a collection of "little old ladies in tennis shoes" allied with southern segregationists and Minutemen obsessed with putting prayers back into classrooms, getting the U.S. out of the United Nations and opposing fluoridation. Each foray undertaken by the radical Right is believed by them to be an assault on the machinations of an international Communist conspiracy. Fluoridation, school-board elections and Supreme Court decisions all have been pawns in that imagined conspiracy. The radical Right, however, has a more grandiose world view. According to sociologist Gary B. Rush, the Right is basically a myriad of groups which maintain as an ideal the principle of "limited individualism," that is, "the opposition of 'collectivism' in government, international relations, to modern social principles, and modern social structure and operation."[1] Put another way, the radical Right is profoundly concerned about changing social values and styles, because it assumes that individual character is by itself weak and corruptible when void of traditional values. The late historian Richard Hofstadter termed this outlook the "revolt against modernity." For the record industry this revolt has been manifested in the condemnation of popular music.

The Right's original introduction to popular music came by way of a folk-music group called the Weavers, which became an overnight success just as McCarthyism was blossoming into a potent sociopolitical force. With "Tzena, Tzena," "Good Night Irene" and Woody Guthrie's "So Long It's Been Good to Know You," the quartet dominated the popular-music charts of 1950. The junior senator from Wisconsin, Joseph McCarthy, held sway over the news. There were Communists in high places in America, he charged, including the entertainment media. The senator was preoccupied with government bureaus and agencies, so the task of investigating the entertainment world was left to the House Committee on Un-American Activities (HCUA). During their investigations into the subversion of American culture, HCUA called professional witness Harvey Matusow, who claimed that the Weavers were Communists. After this "identification," and a similar charge in *Red Channels*, a guide to the political reliability of entertainers, the Weavers were blacklisted from the media and finally forced to disband at the peak of their popularity. Outside of Matusow's testimony, which later he recanted, and the *Channels* citation, there was no evidence to support the charge. Several members of the group—Pete Seeger and Lee Hays—had on occasion appeared before left-wing audiences, but this did not make them card-carrying Communist party members. Ironically, those ties that *did* exist between the Weavers and the CPUSA were never aired either before HCUA or in *Red Channels.* In 1950 mere accusation was enough. Having successfully removed the Weavers from the public airways, the Right turned its attention to more pressing matters—the "betrayal of China" and the persecution of Senator McCarthy by the "Eastern liberal establishment."

In time "communism in high places" took a back seat to the issue of school desegregation. The Supreme Court had ruled in the landmark *Brown* decision that segregated schools were unconstitutional and therefore must be eliminated. Coincidentally, 1954 also witnessed the emergence of something called "rock and roll." Rock was a first cousin to what had been called "race" music. This relationship would later become a central issue with the radical Right.

RACISM AND ROCK AND ROLL

For most adult Americans, rock and roll was a loud new irritant that just might lead their children to juvenile delinquency. Several communities attempted to control it by legislating against "record hops," as they would against rock festivals some 15 years later. The prime impetus for the popularity of the music was the medium of film. *Blackboard Jungle* was the story of a middle-class white high-school teacher laboring in the vineyards of a New York ghetto school. Its theme music was Bill Haley's "Rock Around the Clock." The significance of this film was astronomical. Frank Zappa, years later, recalled: "I didn't care if Bill Haley was white or sincere . . . he was playing the Teenage National Anthem and it was so LOUD I was jumping up and down. *Blackboard Jungle* . . . represented a strange sort of 'endorsement' of the teenage cause: 'They have made a movie about us.' "[2] The impact of "Rock Around the Clock" was such that in a matter of months white "covers" or copies of black rock material all but dominated the "Hit Parade," much to the dismay of traditional crooners. It was artificial but it sold. Elvis Presley was a mixture of all of these elements. His stage dress was from *Blackboard Jungle.* He covered black material leaving much of the original intent. When he sang "Shake, Rattle and Roll" no one thought he meant dancing. Efforts were made to stop Elvis "The Pelvis" by various parent-teacher groups with some success. Ed Sullivan broadcast only the upper half of the famous torso. In Florida, the police insisted he stand still. The

Right concurred, but dissented as to the true meaning of the new popular musical trend.

Asa Carter, executive secretary of the North Alabama White Citizens Council, told the *New York Times* that the National Association for the Advancement of Colored People (NAACP) was "infiltrating" southern white teenagers with rock and roll. (The NAACP had been instrumental in pressing the *Brown* case to the Supreme Court.) Carter proposed that his organization survey juke-boxes and radio stations so as to purge those sources of "immoral" records. He went on to urge that deejays and coin operators that violated his ban be publicly harassed. Lacking the legal support afforded some northern antirock forces, Carter met with considerable opposition from industry people. A local record distributor, Harry Hurrich, retorted, "I consider Carter's proposal an invasion of the freedom of liking what you want to."[3] A programmer at a local radio station replied, "the only dictation in our business is that of our listeners. Carter's statement . . . is absurd." Roy Wilkins of the NAACP, obviously not a rock-music buff, equated it with disease and nuclear radiation, while denying the charge: "Some people in the South are blaming us for everything from measles to atomic fall out."[4] *Billboard* said, "Teenagers are unanimous on two points. They like rock and roll and they don't want it taken off the machines."[5] This rather obvious point did not dissuade rock's southern opponents. The Citizen's Council of Greater New Orleans printed a handbill announcing:

> The screaming, idiotic words, and savage music of these records are undermining the morals of our white youth *in America.*
>
> Call the advertisers of the radio stations that play this type of music and complain to them!
>
> Don't Let Your Children Buy, or Listen To, These Records.

But they did, and the Right's attempt to link rock and roll with the school integration decision failed. Rock itself was defused as a political issue with its absorption by "American Bandstand." Presley's engineered image change from "hood stud" to church-going G.I. left the Right with nothing to do except concern itself with the reappearance of Pete Seeger, the Weavers and the folk music revival.

MARXIST MINSTRELS

When Seeger was barred from the mass media in the 1950s, many of his "progressive" supporters already had gone underground or fled the political scene because of the invasion of Hungary by the Soviet Union (1956) and the famous Khrushchev "secret speech" the same year at the 22nd Party Congress. All that remained for the charismatic folksinger was the college circuit where phone calls from the American Legion went unheeded. Going to a Seeger concert became an act of political courage. Seeger cultivated collegiate interest in the songs of Leadbelly, Woody Guthrie, the Weavers and in traditional folk material. His activities infuriated the Right, especially after folk music became a national fad of several years duration.

Seeger was a prime mover in the folk-music revival and was accepted by collegiates and young people, outside of the South, regardless of his alleged Communist sympathies and his citation by the House Un-American Activities Committee for contempt of Congress. The Right devoted a considerable amount of press space to the folksinger and his descendants, including Bob Dylan. Dylan played a central role as villain. He *was* the link between folksinger Pete Seeger and the Beatles. Jere Real, writing in the John Birch Society organ *American Opinion*, went through the usual congressional and right-wing citations "proving" that Woody Guthrie and especially Seeger were Kremlin agents. He did not stop with People's Songs, Inc., but also indicted Bob Dylan as a "student of old time Communist Woody Guthrie." He continued to portray

Dylan's songs as "typical . . . filled with the bitter polemic which characterizes the Communist folksong."[6] The recitation of these charges was not particularly important in themselves since displeasure with folk-singers has been a traditional rightist position dating back to pre-World War II days. The linkage was dubbed "folk-rock" by *Billboard*'s Aaron Sternfield and came to the fore in 1965, much to the consternation of both segments of the Left and Right. The Left in many cases felt rock an unworthy bearer of political themes. The Right saw it as an unholy alliance of civil rights and communism. This was the year that the John Birch Society and the Billy James Hargis's Christian Crusade "discovered" rock and roll. The events which engendered this attention hinged on the introduction of "protest material" into the previously apolitical Top 40 and the Beatles alleged anti-Christ posture.

On August 21, 1965, a song entitled "Eve of Destruction" climbed to the 58 position on the *Billboard* Hot 100 chart. The song was in the folk-rock genre, pioneered and developed by the Byrds and Bob Dylan, fundamentally a wedding of contemporary and topical lyrics with a subdued 4/4 rock progression, maximizing the poetic or political statement. The sentiment of "Eve" was that the world was on the brink of nuclear war and would be destroyed unless mankind came to its collective senses. P. F. Sloane, the song's 19-year-old composer, defined its message as "a call to arms. We're on the eve of destruction and it doesn't have to be that way." He told another interviewer that the song was indicative of "decaying everywhere. . . . Society is so confused. There are triple roadblocks and detours whereever you go, and no one knows which road to travel. The Bomb? It's like a cloud hanging over me all the time."[7] The song immediately provoked a controversy. Some broadcasters wondered if "an entertainment medium should be used for propagandistic purposes?" Folkniks denounced it as commercialization of protest. For the Right, it was a call to arms. On September 9, "Eve" reached the exhaulted *Billboard* top ten. This prompted a massive letter-writing campaign to the media. In California, the Citizens for Conservative Action and the Young Republicans for a Return to Conservatism petitioned the Federal Communications Commission, contending that the song was in violation of the "fairness doctrine." There was even some talk of the Beach Boys or some other major group recording a reply. None did, although the Spokesmen did release an answer song, "The Dawn of Correction," which in industry jargon was a "stiff." The letter-writing campaign threatening an economic boycott was partially successful. The American Broadcasting Co. forbid its affiliates to air the song. Many disk jockeys echoed Bob Eubank's statement: "How do you think the enemy will feel with a tune like that No. 1 in America?" "Eve" generated a number of imitations dealing with high-school dress codes and superficial statements about ghetto conditions. After 11 weeks the song dropped off the charts. The Right's indignation was not stilled, primarily due to the efforts of Reverend David A. Noebel.

Noebel began his career in the radical Right while a student at the University of Wisconsin, where he taught fundamentalist Bible classes off campus. He was recruited into the Christian Crusade by its founder, Billy James Hargis, and quickly rose in the movement's hierarchy. Lecturing as a bespectacled neighborhood high-school coach, he lent his voice to those fighting the popularity of folk music. At first, he exhibited the by now time-tested posture charging that folk-music books and records used in the schools were corrupting the minds of unsuspecting children. He wrote several tracts charging that Young People's Records—now owned by *Good Housekeeping*—and the publishers of the *Fireside Book of Folk Music* were Communist fronts. These accusations had been raised on several previous occasions by various southern California right-wing newspapers and were not terribly original except to those outside of the Los Angeles area. Noebel's campaign did establish him as *the* Crusade authority on the impact of music upon youth. With these credentials Noebel attempted to send the

Beatles back to Liverpool and Bob Dylan packing to Hibbing, Minnesota.

In 1965, Noebel produced a pamphlet titled *Communism, Hypnotism and The Beatles: An Analysis of the Communist Use of Music.* In a style that would become his trademark, Noebel presented a manifesto with the air of a behavioral psychologist. The 26-page pamphlet contained ten pages of obscure footnotes ranging from Pavlov to HCUA publications to a television guide purchased at a Rexall Drug Store. The essence of this little book is captured in his statement that: "To understand what rock and roll in general and the Beatles in particular are doing to our teenagers, it is necessary to return to Pavlov's laboratory. The Beatles' ability to make teenagers take off their clothes and riot is laboratory tested and approved. It is scientifically labeled mass hypnosis and artificial neurosis."[8] Noebel further suggested that the Liverpool foursome were acting in the interest of the Soviet Union by weakening the moral fiber of the nation's youth, thus rendering them useless in the fight against communism.

The motivation for this attack appears to have been apparently triggered by an offhand remark by Derek Taylor, then the Beatles press aide, to the effect, "They're completely anti-Christ. I mean, I'm anti-Christ as well, but they're so anti-Christ they shock me." In a radio address from the United Kingdom, Billy James Hargis picked up on this remark saying. "The beatnik crowd, represented by the Beatles, is the Communist crowd." Agents of the anti-Christ were employing a subliminal form of musical brainwashing or propaganda, which Noebel claimed would lead to a massive "teenage mental breakdown." In his book, he warned: "Cybernetic warfare is the ultimate weapon and we can't afford one nerve-jammed child. Throw your Beatle and rock and roll records in the city dump. We have been unashamed of being labeled a Christian nation, let's make sure four mop-headed anti-Christ beatniks don't destroy our children's emotional and mental stability and ultimately our nation." In a follow-up work, *Rhythm, Riots and Revolution*, the Christian Crusader attempted to develop a cohesive explanation and causal relationship wedding the Communist conspiracy, folk music, rock and popular music and its singers. Folk music and rock, he wrote, had primitive African roots. Rock particularly exhibited mindless sensual rhythms, made all the more dangerous by the lyrics of Seeger, Guthrie, Ochs, P. F. Sloane and Dylan. To support this argument, Noebel presented a seemingly scientific comparison of two small-sized cities: Paducah, Kentucky, and Cape Girardeau, Missouri. In one community rock and roll was a pervasive part of life, whereas the other city was relatively free of its influence. The combined rate of illegitimacy, school dropouts, fatal auto accidents, burglaries and vandalism was, according to Noebel, "fifty percent higher than it is in the city where good dance music rules."[9]

Political lyrics made rock and roll even more dangerous. "Eve of Destruction," Noebel claimed, was a case in point since it included words which "are obviously aimed at instilling fear in our teenagers as well as a sense of hopelessness. 'Thermonuclear holocaust,' 'the button,' 'the end of the world,' and similar expressions are constantly being used to induce the American public to surrender to atheistic international Communism." With these two works and a series of articles in *Christian Crusader*, Noebel established himself as the Right's leading authority and spokesman on musical subversion. Unwittingly, several music-world personalities appear to have added fuel and legitimacy to Noebel's accusations.

John Lennon, in an interview printed in the London tabloid *Evening Standard*, remarked that the Beatles were "now more popular than Jesus." The remark referred to the declining influence of the Church of England. As reported in the American press, the observation revived the Right's antipathy for the group and rock music. The statement was circulated widely throughout the Bible Belt, resulting in several public burnings of records under the aegis of the KKK and the Citizens Councils. Fundamentalist radio stations vowed never again to air Beatle records. The Beatles were burned in effigy in many sections of the rural South. There was some discussion of postponing their American tour; however, promoters, mayors and local officials argued there would be trouble from irate fans if any concerts were cancelled. The Beatles' overall popularity and the publication of the entire interview greatly mitigated the impact of the remarks, as few could objectively dispute the notion that the Beatles did outdraw and receive more attention than the Church of England, something many English churchmen readily conceded. The incident quickly passed from public memory except in the tracts published by the Right. Noebel, in yet another analysis of the Beatles, returned to the affair some three years later. Besides labeling the quartet the anti-Christs, he also found them in large measure responsible for the rise in drug abuse in the United States.

DRUGS AND POPULAR MUSIC

The passivity and introspection believed to be a consequence of marijuana smoking, coupled with the addictive features of various amphetamines and heroin, fit comfortably into Noebel's schema that the purpose of Dylan, the Beatles and others was to incapacitate the young. Unlike the "made in Moscow" thesis, the association between music and drugs had some basis in fact.

Luria Castell, a founder of San Francisco's Family Dog, called the city an "American Liverpool." She saw the bay city as the only metropolis capable of maintaining a "scene" similar to the one which gave rise to the Beatles and the Mersey sound. While certainly not the only ingredient, the dominant social glue of the Haight-Ashbury scene was the drug culture. Kesey's dictum of "being on the bus" during the Trips Festival period was primarily derived from dropping LSD. Consequently, a good portion of the music emanating from San Francisco was *drug oriented*, an influence which quickly permeated Los Angeles bands such as the Buffalo Springfield, the Byrds and the Seeds, who frequently appeared in San Francisco. In most cases the music was *complementary* to the acid or pot itself. The instrumentals were prolonged and improvised akin to the jazz riffs of the beat days of North Beach. Various devices to emphasize higher octaves and lower basses were employed to highlight the experience. To those "off the bus" the songs no doubt sounded a bit long and somewhat strange. The material of the Grateful Dead, Sons of Champlin, Quicksilver Messenger Service or the Jefferson Airplane, mixed with strobe lights and color slides, provided further stimuli to the drug itself. As Donovan would write, "Fly Jefferson Airplane gets you there on time . . . Captain High at your service." Lead guitarist Jerry Garcia of the Dead was aptly nicknamed Captain Trips. Minus the McLuhanesque affections, much of the music sounded rather innocent with the overt exception of the Airplane material, especially "White Rabbit," which remains the archetypal drug song. Folk-rock groups outside of the Haight-Ashbury also toyed with this theme. In Los Angeles groups calling themselves the Seeds and the Doors emerged. The latter group chose its name from the Aldous Huxley book *Doors of Perception*, which chronicled his experiences with peyote and mescalin. There is little doubt that from 1965–67 a number of West Coast groups had some connection to the drug subculture; however, their advocacy of narcotics was another matter. With increasing awareness of the "hippie phenomenon" Sunday supplement writers, ministers and "moral entrepreneurs" in 1966 began to associate popular music with drugs. In the beginning, critics ignored the obvious Trips Festivals and concentrated on ambiguous Dylan songs such as "Mr. Tambourine Man" and "Rainy Day Woman 12 and 35," which contained the chorus "everybody must get stoned." The Byrds, who began by covering Dylan songs, including "Tambourine Man," added "Eight Miles High" to their repertoire to further fan the flames. The defense offered by the Byrds that their song referred to an airplane flight over London was ignored. Their detractors insisted that it was indeed a drug song. Donovan's album *Sunshine Superman*, the Amboy Dukes' *Journey to the Center of the Mind*, the Beatles' *Sgt. Pepper's Lonely Hearts Club Band* and the Jefferson Airplane's *Surrealistic Pillow* furthered the rock *qua* drug syndrome. The Jefferson Airplane's "White Rabbit," taken from their album, was based on the Lewis Carroll character in *Alice in Wonderland* and advocated the expansion of an individual's awareness state or consciousness:

> One pill makes you larger
> And one pill makes you small
> And the ones that mother gives you
> Don't do anything at all
> Go ask Alice, when she's 10 feet tall.

The song, using a bolero tempo, ends with a crescendo urging the repeated cry of "feed your head." Very few songs played on AM radio made similar statements. After 1967, and the disintegration of the San Francisco Summer of Love, the drug song phenomenon subsided. Only "Don't Bogart Me," featured in the film *Easy Rider*, and Brewer and Shipley's "One Toke Over the Line" transcended the esoteric underground networks. At yet another level folk-rock artists such as Jamie Brockett ("The Legend of the U.S.S. *Titanic*"), Arlo Guthrie ("Flying Into Los Angeles"), Tom Paxton ("Talking Vietnam Pot Luck Blues") and John Prine ("Illegal Smile") have toyed with the relationship of grass to the law and other social institutions. In 1969, two years after its nadir, the Christian Crusade, the John Birch Society and other extreme Right organizations took up the banner of rock as drug music.

Interpretations of "Along Comes Mary" or "Lucy in the Sky with Diamonds" were esoteric, for moral entrepreneurs could easily have confined themselves to Donovan's *Sunshine Superman* album or the Jefferson Airplane's *Surrealistic Pillow*, which they discovered some three years *after* their first appearance. Even Agnew's famous Las Vegas news conference

Exhibit 8.1

CHARTED "DRUG SONGS" CITED BY CRITICS, 1965-1969

Name	Title	Date of Appearance	Position	Weeks on Chart
Amboy Dukes	"Journey to Center of Mind"	6/29/68	16	12
Association	"Along Comes Mary"	6/04/66	7	11
American Breed	"Bend Me, Shape Me"	12/02/67	5	14
American Breed	"Step Out of Your Mind"	6/03/67	24	9
Beach Boys	"Good Vibrations"	10/22/66	1	14
Beatles	"Strawberry Fields Forever"	2/25/67	8	9
Byrds	"8 Miles High"	4/09/66	14	9
Byrds	"Mr. Tambourine Man"	5/05/65	1	13
Bob Dylan	"Rainy Day Women 12 & 35"	4/16/66	2	10
Donovan	"Mellow Yellow"	11/12/66	2	12
Donovan	"Sunshine Superman"	7/30/66	1	13
Electric Prunes	"Had Too Much to Dream"	12/10/68	24	6
Esquires	"Get On Up"	8/19/67	11	15
Fifth Dimension	"Up-Up & Away"	6/03/67	7	12
Jimi Hendrix	"Purple Haze"	8/26/67	65	8
Jefferson Airplane	"White Rabbit"	6/24/67	8	10
Lovin Spoonful	"Full Measure"	1/07/67	87	3
Nitty Gritty Dirt Band	"Buy For Me the Rain"	4/08/67	45	7
Peter, Paul and Mary	"Puff the Magic Dragon"	3/16/63	2	14
Rainy Daze	"That Acapulco Gold"	3/11/67	70	4
Raiders	"Kicks"	3/19/66	4	14
Rolling Stones	"Get Off My Cloud	10/09/65	1	12
Rolling Stones	"Jumpin' Jack Flash"	6/08/68	3	12
Rolling Stones	"Lady Jane"	7/23/68	24	6
Rolling Stones	"Mother's Little Helper"	7/09/66	8	9
Steppenwolf	"Magic Carpet Ride"	10/05/68	3	16
The Who	"I Can See For Miles"	10/14/67	9	11
The Who	"Magic Bus"	8/10/68	25	9
Ian Whitcomb	"You Turn Me On"	5/22/65	8	13
Yardbirds	"Over, Under, Sideways, Down"	6/25/66	23	11
Yardbirds	"Shapes of Things"	3/19/66	11	11
Yellow Balloon	"Yellow Balloon"	4/01/67	25	10

echoing the famous opening lines, "One pill makes you larger/And one pill makes you small" did not take place until 1970. In 1966 and 1967 the Right was still preoccupied with the wayfaring minstrels Pete Seeger, Joan Baez and the Beatles.

Noebel continued his attack with articles such as "Columbia Records: Home of the Marxist Minstrels," which appeared in *Christian Crusade Weekly.* The Crusade also released several record albums featuring Reverend Noebel discussing his favorite topic, the Communist control of popular music. Noebel's thunder was taken up by a young musician, Bob Larson, who was converted to fundamentalism by country singer T. Texas Tyler. David Wilkerson, author of *The Cross and the Switchblade*, persuaded Larson to enter the ministry. In 1967 Larson published *Rock and Roll: The Devil's Diversion*, in which he portrayed himself as a professional guitarist—prior to his conversion—who now tells all about the sin-ridden genre of rock. In one section Larson talks about how record-company executives demanded he write immoral lyrics to songs, and he observes "those songs that I wrote seem tame compared with the morally degenerative lyrics of today's rock songs. . . . Lyricists fancy themselves to be part poets. They're using existential themes of life, death, loneliness, alienation, and existence. War, the pill, drugs, and promiscuity are all a part of a music that is a complete expression of its time and its audience."[10] Larson, using his personal experiences, complemented by the usual gaggle of inconsistent footnotes, touches upon most of the major themes found in the White Citizen's Councils and in Noebel's work: the subliminal impact of rock, the advocacy of immoral acts and so on. Even the racial connection is present: "The same coarse bodily motions which lead African dancers into a state of uncontrolled frenzy are present in modern dances. It is only logical, then, that there must also be a correlation in the potentiality of demons gaining possessive control of a person through the medium of the beat." Larson attributes the source of this material to missionaries who have returned from the primitive jungles of Africa. At the end of his book is found the "Anti-Rock Pledge."

THE ANTI-ROCK PLEDGE

CONFESSING my faith in Christ and desiring to communicate His love and truth to my generation, and

RECOGNIZING that many of the songs and singers of rock music express and promote a morality and life-style contrary to the highest of Christian principles,

I HEREBY PLEDGE MYSELF TO THE FOLLOWING:

1. I will abstain from voluntarily listening to rock music so that I may adhere to the admonition of the Apostle Paul to "Think upon those things which are pure, honest, just, lovely, and of a good report." (Philippians 4:8)

2. I will destroy all rock records and tapes in my possession as an outward, symbolic act signifying my inner dedication to conscientiously discriminate as to the records I buy and listen to. (I John 5:21)

If after reading this book you can take the above pledge, please fill in the blanks below and send this signed pledge to :

BOB LARSON
BOX 26438
DENVER, COLORADO 80226

- -

age	name and address	date
1. ________	______________________________	______
	______________________________	
	______________________________	

Devil's Diversion, revised several times, has reportedly been quite successful. Larson followed up this book with three more: *Hippies, Hindus and Rock & Roll*, *Rock and the Church* and *The Day Music Died* which outline the role of the music in the growth of the counterculture and its infiltration into Christian worship.

Another ex-musician and a faculty member at "America's largest fundamental Christian school," Bob Jones University, Frank Garlock published *The Big Beat: A Rock Blast* echoing the charges Noebel and Larson had popularized: "Rock music is the devil's masterpiece for enslaving his own children. By the grace of God, let's keep him from also using it as a tool to weaken the children of God so that they are powerless to win this generation to Christ."[11]

Two years *after* residents had declared Haight-Ashbury dead, the radical Right launched its main offensive against rock and roll. In film, record, pamphlet, book and article the cry went out, "Pot, Rock and Revolution." Constructive Action, Inc., located in Whittier, California, the birthplace of Richard M. Nixon, made available a 30-minute full-color film entitled "The Pied Pipers." Rock groups, according to the film, were the Pied Pipers leading American youth into the narcotization of drug use, and the Beatles were prominently featured. David Noebel published another book the same year titled *The Beatles: A Study in Drugs, Sex and Revolution*, which restated his earlier position. By 1971 the booklet had gone through five printings. The less extreme John Birch Society also joined the battle. Gary Allen's "The Music: There's More To It Than Meets the Ear," placed *American Opinion* foresquare behind Noebel, Larson and Frank Garlock. "Rock singers are in constant communication with our teenagers," he wrote, "promoting attitudes and ideas which, if they were aware of the message, would blow the minds of most parents."[12] The article, of course, went on to alert parents as to what Allen thought rock music was saying: "Listen to the Beatles' new hit about how great it is to be out of America and 'Back in the USSR.' " Allen continued through the rote citations of Dylan's connection with folk music, acid-rock and the subliminal power of music. He did add a new twist to the Right's perception of rock, exclaiming that *National Review*, the conservative magazine, had totally misinterpreted "Revolution" by the Beatles. William F. Buckley's publication had said that "Revolution" was a put-down on violence and radical politics. Not so claimed Allen. Instead, " 'Revolution' takes the Moscow line against Trotskyites and the Progressive Labor party."

National Review responded with its own authority on youth culture and Trotskyist tactics, Phillip Abbott Luce. Luce was one of the original members of Progressive Labor party who was expelled from the movement. He later disavowed his previous associates and became an "informed" witness before congressional investigating committees and right-wing rallies. In "Are the Beatles Termites?: The Great Rock Conspiracy," Luce accused Allen and the John Birch Society of campaigning against the Devil with ridiculous footnotes and totally misrepresenting the Beatles and rock music. "Back in the USSR," he explained, is a "total put-on" which did not laud the Soviet Union. He reaffirmed the validity of *National Review*'s original interpretation of "Revolution," citing a Young Americans for Freedom review which observed, "Musically and polemically the Beatles urge the generation they helped create to free its mind from revolutionary enticements." Luce cynically added, "Perhaps it would be advisable for Mr. Allen and his 'hip' friends to ignore rock and roll stations."[13]

As the John Birchers and *National Review* were having one of their sporadic internecine ideological spats, a Michigan minister was staging record burnings. Reverend Riblett of Garden City built a seven-foot cross made of rock-and-roll records contributed by his congregation and set it on fire. Part of his explanation for this action was "The Beatles are an immoral bunch and I guess all of 'em have been convicted of marijuana smokin' and heaven only knows what else. I don't think it's the greatest idols for our teenagers to look up to."[14]

Unlike most radical Right charges the drug-song issue was taken over by a number of more dignified public figures and politicians. The late Congressman James Utt frequently inserted Noebel's charge of Pavlovian brainwashing into the

Congressional Record. Former California Superintendent of Schools Max Rafferty echoed the same charges. Television entertainer Art Linkletter, following the suicide of his daughter, charged that rock's advocacy of drugs was an important factor in her death. Linkletter told one congressional subcommittee that the Beatles were "a terrible example for youth," a charge he has repeated often on the lecture circuit and in print. President Nixon bestowed a public service award upon the celebrity for his antidrug activities.

Former Vice-President Spiro T. Agnew injected this argument into the 1970 congressional campaign. While denying that the Agnew speech had any influence, the Federal Communications Commission, several months later, issued a warning to radio broadcasters to the effect that they would be responsible for the lyrics they put on the air. We will return to the relationship of the FCC to popular music in the next section.

The Agnew statement and the FCC warning were hollow victories for the Right, since the drug-music problem by 1970 was virtually nonexistent, as both *Rolling Stone* reporter Ben Fong-Torres and then FCC Commissioner Nicholas Johnson reminded the public. *Sgt. Pepper, Surrealistic Pillow* and *Sunshine Superman* were all buried in the symbolic coffin commemorating the death of the Haight-Ashbury. The Beatles at this time were on the verge of their famous breakup, and Donovan was now an ardent antidrug spokesman. By 1970 the prodrug song was all but a novelty left to folksingers and basically addressed pot smoking rather than "speed" or "smack." Indeed, as Commissioner Johnson observed in a reply to Vice-President Agnew, there were as many antidrug songs in 1970 as there were in favor of its usage. Perhaps the most telling criticism against the "rock turn-on" thesis is that there is no real evidence to support this contention. Conversely, the few existing studies on the influence of songs indicate large portions of those sampled denied that popular music had any effect upon their sociopolitical attitudes. In one study of Canadian high-school students, 81 percent felt songs had no influence on them. Only .031 percent felt the predominant theme in popular music was drugs. In a college survey, 90.3 percent of the respondents reported no change in their attitudes and life-styles as a result of what rock songs were saying.[15]

A more significant figure perhaps is that the Right's own documentation finds less than 30 examples of so-called drug songs. Gary Allen's often-cited number of 28 is considerably less than one-half of the single material released in one average week in the record industry, yet his sample is derived from a four-year time span, which renders the figure an infinitesimally small portion of one percentile. Despite these figures the drug-song conspiracy continues to be a popular topic in right-wing circles with films, records, tapes and lectures all addressed to this question.

SEX AND ROCK AND ROLL

The advocacy of promiscuous sexual relations is another charge directed at rock music by the Right. Early rhythm and blues songs, as noted, had overtly sexual lyrics. "Roll All Night Long" and "Work With Me, Annie" meant just that. These songs had nothing to do with dancing, as the later "covers" by Pat Boone, Georgia Gibbs, Teresa Brewer and others tended to imply. Elvis Presley's lyrical material in most cases was rather innocent; however, his stage presence did in fact have a strong sexual overtone. Presley's gyrations, word inflections, "Ah Wannnn...t you, Ah Neee....d you..." all conveyed the sexual intentions of a hillbilly stud. On the other hand, Dick Clark's tutelage over the music as well as the Beatles' "I Want To Hold Your Hand" image generally presented a most wholesome portrait of rock. In time, as another Beatle song indicated, "love" became "more than just holding hands." Songs, particularly those in the so-called underground category, began to address the topic of sex in interpersonal relations. Performers such as Mick Jagger, Iggy, David Bowie and Jim Morrison combined both the lyrics and the rhythm and blues era with the bump and grind utilized by Elvis Presley. Jagger's interpretation of "King Bee" left little to imagination. Songs such as "(I Can't Get No) Satisfaction," "Light My Fire" and "Good Lovin" were the exception on the *Billboard* charts of 1965 through 1968. As with the overtly drug-oriented songs, pieces such as "Let's Spend the Night Together" or "I'll Be Your Baby Tonight" usually were confined to the underground stations or private home stereo systems.[16] Not even the most liberal radio-station programmers would play the "Fish Cheer" by Country Joe, John Lennon's "Working Class Hero"—with the "word"—or the Fugs' "Wet Dream." The Right's interpretation of sex images in rock did not comment on the de facto radio censorship. David Noebel observed, "rock and roll is a necessary ingredient of the sex revolution." Gary Allen saw it as an open exhortation "to indulge in illicit sex acts . . . [that] . . . are also a factor in the demoralization of youth." To support this connection the right-wing press frequently cites the now-famous Jim Morrison "indecent exposure" case in Miami Beach.

Jim Morrison, the lead singer of the Doors, re-enacted the role that first brought Presley to public attention. Both on record and on stage he became a purveyor of sensuality. The Doors' first and biggest hit record was "Light My Fire." Wearing tight black leather pants or a snakeskin suit, Morrison took pleasure in eliciting the same shrieks and screams which had characterized Presley and Rolling Stones appearances in years past.

On March 2, 1969, Morrison, according to his manager Bill Siddons, was putting on "just another dirty Doors show" for a Miami audience. This time Morrison was charged by the local police with "lewd and lascivious behavior in public by exposing his private parts and by simulating masturbation and oral copulation." This was not "just another" performance. The reaction to this incident was overwhelming and somewhat unexpected. A local reporter commented:

"They'd crucify him if they could, they're so worked up." The *Miami Herald* called Morrison "The King of Orgasmic Rock" and pictured him as being "hypnotically erotic" and as "flaunting the laws of obscenity, indecent exposure and incitement to riot." The Crime Commission of Greater Miami called for an investigation into the concert and why it was allowed to take place in the area. The State Attorney's Office issued warrants for Morrison's arrest. The mayor of neighboring Jacksonville cancelled a forthcoming Doors concert. Finally, the entire tour was scrapped. Morrison was subsequently tried in Dade Criminal Court and found guilty of drunkenness and exposure. He was acquitted of all other charges.

This event mobilized what one reporter termed a "decency movement." Mike Levesque, a 19-year-old football player at Miami Spring High, organized a Rally for Decency with the aid of the Catholic hierarchy, which was held on March 23 at the Orange Bowl. There, 30,000 people, half of whom were adults, attended the rally to see and hear Jackie Gleason, Kate Smith, Anita Bryant and the Lettermen. "Longhairs and weird dressers" were not allowed to attend. Numerous religious organizations were present. The American Legion distributed 10,000 small American flags as young speakers gave three-minute orations on "behalf of goodness and virtue." Down With Obscenity signs dotted the audience. Jackie Gleason told the crowd, "I believe this kind of movement will snowball across the states and perhaps the world." President Nixon sent Mike Levesque a letter of support. George Wallace appeared at a "Youths for Decency" rally at Enterprise, Alabama. Several other such affairs took place in Cincinnati and Baltimore. The Baltimore rally attracted 40,000 youths to hear five rock bands characterized by one participant as "second-rate . . . even for Baltimore." The concert ended in a violent race riot. Plans for future "decency" rallies did not materialize. The short-lived "decency movement" operated at several levels of consciousness. Levesque represented one of these. He told one interviewer, "I like the

Doors' *music*. And I like a lotta good groups. I mean, I'm not like a guy who just likes Rickie [sic] Nelson or somebody like that. I like all these modern groups."[17] What he objected to was the sentiment offered by some rock performers who had "nothin' constructive to say" about America. The more radical rightists found rock to be a more Machiavellian symptom of the moral deterioration of youth. The fact that no rock groups were represented at the original Rally for Decency is illustrative. As Reverend Riblett explained, "Rock and roll is the devil's diversion. It's been traced back to the jungle drums. That's where it all comes from. The head hunters use the same beat before they go out to hunt heads and all this." David Noebel, perhaps, best summarized the relationship of the Right to rock saying, "Present day rock is having a holiday ridiculing religion and morality while at the same time glorifying drugs, sexual promiscuity, and revolution—and all the time claiming to do so under the guise of art!"[18]

GOD-ROCK AND THE RIGHT

By mid-1971 nearly all of the threats perceived by the radical Right from popular music had disappeared. Bob Dylan was past protesting, acid-rock was history and the Beatles were not "more popular than Jesus." They no longer existed, and the most popular album in America was *Jesus Christ Superstar*. Even Billy Graham had a kind word for rock and roll, which he had rejected some years previously. He told the *Los Angeles Times*, "A lot of rock music is basically religious music . . . we don't realize how serious our young people are."[19] Throughout the New Community, "Jesus People" were beginning to appear, making witness to the glory of the son of God in a manner reminiscent of zealous Jehovah's Witnesses. Many denominations welcomed this more serious interest in Christianity on the part of the young. A Catholic lay leader, observing the Jesus People, explained to a *Time* reporter, "We are on the threshold of the greatest spiritual revival the

U.S. has ever experienced."[20] Even Jesus-rock bands were emerging. Many segments of the Right treated this phenomenon with considerable disbelief and bewilderment, and some groups with a fundamentalist theological bent raised objections to the portrayals of Christ in drama and in song.

Again, David Noebel led the charge. *Jesus Christ Superstar*, he claimed, "is blasphemous, sacrilegious, irreverent, profane, desecrating, apostate and anti-Christian."[21] The humanization of Christ he reasoned was the work of unbelievers. He concluded a lengthy indictment saying, "Those who thought John Lennon was right were wrong; and those who think Rice and Webber [the producers] are an improvement over Lennon are also wrong. The Great White Throne will someday reveal just how wrong they were." This last allusion was directed toward liberal Christians who applauded *Superstar*. The *Superstar* campaign did not generate the furor that anti-Beatles efforts had. *Christian Crusade Weekly* did publish occasional barbs against Broadway and God-rock but with—for them—considerable restraint. Some six months after the Noebel charges, another reader inquired about the Crusade's position on the musical *Godspell*. "Crusader's Action Line" replied that while the play was "blasphemous" it was an accurate but trite portrayal of the life of Christ. Little further mention of God-rock was made for nearly three months until another letter appeared asking about the "Jesus Watch." The reply was negative attributing the watch to the *Jesus Christ Superstar* crowd. The play was characterized as having brought "Christ down, and it has done very little to exhalt him." This answer was mild in comparison to the follow-up material from David Noebel and Billy James Hargis. This was unusual, as Hargis normally left musical affairs to Noebel. Noebel began the assault by attacking the Broadway stage and its anti-Christian and American material especially as found in *Hair*, which Noebel believed dealt with "pot, homosexuality, fornication, nudity, astrology, anarchy, anti-patriotism, and playboy-love." During the first week in March 1972, *Jesus Christ Superstar* opened in Tulsa, Oklahoma, the Crusade's home base, to a capacity crowd of over 6,000 people. Hargis was enraged, urging all Christians to leave any church which would sanction such a "satanic production" which treated "Judas [as] the hero, Jesus and His Apostles [as] drunkards, Mary [as] the secret lover of the Lord. . . ."[22] In the same issue of *Christian Crusade Weekly* readers were urged to join the Seventh Day Adventists in combating the production. Noebel's original barrage was reprinted to add further ammunition to the Hargis denunciation. Again, the campaign did not get off the ground.

Noebel plans to revise his magnum opus *Rhythm, Riots, and Revolution*, to be renamed *The Marxist Minstrels*.

It is tempting to dismiss the Noebels, Larsons and Allens as right-wing crackpots or opportunists. Gordon Friesen, the editor of *Broadside* (NYC) and a frequent target in Noebel's books, writes: "I have a young relative who knows Noebel personally. He describes him as a cynic who 'was laughing his head off' at the thought of people gullible enough to fall for the crap he was laying down in *Rhythm, Riots, and Revolution* That's the kind of a cat you are dealing with." To this Noebel might reply, "Oh we laugh at ourselves all the time and we have a lot of fun doing what we are doing, but we still think it's very serious business."[23] University of Texas historian Jerome Rodnitzky offers a more convincing explanation: "Sheltered in places like Tulsa, Oklahoma, and viewing the young from afar, it is perhaps too easy for them to see the new youthful life-styles as aberrations imposed by alien and allegedly hypnotic forces such as the Beatles. Noebel's book, thus, tells far more about the Christian Crusade than it does about the Beatles."[24] Surprisingly, Phillip Luce joined with the professor, accusing Gary Allen of myopia and paranoia: "Some writers at *American Opinion* . . . relate everything they dislike or don't understand to the thrust of the Illuminati (presently referred to as THE INSIDERS). The Illuminati preside over The Conspiracy and The Conspiracy extends even into record stores and radio stations."[25] Both Rodnitzky and Luce seem to be saying that in a complex world simple answers are attractive, especially for those who do not understand it.

Happily for the recording industry, the radical Right's ability to impose its will is not uniform. Outside of its own small constituency, generally confined to rural regions and one or two cities, it is powerless. An occasional letter to a program director will have little effect if the "offensive" record or artist has public appeal. The anti-Beatles campaign is but one evidence of this phenomenon. Lacking the power to impose its will, the radical Right has been forced to send its protests to the agency which has regulatory power over the supreme cultural gatekeeper: the broadcaster.

FCC: THE AMORPHOUS PRESENCE

To place its sound before the public the record industry must contend with many overt barriers. The Federal Communications Commission is a gray eminence lurking in the background. The regulatory agency has no immediate control over the record companies, but it does have considerable authority and influence upon broadcasters, the gatekeepers of pop, who depend upon the agency for their operating licenses.

The commission, established in 1934, regulates interstate and foreign commerce in communication by wire and radio. It is prohibited by law from engaging in prior censorship of broadcast material, yet FCC's own guidelines indicate "no application for a broadcasting license will be granted unless the Commission finds that the *public interest, convenience, and necessity* will be served by such a grant." The right to interpret the "public interest and convenience" accounts for the considerable power the commission exercises over the broadcast media. The commission expects radio and television to address "the problems, needs and interests" of the community which is serviced. Beyond these general boundaries there exist few objective guidelines as to the proprieties and etiquette of programming. The very amorphousness and uncertainty of the policy provide the commission's social control over radio and television. Not exercising prior censorship, the commission only acts after it has received a complaint or discovered some wrongdoing. The ambiguity of the situation has forced many station managers into a highly defensive posture in all areas not clearly outlined by the commission. Popular-music programming has historically been one of these anomic spheres.

Prior to the turbulent 1960s, commissioners were not confronted with material that might be labeled offensive to community mores or standards. The lyrics of the swing and postwar crooner periods were innocent by any but the most austere standards. The not-so subtle rhythm and blues songs of the early 1950s such as "Baby Let Me Bang Your Box" or "Work With Me, Annie," addressed to urban blacks, were ignored by the commission. Double-entendre rock lyrics on Top 40 stations also escaped scrutiny. The inaction of the commission prior to 1971 is partially attributable to the "June, spoon, moon" nature of AM programming. Pop was mainly "our song." Radio stations just did not air controversial material on entertainment shows. Pop music was clearly identified as being in that category. The Noebels, Allens and Larsons had not yet articulated "pop" artists as the termites of American society.

During the sixties, the FCC affected and adjusted the relationships between the radio programmer and the record company. The commission was a prominent and vital catalyst in investigating and catapulting into headlines disk jockey "consultantships" and Clarkola. The disclosures did alter the "play for pay" method of breaking acts. Commission actions and rulings also have altered competitive relations between stations in some markets. In July 1962 the commissioners denied sportsman Jack Kent Cooke's petition to continue operation of KRLA-Pasadena due to deceptions in broadcasting practices, especially promotional contests. This decision created an imbalance in the Top 40 market in the Los Angeles area. The action ultimately figured in the RKO purchase of KHJ-Los Angeles and the birth of boss radio. Four years later the commission temporarily sanctioned KYA-San Francisco for "inadequate policies and practices for control of program material." The implication of only a year license renewal was that payola or "plugola" was being practiced. This action prompted some station personnel to begin thinking about alternatives transcending the confines of boss radio. Several months after the original ruling the FCC granted the offending station the usual three-year extension. The exoneration of KYA did not affect further experimentation in the San Francisco radio scene, allowing it to continue at least on the all-night Russ Syracuse show.

These minor housekeeping decisions were dwarfed by the historical simulcast decision which drastically altered FM programming fare. The Federal Communications Commission ordered, on October 15, 1965, that licensees of FM stations in the cities containing over 100,000 population cease devoting more than 50 percent of the FM broadcast week to programs duplicated on AM stations owned by the same licensee in the area. This edict impacted upon nearly 200 of 551 commercial outlets operating in urban communities. Broadcasters subject to the ruling vigorously opposed the public notice, but to little avail. On New Year's Day 1967 the unpopular order went into practice. The result was an increase in specialty broadcasting on the FM channels. Classical and country and western music received greater exposure, but rock and roll was the major beneficiary of the FCC action. The major casualty was middle-of-the-road material, a prominent feature of the simulcast. Following the decree, pop-music programming constituted 29 percent of FM broadcast format in America's 50 largest cities. Outside of these major metropolitan zones 29 percent of FM programming was pop-music oriented. The simulcast action of the FCC opened up for record companies large segments of valuable air time in which to expose product. The release from all-pervasive clock allowed broadcasters, who could no longer rely upon the usual 2.37 minutes Top 40 fare appearing on the AM outlet, to experiment with longer LP selections in order to fill their new play lists. This paved the way for the emergence of "free-form" broadcasting on major FM stations.

Opinion manipulators have discounted the political value of radio, in part due to the demographics associated with the medium. Television traditionally has reached large numbers of older viewers eligible to vote. David Monroe Miller, president of Contemporary Communications, an advertising agency specializing in "opinion ads," notes, "Radio audiences are not composed of the kinds of persons you want to reach."[26] In support of this observation, a junior college student when queried about the "Eve of Destruction," replied, "Protest songs show no class. Songs should be written for *entertainment*." Sociological studies have repeatedly noted the universality of this sentiment. A large number of Top 40 listeners do not want "their" music to be concerned with social issues. Prior to the enfranchisement of the 18-year-old voter most opinion advertisers would consider Top 40 spots a waste of campaign funds.

The "Eve of Destruction," the pioneer statement of protest to climb the *Billboard* charts, altered the apolitical nature of air fare. Several right-wing organizations in California petitioned the FCC, arguing that "Eve" had violated the "fairness doctrine." This doctrine urges that a station "having presented one side of a controversial issue of public importance [the station] make reasonable efforts to present opposing sides of the issue in his overall programming." The agency did not impose fairness doctrine to popular music. One explanation may be that most stations conform to the vague stipulation that "opposing views need not be presented on the same program or even in the same series of programs, so long as an effort is made in good faith to present contrasting views in the station's *overall programming*." This means that one 30-minute conservative speech could offset ten air plays of "Eve" or "Ohio." Obviously, popular music was best left outside of the umbrella of the nebulous "fairness doctrine."

The rise of the counterculture as manifest in rock music and free-form radio found segments of the broadcasting medium attempting to challenge community mores and conventional wisdoms. In time, the use of some popular Anglo-Saxonisms would be voiced on FM radio. Sex, drugs and other previously taboo subjects would receive equal attention. The question for the government became, as in pornography cases, "What comprises community standards?" This question the FCC has never adequately interpreted, much to discomfort of programmers who recall that "no license will be granted or renewed unless the Commission finds that the public interest, convenience, and necessity will be served." This regulatory power, as constitutionally vague and questionable as it may be, is a fact of life for the broadcaster. The commission did fine one FM station which broadcast Jerry Garcia's use of a "taboo" word during an interview. The statement of censure indicated that the commission welcomed a court opinion adjudicating its action, but the defendant station chose to pay the fine, leaving the question of content review untested. During the drug-lyric controversy, several lawyers offered to represent any radio station willing to contest the FCC's authority. None of the major commercial stations accepted the offer. One of the attorneys told *Rolling Stone*, "We also need a plaintiff station, but most stations want to stay out of trouble and make money."[27]

"FCC DISCOVERS DOPE DOES DARNDEST THING"

Six months after the Agnew drug-lyric speech the FCC issued a public notice, "Licensee Responsible to Review Records Before Their Broadcast." The announcement cautioned broadcasters that whether:

> a particular record depicts the dangers of drug abuse, or, to the contrary, promotes such illegal drug usage is a question for the judgment of the licensee. The thrust of this *Notice* is simply that the licensee must make that judgment and cannot properly follow a policy of playing records without someone in a responsible position . . . knowing the content of the lyrics.

The document warned programmers that failure to exercise adequate control over broadcast material would raise "serious questions as to whether continued operation of the station is in the public interest." Disclaimers by the governmental agency that the notice was not a form of a-priori censorship went unheeded by many radio stations, which interpreted the statement as repressive. Former Commissioner Nicholas Johnson validated this feeling, objecting that the notice "strikes out blindly at a form of music which is symbolic of a culture which the majority [of FCC commissioners] apparently fears—in part because it fails to comprehend it. If the majority were in fact concerned about drug abuse, it surely would not choose to ignore song lyrics 'strongly suggestive of, and tending to glorify' the use of alcohol, which is the number one drug abuse problem in this country." Dick Starr, program director at Top 40 station KYA-San Francisco, concurred, "It smacks of censorship, and it'll create a lot of busy work. I'll have to ask for lyric sheets if it goes that far."[28] The FCC replied, denying that their notice was restrictive. Instead, as Commissioner Robert E. Lee claimed, all that was being asked was "the Broadcast Industry meet its responsibility of reviewing records before they are played." Tracy Weston, an attorney specializing in civil liberties in the broadcast media, contended the reminder was ambiguous, "because the FCC has not had the guts to come out and say what they really mean. They are trying to scare private stations into doing the censorship themselves and avoid the trap."[29] Weston's reasoning had some merit; FCC Notice 71-205 did imply that failure to correctly screen lyrics could affect the "continued operation of the station."

Radio stations being licensed by the FCC were now placed in the position of making sociopolitical judgments above and beyond their usual esthetic ones. Numerous record, as opposed to radio, industry people objected. Sergio Mendes, leader of Brasil '77, stated, "Drug-oriented lyrics many times are a matter of interpretation. Who is going to translate the lyrics?"[30] Max Leon, owner of two radio stations, added, "It is impossible to crawl into any writer's head to find out exactly what they mean."[31] The broadcasters generally complied with the FCC statement. The Storz chain demanded printed lyrics to singles submitted for their play lists; other chains and stations followed suit. George Williams, with stations in North Carolina and Alabama, told *Billboard* he would even "call someone connected with the record" to get the correct interpretation.[32] The industry complied with these requests. Most albums contained the printed lyrics to the songs on the record. More controversial fare usually contains a reminder to program directors to screen the particular cut before providing it air play. For most PDs such a warning is totally unnecessary. Printed lyrics do not solve the problem, as English rock singer Spencer Davis observed: "Lyric sheets will not help. A lot of people read things into lyrics. Look at the stir during the Charles Manson trial about the words to certain Beatles tunes like 'Helter Skelter' and 'Sexy Sadie.' "[33] Davis could easily have added "Lucy in the Sky with Diamonds" to his list of examples of difficult to interpret songs. Critics have all pointed to the acronym "LSD," in the title. Lennon and McCartney both deny that the song is about acid, while admitting that a few of their other compositions have drug-oriented themes. There is little reason to disbelieve them about "Lucy." The problem of interpretation intimidated stations, making them more cautious in the construction of their play lists. WDAS-Philadelphia, in response to the order, removed "Let It Bleed," "Comin' into Los Angeles," "Small Circle of Friends," "Needle and Spoon" and "I Am the Walrus" from their record library. WKBW-Buffalo blacklisted "White Rabbit," "D.O.A." (an antidrug song), "Monkey Man" and "Eight Miles High." KADI-FM in St. Louis pulled three songs off their play list.

The major casualty of the FCC notice was Brewer and Shipley's charted song "One Toke Over the Line," which according to them admittedly was a "cannabis spiritual."[34] Top 40 stations refused to air the record when they discovered "toke" meant a puff on a marijuana cigarette. Major AM outlets in New York, Chicago and Dallas removed the song from their play lists, despite its high position in local and national ratings. The FCC's claim that it did not censor material for the music industry was a hollow statement. A handful of broadcasters resented the interference of the FCC in their programming policies. Precious few challenged the offensive government action; in fact, numerous program directors welcomed the guidelines. WNBC's program director, after removing "Toke" from his play list, explained, "The FCC only makes clear what I've always done anyway."[35] This assertion had considerable merit, as many AM stations were in fact refusing songs with any type of irritation factor, albeit esthetic or sociological. The FCC order was primarily directed at the "more free-form" stations which did air controversial material. AM stations rarely ventured into "irritation" zones. The record companies were "odd man out" in the "drug lyric" fracus. Neil Bogart, then president of Buddah Records, which catalogued "One Toke Over the Line," could protest "the airways fully belong to the people. How do you justify pulling a record that's so heavily requested by the people." But, there was nothing else he could do. No radio-station owner would jeopardize his license or engage in an expensive court suit to increase Buddah's profit margin. Indeed, as one program director put it, "I think the FCC is going after record companies, and they can't get at them so they're going through us." This reply aptly reflects radio's view of record companies, "why should they take a risk merely to fill the corporate coffers of CBS or the Kinney Corporation?" *Billboard* captured the broadcasters' attitude in announcing the FCC notice:

> Many major broadcasters, who prefer to keep anonymous, say that the FCC has no right to impose this type of censorship upon radio stations—that it's a violation of the first amendment. But most broadcasters are reluctant to march against the FCC *because they are afraid to imperil their frequencies.*
>
> There is considerable speculation that some station will eventually challenge the FCC on its new dictum. But high legal costs may be a deterrent. The general feeling, too, is that most stations will go along with the new demands.[36]

One radio station, WBAI-New York, a member of the controversial Pacifica network, filed a petition with the FCC protesting the notice. Edwin Goodman, the station manager, explained, "We have no intention of changing our programming in any way and will continue to broadcast songs which might be construed by someone as advocating the use of drugs. After all, someone might construe the lyrics of 'Tea for Two' as advocating drugs."[37]

WBAI was joined by several networks and finally the Record Industry Association of America (RIAA) in disputing the FCC action. The *New York Times* and several trade publications reprinted former Commissioner Johnson's forceful dissent from the original notice. The commission action also generated a considerable amount of protest mail. On April 16, 1971, some five weeks after the *Licensee Responsibility* statement, the commission issued a clarification which stated, "Any attempt to review or condemn a licensee's judgment to play a particular record is . . . beyond the scope of federal regulatory authority with perhaps the exception of the so-called 'clear and present danger' test." This was, as Nicholas Johnson noted, a "significant retreat" from the earlier statement. However, the broadcaster still remains liable for the material that is aired by his station. Conversely, Leonard Weinless, the FCC's chief information officier, writes, "The FCC takes no position on lyrics. No action has been taken against stations on the basis of song lyrics." This does not guarantee that the commission will not at some future date.

Nearly 18 months after the "Responsibility" statement, with Tracy Weston as their attorney, Yale Broadcasting (WYBC-FM) and the National Coordinating Council on Drug Abuse petitioned a three-judge U.S. Appeals Court for a clarification. Weston told the judicial panel that broadcasters at present must review the lyrics and ferret out the meanings of songs which are frequently ambiguous and determine if they "promote or glorify" the use of drugs as well as establish if the song is in the public interest. He presented 150 pages of affidávits outlining the disruptions in the broadcasting industry due to the "Responsibility" edict. The attorney urged that the FCC's refusal to outline their standards as "an invitation to take the risk." Presiding Judge Spotswood Robinson appeared to support Weston's position, telling the FCC counsel, "I don't want the FCC to speculate—but to be definite."[38] FCC Counsel Marino replied the broadcaster "must have some expertise" and that the commission does not want to second-guess the licensee, however, the FCC must act on listener complaints. He found this approach superior to publishing a list of unacceptable songs. Judge Richard Wilkey cautioned Marino that, "I didn't mean anything like a listing of recordings, but more precise guidelines for the broadcaster." Judge Robinson concluded the hearing observing that the vagueness of FCC rules may be "an impairment of civil rights." The sympathetic questions of the judges were misleading. In January 1973 the three-judge panel upheld the FCC. The commission, they argued, had not revoked any license for violation of its controversial notice. Ironically, the court absolved the broadcaster of some of the prescreening responsibility because of the quality of popular music. In their opinion;

> Some lyrics of sounds are virtually unintelligible. To the extent that they are completely meaningless gibberish . . . they, of course, do not communicate with respect to drugs or anything else and are not within the ambit of the Commission's Order.

Nonetheless:

> At some point along the scale of human intelligibility, the sounds produced may slide over from characteristics of free speech, which should be protected, to those of noise pollution, which the Commission has ample authority to abate.

The noise pollution is the gist of what the FCC was opposed to. As the court restated, "the main thrust of the Commission's Order is that whether a song presents the banal observations of a moon-struck adolescent, resembles two enraged alley cats fighting in a garbage can, or contains the subtle reflections of a master poet, a licensee may not broadcast ignorant of the content of his programming."[39] Several months later Appeals Court Chief Judge David L. Bazelon, a noted civil libertarian, objected to the decision. he wrote, "This case is ripe for judicial review." The case went to the Supreme Court, which refused to review the 1971 antidrug edict of the FCC. Two justices dissented. Justice William O. Douglas wrote, "Under our system, the government is not to decide what messages, spoken or in music, are of the proper 'social value' to reach the people."[40] By its inaction, the Court let stand the power of the FCC to determine content.

For the broadcaster, the FCC is the sword of Damocles hanging precariously over his microphone and license. It is the very unclear posture of the commission which in fact excludes much material from the airways. The commission took no formal action against several stations which aired John Lennon's "Working Class Hero" or NET for telecasting "San Francisco Rock: Go Ride the Music" which features the Jefferson Airplane's "Volunteers" with the complete text. Despite this inaction most program directors adopted KMET's Warren Duffy's position: "We're not willing to risk a license and all the other things we're trying to do for one word."[41] This anomic or unstructured relationship between radio and the FCC exaggerates the delicate balance between artistic freedom and the practicalities of breaking a record. Lou

Reed, then with the "suspect" Velvet Underground, commented, "All we need is a hit single, but nobody will play our songs." In this manner the amorphous presence of the Federal Communications Commission is a shadowy gatekeeper of material transcending ordinary Top 40 fare. Record companies, as Stan Cornyn suggests, are "ticket sellers" in search of customers, and consumers do not purchase what they do not hear. There are esoteric taste cultures which support performers of avant-garde material such as the Dolls, Mothers of Invention or the Bonzo Dog Band. These are specialty acts and are not expected to be "hit bounds." The real difficulty lies in the gray area of double meaning.

A program director, knowing a regulatory agency will evaluate his judgment, can adopt a conservative stance vis-à-vis songs open to various interpretation. "Lucy in the Sky With Diamonds," "Eight Miles High" and "Mr. Tambourine Man" all have been cited as drug songs despite the protests of their creators. Moral entrepreneurs may see an innocent song in the same light as the Illinois Crime Commission. "Yellow Submarine" by the Beatles may mean "street jargon for yellow, barbiturate capsules" or "Puff the Magic Dragon" by the folksinging group Peter, Paul and Mary may be interpreted to mean "smoking marijuana and hashish." Considering the diverse interpretations, some broadcasters no doubt will take the safest course of action and not play these innocuous ditties. One midwestern program director observed, "Why play a song likely to turn off a listener, when I can air something else?"

The presence of the FCC for the record industry creates another barrier added to that of the formal gatekeeper. The government agency becomes yet another dam the recording company must cope with. This powerful agency, unhappily for the record makers, is at odds with some taste publics the industry wishes to service.

Rolling Stone, a magazine believed attuned to the non-Top 40 youth market, has strongly attacked the timidity of broadcasters. The basic premise of the magazine's dissent was aptly articulated in its second issue by disk jockey Tom Donohue: "The music has matured, the audience has matured, but radio has apparently proven to be a retarded child."[42] It is in this spirit that the January 21, 1971, editorial was addressed to program directors and station managers:

> Where are the courageous and responsible men who have become rich broadcasting the music of the young in the past decade and who now advertise so expensively how "committed" to the music and ideals of a new generation they are? We address ourselves to the program directors, station managers and disc jockeys and to the men in New York City who direct the corporate activities of either the Metromedia Radio Network or the ABC-FM network, both of them owners of chains of at least five commercial "underground" rock stations in the major cities of the United States.
>
> Surely these two companies—and any owners of smaller broadcasting corporations who might also join in—can easily afford the relatively small legal fees necessary to play "Working Class Hero" and defend it in front of the Federal Communications Commission and, if necessary, in the Federal Courts, where certainly that ban would be overturned. And once and for all end the nonsense of the great popular art of our time being censored from public broadcast—when it refers to drugs or uses common language—because it deals in honesty and reality.

Record-company executives, perhaps sharing much of the *Rolling Stone* editorial writers' sentiments, have been extremely cautious in dealing with the relationship of the FCC to their product. Mike Maitland of MCA, in the best of political rhetoric said, "If I am totally aware that something harmful was being put into a lyric, I'd try to stop it. Most of the time we don't know when we are being *put on* and that can go for the hippest label."[43] Joe Smith of Warner Brothers observed, "The shakers and movers in this business don't sit around dreaming up campaigns to sell cocaine, nor do writers think of clever ways to refer to drugs in their songs." A more candid reply came from Al Bennett, former Liberty-UA president. It would have to be "a business judgment" he said. Irwin H. Sternberg at Mercury echoed this approach, "I don't think we [record companies] have the right to decide what is moral. The public should decide what is good and bad." While civil libertarians would no doubt applaud this statement, radio-station directors, with one eye on the frequency license, are not so courageous.

The record company's task, then, is somehow to persuade station managers that controversial material is not offensive to their listners *regardless* of the FCC. One interesting example of this process was to be found in the "D.O.A." controversy. Bloodrock's "D.O.A." was the musical account of a drug overdose. Toward the end of the song a sirenlike sound was produced. Many radio stations were hesitant about airing the song due to an alleged FCC notice (70–930) which reportedly banned simulated sirens in broadcasts due to the fear of possible automobile accidents and other public hazards. Capitol Records and Bloodrock producer Terry Knight attempted to persuade PD's to broadcast the record on the basis of its alleged popularity, the notice notwithstanding. Bill Gavin's tip sheet reported "Phenomenal phone response wherever played plus big sales. Gruesome content has blocked most major station air play, but KINT-El Paso programs it as a public service and reports good reaction from several drivers who said they drove more carefully after hearing it on their car radios." Capitol reproduced this statement in a mailing to radio stations. Knight, then riding the crest of his industry influence as the producer of Grand Funk Railroad, told broadcasters, "To question whether this record should or should not be aired on the basis of a sound effect is both ludicrous and irresponsible. The fact of the matter is clearly that the song 'D.O.A.' is high on all of the national singles charts." Having cited the "get behind the record" ethos, he continued;

> It should be now be clear that the song has established its popularity and status from legitimate consumer response. At this point, for a programmer to consider not giving airplay to this

> song on the basis of his personal opinion of a sound effect which is an integral part of the song is to establish himself as sole judge and censor of his audience. We must not allow ourselves or our programmers to misuse the power with which they have been entrusted by telling the public what it may or may not hear after that public has legitimately substantiated and voiced its majorative approval. Putting it quite simply, the record is established as a hit and deserves to be aired by programmers with an obligation to program 'hit' material. Capitol will continue to support both the single and album to the fullest extent.

While a considerable amount of this appeal is industry "hype" the basic dilemma of the record company is clear. For a song to be popular it must receive air play. A possible FCC citation is generally threat enough to keep a record off the air. Consequently, the record companies, once again, must exhibit proof of public support for their product in order to motivate timid PDs into getting the needle on the record. Another ploy utilized by Capitol to further publicize the controversial record was a series of antidrug spots by Bloodrock. While decrying the menace of drug abuse, the spots also generated exposure. On March 8, 1972, three days after the public notice on "licensee responsibility," Terry Knight announced that another of his acts had taped a series of 10-second spots like "Hi: this is Mark Farner of Grand Funk with a word to my Brothers and Sisters. A clean world begins with a clean body . . . don't pollute yours with hard drugs." The residual purpose of the Grank Funk spots was to introduce them to an audience unaware of them. Grand Funk had not yet enjoyed a Top 40 hit. The action also provided stations with visible material that they were "fighting the drug menace."

The industry's insistence that radio listeners are more attuned to their product than program directors is a difficult thesis to substantiate to broadcasters. The sentiment that "most people are unhip" pervades the radio medium. The FCC's presence only makes this feeling more of a reality.

The problem is what to do about the "hip" segments of the audience. Some portions of pop, much of it not aired on Top

40 radio, does reflect segments of the youth market that are in the progressive category. As "ticket sellers" the record companies are anxious to serve the older college and alternative culture people, but it is precisely this group at which, as former Commissioner Johnson suggests, the FCC's drug-song notice was directed. As one observer noted, "Freaks buy records too." Dr. David Smith, director of the controversial Haight-Ashbury Medical Clinic, told *Billboard* Radio Programming Forum in 1970: "Music—particularly pop music—tends to be a reflection of the times. It is very questionable what comes first: Does rock music influence drug taking, or do people who are participating in drug use like to listen to music?"[44] The exact number of people under 30 using drugs is almost impossible to ascertain. Figures run from 20 to 50 percent for marijuana use. One study reported that 45 percent of the high-school students in New York City occasionally toyed with "psychoactive" drugs. At the college level some observers feel that "more students smoke dope than do not." Few would deny that drug use, especially marijuana smoking, is prevalent among young people. There is a relationship between this collectivity and pop music. Sociologist Erich Goode reports that 90 percent of the pot smokers he studied said listening to music was a richer and more rewarding experience when high. Some unpublished materials seem to hint at some correlation between "drug use and the appreciation of more progressive air fare." No causality is inferred, that is, drug lyrics have not been found to cause drug use. The dilemma of the record companies here is clear: Dope smokers and pill poppers buy records. The record companies are quite happy to sell them product, whatever its content. The FCC, with its power over broadcasters, interdicts the traditional buyer-seller relationship. Records, as Terry Knight has proven, can be sold by "word by mouth" rather than by radio or press exposure; however, only rare acts find this mode of communication effective. The FCC has handled the PD yet another cop-out that the road promo man must now cope with: "I can't play *that*. I could lose my license."

The impact of the radical Right and the FCC upon the record industry is problematic. Neither possesses the power of program directors or company accounting departments. Nonetheless, depending upon geography and political climate, both the Right and the FCC have influenced musical fare in America. Fear of these entities forced CBS to remove Bob Dylan's "Talking John Birch Society Blues" from his second album and from the Ed Sullivan program. Pete Seeger was blacklisted from commercial radio and television for nearly 17 years. Ed Sullivan changed the title of the Rolling Stones' "Let's Spend the Night Together" to "Let's Spend Some Time Together." Barry McGuire's "Eve of Destruction" and Crosby, Stills, Nash and Young's "Ohio" were blacked out in many sections of the country. In the case of "Eve" it is fair to say that it broke *despite* fearful station managers and program directors. Alternative media have in the late 1960s augmented the structures of AM radio; however, some of the same political pressures are visible. Many AM Top 40 broadcasters own and operate an FM outlet. Other FM stations are part of Metromedia or the ABC chain, which supervise play lists in some cities. Metromedia policy has consistently been to air antidrug songs. Allen Shaw of ABC told *Billboard*, "We have always had the policy of avoiding advocating addictive drugs to our listeners whether through music or our air personalities."[45] The interference of the Right and the FCC only further complicate the already Herculian task of reaching the "folks out there."

Notes, Chapter 8

1. Gary B. Rush, "Toward a Definition of the Extreme Right," *Pacific Sociological Review* 6 (Fall 1963); 73.
2. Frank Zappa, "The Oracle Has It All Psyched Out," *Life*, June 28, 1968, p. 85.
3. Quoted in "Segregationists Would Ban All Rock, Roll Hits," *Billboard*, April 7, 1956, p. 130.

4. Quoted in "Segregationist Wants Ban On 'Rock and Roll,'" *New York Times*, March 30, 1956, p. 39; also see "Deep South R&R Hassle," *Billboard*, Arpil 7, 1956, pp. 20, 133 and "Jim Crow Chief Hits at Rock and Roll," *Melody Maker* 31 (May 13, 1956): 7.

5. "Segregationists Would," p. 130.

6. Jere Real, "Folk Music and Red Tubthumpers," *American Opinion* 7 (December 1965): 24. See R. S. Denisoff, *Great Day Coming: Folk Music and the American Left* (Urbana, Ill.: Unniversity of Illinois Press, 1971), pp. 151–63.

7. Quoted from "The Children of Bobby Dylan," *Life*, November 5, 1965, p. 44 and "Rock 'n' Roll: Message Time," *Time*, September 17, 1965, p. 102.

8. David A. Noebel, *Communism, Hypnotism and the Beatles: An Analysis of the Communist Use of Music* (Tulsa, Okla.: Christian Crusade Publications, 1965), p. 10. For other explanations of Beatlemania, see Evan Davis, "The Psychological Characteristics of Beatle Mania," *Journal of the History of Ideas* 30 (April-June 1969): 273–80; Ralph J. Gleason, "The Teen-Age World of Beatlemania," "This World" section of *San Francisco Chronicle*, August 29, 1965, p. 41; and "Inside Beatlemania," *San Francisco Chronicle*, February 17, 1964, p. 9.

9. David A. Noebel, *Rhythm, Riots, and Revolution* (Tulsa, Okla.: Christian Crusade Publications, 1966), p. 112. I wish to thank Mark Levine for bringing this example to my attention.

10. Bob Larson, *Rock and Roll: The Devil's Diversion* (McCook, Nebraska: Bob Larson, 1966), p. 19.

11. David A. Noebel, *The Beatles: A Study in Drugs, Sex and Revolution* (Tulsa, Okla.: Christian Crusade Publications, 1969), p. 21.

12. Gary Allen, "That Music: There's More to It Than Meets the Ear," *American Opinion* 12 (February 1969): 49.

13. Phillip Abbott Luce, "Are the Beatles Termites? The Great Rock Conspiracy," *National Review*, September 23, 1969, pp. 959, 973.

14. "The Anti-Rock and Roll Crusade: An Interview with a Real White Panther," *Creem* 2: 9.

15. There has been very little research conducted in this area. Dr. Patricia Schiller, executive director of the American Association of Sex Educators and Counselors suggested from a study of 400 pregnant and 91 nonpregnant girls ages 12 to 21 that "some songs excited them to take part in sex play and sometimes love making."

See "Rock, Soap Operas Called Sex Turn-Ons," *Los Angeles Times*, March 8, 1970, p. 15, section D.

16. As noted in chapter 4, there is little incentive for an artist or a recording company to release a record that will not receive air play, thereby insuring its failure. Consequently, most so-called controversial songs have emanated either from established stars such as the Rolling Stones, the Doors and Bob Dylan, who can rely on album sales regardless of air play. On the other hand, specialty acts such as the Fugs ("Wet Dream") or the Mothers of Invention ("Suzy Creamcheese") have appealed to those in the underground audience.

17. John Burks, "Jackie Gleason is Really a Great Man," *Rolling Stone* 23 (May 17, 1969): 1, 6.

18. Noebel, *Beatles*, pp. 25–26.

19. Quoted in Dorothy Townsend, "Graham Links Lure of Rock Music to Religious Search," *Los Angeles Times*, December 30, 1970, p. 3.

20. Quoted in "The New Rebel Cry: Jesus is Coming!" *Time*, June 21, 1971, p. 59.

21. David A. Noebel, "One Christian's View," *Christian Crusade Weekly*, April 11, 1971, p. 1.

22. Billy James Hargis, "U.S. Takes to 'Superstar'," *Christian Crusade Weekly*, March 5, 1972, p. 1.

23. Quoted in David Batterson, "Lennon as Lenin, *Creem* 4 (November 1972): 33.

24. Jerome Rodnitzky, "Book Review: The Beatles," *Popular Music and Society* 1 (Spring 1972): 178.

25. Phillip Luce, "Termites," p. 959.

26. Quoted in Robert J. Gwyn, "Opinion Advertising and the Free Market of Ideas," *Public Opinion Quarterly* 34 (Summer 1970): 249.

27. Quoted in Ben Fong-Torres, "Radio: One Toke Behind the Line," *Rolling Stone* 80 (April 15, 1971): 10.

28. Quoted in Ben Fong-Torres, "FCC Discovers Dope, Does Darndest Thing," *Rolling Stone* 79 (April 1, 1971): 6.

29. Quoted in Fong-Torres, "Radio," p. 10.

30. Quoted in George Denemeyer, "FCC Lyrics Notice Blasted by Artists," *Billboard*, May 1, 1971, p. 8.

31. Quoted in Bob Glassenberg, "Lyric Rule Poses Stiff Question," *Billboard*, March 20, 1971, p. 29.

32. Claude Hall, "Storz Follows FCC Rule—Demands Lyric with Disk," *Billboard*, April 3, 1971, p. 8.
33. Quoted in Kenemeyer, "Lyrics Notice," p. 8.
34. Quoted in Fong-Torres, "Radio," p. 10.
35. "WNBC Bars Lyrics as 'Drug-Oriented'," *New York Times*, March 27, 1971. p. 45.
36. Glassenberg, "Lyric Rule," p. 1.
37. "WBAI Criticizes Ban On Drug Songs," *New York Times*, April 6, 1971, p. 65.
38. Quoted in "Appeals Court Argues Drug Lyrics Policy," *Billboard*, November 4, 1972, pp. 3, 86.
39. Court opinion quoted in Mildred Hall, "Court Decision on Drug Lyrics," *Billboard*, January 20, 1973, p. 66.
40. Quoted in "Drug Lyrics Appeal Fails," *Billboard*, October 27, 1973, p. 6.
41. Quoted in Ben Fong-Torres, "Lennon's Song: The Man Can't F**K Our Music," *Rolling Stone* 76 (February 18, 1971): 6.
42. Tom Donohue, " 'A Rotting Corpse Stinking up the Airways,'#" *Rolling Stone* 2 (November 23, 1967): 14.
43. Eliot Tiegel, "Curb Stirs Meat—Morals on $$?" *Billboard*, November 14, 1970, p. 10.
44. Lee Zhito, "Music Trips Up Drug Culture," *Billboard*, November 6, 1970, p. 70.
45. Glassenberg, "Lyric Rule," p. 27.

9.

THE FOLKS OUT THERE

Music is love and love is music,
If you know what I mean
© *Songpainter Music (BMI)*

Popular music is a Janus-like figure. Simultaneously it has a special magic or no appeal at all for small clusters of fans. The interplay of these two faces creates the demographic dynamics and content of popular music. Music, as any cultural artifact, does not exist in a vacuum; people read into it a rainbow of meanings. Some parents see pop basically as music for their teenage sons and daughters, a sound they will shortly outgrow. For others, popular music may be a vessel of social, cultural or political change; the slogan "rock revolution" is but one manifestation. The Right's "Beatles as termites" thesis and the Rainbow people's "trans-love energy" life-style are other examples. Rock music is presented as a revolutionary form of psychic energy. For most individuals, however, these opinions simply transcend the everyday role of music as entertainment, companionship or as a nexus of camaraderie.

Music is a sensate or emotional medium. Without words, it is a totally experiential form of communication. Anthropologist Claude Levi-Strauss defines music as "a means of communication. . . . But this kind of language cannot be translated into anything else, except itself. You can translate music into music . . . you cannot translate music into speech."[1] Lyrics add another dimension, in that songs combine the emotional with Hegel's rationality of language. Lyrics, minus music, are poems or editorials whereas music minus words merely is a state of feeling. A song ties these two ingredients into a new form. Traditional song-writing teams such as Rodgers and Hammerstein and David and Bacharach unite melodic rhapsodies with equally mood-creating word sets. In less-structured genres such as blues, country and folk music, words and sentiments are wedded to time-worn musical patterns. Listeners rarely find Louisiana 32-bar blues progression a happy motif. Nor would an up-tempo song proclaiming the "Death of an Angel" or "The End" be a happy song.

Music functions at a minimum on two basic levels of appreciation: the intellectual and the experiential. The intellectual or conscious plane is verbal. Word symbols conjure up visions that are products of linear and analytical thinking, either reinforced or neutral to the instrumentation. Music alone operates at the subjective-emotional level. Ideally, the impact of Bach, Brahms or Beethoven should not be intellectual. Music becomes multi-dimensional when intellectual considerations are superimposed upon it. Kids seem quite content to allow the "beat" or the "sound" to sweep over them while studying, talking on the telephone or reading a book or magazine. The normative aspect of popular music is experiential. A writer conducting an informal poll of Los Angeles area children and young adults reported "nine out of ten said 'It makes me feel good!' "[2] In the 1930s the slogan was "It don't mean a thing if it ain't got that swing." Teenagers on the "Dick Clark Show" for a decade expressed their appreciation by exclaiming, "It's got a good beat, you can dance to it." English social scientists Stuart Hall and Paddy Whannel assert, "Though there is much to be learned from the lyrics of pop songs, there is more in the *beat* (loud, simple, insistent), the *backing,* (strong, guitar dominated), the *presentation* (larger-than-life, mechanically etherealized), the *inflections* of voice (sometimes the self-pitying, plaintive cry and later the yeah-saying, affirmative shouting) or the intonations. . . ."[3] More simply, Rolling Stone Mick Jagger says, "I don't think lyrics are that important."[4] It's the music, not the words.

Popular music has been called a revolt against reason, and perhaps it is. It is direct and gutsy and speaks to the senses. One multimedia show significantly announced itself as The Beatles: Away With Words. Their ad stated, "To *describe* it is impossible . . . to *experience* it is essential! And so it is, my friend. There are no words to describe the sensation that overwhelms you. . . ." Statements such as "it's our song" or "you can dance to it" all highlight the emotional experiential face of music. In juxtaposing the sensate versus the rational there is much to support Marty Cerf's contention that popular music "is not intellectual, it's emotional." A survey directed at college students found that only .02 percent were primarily concerned with lyrics, as opposed to 22 percent who liked the music and 76 percent overwhelmingly chose the entire "sound." Singer Neil Diamond estimates that only 10 percent of his fans listen to lyrics.

In a survey of secondary-school students in a suburb of Vancouver, Canada, 83 percent of the students indicated that they would dance to any song having a good beat, regardless of what it said. Studies by sociologists once again reinforce the argument that the intellectual involvement of both secondary and collegiate audiences with "message" or protest songs is minimal.[5] The high-school students, in less than half the cases, were able to interpret correctly the meaning or message in songs labeled as protest.

The importance of these findings is stressed by the report that high-school students desired less songs dealing with "drugs, school is dull, parents' lack of understanding, and social problems" and more dealing with "love and understanding."[6] In the mid-1960s, some junior college respondents expressed considerable displeasure with the inclusion of political and controversial material on the Top 40 stations. Several replies indicated, "From a musical standpoint they hit rock bottom. They don't add anything to the arts." From these scattered studies the implication is clear that popular music serves first and foremost as an entertainment medium, one believed removed from the political arena.

These findings should not obscure the high poetic quality or the sociological significance of many contemporary lyrics. However, certain esthetic judgments enter into any discussion of lyrical merit. Because of this only certain taste groups appear to "be into" the social significance of songs. The *Chicago Tribune Magazine* in August 1973 underlined this fact in a story about a poorly attended concert. The article was titled "What if Kris Kristofferson gave a concert and nobody came?"

Music, for the majority of teenagers and adults, consists of nonobtrusive sound which is ideologically neutral. In itself, popular music exhibits both sensate and supportive verbal or symbolic material generally associated with the romantic love motif. James Taylor's compositions, no matter how introspective and simple, contain all the elements of a lush, well-orchestrated Eddie Fisher rendition of "I'm Yours." "You've Lost That Lovin' Feeling," "Wild Thing" and Stephen Stills's "Suite: Judy Blue Eyes" are all statements of a rejected lover as full of bitterness and self-pity as anything recorded in the "set 'em up Joe" Judy Garland and Frank Sinatra torch ballads. Despite the substantial change in the rhetoric and style of popular music, its basic elements have remained remarkably similar.

Music universally is an artifact of courtship. It is the "language of love." Primitive puberty rites feature drums and other instruments to welcome children into the world of adulthood. As an accompaniment to dance throughout the ages, music has been a valuable aid to the sexual maturation of youth. Paolo Mantagazza, the Italian anthropologist, documents in detail a number of native rites which utilize "dances, songs and music that are none too decent [which] provide a festal accompaniment to this consecration of the woman."[7] Less direct means of courtship in Europe and the United States were aided and abetted through the use of music. "Play party" songs in areas of Appalachian Mountains, where dancing was forbidden, have at close scrutiny sexual connotations. Mitch Miller explicated this feature in the *New York Times*:

> The appeal of popular songs is primarily to young people in love. When these young people marry and grow older, they look back fondly on the songs of their courting days. Singing middle-age love a bit less enchanting or settling down to a more mature kind of relationship, they believe the new songs they hear just aren't as appealing as the ones they remembered from the days of youth.[8]

Married couples' request for a band or piano player to play "their song" at anniversary dances or festivities aptly demonstrates the close connection between music and sexual maturation. Critic Richard Meltzer sees pop as "background makeout music, where albums serve to cover up anything one in another room might hear."[9] The other uses of music in the dating rite hardly require further elaboration, after the spate of beach party movies, 1940s musicals and more recently, rock festival news bulletins.

The sexuality of popular music is not the same thing for all popular-music fans. The sexual development of the record buyer strongly influences the kinds and types of music purchased. Indeed, the relationship of the music to the listener is colored by the courtship function. The affinity of the preteen school-girl for a singing idol is much different from that of her older sister and brother who may like the James Gang, Cat Stevens or Joni Mitchell. The college students' approach to popular music and that of young married couples is again unlike that of their younger counterparts. Age is an important component in determining musical taste; however, a more important factor may well be that of sexual development or a person's relationship to those of the opposite sex. The nine-year-old girl who explains her interest in David Cassidy or Donny Osmond means much more than, "I just like him" by her answer. The "liking" of a teen idol is the beginning of a preteenager's participation in popular music.

POPULAR MUSIC AS RITE OF PASSAGE: THE BUBBLEGUMMERS

America has no initiation rite to guide the individual from childhood to adult status. No ceremonies exist to celebrate passage of the person from the innocence of toys, trucks and dolls to puberty, dating and marriage. Popular music, especially for young girls, serves as a rite of passage from Raggedy Ann to boys. Girls between the ages of nine through 12, an age bracket rapidly expanding to include six-year-olds, purchase a lion's share of singles in the United States. Teenagers as a whole, it is estimated, buy at least 60 percent of the singles sold. The type of record purchased by the nine- to 12-year-old girls customarily falls into the "teen idol" category. As one crop of teenyboppers graduates to actual dating, their younger sisters take their place. A new idol ascends as the object of teenscream, while the old one is discarded along with the old "kid stuff," fan magazines and wall posters. After the age of 12 or 13, adolescent tastes lend to reflect Top 40 programming. Boss radio becomes an integral part of their waking hours.

"When I was a boy," said Elvis Presley, "I was the hero in comic books and movies. I grew up believing in that dream. Now I've lived it out. That's all a man can ask for."[10] The role of idol is partly truth, partly fiction, but primarily fantasy. Billy Mernit, an aspiring young rock singer, projects, "I'll get into the fantasy, the 'show' level of gigs, and that way it can't be confused with my more private realities." Upon the idol are heaped the hopes, wishes and desires of their fans. Idols are symbols, suitors and rebels for bubblegummers—the nine- to 12-year-olds called "nubies" (prepuberty) by the industry—who use them to fulfill their emerging curiosity about boys. Idols are "paramours in absentia."[11] A *TV Guide* writer presented the idol as one appealing "to that twilight zone between childhood and maturity when girls from 6 to 16 start to become interested in boys but don't know why. His youthful idolators are reaching out for a shy, good-looking boy who sings about puppy love and acceptance, who gyrates in a manner that looks 'groovy' but is not overtly sexy."[12] Bobby Sherman, when the object of bubblegum affection, said, "I'm part of the process of becoming mature for these girls."[13] Teen idols in the record industry are unique in that they are total personality packages who incidentally sing, as opposed to the regular pop act that concentrated upon making music. Not infrequently teen idols become singers *after* becoming national heartthrobs.

The essential ingredient of the idol is his role as fantasy object. "However much," writes George Melly, "they scream outside stage doors or besiege hotels and airports, they need to believe in the non-reality of their idols, and give the impression of being secretly relieved to be held back as this allows them to avoid putting their faith to the test."[14] Fantasies must not be compared to reality, otherwise they are shattered.

The idol is remote, and in distance there is safety. Psychiatrist Stanley E. Willis observes, "A critical factor in a celebrity fantasy is the total unavailability of that celebrity. It is the unavailability which keeps the illusion safe from the chilling discovery that the idealized image is, in fact, not ideal and experience less than its fantasy form."[15] The barrier between the celebrity and audience is a dominant feature of his career. Elaborate security precautions are utilized to protect the performer from the milling, screaming and nearly hysterical fans. Security precautions for the Beatles rivaled those of the president of the United States. Bobby Sherman's manager printed up a booklet for concert promoters blueprinting plans for his protegé's escape. The pamphlet also outlined extensive backstage security measures. David Cassidy usually is whisked away from a concert hall in a nondescript Volkswagon while hiding under a blanket; a conspicuous $120-a-day rented limousine diverts his pursuers' attention. The Beatles, the Monkees, Elvis and the Rolling Stones all had elaborate plans designed to keep fans a safe distance from them. The motto is, "look, buy, but do not touch." All these precautions remove the possibility of the fantasy being ruined by the cold reality of flesh and blood.

"Television is bigger than life," it is said. All of the major idols in popular music during the last two decades, beginning with Eddie Fisher, were brought to public attention through the medium of television. Six of the nine major idols had regularly scheduled television series such as "Ozzie and Harriet" "The Partridge Family," and "The Monkees." All of the idols were initially provided exposure over the tube: Elvis Presley's big break was on the Saturday night Tommy and Jimmy Dorsey hosted "Gleason Show"; "American Bandstand" transformed television into a calculated vehicle by which to create teenage rock stars; the Beatles launched their first American tour on the Ed Sullivan program; the Monkees were synthetically created rock idols. Following these successes, a regular television series was considered requisite for creating teen idols. Performers were then sought out for the role. David Cassidy came to public attention through a bit part on the "Marcus Welby, M.D.," series. However, as Wes Farrell indicates, "nobody had asked him if he could sing."[16]

With the exception of Elvis Presley and the Beatles, both unique talents, teenage idols have been more an artifact of television than of records. Elvis, of course, became a motion picture star. The Beatles were featured in an animated television series, as have many of their bubblegum successors. Records are but one aspect in the midst of love kits, posters, photos, magazines and other mementos. Bobby Sherman's record sales grossed $20 million, but the entire "Bobby industry" earned $35 million. Records only accounted for 20 to 30 percent of David Cassidy's annual $250,000 salary. Unlike performers addressed to older audiences where the music is primary, the idol is the total product that is packaged, and television makes this promotion possible. It allows the performer to forego many of the arduous paths confronting the less glamorous act. He does not have to contend with the usual gatekeepers who have little interest in attracting bub-

Exhibit 9.1

TEEN SCREAM CYCLE: ROCK AND ROLL ARTISTS AND TELEVISION, 1952–1974

1952	Eddie Fisher	"Coke Time"
1956	Ricky Nelson	"Ozzie and Harriet"
1961	Fabian, Avalon, Anka, etc.	"American Bandstand"
1964	Beatles	Introduced on "Ed Sullivan Show"
1967	Monkees (Davy Jones)	"The Monkees"
1969	Bobby Sherman	"Shindig," "Bobby Sherman Show," "Getting Together," "Here Come the Brides"
1971	David Cassidy	"Partridge Family"
1972	Donny Osmond	Regular on "Andy Williams Show"

blegummers to their radio stations or magazines. Nine-to 12-year-old girls may purchase pictures, love kits, concert tickets and singles, but advertisers generally prefer a more affluent listener or reader. Television creates, popularizes and promotes the performer as personality, not as singer or musician. The classic illustration of the contrived recording star is the act called the Monkees.

In order to capitalize on the success of the Beatles, Bert Schneider, Robert Rafelson and James Frawley of Screen Gems plotted a television series based upon the film *A Hard Day's Night*. Four young men were recruited to "romp" or improvise through a television series. The Hollywood trade papers ran an ad announcing, "Four insane boys, 17–21, with courage to work." The name of the group could well have come from the proverb, "monkey see, monkey do." Even the overnight act's name "Monkees" was a parody of the misspelled Beatles (as opposed to beetles). Davy Jones, Mickey Dolenz, Peter Tork and Mike Nesmith, signed for the group, were paid $500 per week despite the awkward fact that they were not rock musicians. Their original records were performed by studio musicians, yet these curious conditions did not prevent the unit from selling six million singles and eight million albums in a four-month period after the airing of their weekly television series. The Monkees received 20,000 fan letters a week. Surrounding the television act was an entire industry geared to the bubblegummers. Chuck Laufer, the publisher of *Tiger Beat*, a fan magazine, recalls: "When the Monkees came along in 1966, I began to see the direct connection between magazines and TV. I worked out a deal with Screen Gems. We began to sell a lot of books and photographs and posters."[17] At Screen Gems, Ward Sylvester, a graduate of Harvard Business School, discovered Bobby Sherman, who was a *Shindig* veteran making a guest appearance on the then increasingly low-rated Monkees show. Sherman became the first in a series of packaged solo artists whose prime base of operation was a television series. "Getting Together" and the "Bobby Sherman Show" were "built-in commercials" for the "Bobby industry," as it was called. The Bobby Sherman–David Cassidy phenomena were parallel to the string of fleeting idols who lipsynched their way to fame on the "American Bandstand" program shortly after Presley's departure for two years in the Army. Even though they were older, Sherman and Cassidy looked 15 or 16 years of age. Both were slight of build and medium in height, and both possessed a quality imperative for teen-idol status: role ambiguity. The liner notes of the Shadows of the Knight first album outline this contradiction: "If you invited them over for dinner, your parents would, at first, have you examined or call the police or run screaming to the neighbors. If your parents stayed around, they would find that the Shadows are polite, quiet, considerate and that they might even grow to like them." Elvis and all of the other real or aspiring teen idols have this confused image, which provides the illusion of revolt against parental values. Parents see the flirtation of their young daughters as a passing phase. In their remarks about pop music, parents may convince the idol worshipper that she is actually rebelling. Megan Rosenfeld of the *Washington Post* observed that this image combined "respect for parents and a happy family with a smattering of rebellion (long hair . . .). They get into scrapes, but everything turns out happily because they are basically good honest and cute. The idols are expected to be as untouchable in real life as they are on TV."[18] Elvis, while the Hell's Angel on stage, was characterized in fan magazines as a church-going young man who was a devoted son and patriot and a frequent contributor to charity. The Beatles were similarly pictured as playing dual roles. Sociologist Renée Clair Fox described them: "They appear to be good boys who nevertheless dress and pose as bad ones—London's Teddyboys. And their fancy, Edwardian-style clothes [sic: Elektra's Sally Stevens states the "rags were Pierre Cardin"] suggest a sort of sophistication which contrasts with their 'home-spun' commoner style of performance."[19] The Monkees, in a similar vein, were zany but decent rogues. Bobby Sherman says, "My songs never have any hidden references to drugs or sex. When I sing 'I Love You, Baby,' or 'Will You Be Mine' the connotation is always strictly romantic."[20] David Cassidy's "I Think I Love You" and Donny Osmond's "Go Away Little Girl" are equally innocent. Both depict an uncertain teenager trying to cope with the emotion of love. These songs mirror great "first kiss" debates found in fan magazines specializing in the bubblegum market. While the teenage idol is certainly not a threat to cherished American institutions, he is not a part of the immediate world either. Idols, clothed in fantasy and glamour, are highly mercurial commodities.

The relationship of the teenybopper or bubblegummer is taken directly from the romantic love novels of Sir Walter Scott, poems of Elizabeth Barrett Browning or Erich Segal's *Love Story*. The familiar elements of "June, spoon, moon" are all present. "She has posters of him all over her room and kisses them every night," said a mother of a seven-year-old girl. Teen idols receive a tremendous amount of fan letters proclaiming devotion. David Cassidy received, at the height of his popularity, approximately 3,000 pieces of mail weekly.

One letter to him said, "I've always dreamed I was going steady with you, but now I blush whenever I think about it. I heard you are 20 years old." Gloria Stavers of *16* magazine explains these feelings: "It's an oral age for the girls. Their idea of sex is malts and hamburgers, a kiss. It's a romantic thing, not physical or orgiastic. They think of their idol as a teddy bear, a blanket, a cuddly thing."[21] More typical responses to bubblegum music stars involve the word "like" instead of "love"!

> I like Donny Osmond Because: Although I've never seen him in real life, he seems to be a real neat guy on and off stage! Their whole group dance neat! Donny has a very nice voice and a very nice personality. He's very handsome if I do say so myself.
>
> —*Beth, Age 10*
>
> I Like Donny Osmond Because: I like his voice and all of his songs, I like his personality and I think he is cute and very nice. I like the way he dances when he sings, and I really like all of his clothes. I like his brothers, also.
>
> —*Cathy, Age 10*

Fantasies have a way of becoming realities. This is the bane of "nubie" idols. The idol introduces the pre-adolescent female to a "love" object; as with Barbie dolls, roles are learned along with many half-truths. But, as *Flip* editorial director Valerie Gerger states, "These little girls have a lot to give and they must channel it somewhere."[22] Time and maturation impact upon the bubblegummer, and few idols remain in that position for any length of time.

The awareness of the teen-scream cycle is relatively new. Davy Jones in 1967 told an airport news conference:

> The Monkees are getting the same enthusiasm and fan fever that greeted the Beatles. I think the Beatles are tired out now and the Rolling Stones sing questionable songs. The British scene in America is dead as a dodo and it'll be a new year for single singing stars. The Monkees hit it big because the Beatles are on the way

> out, not everyone wants to go on listening to the Hermits singing about Mrs. Brown or the Stones singing rude songs. We came along at the right time and hit lucky. But we'll be one of the last groups to hit it big in America.

The success of the imitation Beatles blinded them and their merchandisers to the transitory nature of top idol status. *Flip* magazine, for one neglected the decline in their fan mail and lost $50,000 due to its continuing support of the foursome while Bobby Sherman was ascending the bubblegum charts. Now fan magazines monitor TV shows in search of new potential stars. Sherman's reign was tied to his television appearance, and the cancellation of his weekly show was followed by a sharp drop in fan interest. In May 1972 Gloria Stavers predicted to *Rolling Stone*, "David's passed his peak already. But his effect will last until the end of the year." In September of the same year the Record Industry Association of America (RIAA) announced that the Osmonds had earned ten gold records in one year, breaking the Beatles' mark of nine. A new teen idol, Donny Osmond, displaced "The Partridge Family"'s ace. The ever-changing cycle is perhaps a partial reflection of the fickleness of 12 and 13-year-old girls who outgrow their idols. A fan wrote *Tiger Beat*:

> For a long time Bobby Sherman has been my special fave, but then David Cassidy came along and my heart was torn between the two. But everything worked out fine, because one half of my heart is for Bobby and the other is for David.

The fantasy is replaced by the reality of dating. "By the time they're 16," says Chuck Laufer, "they're having dates, and they don't need them anymore." One sophisticated teenager concurred. "When you're 13 and have had a real date, you don't go in for crushes anymore." Another teenager disclaimed David Cassidy, "It's the thing to say you can't stand him."[23] Reality and the pressure to conform find idols being discarded with growing rapidity. In the bubblegum world of popular music, taste generations are not 15 or even seven years in duration. The average taste generation is less than three years. David Cassidy acknowledged, "There are just a couple of years of this sort of thing."[24] Preteens reject the idols of their older sisters and adopt their own. Only Elvis Presley was able to carry a significant number of admirers through his numerous stylized MGM soundtracks. There is some evidence "Elfans," as Jerry Hopkins calls them, have changed over the years. The girls that screamed and fainted when the singer wiggled to the strains of "Heartbreak Hotel" on stage got married or went off to college and adopted the Kingston Trio in the late 1950s. A different group of teenagers flipped over the more subdued, nearly operatic, "It's Now or Never" in 1960. "Suspicious Minds" and "In the Ghetto" some nine years later, as well as his touring, revived interest in the singer. The Elfans in the United States reflect this distribution. In England, one-third of the members of the Presley fan club are over 20, with a good number of them in their late twenties or early thirties; the rest are teenagers. The Beatles, now without an American fan club, exhibited a similar progression. The "I Want to Hold Your Hand" jelly-bean tossers were a different bunch than the more intellectual *Sgt. Pepper* fans. Continued fan loyalty, even of the kind generated by Elvis and the Beatles, is rare in popular music. In soul, country and western, jazz or the classics this is not the case. The pop-music teen idol, however, is thrown away like an old shoe. It is not fashionable except during class reunions or nostalgia crazes to reminisce over the awkward years of adolescence. As music becomes the language of love in the teenager's life, it becomes the backdrop for courtship, and ceases to be the central feature or focus.

YOU CAN DANCE TO IT: THE TEENYBOPPERS

The teenager's flirtation with pop music does not cease the moment of her date, as one 15-year-old Beatle fan indicated, "Even though I love John [Lennon] so much, it didn't stop me chasing other boys at school." As do most adolescents, this young lady no doubt moved away from her fantasy relationships with the Beatles. Even in the nostalgia-ridden 1950s of black leather jackets and acrobatic rock and roll, the idiom did not enjoy an exalted place. A 1958 survey of Chicago teenagers reported that girls, by a 3 to 1 margin, spent their time in pop-music related activities. Some ten years later a sample of Florida high school students revealed 65.3 percent of the girls were most heavily into pop as opposed to 34.7 percent of the boys. George Booker, who conducted this survey, described the typical music fan. "The teenager most apt to be listening to the radio is a thirteen year old girl with a transistor radio. She is most apt to be of low intelligence and make low grades in school. Her favorite type of music is rock 'n' roll and she is relaxing when she listens most."[25] Few parents would argue with this stereotyped image of their daughter with the radio "growing out of her ear." This caricature of the teenager doesn't last long; only the exceptional teenager continues a close relationship with popular music. A teenager in the 1950s told a survey team "there is no swooning over rock and roll singers. It is the drapettes and the unaccepted girls who are in fan clubs and swoon over these singers."[26] In 1972, 17-year-old Penny Bergman explained her attendance at a David Cassidy concert to a *New York Times* reporter, "I Ought to have a sign saying 'Jerk' pinned on me. If the kids at school hear about this! I wouldn't tell them I was coming. He's known as a teenage idol. I'm too old."[27] Penny Bergman's interest in David Cassidy was uncommon. She was a nonconformist to her adolescent peer group. A New York 17-year-old should be into the Allman Brothers, Humble Pie, Grand Funk, Alice Cooper or Black Sabbath. "Music freaks," even among teenagers, are statistically a small unit. Adolescents spend time where music is an idiom for individual or group activities as going to dances, but for most it is mere background noise. A music educator finds "relaxing," dressing and grooming, performing household chores, studying, dating and driving as the major functions accompanied by popular music. These activities center around "getting ready for school" and "coming home." Both the Chicago and Florida studies suggest that as teenagers become *more* involved in social life their interest in pop music wanes. Dances and concerts are social events, whereas music is part of a total experience. A question which baffled Capitol Records executives, most rock writers and radio station personnel was "Why is Grand Funk popular?" So far few if any persuasive answers have been offered. Dennis Killeen at Capitol explained, "None of the project people who worked on Grand Funk were into Grand Funk. They didn't sit in their offices listening to the records thinking this is really super. Not one." The rise of super-loud bands such as Black Sabbath, Uriah Heep, Bang and Alice Cooper in the early 1970s is difficult to explain. Rock writers have called this type of music punk-rock, underlining its totally experiential character as well as its teenage audience. The rise of punk-rock is generally seen as a generational phenomenon. A copywriter at Warner Brothers observed, "Many of the important rock people of the last decade have turned 30, along with the people who moved into the record industry with them. Most 'legitimate' rock forums represent the 20- to 30-year-olds, whose tastes are eclectic, specialized and unfrenzied." The age factor has not escaped many. Writer Richard Goldstein, after attending a Grand Funk concert, wrote:

> The people who came out to see Grand Funk perform are the young who offer perfunctory allegiance to Dylan and the Stones, but who really have no feeling for the context of that music, who have no sense of the Sixties. These people are looking for a new set of guidelines. . . . What is significant about this band is its audience which consists of people just coming into their own. People between the ages of fourteen and eighteen are a hidden source of energy, precisely because they have no vested interest in popular culture, except as it reflects their immediate needs.

Lenny Kaye characterized Grand Funk as "a big fan club. The best . . . fan club in the world."[28] The concert is the tribal gathering of the club. A central feature of punk-rock is its primary appeal as a concert phenomenon. Grand Funk sold out Shea Stadium, which seats 55,000 people in 72 hours. Record sales come after concerts. Tim Ferris of *Rolling Stone* asked some of the patrons at that historic event about Grand Funk's records; most replied that their concerts were better. The rise of Black Sabbath, an equally loud band, has generated equal statements of disbelief. A Warner Brothers executive attempted to explain the unexpected acceptance of Black Sabbath, commenting: "I've been driven out of places by the noise. They play to a young crowd, 14–17 years old, but who knows how they hear about them? The word just gets around that this is a group to go see."[29] Another Warner spokesman writes, "The times they are a-changing, as evidenced by Black Sabbath and groups like Grand Funk Railroad (though they have had the benefit of long and strong concert tours and monstrous record company hype)." Still, the question of why 14-year-olds and others go to hear them remains open. A journalist at one Black Sabbath concert reported many people there did not appear to like the band, but attended because it was something to do. This observation suggested that punk-rock may be just another form of background noise. Alice Cooper explained, "A young audience usually comes stoned. Most of them come there wiped out of their heads. When they see us they're convinced we are mad. . . . We give the audience an enormous number of images . . . so fast that they really can't possibly digest the whole thing."[30]

Less elaborate performances generate similar reactions. The Market West is a typical Midwest club where people go to drink or to find a friend for the night. People sit at long cafeterialike tables drinking 3.2 beer or watered-down booze in red, white and blue paper cups marked Pepsi-Cola. Waitresses patrol the narrow aisles taking orders and delivering more Pepsi cups. The bandstand, nearly buried in wires and speakers, is nestled in the far corner of this darkened cafeteria. A living-room sized area is reserved for dancing, the main ring for scoring.

Lima is just one of those small towns found along interstate highways. It's Saturday night and 18-year-olds go to the Market West and several clubs like it. They come in pairs, or threes, to talk and sip beer. It's a relatively cheap way to spend the evening. After a few pitchers of beer, the sport begins with guys flirting from aisle to aisle asking girls to dance, all for $2.50 admittance charge.

The band appearing at the club that night is above average, having toured with Humble Pie, Black Oak Arkansas and Three Dog Night. The material they play is geared directly for nightclub consumption. Songs are taken from Grand Funk Railroad, Humble Pie, Mountain and several other hard-rock bands. The audience here is a bit older than at Black Sabbath concerts due to the 3.2 beer served on the premises.

At 10:00 P.M. the set begins. Occasionally couples get up and dance—two, maybe three couples. People mill in the narrow aisles, clutching the ever-present Pepsi-Cola cups. Barbiturates or "downers" are openly passed around. Patrons nod to the music, not dancing or applauding, just being there. The introductions to songs are blurred by the crowd noise. The first 50-minute set ends with "Bobby McGee." As the evening wears on, booze and downers begin to take effect as the dancers multiply. "Clap your hands," urges the lead singer, "C'mon everybody." A few do. As the beer flows the tempo picks up. The aisle-cruising increases. To fast-paced songs, couples—immobilized statues—sway against one another. Time is out of synch as "Still of the Night" dancers move to a requested Grand Funk song. As the second set moves on the cruisers become less steady and glassy-eyed, wandering up and down. A burly student with long hair stumbles, spilling beer and grabbing at girls not yet spoken for. A fight breaks out. The band's $40-a-week road manager or equipment mover says, "Make sure I'm not going to get this again," pointing to his swollen jaw. He was floored in a club brawl in Charleston the week before. The modern-day combatants are entangled and the best goes on. The band's rendition of the Roberta Flack ballad "The First Time" cannot be heard beyond the front row. The band is a human jukebox. By 1 A.M., the small dance floor is packed—the evening's alliances are made. An auburn-haired girl greets countless males as they pass with their dates. They anxiously say hello and hurry off. Why did she come? "Because all my friends come here . . . ain't nowhere else to go." A friend interrupts, "I hate the place . . . I try to have a good time." Two guys at the bar come to "meet friends . . . pick up girls, you know." One waitress explained, "they come to dance, drink, who knows." No one mentions the music.

Scenes like the one at Market West or Shea Stadium are the rule in the so-called punk-rock idiom. Clubs and concerts replace the festivals which reigned supreme during the Woodstock craze. The music becomes a magnet to attract teenagers and some noncollege youths into social situations. The band itself is just another component of the environment. As Terry Knight told Bob Hilburn, the posture of Grand Funk was communal: "We are part of you. We are your voice." The loud music adds to the milieu because it overcomes the need for fixed attention by the audience. Nothing is lost while cruising, talking or doing something else. Punk-rock is not simply entertainment, either at the level of the teen idols or that of plain background noise afforded by a radio or phonograph or even a live dance band.

The popularity of punk-rock is affected by its social implications. It is music designed to be played at concert halls with the fans an important adjunct to the music. People attend these concerts both for the music and to interact with their friends and dates. The loudness of the music allows the listener to mentally tune in and out with ease. The social aspects of punk-rock have been underlined by a number of audience surveys which find that peer-group pressure and social activity are important in the development of musical preferences among adolescents. Sociologists John Johnstone and Elihu Katz in the late 1950s found that frequent dating influenced the type of songs a teenager enjoyed. Frequent daters, they reported, "overwhelmingly prefer the 'sad' songs, while infrequent daters like 'happy songs.'"[31] Why this is, they did not explain. Participation in the courtship rite does not appear to have an effect on taste. A recent Ph.D. dissertation completed at Notre Dame University added another dimension to the punk-rock phenomenon. It was reported that loud rock was essentially a "mood establisher," "atmosphere setter" or "crucial socializing element." Here the music "would not serve as the focus of attention, but provide the setting in which interaction could occur."[32] This description appears to fit the punk-rock concert; however, it can also describe other live performances that serve as catalysts for getting people together.

The punk-rock phenomenon is very much a part of the courtship process of the middle-teen or teenybopper. Loud rock-and-roll bands provide background noise for the dating game, allowing an almost schizoid dispersal of attention. Her date, now, gets as much attention as Ian Hunter, Mark Farner, Peter Frampton, Alice Cooper, David Bowie or David Byron. Equally important, punk-rock is an age-identification symbol, isolating the teenybopper from the Donny Osmond fan of the older *aficionado* of the more cerebral James Taylor or Cat Stevens. Grand Funk Railroad's repeated practice of addressing the audience as "brothers and sisters" underlines the "them" versus "us" ethos of the music. Black Sabbath is more sophisticated than Donny Osmond but has "more balls" than the whimpy folk-rockers, argue the proponents of punk-rock.

After high school, shifts in music tastes and record buying habits appear to take place. In 1964 the RIAA told National Association of Broadcasters that teenagers accounted for 60 percent of rock-music sales. Those over 25 years of age purchased less than 20 percent of the same musical style. The same report found that 60 percent of ten-year-olds spent their record money on popular music. At the age of 15, there was a drop to approximately 40 percent, and by the age of 20 this percentage was cut in half. Five years later, this figure is once again cut in half. Other less complete surveys have noted identical shifts in consumption habits. The main difference between 1964 and 1972 is the expansion of the popular music age group. Many forms of specialty material such as jazz, folk music and several strains of country music have now been subsumed into popular music, thus expanding the preference chart as well as continuing it into the middle twenties and in some cases the early thirties. Russ Soloman, owner of the Tower Record chain in California, says, "The point is 'kids' are older, but their tastes are the same as today's teens. Five or 10 years ago the customer in his early twenties would not be a pop-rock customer, but he sure is now. He's buying the musical entertainment he has been brought up on . . . and he loves it."[33] In Exhibit 9.1, those under 20 preferred pop fare in 86 percent of the cases, while those in the 26-to-28 category opted for it in 57 percent of the cases. Thirty-eight percent of those over the watermark of 30 favored popular music genres. This is much higher than the ten percent in the RIAA report some eight years before. Still, the consumer engaged in the courtship process is the cornerstone of the pop-music industry. For example, the bubblegummer infatuated with Donny Osmond buys most of his singles; the male, upon reaching a similar consciousness of sex, begins to purchase long-playing albums with which to pursue this new interest. Age and sex are key factors in discussing the figurations of record purchasing during the courtship years; however, one intervening factor in recent years has emerged: higher education.

WE ALL LIVE IN AN IVY-COVERED SUBMARINE: THE COLLEGIATES

The American higher education system has been called the "world's most expensive babysitting service in history." One need not agree with this characterization to realize that the growing emphasis upon college and university training has

Exhibit 9.2

AGE AND MUSICAL PREFERENCE BY COLLEGIATES (1970)

	17-19	20-22	23-25	26-28	29+	TOTAL
Folk	20 .24	104 .36	58 .30	29 .25	25 .18	236 .29
Motown	19 .23	34 .12	29 .15	17 .15	22 .16	121 .15
Rock	32 .39	74 .26	40 .21	20 .17	6 .04	172 .21
Jazz	3 .04	25 .09	18 .09	14 .12	19 .14	79 .10
Classical	4 .05	27 .09	30 .15	23 .20	44 .32	128 .16
Other	5 .06	26 .09	20 .10	12 .10	22 .16	85 .10
TOTAL	83 (1.01)	290 (1.01)	195	115 (.99)	138	821

(N = 821)

prolonged the years of adolescence. The responsibilities of job and family are postponed for at least four years, if not longer. The courtship process is equally extended. Add to this the spending power of those in the halls of ivy and the significance of the college student to the record industry becomes apparent. Most record companies have special college divisions and *Billboard* publishes a weekly "Campus News" page with a column "What's Happening" by Sam Sutherland concerning records broadcast by college stations. Since World War II the campus has become a major consumer for both concerts and records, much to the delight of the music industry.

In a 1955 poll of Atlanta University students, James Conyers discovered that preferred musical styles were: (1) film scores, (2) choral arrangements, (3) popular, (4) classical and

(5) musical comedy. Blues and "hillbilly" were the least popular, ranking 17 and 18 on the scale, although the sociologist did find a growing interest in "modern jazz" in his sample of students "under 20."[34] Conyer's "under 20" students reflected a nation-wide jazz revival on campus which saw Dave Brubeck filling concert halls and gracing the cover of *Time* magazine. The progressive jazz fad, however, did not establish the campus as a major consumer in the eyes of record manufacturers. The jazz version of *My Fair Lady* sold well, but never in the figures of the Miller-created Columbia "belters." A southern Appalachian murder ballad, as sung by a folk-music trio that dressed as if they were going to an Ivy League lecture, awakened the industry to the college market.

On October 5, 1958, "Tom Dooley" an up-tempo folksong, began to climb the national sales charts. The November 17 issue of *Billboard* saw it as the nation's number one single. "Tom Dooley" remained on the charts for 21 weeks and ultimately sold over four million records. Adding to the song's attractiveness was its murky legal status, which allowed the Kingston Trio to pocket all of the publishing royalties from it, much to the chagrin of the folklorist who found the song and his rural informant Frank Proffitt. "Tom Dooley" began a folk-music revival which lasted nearly six years, going through two phases and finally being absorbed by the rock genre in 1965. The prime supporters of the fad were college students.

The college students of the early 1960s were Elvis Presley fans only three or four years before. Pop music had left them for the packaged teen idols of "American Bandstand." Folk music was a kissing cousin to rock-a-billy, with a tradition on many campuses. Pete Seeger had cultivated his garden well during the McCarthy era, when the campus was the only refuge from American Legionnaires bent on shielding the public from the banjo picker. The Kingston Trio and their many contemporaries basically ignored the politics of folk music and presented good "ole" American songs.

Fraternity types and young executives delighted in the humor and gaiety of contrived "folk songs," but others went a step further and discovered the ethnic tradition—"to be folk, you live folk." Little magazines chronicled and expanded the horizons of the new folk fans. *Little Sandy Review* joined *Sing Out*! in judging groups on their "ethnicity" or their ability to imitate the real thing. The New Lost City Ramblers, Charles River Valley Boys and the Greenbrier Boys were the purists, as *Time* called them, and in direct opposition to the original popularizers, the commercializers: the Kingston Trio, Limeliters, Tarriers, Brothers Four and a legion of similar trios. The animosity was deadly serious and thousands of hours and gallons of printer's ink were wasted on the overpowering question: "Was X really folk?" The Trio and the Limeliters did not really care and collected their increasing royalty checks while the folkniks hated them for it. Joan Baez took great delight in mentioning Peter, Paul and "Misery" at her concerts.

The already fragmented revival *personae* was further complicated by the reemergence of the "Guthrie-Seeger" school of political songwriters who congregated around a little mimeographed magazine, *Broadside* (NYC). It was a unique mix: a few elderly ex-Communist party members and fellow travelers, and a lot of young people who were into folk music and saw "a new world a 'coming" but not through any easy Old Left solutions. Dylan published his first song, "Talking John Birch Society Blues," in *Broadside.* Phil Ochs, Tom Paxton, Len Chandler, Gil Turner and scores of guitarists and banjo pickers joined him in writing and singing about the issues of integration and peace. The early politicos shared the ethnics' disdain for the commercializers because they typified the corporate America they desired to change. They also were not overly fond of the ethnics, who were seen as irrelevant and esoteric. Dylan's "Talking New York" aptly outlines this view with "we don't want hillbillies here, just folk singers." Folk music appealed to nearly all segments of the university community. Esoteric classes in folklore became "relevant" and filled to capacity. Professors were besieged with questions as "Why isn't Dylan really folk?" The activists supported singers of protest songs, while the fraternity and sorority parties featured hootenannylike singalongs. Collegiates purchased albums by the Kingston Trio, Limeliters, Chad Mitchell Trio and Bob Dylan, several years before the popular-music audience discovered the albums full of hits by the Beatles and Rolling Stones.

Bob Dylan was the unquestioned superstar on campus. *Esquire* labeled him the bard of the college generation. He was topical, addressing the civil rights ardor of the 1960s as well as the existential condition of man. His defection to rock, while denounced by the more ideologically committed, made the electric sound respectable for many folk fans who had previously considered Beatlemania a form of childhood disease. The Beatles' first American tour found Ivy League students picketing with placards reading "Stamp Out Beatles," "Pass the Bug Repellent" and "Bach Not Beatles." Folksingers such as Joan Baez and Peter, Paul and Mary included rock parodies in their college concerts. The Animals' version of "House of the Rising Sun," a traditional folk song included in Bob Dylan's first album, was received with laments and polemics previously reserved for white "rednecks" and southern sheriffs such as Bull Connor. Bob Dylan changed much of this attitude. While the Byrds reintroduced Dylan to Top 40 audiences with "Mr. Tambourine Man," he in turn made them presentable at student parties. The emergence of the acid-rock bands and the Beatles' growth into *Rubber Soul*, *Revolver* and finally their *tour de force*, *Sgt. Pepper's Lonely Hearts Club Band*, crowned rock as the dominant musical force in the nation's bastions of higher education. Campus radio stations, once a training ground for Top 40 announcers, turned into smaller versions of what was to become free-form FM radio. The stations, of course, were not dependent upon commercials for survival. They could air songs longer than 2.37 minutes. Indeed, some campus stations at Berkeley and Ann

Arbor were broadcasting album material from Simon and Garfunkel, Tom Paxton and Phil Ochs long before Larry Miller's famous KMPX-San Francisco all-night show, whose main audience consisted of San Francisco State College and University of California students. Rock has not driven the folk influence away from the campus, for many college favorites remain in the singer-writer-guitarist idiom. Pete Seeger concerts remain sell outs. A popular folk-rock act working only weekends on campuses according to the William Morris Agency can earn $500,000 a year. James Taylor, Neil Young, Joni Mitchell, Carly Simon and legions of other subdued and musically low-key artists dominated concert tours in university towns during the early 1970s. Top-selling albums were recorded by Chicago, Crosby, Stills, Nash and Young, the Moody Blues, James Taylor and Melanie. The popularity of quasi-jazz and folk acts can be partially attributed to the so-called traditional tastes on campus. The universities spawned both the jazz and folk revivals of the 1950s. Campus program directors have nurtured this tradition as much as boss radio deejays keep bubblegum music alive.

Recent studies suggest that the type of music preferred by collegiates is also determined by their style of dating as well as by the phenomenon of marijuana smoking and pill popping. One can easily carry on a conversation with James Taylor whining in the background. Some of the lyrics easily lend themselves as topics of conversations over soft drinks, beer or what have you. The music is also considered "an enhancer of inner experience." In recent years many students have indicated on questionnaires that they spent time listening to music while "relaxing." At one time "relaxing" meant doing nothing, today it may well be a euphenism for "dope smoking" or taking "downers" or "soapers." One West Coast program director attibuted the playing of a bevy of "downer" bands between the hours of 10:00 P.M. and 2:00 A.M. to his "stoned" audience of college students. There is, of course, no concrete evidence to substantiate this claim, but broadcasters with an 18-plus audience believe this a fact of life and successfully cater to it. They have so far received few if any objections to this programming policy. In David Dees' study of Notre Dame University students he reported that "the music is the center of group activity and establishes the nature of social and personal experience. When drug usage is considered, the use of music was discussed as crucial by some students in its role as a guide for hallucinogenic experience, and as a means for ensuring good or bad 'trips.' " In a footnote he added, "Some students were rather detailed in their discussion of drug-related music, indicating that certain songs were more appropriate for LSD, while others should be played when marijuana is used, and still others should be used with amphetamines."[35] While not identifying the songs associated with specific drugs, campus lore does connect many of the punk-rock bands such as Grand Funk Railroad, Black Sabbath and Uriah Heep with "downers." Donovan's *Sunshine Superman*, Jefferson Airplane's *Surrealistic Pillow*, the Beatles' *Sgt. Pepper* and Amboy Dukes' *Journey to the Center of the Mind* are considered "acid" albums. The preferences of marijuana smokers, given their large numbers, are not uniform. Some prefer groups such as the Moody Blues, while other collegiates indicate guitarists such as John Fahey, Robbie Basho, Leo Kottke and Sandy Bull as ideal mood-setters. Many students listen to what genre they like regardless of the sound. One bluegrass "freak" envisioned Bill Monroe as the man to "get wasted" with. As Exhibit 9.3 indicates, folk music with or without a rock "bottom" is "the sound on campus." As the student becomes mature, his tastes change to the more conventional modes of "easy listening" and in some cases to classical or other more specialized idioms. Age and courtship patterns, again, appear dominant.

Upon graduating from high school or college, the world of "rating and dating" music becomes increasingly a form of background noise for the average person. It is sound that comes from the car radio or something that interrupts the morning and evening news and traffic reports, a sound that obscures the drudgery of housework from 10 A.M. until 4:00

Exhibit 9.3

GENERATIONAL MUSICAL PREFERENCES*

Bubblegummers (9 to 12)	Teen idols:	Donny Osmond David Cassidy Bobby Sherman Monkees (David Jones) Beatles Fabian (Frankie Avalon) Ricky Nelson Elvis Presley
Teenyboppers (13 to 18)	Top 40 (Albums and singles):	*Punk Rock* Mott the Hoople David Bowie Grand Funk Railroad Black Sabbath James Gang Three Dog Night Grass Roots Black Oak Arkansas Rare Earth
College Students (18+)	Albums:	*Folk-Art-Rock* Simon & Garfunkel James Taylor Bob Dylan Carly Simon Moody Blues Others
Easy Listening (24+)	Albums:	Andy Williams Barbara Striesand Al Martino Ray Conniff Singers

* These categories are not always mutually exclusive, as certain songs have transcended age and education classifications.

P.M. Housewives frequently constitute the bulk of the daytime pop-music audience. All of the major ratings services have special categories for women between the ages of 18–34 and 34–49. These listeners are the major married adult record consumers. The importance of married females was graphically underlined by Kal Rudman in *Friday Morning Quarterback*, a radio tip sheet: "I'll take a female audience . . . any age . . . any day! And remember, girls and women love to SHAKE THEIR ASSES . . . and any record that makes a broad shake her ass . . . is a record I recommend to be played . . . because it will be BOUGHT and phone-requested!!!"[36] The married male only occasionally will purchase a record unless it is in specialty area. The highest percentage of record buying by those over the age of 25 is in the genre of the classics. While adolescenthood is expanded by the college experience to the mid-twenties, thus prolonging popular-music interest, less than ten percent of those continue to support the idiom *after* college graduation. Indeed, male adults who are still popular music fans are considered by many people to be "somewhat strange" or in their "second childhood." Record-company executives who make their living from the music are not exempted from this charge. Rudman described industry executives to the *New Yorker*: "They want this one piece of plastic to accomplish for them the realization of everything they want, all their ego-trip needs. . . . Status, emotional problems, financial problems, everything in their whole life. . . . This is the LAST OF THE GOLD-MINE BUSINESSES." A small marginal group of adults interested in popular music in recent years has arisen: professors studying the music form as a legitimate object of scholarly concern.

MR. JONES MEETS POP: THE ACADEMICS

Prior to the advent of *Sgt. Pepper's Lonley Hearts Club Band,* few academics were aware of the differences between Fabian and Muddy Waters. This certainly did not disturb them. Rock music was something frivolous that their students and children wasted time with. As "Yellow Submarine" replaced "We Shall Overcome" at campus protest rallies, a few professors began to ask, "What do the Beatles signify?" Some were led into rock music by Bob Dylan when he traded in his Martin acoustical for a Fender guitar. The emphasis on youth culture and flower children during the late 1960s ignited some professors' curiosities as to "what's happening." J. I. Simmons and Barry Winograd in their book *It's Happening* informed their colleagues:

> The new musicians are the poets and troubadours of what's happening, and their work, as it is disseminated, becomes itself an active social force which shapes and spreads the themes it is describing. As chroniclers, these artists therefore are acting also as innovators and propagandists. As propagandists they still cloak their thoughts behind frequently murky lyrics; words that are vague to censors or parents, but "in" with the listeners. . . . The music has become a chronicle of events and messages, with the latter approaching the esprit of past eras' revolutionary ballads. The words are different, and even though it's difficult to define the antagonists, the force of feeling and craving are all too clear.

They continue:

> These are happening times and the music of these times, more openly and blatantly than most other aspects of the happenings, leads the way to where it's at. With its ties to almost all the current scenes, the new music offers a substantive look at bits and pieces of the hang-loose ethic. It does not pretend to speak for everyone and his brother, but it does speak *to* them if they would just sit down and listen. The fact that this music so well portrays the temper of the generational change we have been discussing is, itself, an open invitation.[37]

A year following the appearance of *It's Happening*, a University of California Ph.D. candidate read a paper titled "For What It's Worth: Today's Rock Scene" before the American Sociological Association. The paper echoed the original "it's happening" argument. Pop became a symptom of the "youth revolt" and a valuable guide to its make up. The Doors and

Beatles joined Dylan and Bach as cocktail party background noise. For some faculty members wishing to identify with the campus protests of the 1960s this was an open invitation to become involved.

A number of academicians accepted the invitation, but on their terms. Rock was analyzed as poetry, art and protest, not as popular music. Numerous articles and several books were written on the subject. Universities at Oakland, Urbana, North Dakota, SUNY, Buffalo and the New School of Social Research initiated courses and classes called Pop Music 1A. The Center for the Study of Popular Culture at Bowling Green University in 1971 began publishing an academic journal addressed to popular music. Despite the surge of interest, the relationship between music and academia is an uneasy one.

American folklorists for decades combed the hills of Appalachia in search of old Scotch-Irish Anglo-Saxon ballads, totally ignoring indigenous native material. It took a maverick scholar like John Lomax to awaken his colleagues to the value of worksongs and chain-gang chants. The relationship of popular music to colleges has been painfully similar. Unfortunately, no pop-music John Lomax graced the 1950s or mid 1960s. Social scientists were aware of what was called "radio music" during the World War II. The Nazi propaganda machine had attracted the attention of scholars at Columbia University who formed the Office of Radio Research, later called the Bureau of Applied Social Research. This bureau churned out a series of monographs, articles and reports on the effect of media upon the public. Robert K. Merton and Alice Kitt, for example, chronicled the influence of Kate Smith on war bond sales. But popular music was not treated kindly by others. T. W. Adorno, a political refuge from Nazi Germany, found pop music to be inferior to classical or "serious" music. For the German scholar, popular music was characterized by "standardization"; hit songs always invoked the same experience and nothing new was ever introduced. Not only did Adorno view the music as static and unchanging, but he also felt it was "antagonistic to the ideal of individuality in a free, liberal society." Adorno continued, "Standardization of song hits keeps the customers in line by doing their listening for them, as it were. Pseudo-individualization for its part, keeps them in line by making them forget that what they listen to is already listened to for them, or 'predigested'."[38] Popular music listeners were passive subjects: "The frame of mind to which popular music originally appealed, on which it feeds, and which it perpetually reinforced, is simultaneously one of distraction and inattention. *Listeners are distracted from the demands of reality by entertainment which does not demand attention either*."[39] These observations haunted nearly all discussions of popular music for several decades. In the academic mind popular music became predominantly simplistic escapism, mass-produced for a passive radio audience which was seen as accepting anything, regardless of its merit. S. I. Hayakawa, David Riesman and Jacques Barzun parroted, in varying degrees, the Adorno paper. Hayakawa characterized the music as "sentimental clichés masquerading as emotion." Riesman portrayed pop as fundamentally "disconnectiveness" broadcast to an "atomized majority." Barzun, author of *The House of Intellect*, lamented the trend toward "noise" and "triviality":

> Popular songs, says one musical director of a recording company, must be aimed at people between the ages of fourteen and twenty-two; it must be 'simple, sad, and sexy' more than that, if we are to believe the master of them that know, Mr. Billy Rose, there are predestined vowel sounds that make for song hits, notably *ooo* and *eee*. Only put those repeatedly close together in a lyric and we drool and dree like Pavlov's dogs.[40]

The attitudes displayed by academics toward popular music were influenced by their age and also by their opposing musical value structure. Adorno, of course, genuinely feared what he saw as the creation of "false consciousness" in radio listeners, which he believed led to societal passivity. For most, pop was merely a mass-produced musical form inferior to the more "serious" genres.

The 1950s evidenced little in the way of scholarly concern with popular songs. Most professional journals ignored it. In 1954 *American Quarterly* included H. F. Mooney's "Songs, Singers and Society," dealing with the shift in popular music tastes. It was prophetic of many studies in the late 1960s, when social scientists of many disciplinary stripes began chronicling the perceived "pop revolution." A special issue of the *American Journal of Sociology* devoted to the study of mass culture did manage to publish two papers dealing with music. One discussed themes found in the lyrics of songs popular in 1955. The other examined the influence of neighborhoods and friendship cliques on musical taste. Bernard Rosenberg and David Manning White co-edited *Mass Culture: The Popular Arts in America*, including S. I. Hayakawa and David Riesman's papers on the mass character of popular music. In the early 1960s there was almost total silence on this subject, except for a few student fanzines such as *Crawdaddy* which began to circulate after Beatlemania had landed on the Atlantic shores. If one read only American academic journals of the time period, one would have to conclude that Beatlemania was a figment of some journalists' imaginations. Ironically, only the highly prestigious *British Journal of Social and Clinical Psychology* took note of the Beatles, reporting A. J. W. Taylor's findings on the reaction of teenagers to the Liverpool quartet's visit to New Zealand. The paper was later reprinted in Marcello Truzzi's introductory sociology text, *The Sociology of Everyday Life*. In 1968, the year record sales surpassed the billion-dollar figure, academics began to take popular music seriously, but on their own terms. *Sociological Quarterly* published an historical analysis of the protest songs of four decades, including those published in *Broadside*. The orientation of the writer was that pop music was politically significant. The most influential work was journalist Richard Goldstein's collection of pop lyrics called *The Poetry of Rock*. Goldstein's anthology quickly became required reading in many freshman courses, especially in composition classes. English professors comfortable with Milton, Browning, Burns, Blake and T. S. Eliot found the lyrics of rock songs, particularly those of Bob Dylan, Leonard Cohen and John Lennon to be the "poetry of the 1960s," ignoring Goldstein's admonition that: "If any volume of major contemporary poetry were set to music and sounded ridiculous, would we blame the poet for his failure to anticipate this contingency? Or would we reason that his words should not be expected to shine in partnership with rhythm and melody. Well, the reverse is also true. *Rock was meant to be heard, not seen*." He further cautioned: "This book violates a timeless pop taboo: it imposes one form upon another. . . . Don't expect a rock lyric to move like a poem."[41]

The difficulties of the pop *qua* poetry stance were explicated in a debate carried in the pages of the *Journal of Popular Culture*, an unconventional academic journal. Geoffrey Marshall, a University of Oklahoma English professor, complained that neither the Beatles nor their record company were treating the English act with propriety. The Beatles' record jackets should be annotated, as were the classics and other forms of high art. Documenting how "shoddily" earlier Beatles' albums were packaged, Marshall urged that:

> They might ask the record companies and the lyric reprint houses to do some of the following things: date the package (the production of the LP and its cover for distribution); identify the date of recording of each band (not the date of issue); proof-read carefully the jacket and all associated printed material for both internal consistency and grammar as well as for accuracy against the words being sung; provide better standards for punctuating lyrics; consider listing personnel and the instruments they are playing as a matter of course. The latter should be mandatory when unusual circumstances are involved—as might happen if Ringo played nonpercussion instrument, or when outside voices are added.
>
> The information requested above would help us take all of pop music more seriously. First steps might be taken. (On The Rolling Stones' newest album, "Beggar's Banquet" there are no indications of The Rolling Stones' names, no indication of how many

> of them there are—unless the jacket picture is definitive—no indication of what instruments they play, if any.) This is not taking pop music seriously.[42]

The professor's protestations underlined his concern that popular music—or at least the Beatles' songs—was art and deserved high culture status. Carl Belz, a Brandeis art historian, in the *Story of Rock*, made a similar point, declaring the Beatles as the high art of the 1960s. The application of his label, removing its declassé status, obviously meant pop music was worthy of study. Marshall's short article generated a series of replies by other academics. Richard A. Peterson, a Vanderbilt University sociologist, cautioned that "if the study of *popular* music is anything, it is the study of dynamic art-form and not an academic high art cult."[43] Neil Rosenberg, a Canadian folklorist, added, "The Beatles' obligation to the public is to entertain."[44] They are correct. The basic purpose of popular music generally was overlooked in favor of lengthy articles dealing with changes in lyrics, with the musical content all but ignored. The lyrics were either reduced into terms not unfamiliar to readers of Aristotle's *Poetics* or placed into the fabric of the social protest then raging on America's campuses.

In 1969, James Carey, a University of California sociologist, published several articles in *Psychiatry* and the *American Journal of Sociology* arguing that rock music was a reflector of the "new culture." Comparing the 1957 Chicago study of courtship themes in lyrics to those of 1966, Carey observed: "The fact that there is a distinctive set of beliefs associated with a large proportion of 1966 lyrics may reflect the growing disaffection among younger people who constitute the audience for the new lyrics, or it may simply reflect a change in those who write them."[45] Carey reported a drop of 83 percent to 65 percent of songs that dealt with boy-girl relationships. He also documented a growing concern with autonomy and choice in love relationships in contrast to the "love your spell is everywhere" motif of the 1950s. The researcher admitted that a majority of charted popular songs still dealt with the traditional themes of love and courtship. Robert A. Rosenstone's paper, "The Times They Are A-Changin': The Music of Protest" and Jerome Rodnitzky's "The Evolution of the American Protest Song" mirrored these sentiments. Popular music was ushering in a new culture. As to underline this fact, Rosenstone's paper was included in a special edition of the *Annals of the American Academy of Political and Social Science* dealing with "protest in the 1960s." The reliance upon lyrics to support these arguments has generated criticism. Some have perceived the major change in popular music as fundamentally experiential. Lyrics alone, they contend, do not represent an entire song. John Robinson and Paul Hirsch made the nation's wire services when their findings of the impact of rock-music lyrics and songs were reported at the 1969 meetings of the American Sociological Association. The two University of Michigan researchers announced that 70 percent of their high-school student respondents preferred the "sound" of a song rather than its meaning. More importantly, when their sample of students was asked to interpret eight songs including "Ode to Billy Joe" and "Skip a Rope," less than 43 percent could do so correctly. In one case, "Ode to Billy Joe," only 17 percent understood what was thrown over the Tallahatchie Bridge. Mark Levine and I found university and junior college students similarly unable to comprehend the lyrics to the controversial song, "Eve of Destruction" when it was on the top of the *Billboard* chart. Still, a number of papers appeared on the *power of song* and the new consciousness found in the lyrics. While the so-called power of song remains, for academics, at best an unproven commodity, many academics still use this foil to justify looking at the music. With the decline of the student protests of the 1960s, these analyses have come more to be associated with the role of popular music and the emergence of the counterculture of Consciousness III (see chapter 7). *Youth and Society*, especially, has published many scholarly papers on this subject.

Exhibit 9.4

HOW MANY TEENAGERS UNDERSTOOD HIT SONG LYRICS WITH "MESSAGES"?*

DETROIT	"Ode to Billy Joe" %		"Incense and Peppermints" %		"Heavy Music" %		"Lucy in the Sky" %	
Didn't hear	7		33		31		61	
Heard – no meaning given	14	(15)	32	(48)	28	(41)	18	(46)
Heard – inadequate description	60	(64)	21	(32)	27	(39)	11	(27)
Heard – understood theme	19	(21)	14	(20)	14	(20)	10	(27)
	100	(100)	100	(100)	100	(100)	100	(100)

GRAND RAPIDS	"Ode to Billy Joe" %		"My Condition" %		"Green Light" %		"Skip a Rope" %	
Didn't hear	11		17		27		33	
Heard – no meaning given	14	(16)	28	(34)	19	(26)	21	(32)
Heard – inadequate description	60	(67)	29	(35)	23	(32)	17	(25)
Heard – understood theme	15	(17)	26	(31)	31	(42)	29	(43)
	100	(100)	100	(100)	100	(100)	100	(100)

*Two percentages are given: one for all students and, in parentheses, the percentage of only those who reported having heard the song. A large number of students who had heard the songs did not attempt to describe what the songs meant; many of these students probably were aware of the songs but were afraid to guess in a classroom setting or didn't reply for some other reason. This nonresponse leads to conservative estimates and should be kept in mind in interpreting the percentages.

Source: reprinted by permission from John Robinson and Paul M. Hirsch, "Teenage Response to Rock and Roll Protest Songs," in R. Serge Denisoff and R. A. Peterson, eds., *Sounds of Social Change*, (Chicago: Rand McNally, 1972), p. 227.

While social scientists have been preoccupied with the sociopolitical implications of popular music, their counterparts in the humanities have continued on the pop-as-poetry path. Harold Mosher, Jr., as late as 1972, published a paper titled "The Lyrics of American Pop Music: A New Poetry." Ignoring Goldstein's warning, the English professor concluded, "Although most rock songs have been admired for their music, many of them have lyrics with remarkable poetic qualities. Their form is generally loose, often to accommodate the music. . . . Their art and relevance are renewing poetry and an interest in it. Time and time again in these songs one finds beneath a disarmingly simple and entertaining surface a studied art and considered though organically unified to create something worthy of the name of 'new poetry.' "[46] The insistence of academics on clothing popular music in some acceptable elitist robes is understandable but regrettable. Unfortunately, too few academics appear to appreciate the fundamental nature of the pop music.

One Berea College English professor indicated that Bob Dylan should receive the niagara of attention due to his superior writing ability. Yale, in fact, awarded a fidgety Dylan an honorary degree in music, an event he later immortalized in "The Day of the Locusts." Top 40 songs were discounted. William Schaffer wrote:

> There are hundred talentless hacks for every Dylan at work—but then who is talking about numbers. Dylan is also demonstrably more popular/accessible than most hacks. Even allowing that Top Forty bubblegum standards often outsell him, his works have sold steadily for years and have been repeatedly played on AM radio—they have had a longer cultural life than many other songs.[47]

Another example of an academic's restructuring of the pop music world occurred at the 1972 annual meetings of the Popular Culture Association. At one session a doctoral candidate in folklore from the University of Pennsylvania, read a highly technical paper which simply stated that age, race and class groups have different tastes. During her presentation she asserted that oligarchical record companies dictated what forms of music were to be popular. She charged: "The corporation recording experts began to believe that they could judge the qualities necessary to that universality . . . performers were pressured to alter their styles to fit the multiple group market." This statement triggered a rejoinder from Lewis Segal, then national publicity director for Capitol Records. Segal replied that record companies were in fact businesses and consequently made records attractive to the public taste. They also released material which appealed to specialty audiences, he claimed. The folklorist violently objected and explained to Segal that "he did not understand the record business." The exchange was certainly an example of academic arrogance, and it underlined the problem of the imposition of preconceived meanings onto any social phenomenon, albeit music or toothpaste ads.

In the fall of 1971, as a response to this growing interest, the Center for the Study of Popular Culture at Bowling Green State University gave birth to *Popular Music and Society*, and academic journal. The first issue was a strange mélange of papers by historians, sociologists and *Rolling Stone* editor and writer Jerry Hopkins. The advisory editors include two record-industry executives, Jerry Hopkins and academics representing various fields. The journal has not established a clear identity, at times containing short *Crawdaddy*-type record reviews more suited for a L.A. *Free Press* audience along with highly technical and esoteric papers such as "Responding to Popular Music: Criteria of Classification and Choice Among English Teenagers" or "Demographic Variables and Record Ownership by Collegiates: A Research Note" or "Popular Music and Research Design: Methodological Alternatives." *Popular Music and Society* certainly is not a challenge to any of the trades, prozines or even many of the privately published fanzines. It is basically self-supporting, receiving little aid from the university, yet it continues to survive. *Man and Music* has also appeared advertising itself as "Centering on music as humane occupation of man, the journal considers all facets of musical experience—music history, aesthetics, composition, performance, significant thought about music—in an attempt to reach a valid philosophy of music and the arts and to promote the realization, in the musician, of the importance of the world that exists offstage." Editor Arthur Motycka, a professor of music at Kent State University, sees the journal as directed at examining "the art of music from many frames of reference . . . an admixture of philosophical practice, if you will."

POP MUSIC 1A

The popularity of rock music with students has generated courses at universities in widely divergent parts of the country. The University of North Dakota, Urbana (Ohio) College, Oakland University (Rochester, Michigan), SUNY at Buffalo and the New School for Social Research in New York City have all featured classes in popular music with exotic titles such as "Atomic Youth and the Rock Mushroom," "The Image of American Society in Contemporary Music" and "Progressive Rock Music." B. Lee Cooper's class in "Images" attracted some 26 students who discussed the significance of rock music by "using lyrics from popular songs as contemporary observations about the nature and meaning of American life." Some of the themes were antiwar sentiments, escapism, personal alienation, nostalgia and drug usage. "The students," according to Cooper, "seemed extremely enthusiastic about the course's thesis, content and structure." Michael Luckman's class at the New School found 60 students paying $80 in fees to attend 15 sessions treating the "music of advocacy and of liberation." Luckman invited various promoters, deejays and artists to talk about their role in the industry. His thesis was that rock is the nexus of youth rebellion and the energy center around which all this activity—namely protest and a new life-style—has revolved. He deplores the relationship of rock music to profit-making corporations.[48] Luckman's course was also a success. James Graham's survey course on "Progressive Rock Music" at Oakland University generated a mixed reaction; students did not appear to take the class seriously. In an end-of-the-semester memo, the instructor summarized his feelings: "Partly because of an unusually high set of expectations, I have been disappointed in [the class] and troubled by indications that many people's interests in 'progressive rock' have not been significantly expanded during the semester. . . . It has been difficult for me to assess people's intellectual growth in this course because we all had our own starting points and goals." One of the problems encountered by Graham, no doubt, was the basic anti-intellectualism of rock music. Rock and, indeed, pop is not a cerebral idiom. The usual course framework frequently breaks down into opinion sessions and evokes a democracy rarely seen in the college classroom. Only when the traditionalism of technique (such as rock as poetry) is reintroduced does the professor regain his stature. Despite all the problems and deficiencies, classes in popular music seem destined to proliferate. This will not be due to a revolutionary consciousness entering the academy, but rather the very practical consideration of attracting students. As the postwar crop of entering freshmen declines, administrators will increasingly search for devices to lure graduates and noncollegiate people back into the classroom. Popular culture classes have proved to be effective academic bait. Popular music will be part of this rebuilding campaign. By sheer body counts the academics seem to become yet another constituency in the popular music arena. What impact if any they will have on taste remains an open question colored by several other potential trends bubbling around the popular-music charts.

GETTING IT TOGETHER

Stan Gortikov, the president of the RIAA, in 1973 said "Today music is everywhere." The world of popular music at the time was enjoying an unprecedented success. Record-company executives and merchandisers were happy with their two-billion-dollar volume and looking forward to even greater successes. The key reason for this optimism was the nature of their record-buying market. Irving Louis Horowitz suggested in 1971 that rock music had fragmented into many taste groups. "Rock is dying," urged the Rutgers sociologist, "because it has matured and its fans have become self-selective. They sit intently and listen to complex guitar arrangements and improvisations." He added, however, "Young teenagers find it very difficult to follow this improvisational music because they do not have background experience with rock. . . . Young teenagers don't like to sit and listen anyway. They want to move."[49] Horowitz's description of the changes in popular music have proven quite correct. Popular music, with rock still the dominant genre, has split into many other manifestations. Bubblegum music now has as much support as ever. Donny Osmond *surpassed* the annual sales of both Elvis Presley and the Beatles, yet many people tuned into pop were only vaguely aware of this preteen phenomenon. The popular-music audience has expanded; it now includes a rainbow of tastes and preferences which continue to grow. In future years it is quite conceivable that the popular-music audience may jet into the 6 to 50 range.

There are many factors contributing to this growth. The expansion of the courtship years has prolonged the need for romantic background noise. This trend found both in college and the so-called singles phenomenon adds a vast number of consumers to the ranks of record buyers. The prediction that married people will be a minority in a decade, while derided from many a pulpit, brings joy to the hearts of the record retailers. If prevous buying habits are of any value, postponement of marriage means more record sales.

This sociological trend is complemented by the nature of the music itself. As Horowitz suggests, a segment of the popular-music audience is now attuned to listening. This is especially true with young adults. These individuals look for content and read serious analyses of the music by cultural commentators and observes of the "scene." A good deal of the rock press is addressed to this audience. It is this group that purchased Jonathan Eisen's two volumes of the *Age of Rock* and Charlie Gillett's *Sound of the City*. The listeners spend over $20.00 a month on records. Ninety-seven percent listen to FM radio; 60 percent attend at least one music concert a month. They tune in four hours a day to their favorite radio station. Most own sound equipment including tape decks or cassette players. The popularity of singer-writers Kris Kristofferson, John Prine and Mickey Newberry is attributable to this group. Esoteric artists such as John Fahey, David Bromberg, Leo Kottke, Randy Newman and a legion of others also depend on Horowitz's "listeners."

Another cause for record-industry joy is the increasing popularity of country music. Affluent city dwellers in increasing numbers are tuning into country music. The wedding of country and popular music in the early 1970s has tremendous implications, even if the Nashville sound does not push rock off into a demographic corner.

The popularity of country music has expanded from 5 percent of the record and tape sales in 1963 to 16 percent in 1969, surpassing all genres except "rock and underground." In 1973 country music commanded 17 percent of the total record-buying audience; 51 percent of all singles were in the country genre; 37 percent of all of RCA's sales were country sound. What is more important is that one-third of record consumers between the ages of 20 through 29 prefer country music. Among higher income groups this rise is further reflected with 21 percent of those over the $12,000 income level preferring the products of Nashville and Bakersfield. The increasing affluence of country music fans has allowed them to buy $350 million worth of records in 1973.

With this buying power country and western has made a significant dent in the pop market. Many industry people see a merging of the country and pop markets into one. This of course could start a new popular-music trend. Some record companies already have their promotional people servicing both pop and country on the same basis. Pop product is sent to country stations and country product is shipped to MOR and Top 40 stations. Frank Mancini, vice-president of promotion at RCA, reminds people that John Denver's song, "Country Roads," originally broke on the country and western stations before becoming a smash pop hit.

The growing preeminence of country music augers greater stability, perhaps, for the popular music field. The tremendous loyality to country artists has historically guaranteed a return of most of their records. Chet Atkins says that a country artist can live on "one hit for many years." This sustained interest could greatly strengthen the upper reaches of the pop-music audience.

As Nashville increasingly becomes tied to the mechanics and ideology of the parent offices in New York and Los Angeles, one can only guess at the consequence of the relationship between the pop market and country music. Many Nashville executives point with pride to the lack of interference from outside. An ABC-Dunhill producer said, "I never talk to Lasker unless I call him." Nonetheless, as in the areas of rhythm and blues and folk music, no specialty genre in its pure form has ever become the dominant popular music style. It will be interesting to see if Nashville can manage to enjoy the best of both possible worlds.

Bill Williams, a local *Billboard* writer, acknowledges Nashville's awareness of the problem. The lure of pop-music profits seems too strong, however. Top country artists sell 400,000 albums; pop-music superstars double or triple that figure per release. Many country artists are quite anxious to follow Tammy Wynette, Charlie Rich and Tanya Tucker into this lucrative arena.

The soul sound is as viable as its Nashville counterpart. Many black artists sell in the 400,000 figures. Many songs from Philadelphia and Detroit cross over into the popular-music world. Indeed, black crossover is greater than country music. At any given time 25 to 40 percent of the artists represented on the *Billboard* Hot 100 singles chart are black. Black artists capture around 15 to 20 percent of the albums slots in *Billboard*'s "Top LPs and Tape" section. The number of soul singers who do well on albums charts is smaller. Diana Ross, Curtis Mayfield, Stevie Wonder, Isaac Hayes and a few other superstars are most frequently found on pop charts.

A number of factors work against any major wedding of soul with the popular-music genre. The most obvious is the black consciousness inherent in much of the soul genre. Many whites either do not understand or appreciate it. The root of gospel do not fit the esthetics of some; the lyrics in other instances may be too strong. Some people resent music being used for politics or protest. Blacks, on the other hand, simply say "right on" to the rhymes and sentiments of the Temps, James Brown and others. Attitudes and tastes, however, can change.

Unlike Nashville companies, which have enjoyed the comfort of being independent entities within large pop-record companies, the soul industry has been largely a product of independent entrepreneurship. In the 1950s Imperial, Chess, Atlantic and Veejay were developed by white businessmen for the black and later the youth market. After some unhappy experiences with the rock market of the 1950s, black music reverted to the ghetto and the hands of black entrepreneurs. A few whites—Jerry Wexler, Marshall Chess and Ahmet Ertegun—stuck with the soul market, but the 1960s belonged to Barry Gordy at Motown. Motown did not depend upon the popular music market for its profits. If the Miracles, Supremes or any other Motown artists made the *Billboard* Hot 100 it was considered gravy. Gordy was primarily servicing the black community.

The "community" aspect of soul has produced several structural barriers. The underlining ethos of soul is life in the ghetto. All of the frustration, suffering and injustice are expressed in the music. The music also provides a vehicle through which both psychological and actual escape is made possible. One can leave the ghetto and become another Marvin Gaye, James Brown or B. B. King. All one need do is *make it*. The competition therefore is fierce, with many persons preying on the desire of young artists. Consequently, the rules of the game in the soul market can be quite rough. Soul is not a Hobbesian war of each against all, but conditions in this market do spawn a number of sharpies at all levels, including record companies and radio-station people.

The soul industry is funadmentally a series of record labels competing for air play on a small number of stations. In many respects the soul market reflects the state of pop music in the mid-1950s, When companies with limited resources competed for a few slots of air time. For the early part of the 1960s it was Gordy and the Motown label versus a large number of independents ranging from "one-shot wonders" to Atlantic. Given the state of this market many of the pop "majors" had little desire to become involved in such an explosive field which seemingly promised limited profits. The cost of doing business in the soul market, given its high degree of competition, was not to the liking of many corporation executives, especially after the payola scandals of the early 1960s.

In the latter half of the 1960s, with the infusion of large amounts of conglomerate capitol and the growing awareness of black consumer dollars, many of the majors entered the soul market. Columbia took over the distribution of several black labels. RCA, United Artists and ABC Records signed a number of black acts, while Warner, Capitol and Metromedia temporarily held back. By the 1970s, the state of the soul market was a replica of the pop-music scene of 1958 and 1959. Large companies with huge promotion and publicity staffs competed with undercapitalized small labels, and the methods of competition in some cases also returned to the payola era. Some small companies that could not afford some of the standard methods of doing business, once again found it easier to simply give cash or sealed product to deejays in payment for air play. A few of the majors felt it necessary to follow suit. The messy practices have made many record companies leary of the soul field entirely. Metromedia has continued to stay away from this area. Capitol has stuck its corporate toe into the turbulent waters but has never really climbed in. Until recently A&M has all but ignored the soul market.

While there is money to be made in soul, it is predominantly a singles market. Major record companies are primarily concerned with album sales. Singles sell albums. This is the reason promo guys climb all over themselves at Top 40 radio stations. Breaking the single is important because it will sell the album. Consequently this second fact of economic life again goes against the corporate philosophies of many major companies. As Ron Saul suggested, "albums is where the money is." The cost of doing business, pop-music tastes and consumer habits are some major obstacles to a total linkage of the soul and pop markets.

The MOR market is also a major hope of record-company executives. Stan Gortikov feels that adults who were weaned on Elvis and the Beatles will continue to support this type of music regardless of their age. This would effectively link the MOR field with that of the pop market. As we have seen, some stations already use a mixed chart of MOR and pop material. The Jacobs conveyer belt partially relies on this taste composite. The golden oldies weekend is also a direct reflection.

Despite all the positive trends there exists a vast untapped audience for popular music. The fact that 502,000 albums find a buyer and are certified "gold" is not terribly impressive when one realizes that there are over 60 million potential record buyers. Records like *Sound of Music* and *Tapestry*, selling over 10 million copies, are extremely rare. Several factors seem to account for the hit-and-miss nature of the record business.

Public tastes are capricious. Fads and crazes come and go. The record industry is frequently behind a taste movement rather than in front of it. Most of the majors rejected rock and roll in the 1950s; Capitol turned down the Beatles in 1963. Part of the problem is that the industry is removed from "the street" and "the folks out there." The everyday mechanics of the record industry separate it from its audience. Touring acts rarely see anyone except people in the industry. Executives guarded by secretaries, assistants and, at Columbia, armed security people, rarely are exposed to "the folks." Furthermore, the industry is located mainly in Los Angeles, New York and Nashville. The record industry is not totally isolated, but it would benefit from greater awareness and interaction with its consumers.

One way of doing this, of course, is to adopt practices current in other entertainment media. Audience preferences and market research are at a primitive level at most record companies. Several of the majors boast research budgets of less than $35,000 per year. Many companies have none. Television networks spend in the vicinity of $175,000 to $225,000 profiling one television program.

The resistance to these techniques in the industry is partially due to its very successes. "We must be doing something right to be a $2 billion a year business" is a statement frequently heard in the record industry. This is absolutely correct. However, the industry might do much better with greater awareness of buying and listening habits.

An industry as individually oriented as the record business believes more in "gut feeling, seat of the pants" than hard, cold statistics. This has led to the many successes of the industry—and to some of its monumental flops. Individuality in creativity is essential, yet it can be counterproductive in everyday business affair. For example, the very individuality spark that created Atlantic Records, A&M and all of the other successes has also contributed to many industry problems. RCA's unique vision of creating 20 million exclusively 45 rpm record players found the entire industry adopting two speeds, 45 and 33⅓, when logic and economics suggested that the one speed is the most practical. A similarly confused state exists today in the very lucrative area of quad systems. The individuality of many different departments frequently keeps a record from breaking out as a hit. Individuality has plagued the music industry's effort to pass an effective copyright and antipiracy law. Capitol producer Joe Allison quips "a camel is a horse designed by record men."

It would be very unfair to end on this note. Many industry problems are outweighed by successes. A $2 billion industry is not to be put down as incompetent. The record industry is not a total rip-off nor is it a pillar of virtue. It is many things to many people. To many it represents a path to paradise. It is one of the last refuges of the "rags to riches" philosophy. Most definitions of this industry are misleading. The blind-men-and-the-elephant analogy may be suitable, or Kris Kristofferson's "Pilgrim 33": "He's a walking contradiction, partly truth and partly fiction" taking every wrong direction but getting eventually where he wants to go.

What is even more important is that nearly every American under the age of 50 grew up under the influence of recorded popular music. It could have been swing, ballads or rock of several varieties, but it was recorded music. Any industry that touches so many people deserves serious attention. Despite the many economic and sociological aspects of popular music, it may have been best summarized by the hit-making team of Mann and Goffin who wrote in "Who Put the Bomp":

I'd like to thank the guy
Who wrote the song
That made my baby fall in love
With me

Notes, Chapter 9

1. Quoted in George Steiner, "A Conversation With Claude Levi-Strauss," *Encounter*, April 1966, reprinted in Mitchell Good-

man, ed., *The Movement Toward A New America* (Philadelphia: Pilgrim Press, 1970), p. 372.

2. Jerry Hopkins, *The Rock Story* (New York: New American Library, 1970), p. 7.

3. Stuart Hall and Paddy Whannel, *The Popular Arts* (New York: Pantheon Books, 1965), p. 282.

4. Jonathan Cott and Sue Clark, "Mick Jagger Interview," *Rolling Stone Interviews*, (New York: Pocket Books, 1971), p. 163.

5. John Robinson and Paul Hirsch, "It's the Sound," *Psychology Today* 3 (October 1969): 42–45 and R. Serge Denisoff and Mark H. Levine, "The Popular Protest Song: The Case of the 'Eve of Destruction,'" *Public Opinion Quarterly* 35 (Spring 1971): 117–22.

6. Ibid., p. 45.

7. Paolo Mantegazza, *The Sexual Relations of Mankind*, trans. Samuel Putnam (New York: Eugenics Publishing Co., 1935), p. 6.

8. Mitch Miller, "June, Moon, Swoon and KoKoMo," *New York Times Magazine*, April 24, 1955, p. 19.

9. Richard Meltzer, *The Aesthetics of Rock* (New York: Shoestring Press, 1970), p. 157.

10. Quoted in Judith Sims, "At Last—The First Elvis Presley Movie," *Rolling Stone* 121 (November 9, 1972): 10.

11. Bill Doherty and George Uhlman, "Kiddy Rock," *Rock*, April 10, 1972, p. 15.

12. Diby Diehl, "Bob-b-e-e-e-e-eee: A Portrait of Bubblegum Charisma," *TV Guide*, December 25, 1971, p. 18.

13. Quoted in ibid., pp. 18–19.

14. George Melly, *Revolt Into Style: The Pop Arts* (Garden City, N.Y.: Anchor Books, 1971), p. 39.

15. Stanley E. Willis, "Falling in Love With Celebrities," *Sexual Behavior* 2 (August 1972): 3–4.

16. Quoted in "Pop Records: Moguls, Money and Monsters," *Time*, February 12, 1973, p. 65.

17. Quoted in Dwight Whitney, "It's Practically a Branch of the U.S. Mint," *TV Guide*, July 15, 1972, p. 25.

18. Megan Rosenfeld, "The Selling of the Bubblegum Kings (Oh Donny, Oh Donny, Oh!), *Toledo Blade Sunday Magazine*, October 1, 1972, p. 12.

19. Quoted in "Inside Beatlemania," *San Francisco Chronicle*, February 17, 1964, p. 9.

20. Quoted in Diehl, "Bob-b-e-e-e," p. 19.

21. Quoted in Robin Green, "The Naked Lunchbox: The David Cassidy Story," *Rolling Stone* 108 (May 11, 1972): 42.

22. Rosenfeld, "Bubblegum Kings" p. 15.

23. Statements of fans from Angela Taylor, " 'David!' They Yelled, and Parents Quietly Paid," *New York Times*, March 13, 1972, p. 44.

24. Quoted in Leslie Raddatz, "Dear David—I am 9 Years Old," *TV Guide*, May 22, 1971, p. 27.

25. George Allen Booker, "The Disk Jockey and His Impact on Teenage Musical Taste as Reflected Through a Study of North Florida Cities," Ph.D. diss., Florida State University, 1968, p. 89.

26. Quoted in James S. Coleman, *The Adolescent Society: The Social Life of the Teenager and Its Impact on Education*. Glencoe: The Free Press, 1961), p. 126.

27. Taylor, "David" p. 44.

28. Lenny Kaye, "To Live Outside the Law You Must be Honest," *Creem* 3 (November 1971): 75.

29. Quoted in Robin Green, "How Black Was My Sabbath," *Rolling Stone* 94 (October 28, 1971): 42.

30. Quoted in Timmy Ferris, "Alice Cooper's Beer Bottle Polka," *Rolling Stone* 125 (January 4, 1973): 18.

31. John Johnstone and Elihu Katz, "Youth and Popular Music: A Study in the Sociology of Taste," *American Journal of Sociology* 62 (May 1957): 565.

32. David Regan Dees, "On the Theory of Art: A Structuralist Analysis With Example[s] From Contemporary Popular Music," Ph.D. diss., Notre Dame University, 1972, p. 200.

33. Russ Solomon, "Solomon: Inventory Depth Counts," *Billboard* May 23, 1970, p. 21.

34. James E. Conyers, "An Exploratory Study of Musical Tastes and Interests of College Students," *Sociological Inquiry* 33 (Winter 1963): 58–66.

35. Dees, "Theory of Art," p. 201.

36. Quoted in George S. Trow, "Money Music," *New Yorker, December 23, 1972, pp. 37–38.*

37. J. I. Simmons and Barry Winograd, *It's Happening: A Portrait of the Youth Scene Today* (Santa Barbara: Marc-Laird Publications, 1966), pp. 157–58, 165.

38. T. W. Adorno, "On Popular Music," *Studies in Philosophy and Social Science* 9 (1941): 25.

39. Ibid., p. 37.

40. Jacques Barzun, *Music in American Life* (Bloomington: Indiana University Press, 1956), p. 90.

41. Richard Goldstein, *The Poetry of Rock* (New York: Bantam Books, 1968), pp. xi–xii.

42. Geoffrey Marshall, "Taking the Beatles Seriously: Problems of Text," *Journal of Popular Culture* 3 (Summer 1969): 33.

43. Richard A. Peterson, "Taking Popular Music Too Seriously," *Journal of Popular Culture* 4 (Winter 1971): 593.

44. Neil V. Rosenberg, "Taking Popular Culture Seriously: The Beatles," *Journal of Popular Culture* 4 (Summer 1970): 53.

45. James Carey, "Changing Courtship Patterns in the Popular Song," *American Journal of Sociology* 74 (May 1969): 731.

46. Harold F. Mosher, Jr., "The Lyrics of American Pop Music: A New Poetry," *Popular Music and Society* 1 (Spring 1972): 174–75.

47. William J. Schaffer, "Coffee Lounge: A Forum of Opinion," *Popular Culture Methods* 1 (1972) 2.

48. Quoted in McCandlish Phillips, "Rock Makes the Academic Scene," *New York Times*, April 5, 1971, p. 31.

49. Irving Louis Horowitz, "Rock on the Rocks or Bubblegum Anybody?" *Psychology Today*, January 1971, p. 61.

BIBLIOGRAPHY

Citations throughout the book have generally been used to identify sources for quotations. Therefore, it may be helpful for those wishing to further pursue the subject of the popular-music industry in America to know about other more generalized statements about trends and events in the medium. What follows is only the tip of a very large bibliographical iceberg. A good place to start is with Neil V. Rosenberg's "Rock Books: An Incomplete Survey," JEMF *Quarterly* (Spring and Summer 1972) which introduces the reader to some of the current literature that is available. After that, where one searches is based upon what issues are of concern. The trades, *Billboard*, *Cash Box* and *Record World* are very helpful in following the economic and merchandising trends in the record industry. The so-called rock and specialty press keeps up with "what's happening" as best they can. The major papers are *Rolling Stone*, *Zoo World*, *Rock*, *Creem*, *Crawdaddy*, *Phonograph Record*. *Downbeat* dominates in the jazz world. *The Journal of Jazz Studies* is important. *Bluegrass Ltd*. and *Blues Ltd*. are addressed to the obvious audiences. *Soul* and *R&B* cover black music. Bill Ivey's *Journal of Country Music* is important. *Sing Out*! continues as the folk-music publication. Depending on taste there exist many fanzines dealing with them; these were discussed in chapter 6. Two scholarly journals publish material dealing with this subject: *Popular Music and Society* and *Music and Man*. The first journal leans heavily toward the social science approach while the latter is more in the humanistic tradition of academic departments of music and English. The reader should look at most of this with a jandiced eye. Much of it is so generalized as to be almost useless. Some of the material is very esoteric. The task of integration is left to the student of popular music.

The English press has been more concerned with the basics of popular music than has its American counterpart. George Melly, *Revolt Into Style* (Anchor Books), Tony Jasper, *Understanding Pop* (SCM) and Richard Mabey, *The Pop Process* (Hutchinson Educational) all deal with it as an adjunct to youth culture.

Good summary histories of popular music are David Ewen, *The History of Popular Music* (Barnes and Noble), Roland Gelatt, *The Fabulous Phonograph* (Appleton Century), Sigmund Spaeth's *History of Popular Music in America* (Random House) and James J. Fuld, *American Popular Music,* 1875–1950 (Musical Americana). The classic works dealing with particular eras are Isaac Goldberg, *Tin Pan Alley* (John Day), Larry Freeman, *The Melodies Linger on* (Century House), George Simon, *The Big Bands* (Macmillan), David Ewen, *Rise and Fall of Tin Pan Alley* (Funk and Wagnalls) and Charlie Gillett, *The Sound of the City* (Outbridge and Dienstfrey). H. F. Mooney's "Popular Music Since the 1920s: The Significance of Shifting Taste," *American Quarterly* (1968), Richard A. Peterson and David G. Berger, "Three Eras in the Manufacture of popular Music Lyrics," in Denisoff and Peterson, eds., *Sounds of Social Change* (Rand McNally) and Russell Nye's chapter in *The Unembarassed Muse* (Dial Press) are short pieces hitting the high points of popular music's American evolution.

Charles Reich's *Greening of America* (Random House) is the most popular text dealing with popular music as a focus of generational conflict.

The pop music and generational rebellion theme is all pervasive. See especially J. Frederick MacDonald, "Hot Jazz, The Jitterbug, and Misunderstanding: The Generation Gap In Swing, 1935–1945." *Popular Music and Society* (Fall 1972) and

R. Serge Denisoff and Mark Levine, "Generations and Counter Culture: A Study in the Ideology of Music," *Youth and Society* (September 1970), also see the first two articles in Greil Marcus, *Rock and Roll Will Stand* (Beacon Press).

On the demographics in popular culture, see Herbert Gans, "Popular Culture in America" in Howard Becker, *Social Problems: A Modern Approach* (John Wiley and Sons). His notions are applied to popular music in R. Serge Denisoff and Mark Levine, "Youth and Popular Music: A Test of the Taste Culture Hypothesis," *Youth and Society* (December 1972). There are literally hundreds of thousands of books, articles, and biographies dealing with the theme of "from rags to riches" by a pop-music star. Little attempt has been made to address the actual processes of the occupation of record artist. James Coffman's " 'Everybody Knows This Is Nowhere': Role Conflict and the Rock Musician," *Popular Music and Society* (Fall 1972) examines the competing forces the performer must cope with. Teddy Bart's *Inside Music City* U.S.A. (Aurora Press) describes the steps of "making it" in Nashville. Jerry Hopkins' chapter on the rise and fall of the Buffalo Springfield in *The Rock Story* (Signet) is invaluable on the subject of internal feuds that develop in successful acts. *Forbes* looked at the potential profits of rock stardom in "The Rockers are Rolling in It" (April 15, 1973). Patrick Salvo's "On The Road Again," *Rock* (June 7, 1972), is one of the better treatments of the joys of touring. There are many more especially of the Rolling Stones' American visits. The difficulty with the Stones' tours is that they are not typical. Few acts are afforded the luxuries and attention flowered upon this "super" group. The reader is directed to the many interviews with acts published in the rock press. *Rolling Stone* and *Phonograph Record* are perhaps the most savvy. Peter Guralnick's *Feel Like Going Home* (Outbridge and Dienstfrey) and Michael Lydon, *Rock Folk* (Dial Press) are nice collections of selected musicians. Robert Somma's *Nobody Waved Goodbye* (Outerbridge and Dienstfrey), dealing with the death of Janis Joplin, Jimi Hendrix and Brian Jones also treats with some of the pressures pushed upon a superstar. Jerry Hopkins' *Elvis* (Simon and Schuster) and Anthony Scaduto's *Bob Dylan* (Grosset and Dunlap) present two very different reactions to the life of an idol.

The August 1972 issue of *Crawdaddy* includes a series of limited but revealing articles dealing with agents, managers, artists' attorneys and contracts. The standard industry source of contracts and terms is Shemel and Krasilovsky's *This Business of Music* (Billboard Publishers). The rise of music conglomerates has received considerable attention. "$2 Billion Worth of Noise," *Forbes* (July 15, 1968), Hans W. Heinsheimer, "Music From the Conglomerates," *Saturday Review* (February 22, 1969) and Mike Gross, "Music Rumbles—Wall St. Tumbles," *Billboard* (December 6, 1969) are especially revealing despite their compactness. As cited in chapters 3 and 4, a number of individual companies have been profiled in both the rock press, trades and in *Forbes and Business Week*. Statements in these business-oriented publications frequently are very revealing because the company spokesman is not trying to build a street image.

Everybody talks about excessive product, but few analyses are available. Jody Breslaw's "New Releases: Quantity and Quality in a Gambler's Market," *Rock* (July 5, 1971), is a short statement of the problem, as is "Pop Records: Monguls, Money and Monsters," *Time* (February 12, 1973).

The vinyl crisis has been an on-going concern in the trades since fall 1973. A short introduction to the situation is "Vinyl Shortage Slows Record Industry," *New York Times* (January 7, 1974), p. 40.

Ratings of how the individual record companies are faring in the album and singles market are published in *Billboard* semiannually. The reader should look in the January and July issues.

The best statement, however dated, on trends in the record industry is Rolf Meyersohn and Elihu Katz, "Notes on a National History of Fads," *American Journal of Sociology* (1957). Also see sections on "teen idols."

Outside of Richard Williams's musical biography of Phil Spector, *Out of His Head* (Outerbridge and Lazard), there are few complete treatments of this role. The best analysis of the conflicting demands made upon a producer is Richard A. Peterson and David G. Berger's "Entrepreneurship in Organizations: Evidence from the Popular Music Industry," *Administrative Science Quarterly,* March 1971. Garry Sherman in a four-article series in *Billboard* published in December of 1967 outlines the various problems and demands posed upon the producer. *Audio* and *Downbeat* magazines have in the last several years published a number of articles dealing with the technical aspects of record mixing. See especially John Woram's discussion of recording and mixing in the May and June issues of *Audio* in 1969. For a discussion of "in-house" producing see "Can a Modern Day Producer Find Happiness in a Record Company's A&R Department?" *Circular* (March 4, 1974).

Discussions of marketing techniques can be found in the trades as well as in *Advertising Age* and several other ad journals. George Uhlman's "Soft Peddling Albums Ain't That Easy," *Rock* (April 24, 1972) and Algin B. King, "The Marketing of Phonograph Records In the United States: An Industry Study," Ph.D. diss., Ohio State University, 1966, provides further information. Also see *Billboard* (November 3 and 10, 1973) on how record companies spend their ad money.

The subject of cutouts, not surprisingly, has been all but confined to the trade press. Lenny Goldberg's "Inside Record Distribution," *Rock* (March 1, 1971) is one of the few written for nonindustry people—with definitions of so-called technical terms. An excellent discussion of the "return" problem is found in *Billboard* (May 10, 1973), p. 1.

Bill Randle's unpublished Ph.D. dissertation "History of Radio Broadcasting and Its Social and Economic Effect on the Entertainment Industry, 1920–1930" (Case Western Reserve University) is the most authoritative examination of the early days of radio. Sadly, no one summary work has continued where the Cleveland disk jockey left off. Arnold Passman's *The*

Deejays (Macmillan) is a readable but superficial treatment of the evolution of the radio record spinner. Jerry Hopkins's chapter dealing with boss radio in *The Rock Story* (Pocket Books) is excellent but timebound. Tom Nolan's "Underground Radio" and Harry Shearer's "Captain Pimple Cream's Fiendish Plot" reprinted in Jonathan Eisen's *Age of Rock*, vol. I (Vintage Books) are also worthwhile. Michele Hush's "The Anatomy of a Hit Record" *Rock* (February 25, 1974) is an outstanding case study. The best source for information about deejays is the "Vox Jox" page in each issue of *Billboard*. Claude Hall's interviews with radio industry leaders are especially insightful.

Material on record critics and rock writers is perhaps the most poorly documented of all the subjects discussed herein. Journalists have rarely been paid to write stories about themselves. John Landau's series of three *Rolling Stone* articles; Patricia Kennedy's *Rock* magazine critique; and especially Chet Flippo's history of rock journalism cited here are perhaps the best statements on the subject. Examples of various dominant writing styles found in the early issues of *Crawdaddy* and *Rolling Stone* can be found in Paul Williams's *Outlaw Blues* (W. W. Norton), Richard Goldstein's, *Goldstein's Greatest Hits* (Prentice-Hall) Jon Landau's *It's Too Late To Stop Now: A Rock and Roll Journal* (Straight Arrow Books) and Richard Meltzer, *Aesthetics of Rock* (Shoe String Press). *The Rolling Stone Record Review* (Pocket Books), despite its historical organization, does provide a representative sample of rock criticism. The April 1973 issue of *Coast* magazine featured a portrait of influential rock writers. Greg Shaw in several publications, including his own *Who Put the Bomp*, has compiled lists of fanzines throughout the world. See *Creem* (June 1971) and *Crawdaddy* (May 1972). Unfortunately, most rock fanzines and prozines are not on microfilm. Consequently, it now takes considerable digging to find early issues. One repository is the Bowling Green State University Library, which houses incomplete collections of many rock music magazines. William Schurk is the keeper of these treasures in the Audio Division of the Library.

Two volumes deal with the traditional political use of music. See Frank Kofsky, *Black Nationalism and the Revolution in Music* (Pathfinder Press) and R. Serge Denisoff, *Sing a Song of Social Significance* (Bowling Green Popular Press). *Broadside* (NYC) remains the dominant outlet for songs of protest as well as articles and reviews. Discussions dealing with popular music and politics abounded in the underground press. Especially see early issues of *Creem* before it became a magazine. Also, the *Ann Arbor Sun* published by the Rainbow People's party has a wealth of interesting material. Kenneth Westhues's *Society*'s *Shadow Studies in the Sociology of Countercultures* (McGraw-Hill Ryerson, Ltd) contains a good bibliography of scholarly papers on the so-called counterculture. David Horowitz et al., *Counterculture and Revolution* (Random House) provides a quick review of this phenomenon. For further accounts of the Detroit rock scene of the late 1960s, see John Sinclair, *Guitar Army* (World Publishing) and John Sinclair and Robert Levin, *Music and Politics* (World Publishing Co.), John Lombardi, "Of Energy & Grease & Mao & John Sinclair," *Rolling Stone* (February 21, 1970) and Greg Shaw, "The Back to the Roots Rock 'n' Roll Movement," *Rolling Stone* (October 28, 1971). An interesting piece on the organization of a cooperative record store is found in John Morthland, "How To Start a Co-Op Record Store for Fun, Liberation, and No Profit," *Rolling Stone* (March 7, 1970).

The two best works on rock festivals are Jerry Hopkins's *Festival: The Book of American Music Celebrations* (Collier Books) and Richard A. Peterson's "The Unnatural History of Rock Festivals: An Instance of Media Facilitation," *Popular Music and Society* (Winter 1973).

The muddy and murky world of concert promotion is partly covered in the trade papers. *Billboard*'s *Campus Attractions*, published annually, explicates some of the mechanics of this area. Bill Graham's farewell press conference is quite helpful, see "Fillmore East 1968–1971 PEACE," *Rock* (June 7, 1971), also Hemy Edward's interview with Bill Graham, "The Promoter: Money Hawks, Graham Talks," *Crawdaddy* (August, 1971).

William Livingston, "Piracy in the Record Industry," *Stereo Review* (February, 1970), is one of the better articles on this subject. Also see Charles McCaghy and R. Serge Denisoff, "The Criminalization of Record Piracy: Analysis of an Economic and Political Conflict," in Denisoff and McCaghy, editors, *Deviance, Conflict and Criminality* (Rand McNally); John Morthland and Jerry Hopkins, "The Bootleg: The Rock and Roll Liberation Front," *Rolling Stone* (February 7, 1970); and Ed Ward, "The Bootleg Blues," *Harpers* (January, 1974).

For a summary statement on the industry's posture toward this problem, see "Piracy Background Shows Giant Push," *Billboard* (February 9, 1974), p. 33. Social scientists continue to search for some link between drug use and popular music. See "The Counterculture Beat," *Human Behavior* (January 1973) and Mike Douse's "Contemporary Music, Drug Attitudes, and Drug Behavior," *Australian Journal of Social Issues* 8 (1974).

Perhaps the most impoverished area of popular music studies is that dealing with its audience. A handful of record companies do have market research data in their files. This they guard very closely. Some data on a very limited and specific basis is available from publishing companies like BMI. *Youth and Society* and *Popular Music and Society* have published some studies dealing with demographics of music tastes. All have been confined to relatively small populations.

A Los Angeles poll of record buyers is reported in three issues of *Billboard* from September 29, 1973, through October 13, 1973. Materials dealing with teen idols is best picked up at the newsstand. David Dempsey's attempt to deal with the Beatles in the *New York Times Magazine* (February 23, 1964) is a nice review of explanations of the phenomenon. The why's and wherefore's of pop music and "punk-rock" are more than adequately treated in the rock press. *Creem* is the best source on "punk-rock." *Rock*, *Zoo World and Phonograph*

Record are also important. Back issues of *Rolling Stone* should also be consulted.

For a glance at what academics are doing in popular music, see *Popular Music and Society*, *The Journal of Jazz Studies*, *Journal of Country Music* and *Man and Music*.

INDEX